A'aisa's Gifts

STUDIES IN MELANESIAN ANTHROPOLOGY

General Editors

Donald F. Tuzin
Gilbert H. Herdt
Rena Lederman

A'aisa's Gifts

A Study of Magic and the Self

Michele Stephen

UNIVERSITY OF CALIFORNIA PRESS
Berkeley / Los Angeles / London

University of California Press
Berkeley and Los Angeles, California

University of California Press
London, England

Copyright © 1995 by The Regents of
the University of California

Library of Congress Cataloging-in-Publication Data
Stephen, Michele.
    A'aisa's gifts : a study of magic and the self /
Michele Stephen.
        p.   cm.
    Includes bibliographical references and index.
    ISBN 0-520-08761-5 (alk. paper). —
ISBN 0-520-08829-8 (pbk. : alk. paper)
    1. Mekeo (Papua New Guinea people)—
Psychology.   2. Mekeo (Papua New Guinea
people)—Rites and ceremonies.   3. Philosophy,
Mekeo.   4. Magic, Mekeo.   5. Ethnopsychology—
Papua New Guinea.   6. Self (Philosophy)—Papua
New Guinea.   7. Dreams.   8. Papua New
Guinea—Social life and customs.   I. Title.
DU740.42.S75   1995
155.8′49912—dc20   94-24807
                                              CIP

Printed in the United States of America

The paper used in this publication meets the minimum
requirements of American National Standard for
Information Sciences—Permanence of Paper for
Printed Library Materials, ANSI Z39.48-1984 ∞

For John Stephen,
the finest and truest of companions

Contents

Acknowledgments

The cooperation, friendship and generosity of the Mekeo people have made this study possible. Although they may not recognize it as such, this book is my tribute to them. In bringing a knowledge of Mekeo ways of life to a wider audience, I hope to give a greater appreciation of, and thus respect for, the richness and complexity of their cultural traditions. In doing so, I have taken great pains not to expose things that might prove dangerous to others. In the view of the old people (*au apao'i*), what is said here is merely "talk" (*niniani mo*), I have revealed only the tip (*onina*). The root (*gome*) is not disclosed; be assured that no one can find here the information necessary to implement *ugauga, mefu, ipaipa, kinapui,* nor any of the other techniques of secret knowledge described here.

For hospitality and help on innumerable occasions during my several fieldwork visits, I thank the Catholic Mission of the Sacred Heart, in particular the Reverend Father Diaz of Beipa Mission. Fieldwork from 1969 to 1971 was sponsored by the Australian National University, Research School of Pacific Studies; from December 1978 to January 1979 by the School of Humanities, La Trobe University; from 1980 to 1982 by the Australian Research Grants Council. I thank each of these institutions for their support.

The final shape taken by this book owes much to the creativity and devotion of the then editors of the Melanesian Anthropology Series of California University Press, Don Tuzin, Gil Herdt, and Rena Lederman, who gave generously of their time and professional knowledge in their initial reviews of the manuscript. The lengthy exchanges that followed, and the several re-writings that resulted from them, were overseen with patience, firm judgement, and most generous assistance by Don Tuzin, to whom I owe much. Without his deep interest and commitment, I might well have been tempted to give up on the project. I thank Bruce Knauft for a most thorough, and yet empathetic, review of the manuscript which has significantly shaped the final form and presentation of this work. My thanks also to J. D. Brown of University of California Press for expert editing of the final product.

To Gil Herdt, a special tribute. I first met him in Papua New Guinea in 1981, while undertaking the fieldwork on which this study is primarily based. For more than a decade I have valued his personal friendship and intellectual companionship; his enthusiasm and support over these many years have influenced all that I have written in that time, but especially this book.

Many others have contributed in less direct but nevertheless significant ways. It is impossible to thank them all but certain names stand out. The late Peter Lawrence, who examined my Ph.D. thesis, was a crucial influence, source of encouragement—and his own work an inspiration—in the direction taken by my post-doctoral research. Edgar Waters guided my early research interests in New Guinea and helped me formulate my first research proposal. Ben Finney introduced me to Melanesian anthropology and guided me through my early fieldwork (1969–1971) among the Mekeo. To my colleagues in the Department of History, La Trobe University—especially to John Cashmere, Inga Clendinnen, David Dorward, Bronwen Douglas, Rhys Isaac, Judith Richards, and Tom Spear and Alan Ward (both formerly of La Trobe); and to Dawn Ryan (Monash University), my appreciation for an intellectual dialogue extending over many years. Perhaps even more important has been the influence of my students at La Trobe, who have always spurred me on by their keen interest, and have taught me far more than I can ever hope to teach them. In acknowledging the many contributions colleagues, students, and friends have made to this book, I, of course, accept full responsibility for its shortcomings.

On a more personal note, I am grateful to my parents, and especially my mother, for always cheerfully accepting the wilful ways of their only child. Special acknowledgment is due to Mercurius for his unique and gracious assistance, and much valued companionship over the long hours in my study spent writing and editing.

I dedicate this book to John Stephen, my husband, who has undoubtedly contributed more than anyone else to it. During my 1969–71 fieldwork he spent a great deal of time helping me conduct a household census, mapping the village, and photographing activities and people. He came to help me set up for fieldwork in 1980, and returned with me in December 1981. His photographs illustrate this book. From the earliest beginnings of my research in New Guinea, to the final word of this manuscript, I have drawn constantly upon his advice, skills, and sheer hard work. Without his endless encouragement, support, and invaluable practical help in so many ways, this book would never have been written.

Introduction

The topic of this book, "magic and the self," may seem an odd juxtaposition of the newest and most old-fashioned concerns in anthropology. Magic is a topic only occasionally discussed in the anthropological literature today, and when it is, it is usually subsumed under the more voguish headings of "ritual" or "symbolism." The very term *magic* conjures images of the armchair anthropologists of the late nineteenth century, Frazer's great opus *The Golden Bough* (1913), out-dated speculations concerning the "primitive mentality," and the fusty tomes of bygone evolutionary theorists. In contrast, the "self" is redolent of the new, the experimental, the postmodernist concerns of the new ethnography (reviewed by Clifford and Marcus 1986; Marcus and Fischer 1986), which strives to find ways to more vividly represent the experience of other cultures and to develop a "cultural psychology" (Shweder 1990) that can transcend the outdated, culture-bound yet globalizing paradigms of the past. Why this strange hybrid of nineteenth-century universalism and postmodern particularism—magic and the self?

The ethnographic aim of this study is to show how what I refer to as "magic" and concepts of person and self are intimately intertwined for Mekeo, a people of central, coastal Papua. That is to say, on the one hand a distinctive cultural view of the self is shaped by cosmological beliefs based upon a magical worldview; on the other, the beliefs and rituals of Mekeo magic serve to create a particular kind of awareness and experience of self—thus they are the very means of creating self.

Self is a problematic term frequently bandied around in current anthropological debate (the literature, now extensive, is reviewed by Hallowell 1967; Clifford 1982; Shweder and Bourne 1984; White and Kirkpatrick 1985; Doi

1986; Strathern 1988; Herdt 1987, 1989a; Herdt and Stoller 1990; Whittaker 1992). By "self" I refer to a person's sense of being an entity (or combination of entities) somehow distinct from others (although connected to them) with thoughts, feelings, needs, and desires that inevitably oppose self to others, no matter how close those others might be. In other words, I am referring to a person's self-awareness or self-identity.[1] I do not assume, as so many cross-cultural studies caution us against assuming (e.g., L. Dumont 1965; Marriot 1976; White and Kirkpatrick 1985; Strathern 1988; Herdt 1989a), that Mekeo selves are conceptualized in the same way as Western selves—indeed much of this book is an exploration of the differences. Yet I do work from the basic assumption that an existential sense of self—self-consciousness or self-awareness—as a center, however shifting, of thought, feeling, and desire, is a universal of the human condition; indeed, it is this self-consciousness, rather than a capacity for tool making, language, symbolic representations, or any other characteristic, that primarily distinguishes humans from animals.

My concern is with this existential sense of being a person, somehow differentiated from others, and how this sense of I/me is realized both in the system of Mekeo cultural beliefs and in the lived experience of actual Mekeo persons. That the category of the "self" is a problematic one, and is inevitably misleading when applied to other cultures, is certainly true. Yet since this whole study is in effect an extended exploration of how our Western category compares with Mekeo notions, I find it impossible to avoid it. I could use glosses such as "face," "outside me," "inside me," "skin," "body substance," "body surface," "body interior," "dream-self," "hidden self," and so I shall, but I cannot remove the term *self* without my prose becoming hopelessly clogged and unintelligible.

Why should magic provide the focus for an exploration of self-awareness and identity? An important recent study by Fredrik Barth (1987) argues that Melanesian cosmological symbols in general might better be understood as relating to the self rather than to social structure. I have come to similar conclusions here. Since a system of beliefs and rituals that can most easily be identified as magic forms the basis of Mekeo cosmology, it is "magic" that is central to this study. At once, our discussion is placed in danger of foundering against the reef of hoary and inappropriate connotations attached to the very idea of magic both in popular Western culture and within the specialized culture of anthropological and sociological discourse. Obviously my concern here is with the latter, but this removes few difficulties owing to the many negative associations the term *magic* carries—labels condescendingly applied to modes of thought deemed primitive, archaic, and childish. As Tambiah (1990) cautions, it is a concept that has emerged from historical processes specific to Western culture and thus remains inherently problematic as a "baseline" from which to translate the modes of thought of other peoples and times. Unless I intend this book to be a thorough "deconstruction" of the term, would I not be better to eschew all reference to it, and simply refer to Mekeo cosmology, ritual, and belief, which are currently more neutral terms?

Although my aim here is by no means so ambitious as to provide a thorough deconstruction of the anthropological concept of magic, I do hope to be able to shed different light on our present understandings of what it entails. Magic, despite its drawbacks, is still a useful concept in identifying a particular kind of cosmology, ritual, and belief. When used within anthropological discourse, it is understood to refer to a belief system that assumes that through specific actions on the part of a human agent, involving incantations or spells and the use of magical substances and the performance of specified ritual actions, desired changes can be brought about in the material world. Why such an assertion is made, and why it is believed, is in essence the subject of all the debate about magic—from Frazer (1913), Durkheim (1915), Mauss (1966 [1902], 1972), Malinowski (1935, 1961, 1974) Evans-Pritchard (1937) and the innumerable ethnographic studies of magic that have followed in their wake—regardless of whether argument is based on the nature of the "primitive mentality," modes of thought, infantile wishes, theories of the sociology of knowledge, or even ESP (e.g., Winkleman 1979). In refusing to relinquish the term *magic,* I shall, nevertheless, restrict it to refer to the Western analytic concept and avoid it as far as possible when referring to the culturally specific Mekeo system of beliefs and rituals.

Pivoting as this study does on the contrasting perspectives afforded by two separate phases of fieldwork and the disjunctions I discovered between public symbolic representations and the intimacies of private revelations, it inevitably calls into question, and thus makes problematic, the nature of my ethnographic data. It is impossible to give a straightforward description of Mekeo beliefs and action; rather, I must show how it was that particular kinds of information became available to me and describe the interactions shaping my different perspectives. In view of the growing commitment in current ethnographic writing to more interpretative and reflexive approaches, my stance can no longer be regarded as novel. The theoretical grounds for it have been extensively argued by others (Rabinow 1977; Dumont, J.-P. 1978; Crapanzano 1979, 1980; Clifford 1982, 1986; Marcus and Cushman 1982; Geertz 1988; Clifford and Marcus 1986; Marcus and Fischer 1986; Herdt and Stoller 1990). Of the many arguments in favor of this approach, the most compelling in my view is the observation that when the human mind takes itself as its subject, it must devise methodologies and theories very different from those applied to the external, physical world (Jung 1969:216–217; Sartre 1969; Kohut 1971:301–305, 1977:311, 1985:116–118).

Once one adopts this mode, the "I" is inclined to take over and become integral to the whole work, as Marcus and Cushman (1982) have pointed out. Here it becomes the means whereby I introduce my understandings of an exotic culture to the reader. It is by explaining how I obtained my information that

I attempt to give my interpretations authority. In the exploring of individuals' subjectivity it is a means of coping with the problem of penetrating other people's inner worlds. I cannot simply assert Mekeo think this or that, I need to show how they shared their inner worlds with me. Furthermore, it is by reflecting upon Western modes of understanding mind, consciousness, and inner states that I hope to contribute to our general understandings of such. The narrative of my personal process of intellectual discovery, as I gradually moved from public levels of understanding to increasingly private and hidden levels, provides structure to the book as a whole and the plot whereby my ethnography unfolds.

There are dangers in the balancing act this approach requires. For some readers, there will be too much here about I/me; for others, the process of reflexivity will not be developed fully enough. Devereux (1967), for example, maintains that fieldworkers would have to undergo extensive psychoanalysis before being sufficiently aware of their own distortions and projections to achieve an appropriately honed psychological objectivity. As Herdt and Stoller (1990) have pointed out, a fully reflexive approach seems to imply the need to present to the reader a careful self-analysis of the investigator—yet both authors draw back from offering this. No one, of course, can be totally self-aware or in touch with all their unconscious as well as conscious motivations. We can only aim at increasing our awareness without becoming overwhelmed by our "self critical stance" (Crapanzano 1979); this is as much as I attempt here.

Reflexivity—or as Geertz (1988), tongue-in-cheek, dubs it, the "I-witnessing" mode—has its costs. Too great a preoccupation with the means by which one constructs ethnography, Marcus and Cushman (1982) have warned, too myopic an absorption in how one knows what one knows (or can know anything at all), may lead to loss of confidence, negativity, and the abandonment of ethnography as a viable mode of knowledge. Geertz (1988) observes that it is difficult to create new knowledge, and present it effectively and convincingly, when one must call into question each stage of the process. The rhetoric of "I-witnessing" can become a double-edged sword when it is invoked simultaneously as the source of ethnographic authority and as a critical tool to evaluate that authority. Had it seemed possible to do so, I would have preferred to avoid the tight-rope tensions involved. Yet, like Favret-Saada (1980) in her study of witchcraft in provincial France, I find myself in a situation where, in penetrating the "concealed things" of Mekeo esoteric knowledge, it is impossible to withdraw the author from the text: what is told is inseparable from to whom it is told, and only those who participate in the discourse are ever told. My perspective on the man of sorrow and of ritual experts in general is largely the product of my own involvement in acquiring esoteric knowledge; it necessitates putting my own experience in the fore, although my intention is to use this to illustrate what acquiring secret knowledge involves for Mekeo.

Although the very notion of self as an analytic category necessarily entails the "experience of selfhood . . . that occurs in human beings in various cultures"

(DeVos, Marsella, and Hsu 1985:1), this experiential aspect has often been absent in the accounts of Western observers. Recognition of this lack, and of the distortions arising out of an exclusive focus on cultural symbols and normative statements, has been the focus of a number of important studies (including McHugh 1989; Wikan 1989, 1990; and Ewing 1990b). My approach to Mekeo subjectivity explicitly deals with how real people experience their lives and give personal meaning, based on "cultural templates" (Wikan 1990), to the flow of everyday life. My presentation has not been directly influenced by Wikan's work, as I had already completed the final draft of this book before reading it, but I fully endorse her questioning of the low priority given to an anthropology of experience as compared with more conventional approaches and her suggestion that "the lived significance of other people's concerns should be granted as much primacy as those other approaches" (Wikan 1990:xxiv).

Herdt and Stoller (1990) have also drawn attention to anthropology's discontinuous interest in subjectivity and urged development of new approaches and new rigor. They take the insights of depth psychology and use them to help penetrate the secrets of Sambia sexuality and erotics. I, much less methodically and almost by accident, found that for Mekeo, dreams provide a (culturally) natural context for self-reflection and the examination of inner states and feelings. This study cannot pretend to be the "clinical ethnography" practiced by Herdt and Stoller. It is the work of a single scholar who has had no training in clinical psychology or psychoanalysis; it is not based on formal, clinical, interviewing. My approach to subjectivity is ethnographic: my discussions with Mekeo concerning their inner experience were directed at eliciting responses in their own idiom. My aim was to understand as far as possible their inner worlds in their terms.

Essentially, this is a study of Mekeo cosmology and esoteric knowledge as revealed in the lives of actual men and women, both laypersons and ritual experts. Dreams, waking visions, and other subtle intuitive states are a key focus of attention since they are culturally valued as modes of participation in the realm of spirit powers and forces. I also examine how the ongoing events of mundane life are seen to interweave with perceptions of a "hidden" world, and how particular individuals interpret these circumstances. Descriptive ethnography and conventional cultural analysis are thus interwoven with narrative accounts of actual events to reveal the interplay between cultural templates and lived experience. This began as an investigation neither of esoteric knowledge nor of the self; my original intention was to examine dreaming as a mode of cultural creativity. Dreams, however, led—by means of a logic it is largely the aim of this book to explicate—to deeper understandings of esoteric matters and to subtle layers of self-concepts previously unavailable to me. My explorations of these topics and their interrelationship are thus grounded in the subjectivities of Mekeo men and women as reported to me, producing a largely "person-centered" ethnography, although my intent is equally to locate their discourse within a specific cultural context.

My task of ethnographic description is greatly complicated by the fact that once one gains access to esoteric knowledge and to the private worlds of individuals (which is itself no easy matter), the public symbolism and public descriptions given of the cosmological order seem to be overthrown. I must wrestle with the interpretative problems posed by the seemingly contradictory perspectives that emerged from two different phases of fieldwork, one carried out in 1969–1971, the other in 1980–1982. The discrepancies were such that I might easily have concluded I was initially mistaken on many points; during my second extended fieldwork, when I learned the language well enough to converse without interpreters and was at last given access to esoteric knowledge, I was able to get the "real" picture. Here I faced the conundrum that, on the very points at which my new understandings seemed to confound the old, the findings of two other comprehensive and in-depth ethnographies (Hau'ofa 1981, dealing with the same cultural group, and Mosko 1985, dealing with a closely related culture)[2] supported my previous rather than my new understandings. In understanding Mekeo culture one must pay careful attention to those things which are manifest and overt (*ofakae*) and those which are concealed (*ogevake*). Of the latter, there exist yet further layers—the "secret," pertaining to esoteric knowledge, and the "hidden," pertaining to the realm of spirit forces. The point is not that all cultures have a "front stage" and "back stage," that which is produced for public view as the ideal and that which is in fact done—of course they do. Mekeo epistemology and cultural logic posits many layers of things concealed, and according to this cultural logic, one layer contains the opposite of another.[3]

Describing the nature of this ordering is the first challenge. Part I, "From Manifest to Hidden," comprises five chapters. I begin with an ostensibly straightforward description of Mekeo society; chapter 1 outlines things that if not immediately apparent are at least directly observable. The complexities underlying this surface order emerge in chapter 2, which introduces the concepts of *ofakae* and *ogevake*. Here I confront not only problems of different levels of observation and understanding but also bound up with them questions of how one obtains knowledge of things deliberately screened and what the consequences of such understanding are. It becomes essential to explain how my understandings have changed over time and through the vicissitudes of different phases of fieldwork. These issues are the subject of chapters 3 and 4. Once the nature of the material being dealt with becomes clearer, problems of a more general theoretical nature arise. Having gained access to hidden things and to the inner worlds of particular persons, how is one to handle the elusive, ephemeral stuff of private fantasy without bruising or destroying its fragile tissue? These problems are considered in chapter 5, which also outlines my concept of autonomous imagination (Stephen 1989a, 1989c) as a theoretical orientation for the discussion of subjective experience to follow.

The importance of dreaming as mode of special knowledge is examined in part II, "Dreaming and the Hidden Self." Chapters 6, 7, and 8 deal primarily with the experience of ordinary men and women who make no claims to esoteric knowledge, yet these people reveal a subtlety of self-knowledge and an understanding of, and interaction with, the spirit realm that seems to confound distinctions between laypersons and ritual experts.

Part III, "The Sorrows of Knowledge," deals with esoteric knowledge and the consequences of possessing it. The system of knowledge and who has access to it is described in chapter 9. Variations in ritual practice and the distinctive modes of self-awareness developed by adepts are dealt with in chapters 10 and 11. The role of the most powerful and feared possessor of ritual knowledge, the "man of sorrow," is examined at length in chapters 12, 13, and 14. It is through my encounters with a renowned man of sorrow and my own struggles to acquire secret knowledge that I attempt to demonstrate the remarkable self such an individual achieves. Chapter 15 brings to a close the ethnographic data, moving from individual experience back to the potentials for self imaged in cultural symbolism. In arguing that Mekeo cosmological symbols can best be understood in relation to the self, I return to the apparent contradictions between public and private levels of understanding. The final chapter reflects on broader comparative issues, drawing out the interconnections between magic and the self. I conclude that from the perspective of autonomous imagination some pragmatic effects of magic become understandable as a psychological reality, and that the link between magic and self-consciousness is not merely the creation of a specific cultural logic but has a far wider applicability.

In reflecting on the "permeable" and "impermeable" selves Mekeo create in cultural symbol and lived performance, I suggest that simple dichotomies between Western and tribal selves, and assumptions that "individuality" is known only in Western cultures, are misleading since they ignore subtle continuities of experience and desire that are masked by normative, prescriptive cultural representations. I hope to show the rich discourse of subjectivity that emerges in Mekeo reflections on dreaming and on hidden aspects of self that dreaming reveals. I argue that Mekeo esoteric ritual and knowledge go far beyond techniques for merely obtaining power or defending a status quo and are no less than the means of creating a uniquely individuated self capable of forcing its will upon others. I further show that oppositions such as rational/irrational, instrumental/magical, causation/participation, conscious/unconscious exaggerate differences in modes of cultural knowledge and serve to obscure the operation in all cultural productions, be they Western or tribal, of a rich vein of imaginative thought—an autonomous imagination—that is neither introspection nor analysis, yet probably underlies both.

Part I

From Manifest to Hidden

Reality—everything we are, everything that envelopes us, that sustains and, simultaneously, devours and nourishes us—is richer and more changeable, more alive, than all the ideas and systems that attempt to encompass it. In the process of reducing nature's rich, almost offensive spontaneity to the rigidity of our ideas, we mutilate its most fascinating element: its naturalness. . . . We do not truly know reality, but only the part of it we are able to reduce to language and concepts.

Octavio Paz, *The Siren and the Seashell*

1

The Visible Ordering
of Things

Like many ethnographies, this book pursues a mythic path trod by the culture
it purports to investigate. The story of A'aisa, the mythic hero and founder of
Mekeo culture, provides the starting point, and the destination. It is appropriate,
therefore, to retell his exploits here. This is not a complete version, nor an
esoteric version of his story, but rather a bare outline such as is known to all
ordinary Mekeo men and women, and even children.

A'aisa was found by an old woman, Epuke, who picked up a dried branch
from the ground while collecting firewood. She took it home later to find
concealed inside it a small boy. Childless and alone, the old woman adopted
him as her own.

As a boy, A'aisa goes hunting with the adult men. They find nothing, but
little A'aisa, with his special knowledge, bags a huge catch. The men then grab
A'aisa's game from him, pretending it is theirs and take it home, leaving
nothing for A'aisa and his old mother. A'aisa is angry and determined to have
revenge. He invites the women of the village to go fishing with him, but he
tricks them. With his special powers, he steals the women. A huge mountain
grows up under the canoe in which the women and he spend the night, leaving
them stranded there. A'aisa refuses to return the women to their husbands,
despite their pleas. The men come after A'aisa, swearing to kill him and regain
their wives, but as they begin to throw their spears and fire arrows at him,
A'aisa, from the top of the mountain, strikes them down with his powers. The
women weep and loudly beg A'aisa to have pity on their husbands. At last, he
relents and brings the men to life again, and tells them to return home.

Having demonstrated his superior powers and having punished the men for
their meanness, A'aisa now gives them some of his special knowledge. He

confers upon humankind ritual knowledge, and then creates the roles of the man of kindness (*lopia auga*), of the spear (*iso auga*), of cinnamon bark (*faia auga*), and of sorrow (*ugauga auga*). Along with these gifts, he also bestows death upon human beings.

The final episode of A'aisa's story deals with his quarrel with his brother Isapini. Isapini visits his brother but encounters what appears to be a small boy but in fact is A'aisa in disguise. Isapini asks to speak to the boy's father, failing to recognise A'aisa. Whereupon A'aisa is insulted and moved to anger. He decides to kill Isapini's son, his own namesake, A'aisa, with *ugauga* sorcery, thus originating both *ugauga* sorcery and jealousy (*pikupa*). Isapini retaliates by killing A'aisa's son, his namesake Isapini, with his own powers of *mefu* sorcery. The grieving A'aisa leaves Mekeo carrying the decomposing body of his son and searches for a place to bury it. He finally leaves the world of the living for good and makes his abode at Kariko, a hill on the coast toward the west, in the direction of the setting sun, where he still is believed to dwell with the shades of the dead.[1]

A'aisa's gifts to humankind included esoteric knowledge, death, and—as I shall show—self-consciousness. The task of this book is to unravel the threads that, for Mekeo, bind all three.

Although this study is primarily a descriptive ethnography, it is admittedly an unusual one in that it moves away from the social relationships, social interactions and shared cultural beliefs that are the usual focus of the ethnographic endeavor. My subject matter consists of dreams, waking visions, reverie— various kinds of elusive subjective experiences revealing the subtle, almost invisible interaction between the Mekeo mundane order of things and the hidden realm of sacred and cosmic forces. Perhaps this might be regarded as an "ethnography of inner experience," an exploration of the inner worlds of particular Mekeo individuals. Yet this seems too pretentious a label and to promise much more than I can hope to deliver. It would be claiming far too much to suggest a charting of inner experience of the same order as that possible for the ethnographer of the visible, public aspects of a culture. I cannot provide a "thick description" (Geertz 1975c) of Mekeo inner worlds in the sense of a comprehensive and exhaustive analysis of them. At best, I can offer glimpses, evocative rather than definitive, yet still revealing. In short, this book must itself be regarded as exploratory in its methods and approach.

The material on esoteric knowledge, cosmology, dreaming and subjective states which provides the major focus of the book derives from fieldwork carried out in the early 1980s. My understanding of Mekeo culture, however, also draws upon fieldwork done a decade earlier from 1969–1971 (and in several prior and subsequent short visits). The radically different perspectives emerging from these two phases of fieldwork create an antinomy threaded through the whole work. The reader must be ever wary of the movement in the text between these two contrasting perspectives, a tension which I shall not attempt to resolve until the final chapters. It is more usual in ethnographic works to open with at least a brief discussion of the nature of the fieldwork undertaken. I postpone this, however, until chapters 3 and 4 for the simple reason that no brief account will suffice.

Visual Impressions

Inner worlds cannot, of course, be understood in isolation from the public, outer worlds with which they interconnect. My account begins where every ethnographic enquiry, although not necessarily its reporting, must start: with what one can actually observe of Mekeo culture and social action, and with the explanations members give of its workings. Much is revealed in the actual, visible layout of communities. Although changes have occurred over the decades my fieldwork has spanned, the general appearance and tenor of village life in the early 1980s had not altered greatly since the mid-1960s. What is described here refers, unless otherwise specified, to the early 1980s. I follow the convention of an "ethnographic present" to indicate the particular chronological vantage point afforded to me, but obviously changes have occurred since, and are continuing to occur.

Mekeo culture conveys an immediate visual sense of order and harmony—a sense of order underlined in the articulate descriptions Mekeo themselves give of their society. My first impressions of their large, populous villages was of a smooth, measured pace of life. There was an appearance of formality in the structuring of village space and in the calm and dignified manner in which men and women went about their daily tasks. As I learned more, these initial impressions only seemed confirmed. It is a culture where hereditary status plays a large part: everyone seems to know precisely their appropriate place in the scheme of things and are ever conscious of the dangers of forgetting it. Even in the bustle and excitement of grand feasts there is an imposing air of organization, of time-honored ceremonial hospitality and etiquette. In the center of the village, at the clan meeting houses, hosts and guests play their parts urbanely; hereditary clan leaders and elders preside over affairs with impassive dignity. Overall, one cannot fail to gain the impression of a smooth and careful social ordering of things. There has been much recent comment on the emphasis Western cultures give to visual modes of perception and analysis (reviewed by Clifford 1986:11–12) and hence their dominance in ethnographic writing. Nevertheless, I am confident the following chapters will show that concern with appearances and visible surfaces—and what they conceal—are as much a focus of Mekeo cultural interest and elaboration as my own.

Oral tradition tells that the Mekeo people originated in the mountains and then descended to the plains, settling at various locations and driving before them the Waima and Roro people until they occupied all the fertile plains and only the arid coast was left to their enemies.[2] Like their coastal neighbors, the Waima and Roro (Monsell-Davis 1981) and the Nara-Kabadi people located

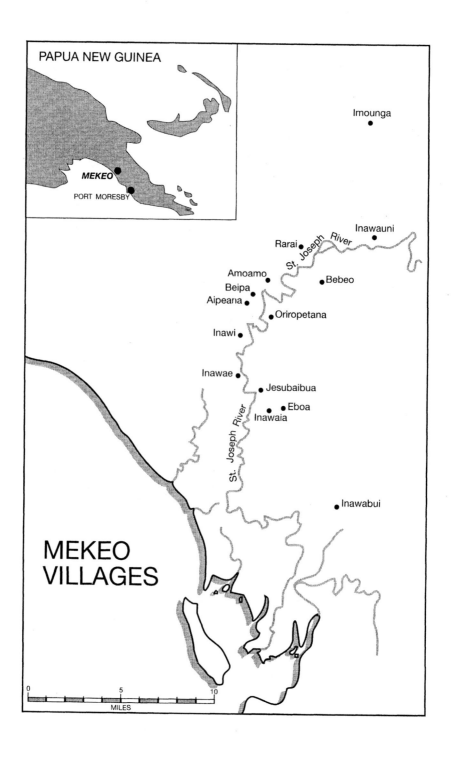

PAPUA NEW GUINEA

MEKEO
PORT MORESBY

Imounga

Inawauni

Rarai   St. Joseph River

Amoamo   Bebeo
Beipa
Aipeana

Oriropetana

Inawi

Inawae
        Jesubaibua
        Eboa
Inawaia

St. Joseph River

Inawabui

MEKEO
VILLAGES

0   5   10
          MILES

immediately to the east (Wilson 1975), the Mekeo are an Austronesian-speaking group. Culturally and linguistically, they are closely related to the Bush Mekeo people, who inhabit the more inaccessible swampy region to the northwest (Mosko 1985). Further north, into the mountains, are the Kuni, and beyond them the Mafulu and other non-Austronesian mountain peoples; to the west are the non-Austronesian peoples of the Papuan Gulf.

Situated between the coast and the mountains, and occupying the richest agricultural land in the region, the Central Mekeo were, and are, in an advantageous position to trade their abundant garden crops for the produce of both coastal and mountain regions and to control access to trade routes between coast and mountains. Since the Second World War, and especially since the opening of the Hiritano Highway to Port Moresby in the mid-1970s, Mekeo have become cash-rich by selling their garden produce and betel-nut harvest in the markets of the capital. Most villages boast locally owned trade stores, and many people own trucks and other vehicles. In the early 1980s there was constant travel to and from Port Moresby as people went to town to sell their produce (this was one respect in which village life had changed notably since the late 1960s, when vehicles were scarce and passable roads were few). Rich in terms of subsistence crops—the staples include plantains and taro as well as many introduced plants—and with the ready availability of cash from the sale of produce in town, Mekeo are not unaware of their advantages over less well-situated, less well-endowed groups such as their coastal neighbors. They are justly proud of their fertile and abundant land and boast of a way of life that gives them everything they need, and more, without excessive labor.

Mekeo live in large nucleated villages, ranging in size from the largest of about 1,000 inhabitants to the smallest of about 130; Mekeo number approximately 7,000. The community in which I conducted fieldwork was the third largest, with a population of just under 900.[3] The region is located on the central Papuan coast, about seventy miles northwest of the capital, Port Moresby. Fourteen villages are situated along the St. Joseph River as it traverses a fertile plain that extends inland from the coastal hills of Waima to the foothills of the mountains to the north. Occasionally, on very clear days, the mountains are visible—steep, craggy, and of a startling intense purple against the tropical sky, almost like a child's painting. There are usually no such vistas, however, and beyond the cleared spaces of human settlement one tends to feel shut in by the surrounding bush, the gardens, or large stretches of cane grass. Perhaps for this reason Mekeo refer to entering the village as "going outside" (*pealai*) or going "out into the open." Cut off from the cooling sea breezes by the coastal hills, the Mekeo plain is intensely hot and humid, and much of it is flooded in the wet season, December to April.

A Mekeo village community is composed of named patrilineal descent groups, each, ideally, with its own hereditary leader (*lopia*) and its own *ufu*, or meeting house.

The *Ufu* are large open structures found in central, prominent positions in the village. They are roofed with thatch (or, nowadays, iron), and are built on posts, as are the domestic dwellings, with broad steps or ladders at the front by which to enter. The dwellings of the members of the descent group, where married men live with their wives and children, cluster behind each group's *ufu*, thus dividing the village settlement into a number of different wards. These divisions are not, however, immediately apparent since the houses of black palm, bamboo, and thatch are built close together in rows along a clear central thoroughfare. This is the *pagua inaega* (literally, the belly or womb of the village);[4] it is usually many yards wide, with the *ufu* of each descent group facing it directly and the domestic houses ranged behind.

Ufu have no walls, and since these structures face the central thoroughfare of the village, what takes place there is visible to all. Mekeo appreciate generosity and largesse, and fortunately they can indulge in it. Anyone, I was assured, might go to any *ufu* (each descent group represented in the village is supposed to maintain at least one) and be provided with food and shelter. As a visitor, I was in fact usually taken by my contacts to one or another of the community's *ufu*, where we would be received with some ceremony. A mat would be carefully spread out for us to sit on, and men would arrive, shake our hands, and sit down to talk and chew betel nut. Women also would come to shake hands, perhaps because I am a woman, but did not stay, although some would soon reappear to bring refreshments which the men served. (The *ufu* is reserved for the men; women can gather in the *ufu* only to mourn a corpse that has been laid there just prior to burial.)

On my first visits to the region in the late 1960s, I was received everywhere with an almost embarrassingly extravagant hospitality. I could not sit down to talk for a few minutes with people I might find on their veranda without someone insisting on preparing a large cooked meal or serving a lavish tea with store-bought sweet biscuits, bread, and tinned meat. Should I protest, people would explain it was the custom and that any visitor should be received in this way. Indeed, it was the special duty of the *lopia* to provide hospitality to all visitors who came to their *ufu*.

A large village is composed of several descent groups and is an impressive sight with its wide open central space and long rows of houses. Such a community, of several hundred inhabitants, conveys an almost metropolitan air (cf. Guis 1936). From either end of the central plaza, tracks or roads lead out of the village. Pigs and dogs occasionally wander across this central space and vehicles drive through it, yet it has an air of formality. As one walks down the plaza, one becomes aware of the scrutiny of the people sitting concealed on their verandas or resting in the shade beneath the houses. There is no shade in the *pagua inaega*, the sun beats down and reflects off the flat sandy ground; no trees, fences, or other encumbrances clutter this carefully cleared and swept area. It is impossible not to feel a little self-conscious and exposed whenever one traverses this imposing, preeminently public space.

A more informal route is the path circling the outer periphery of the settlement. Between the last row of houses and the surrounding bush is a cleared space, but it is a much less tidy one than the central plaza. Some shade is provided by the surrounding bush and the occasional shrub and tree allowed to grow here. This is the village's "backyard"; here are found small sheds and outhouses, fowl yards, pigs and dogs (both of which roam freely but are more likely to be found scavenging here), and people chopping wood, splitting coconuts to feed pigs or make copra, making their way to or from the river (still the community's only water supply in the 1980s) to fetch water or to bathe, or returning from the gardens.[5] Most people in fact move around the village via either this backyard or the space between rows of houses, rather than across the central plaza. This area on the village's periphery extends several yards behind the outer row of dwellings to a natural wall of bush and tall trees. People retire into the shelter of this surrounding growth for defecation, each household using the area just to the back of its dwelling; the domestic pigs that scavenge here dispose of refuse. Many little paths lead through the encircling bush to the river, to the gardens, and to the areas of bush and cane grass stretching beyond. People locate gardens at some distance from the village to avoid the need to construct fences to keep out domestic pigs.

At the very edge of the settlement, where the backyard merges into thick bush, and well separated from the other houses, may be found an occasional small dwelling referred to as a *gove*. In the past, young bachelors and widowers of all ages were required to live in *gove;* throughout both phases of my fieldwork, however, the segregation of unmarried youths and widowers was not strictly observed.[6] Most young men spent the time before marriage away from the village, either at school or in paid employment. Only a few elderly widowers chose to live permanently segregated in this way; in my experience, they were usually individuals identified as powerful and feared ritual experts. Just as one cannot spend long in a Mekeo community without being told something about the duties and functions of the *lopia,* so it is that one is warned about the dangerous presence of the *ugauga,* possessors of death-dealing ritual powers. Such persons are not, however, unidentified bogeymen or despised misfits, as in some Melanesian societies (Stephen 1987b). They are men of rank who employ their lethal rituals to uphold the social order and the authority of the *lopia.* Their location, at the very margin of domestic space in the encircling bush where people hide themselves to defecate, is indicative of the dark forces with which they are said to deal.

A brief examination of the layout of the settlement begins to reveal a sketchy outline of a social ordering (cf. Hau'ofa 1981:chapter 3). At the center of society are the descent group meeting houses, the *ufu,* presided over by the descent group heads, the *lopia*. Ranged behind these public centers of collective activity are the private houses of the adult married men, their wives, and children, as well as unmarried girls and widows. Beyond this middle domestic space, on the periphery of the settlement, are found the *gove*, small shelters occupied by unmarried males, bachelors, and widowers. These marginal males without women are suspected of associating with the *ugauga*, who are reputed to maintain secret dwellings (*fauapi*) deep in the bush, where they are presumed to practice their dangerous rituals.

The orderly, structured sense of space conveyed in the layout of the village is underlined in the controlled movements, gestures, and careful deportment of its inhabitants (cf. Hau'ofa 1981:117–19, 301–302). Men carry themselves tall, heads held high, with straight backs and shoulders, giving the impression of height even in its absence. They move smoothly, creating a very deliberate and careful public presentation of self. Mekeo always contrive to look unruffled. Males pay more attention to grooming and self-decoration than women; indeed, they often convey a dandified, almost effeminate vanity to some European eyes. Mekeo men, however, do not, as European rumor would have it, dress to attract male lovers but, rather, to inspire female admiration. In the Mekeo view, it is men, not women, who must make themselves beautiful to the opposite sex. Fashions change even in Mekeo villages, but in the late 1960s and 1970s, male beauty required a tall, wasp-waisted figure and lightly but strongly muscled limbs. A great rounded halo of hair, carefully teased and trimmed, and a smooth, light brown to yellowish skin, free of all facial and body hair, were also *de rigueur*. Most men either removed their eyebrows entirely, or plucked them to a fine line, giving their smooth, almost oriental, faces with high cheekbones a somewhat haughty expression. On holidays and special occasions, married men dress in close-fitting, ankle-length sarongs of plain bright red, yellow, or blue, cinched tightly at the waist with a fancy belt. Scarfs, bead necklaces, earplugs and earrings, flowers in the hair, and arm bands and leg bands complement outfits worn with a deliberately nonchalant elegance. Young unmarried youths, ever on the lookout for prospective brides, usually take pains to look their best at all times in the hope of attracting female attention. Even elders may go to considerable lengths to present a fine appearance in public. By the 1980s, young unmarried men were adopting more of the European-influenced styles of Port Moresby—tradestore-bought shorts and shirts, jeans and T-shirts—and only older men continued to favor the distinctive attire just described.

Females, including young girls, never lavish much attention on their appearance beyond keeping themselves neat and clean, and there was no change to be observed in female dress in the early 1980s. For a brief time after her marriage, a bride's in-laws customarily decorate, oil, and dress her elaborately so that she can be shown off to all, and during this period as a newly married woman (*amage mamaga*) the bride does no physical work. Women and girls, as they themselves will insist, are usually far too busy to be bothered about unnecessary primping. They cut their hair close to their heads, wear few ornaments, and usually dress in rough grass skirts for gardening and in simple trade-store skirts and blouses for less heavy work. On holidays and special occasions they wear new clothes of bright colors, but never with the calculated effect and studied elegance of the men. Nevertheless, it should not be imagined Mekeo women are colorless drudges. They are confident and assertive in their bearing, they openly boast of their physical strength and are proud of their capacity for hard work. Indeed, young girls are said to be admired more for the strength they display in hard work than for their prettiness. Tall, sturdily built, muscular girls are much admired. Females move purposefully, speak assertively, gesture firmly: even girls give the impression of strong, motherly capability. To an outsider they may evince a straightforward homely honesty, especially compared with the artificiality of dress and makeup common to women in Western cultures, yet there is a reserve and subtlety behind this apparent openness, as there is behind every aspect of Mekeo life. Overall, Mekeo are a handsome people, and what a person lacks in looks can always be made up for by style. Certain individuals, both male and female, are possessed of unique and striking beauty, and such beauty is not necessarily limited to youth.

Gender Relationships

This is a patrilineal society in which group membership, property rights, rank, and ritual knowledge are transmitted through males, and as is common in most Melanesian societies, the important divisions of labor are based on gender. To women fall the continuous backbreaking work of weeding, planting, and maintaining gardens, and carrying heavy loads of vegetables, firewood, and water; they feed the pigs and other domestic animals; they cook, clean, wash, keep the village swept and tidy, and look after their large families. Young unmarried girls usually work even harder at these tasks than married women, as they are not debilitated by childbearing and breast-feeding or hampered by the care of babies and small children. A Mekeo woman longs for the time when she has a daughter old enough to be of real help to her. A middle-aged woman I knew well, who had six handsome sons, was forever telling me how hard her life had been because she had borne only male offspring, who just created work for her. She lived for the day when the eldest would marry and she would have a strong young daughter-in-law to take the burden off her aging shoulders. Another family I knew had several hefty, hardworking unmarried daughters whom the mother did not want to see marry until she had daughters-in-law to replace them. Females are a valuable asset in any household, and are so not only for their childbearing capacities.

In contrast to the daily grind experienced by women and girls, males perform tasks that require short bursts of intensive labor: they clear bush for new gardens, construct fences, build and repair houses, and hunt and fish. Adolescent boys and young unmarried men, unlike girls, are not expected to work hard but are free to spend their time largely as they please. In the past, adolescence was a time when youths devoted themselves primarily to courting and finding a suitable bride (see also Hau'ofa 1981:116–20). For the last three decades or so, however, most boys have spent these years away at school or working for a wage away from the village. Today, men and youths drive trucks and tractors and engage in various business activities, but female labor is still required in any farming activity. Both men and women share the task of taking garden produce and betel nut to sell in town.

Males are not unaware that overall theirs is an easier life; they will tell you that this is just how things are. I have often heard men comment, as we sat back leisurely, chatting in the clan meeting house while sweating women ran back and forth delivering endless platters of cooked food and huge kettles of tea and coffee: "We don't force our girls and women to work, they are happy to do it. Their mothers did it and now they do. Women are proud of their work."

To large extent, women share this view, at least in their public expressions of opinion. They are proud of the vital contribution made by their labor. They point out that without them, life simply could not go on: there would be no gardens, no food, no pigs, no people—nothing. They know their contributions are essential and valued, and they are aware they are valued as persons because of their femininity (and not in spite of it).

The word for female, *papiega* (*papie* = married woman; *ga* = suffix of relationship), has strongly positive connotations. The definition of a nonhuman or inanimate object as "feminine" is its capacity to multiply or to contain additional entities. Something that is male (*maguaega*) is both a single and sterile entity; thus land described as female is fertile and productive, whereas male land is infertile. A truck might be regarded as female because it carries many people, a car as male because it carries only one (or few). A single quartz crystal charm (used in many esoteric rituals) is *maguae* (male); a cluster is *papiega* (female). Women are regarded as more altruistic since they look after others, whereas men are concerned with their own selfish pursuits. Elderly parents of both sexes bemoan the lack of adult daughters to look after them in their old age, just as younger women complain of the lack of girl children to help in daily tasks. Old people declare that sons ignore them and daughters-in-law only look after their own parents; one's best hope of loving care in old age is to have daughters of one's own. Men, both sexes say, have hard hearts (*gua'i ke inoka*), only women are really kind.

Evidently there is in Mekeo culture little of the bitter misogyny or rampant sexual antagonism and anxiety (reviewed by Herdt and Poole 1982) reported for many New Guinea cultures, particularly, though not exclusively, of Highlands cultures. There are no secret male cults from which women are excluded and no male initiation rites; women are not segregated from the rest of the household during menstruation (although they do not cook for others at this time or work in the gardens). Husband and wife normally sleep together, occupying the same dwelling with their offspring; this, however, is largely the result of the influence of the Catholic mission and of other changes that followed pacification and colonial rule (Stephen 1974; Hau'ofa 1981). In the past, married men slept in their *ufu,* leaving the domestic dwellings to the women and children, while unmarried men and widowers slept in the *gove.* Restrictions on the sexes cohabiting apply only during certain ritual practices and for a stipulated time following childbirth.

Despite the relative ease of relations between the sexes, there is not quite the same sense of sexual freedom and open eroticism reported for some coastal and island societies, particularly matrilineal groups such as the Trobrianders (Malinowski 1932). There is a seemingly puritanical streak in Mekeo that can not be attributed solely to the influence of European missionaries, since the coastal Waima, who have been exposed to the same pressures, are renown among their Mekeo neighbors for their open sexual dalliances and for the freedom granted to both sexes in erotic matters. In contrast, Mekeo observe a double standard that is almost Victorian in flavor. Adultery is an expected male pastime, although such things are always kept out of the public eye for the sake of decorum. Women must be faithful to their husbands; moreover, they are said by males to be scarcely interested in sex. Unmarried girls are required to be chaste and are carefully watched over (see also Hau'ofa 1981:120–21). It is not that Mekeo think women are frigid, like the hysterical nineteenth-century Viennese or Victorian lady—Mekeo women are more robust souls. Yet it is thought female sexuality is more slowly aroused, less immediate, perhaps less insistent, than is male desire. Women, in keeping with cultural convention, are so reticent about such matters that I have available only male views. Whatever their innermost erotic desires, Mekeo women do not easily reveal them, but that may add to their attraction in the eyes of males, who believe females are unattainable without special ritual aid to overcome their natural aloofness from erotic pleasure. It is also for this reason that males employ the artifice of self-decoration to acquire a bride; that Western culture reverses this view perhaps gives it an odd piquancy in our eyes.

Sexuality and eroticism, whether in courting, marital relations, or illicit affairs, are matters private and covert in this culture (see also Hau'ofa 1981: 120–24). Both men and women behave with great decorum in public. In most group activities the sexes are usually segregated; men and women are never left alone together unless they are married or are very close relatives. Gestures of affection such as kissing or embracing between adults are permitted in public only in the greetings and farewells of close kin. Young couples must keep their courting secret, and everyone contrives to keep their sexual dalliances out of the public eye. This is not to say, of course, that in small communities, where everyone knows everybody's business, such matters remain unknown for long, but dissembling and disguise is the norm. People tend to speak of these things in veiled terms and innuendo, and not openly in gossip.[7] The tensions of erotic attraction and desire are thus carefully screened behind the smooth, impassive face of the visible social order.

The Social Ordering

The immediate visual impressions of order and structure in a Mekeo community are confirmed by the careful structuring of leadership according to the seniority of birth and lineage, in the formalized but friendly relationships between affines, and in the permanent relationships of reciprocal feast exchanges which link descent groups. The aim of this study is not to reassess Mekeo social organization but merely to provide a brief outline to contextualize the discussion of esoteric knowledge and the self. Inevitably, I do touch upon problems of defining various aspects of social structure, particularly as raised in other studies (Hau'ofa 1981; Mosko 1985), but in terms of the broad outlines being sketched, my picture of Mekeo society varies little from that presented in more detail by Hau'ofa.

Local Groups and Descent Groups

A Mekeo village (*pagua*) is an independent social and political unit, managing its own internal affairs; in the past, the clans combined as a whole to meet the threat of external aggression. The region came under colonial control in the 1890s, and intervillage warfare was brought to a halt by 1900. Local groups, descent groups, and the ordering of social relationships within the community were not seriously disrupted by this external intervention (Stephen 1974; Hau'ofa 1981). Throughout the period I worked in the region, villagers managed their day-to-day affairs with a minimum of interference from the Australian colonial government and, later, the national government.

Within the village settlement, the patrilineal descent groups (*ikupu*) provide the most important focus of social relationships. In principle, each village-based descent group has its own hereditary leader (*lopia*) or leaders, maintains its own meeting house (*ufu*), and directs its own internal affairs. Rights to residential, gardening, and foraging land are based on descent group membership. The members consider themselves to be closely related, as brothers descended from brothers; men build their houses together, contribute to one another's marriage payments, bury their dead in the same ground, and provide mutual help and labor in all manner of tasks. Under the direction of their descent group head, they engage in feast exchanges with other descent groups to mark important social occasions—in particular, death. Women leave their natal group on marriage but retain strong ties with it and continue to participate in various ways in its collective activities. The importance of females born of the descent group is further emphasized in the work obligations that a husband owes his wife's descent group (I will return to this shortly).

I refer to these descent groups (*ikupu*) as "clans" for the sake of convenience. The Mekeo term *ikupu* is used to refer to: a) the separate lineages of a clan, b) clan sections made up of two or more lineages, c) the localized village-based segment of a clan, and d) the clan in the broadest sense as the sum of its village-based segments. Some clans, in the latter sense, have segments in two or more villages. Although the members of all the different village-based segments of the same clan consider themselves to be related, and may maintain special ties with one another, for all purposes it is the village-based segment that is the functioning social unit, and I shall henceforth refer to it simply as a clan. The community in which I lived comprises eleven different named clans. Some of these groups, however, are too small or too weak to have their own leaders and ritual experts, and thus must align themselves with larger clans since only a properly installed clan head can perform the death ceremonies. A large clan, which may have several hereditary leaders and ritual functionaries, is commonly divided into three sections. The internal divisions of such a group may prove to be rather more complex when the lineage structure is investigated via actual genealogies of its members, but according to the stated ideal, and often in fact, a threefold structure prevails. I refer to these internal divisions as "clan sections."

The clan sections are ranked in order of seniority and are usually said to represent the descendants of three named brothers; the precise genealogical links to the founding brothers cannot always be recalled, but often are. The descendants of the eldest brother constitute the senior section of the clan and are usually designated by the term *lopia* linked to the clan name, thus Paisapaisa Lopia. *Lopia* is also the term used to refer to the leader of the village-based clan. The genealogically most senior member of the *lopia* clan section (who is, or should be, the direct descendant of the eldest of the founding brothers) is the most important, the senior (*fa'aniau*), the leader of the entire group. Only the *lopia fa'aniau* can perform the mourning ceremonies. The descendants of the second brother constitute the second section of the clan; this is usually referred to as the Eke, the junior section, thus Paisapaisa Eke. The head of this section, who is regarded as the direct descendant of the second founding brother, is referred to as the *lopia eke,* the junior leader. He is considered to be an assistant to the *lopia fa'aniau,* but maintains his own meeting house, where the men of his section gather. The third clan section, comprising the descendants of the third brother, is the Iso, literally "spear" section; its leader is the *iso auga* (spear man), or *iso lopia.* As the name suggests, he and his section were responsible for leading the group into battle. In the early 1980s, the title and position of war leader still existed in many clans. The head of the war section, like the *lopia eke,* maintains his own meeting house and presides over the internal affairs of his own section. But the death ceremonies for members of the Iso section, as for the other two sections, must be conducted by the *lopia fa'aniau.*

Members of the clan section build their houses together, clustered behind their *ufu,* thus indicating their separate identity within the clan. Often the section comprises a single lineage, and members trace their descent—once again—from three brothers, thus separating lines of descent even within the lineage according to the seniority of birth of a set of founding brothers. Mekeo descent groups can thus be seen to be conceptualized as siblings descended from sets of (conventionally, three) male siblings, rather than from a single common ancestor. Agnatic kinsmen are referred to as one's *aga akina*—brothers senior in birth and brothers junior in birth (to the speaker). Siblings of opposite sex (regardless of one's sex) are termed *afakua.*

As the term *aga akina* (senior and junior brothers) suggests, seniority of birth order is a key principle in the structuring of descent groups. The first-born brother, by virtue of his seniority, is considered to have precedence and authority over his juniors, who owe him respect and obedience. Two brothers (and sometimes two sisters), a senior and a junior, are the prominent characters in many Mekeo myths, as in the myth of A'aisa and his younger brother, Isapini. Social relationships, and conflicts, are culturally conceptualized in terms of relations between senior and junior male siblings rather than between fathers and sons. Indeed, A'aisa, the mythological hero responsible for founding the existing social order, had no father and only an adoptive mother, but he had a younger brother with whom he had a fatal quarrel, leading to the killing of each other's sons.

The close relationship between brothers, which provides the model of ties and obligations that link men, is revealed in the A'aisa myth to contain the potential for bitter and murderous rivalry. Clan histories explain that the present divisions of clan groups into localized segments scattered throughout different villages has come about over generations because of fratricidal conflict similar to that initiated by A'aisa himself (Seligman 1910; Stephen 1974; Hau'ofa 1981; Mosko 1985). Many such conflicts and fissioning of descent groups have taken place within living memory. When an irreconcilable internal quarrel developed, a section, a lineage, or a few individuals belonging to the clan would decide to leave the rest of the group. This involved seeking residence and land somewhere else—sometimes within the same village settlement, thus necessitating an alliance with another existing clan. For example, a quarrel within the Lopia Fa'a section of Oaisaka clan in the 1920s led to two brothers leaving their natal clan and seeking land from Ogofoina, another large clan in the same village. The sons of these two brothers, and their offspring, are now said to constitute a separate clan (*ikupu*), called Ogofoina Lopia Fa'a. Although people agree that the eldest son of the eldest of the two brothers who initiated the break should be the *lopia,* the new group has never mustered the resources to establish its own head, and it relies upon the head of its host clan, Ogofoina, to officiate at mourning rituals.

When breakaway groups moved to different villages or, in the past, founded new settlements, they would, if they flourished, eventually establish their own leaders and become politically and ritually independent while still recognizing their origin from the senior group (see also Hau'ofa 1981). In the process of fissioning, however, the system of segmentary lineages found among African peoples (Fortes and Evans-Pritchard 1940) did not develop since the new group, as it expanded, replicated the ideal structure of clan segments ranked in order of seniority, so as to form anew the ideal threefold structure of senior, junior, and war sections.

Associated with the principle that dictated seniority of birth of male siblings as the basis for the descent group structure, and the expectation that the first-born brother would exercise benevolent influence over his juniors, was an assumption that junior lines would undertake the dangerous, aggressive roles and rituals necessary to defend the group and to punish those who flouted the moral order. The roles of war leader and the lethal rituals of sorcery (*ugauga*) were undertaken by junior brothers and by junior sections of the clan, but they were expected to use their powers at the direction of the first-born brother and, under his benign influence, to serve the common good of the clan as a whole. A tendency toward a proliferation of leadership and ritual roles based on the division of senior and junior lines seems to have motivated a process of internal differentiation into sections within the village-based clan (see also Hau'ofa 1981: chapter 7).

Large clans commonly display the threefold structure just described, but there is an observable tendency, even within the clan section, for further divisions along the lines of senior versus junior. For example, Oaisaka clan in Inawi village has three sections, Oaisaka Lopia Fa'a (the senior section), Lalae (the junior section), and Oaisaka Iso (the war section). The war section, however, is further differentiated into a senior line and a junior line and has recognized senior and junior war leaders (Hau'ofa 1981:193 describes a similar example). In the case of Paisapaisa clan, another large group divided into three sections, the war section, Paisapaisa Iso, is also renown for its possession of the lethal rituals of *ugauga*. The senior line of the war section retained the position of war leader for itself, while passing over to a junior line the knowledge of *ugauga* rituals.

As a village-based clan, or even a clan section, increased in size and moved too far from the ideal of a set of brothers and their offspring, senior and junior lines gradually emerged and established their own leaders and ritual specializations. Thus the stage would be set for a more radical split wherein junior lines might seek complete autonomy from senior lines. With the establishment of colonial control and the imposed peace that followed, local grouping and land boundaries tended to be frozen (Stephen 1974; Hau'ofa 1981); as a consequence it became difficult to found new settlements. Breakaway groups had to re-establish themselves somewhere else in the same village, or in another established settlement where they had to assume a subordinate position in relationship to their host group (as in the case of Ogofoina Lopia Fa'a). A proliferation of leadership roles within the clan section, such as the senior and junior war leaders of Oaisaka clan, was perhaps a way to deal with a situation in which establishment of complete independence for a new group was no longer possible.

Remnants of once-populous and powerful clans, like Ugo in Inawi village, have almost died out and thus no longer have their own leaders. These groups also must align themselves with larger clans possessing functioning *lopia*. Thus a situation emerges in which a few large powerful clans become the foci of clusters of smaller groups. The village that was the site of my fieldwork, with its eleven named clans, consists of three such clusters centering around Ogofoina, Oaisaka, and Paisapaisa clans, with Gagai clan as a single independent group. In terms of their internal affairs, these four groups are independent of one another; each holds its own death feasts and the feasts to install new leaders and inaugurate new meeting houses. The founding clan of the village, Oaisaka (from which the village derives its correct Mekeo name, Oaisaka), is considered to have precedence over the others since it is the most senior. The senior leader (*lopia fa'aniau*) of Oaisaka is considered to be senior to, and therefore higher in prestige than, all the other senior *lopia* of the village. While this might add weight in negotiations, it in fact confers no functionally superior authority.

Every fully functioning independent clan is linked to at least one, and sometimes two or more, other clans, in a special relationship termed *ufu apie,* a rather enigmatic term that has had several readings by different scholars (Seligman 1910; Hau'ofa 1981; and in particular Mosko 1985). Desnoes's "Mekeo Dictionary" (1941:998) defines the term thus: "Friends, the allies with which one intermarries (Les amis, les alliés avec lesquels on se marie)." The literal meaning he gives as, "The *ufu* (clan meeting house) of the other side or: of the other end of the village (L'ufu de l'autre côté, ou: de l'autre bout de village."[8] If the *ufu apie* relationship represents a remnant of dual organization, the problem still stands that there now exists a chaos of such relationships, often involving more than one other clan and often linking clans of different villages; these relationships may be in some cases still operative, in others defunct. On the basis of my own observations of social practice, and the explanations villagers have given, it appears to me the *ufu apie* relationship retains importance because it is a clan's *ufu apie* who are the major recipients of meat and food gifts at its most important feasts. When a descent group installs a new *lopia,* builds a new meeting house, or conducts the ceremony to end the period of mourning for the dead, it is the group's *ufu apie* who are the most honored and most important guests, and it is to them that the best and largest shares of meat and vegetables are presented. It is in fact the *lopia* of the *ufu apie* who must be invited to perform the final ritual acts for installing a new leader and removing mourning for the dead. This is a reciprocal relationship: the *ufu apie* return these gifts and services when it is their turn to hold mortuary feasts and other events. A careful investigation of actual *ufu apie* relationships reveals they can be terminated and new ones formed but, in principle, they are regarded as involving long-established, permanent ties with other groups. The ideal is of balanced reciprocity between allies.

The *ufu apie,* as Desnoes points out, are also considered proper and appropriate marriage partners (see Hau'ofa 1981:166). But marriage choice is not restricted to them, indeed could not be, since one cannot marry into either one's father's or one's mother's descent group. If a man's father had married a woman from an *ufu apie* clan, he could not himself marry into it since that would be his mother's clan. Only the next generation could do so. Brothers-in-law have special obligations to each other in providing labor for feasts, which means that when the *ufu apie* are called upon to be the most important guests at a feast, the *ufu apie* men, who are married to the host's daughters and sisters, have to provide labor for the occasion. Consequently, it is very undesirable for the *lopia* of a clan to marry a woman from his *ufu apie* as this would place him in two incompatible roles: as the chief guest of honor and as a laborer at his *ufu apie*'s feasts!

There are no formal relationships today that link or bind entire village communities to other communities. Relationships that cut across villages are between descent groups or individuals. The term *Mekeo,* as so often the case in Papua New Guinea, is a colonial inheritance, not an indigenous category. It refers to communities who consider themselves to belong to two separate groups, the Pioufa and the Ve'e. Once again the precise nature of this division and its significance in the past is difficult to determine (although it is, of course, of interest when attempting to reconstruct ideal forms of social structure, but that is not my concern here). People today still identify themselves and their villages as either Pioufa or Ve'e (roughly speaking, the division coincides with the West and East Mekeo). This indicates a sense of common origin and stock, of a common cultural inheritance and local history uniting those who identify themselves as either Pioufa or Ve'e. But there are no longer formal institutions of any kind expressing this identity; even in the past, Pioufa villages fought Pioufa, and Ve'e villages fought Ve'e.

Marriage, Affines, and Relations Traced through Women

A person cannot marry into either his or her own clan, or into the clan of his or her mother. When I asked people to explain why marriage within these groups is prohibited, they did not refer to degrees of relationship or the sharing of blood or other forms of body substance. Instead, they explained that if a man were to marry a woman of his own descent group, or of his mother's group, then the people who were making the payments to the bride's family and those who were receiving the payments would be one and the same, which is patently ridiculous and unsatisfactory. For the Mekeo, it all comes down to marriage payments.

Marriage payments are described as compensation for the loss of a woman. Parents are indeed reluctant to allow strong, hardworking girls to marry, as the family's daily subsistence may depend primarily on them, particularly if the mother is getting old, is ill, or has many small children. I referred earlier to a mother who refused to let her daughters marry until she had daughters-in-law to replace them. The father confided he used certain spells and charms to prevent the girls from falling in love and thus being lost to the family. Many people, he assured me, did likewise. In a similar vein, parents discourage their daughters from courting and love affairs, and often beat them for encouraging a suitor's attentions. Girls' relatives do not relinquish their rights to their labor and the offspring they will eventually produce without adequate compensation. (At the same time, the girls themselves, it is said, would feel ashamed and devalued if their families simply allowed them to leave without protest.) Four clans are involved in marriage payments: the groom's agnates, who supply the major part of the payment; the groom's mother's agnates, who provide a lesser portion; the bride's agnates, who receive the largest portion; and the bride's mother's agnates, who also receive a share (see also Hau'ofa 1981:158–159). People observe that a girl's father and brothers look forward to a handsome compensation when she marries.

Marriage takes place either by arrangement between the parents or by elopement when the couple runs off without the girl's parents' knowledge and announces the *fait accompli* of their union. (There was also rumored to be marriage by rape where a girl might be literally kidnapped against her will by a man and then forced to cohabit with him; one very aggressive, surly man, with a generally sinister reputation in the community was said to have acquired his wife in this manner.) Most marriages nowadays are elopements. Marriage thus usually begins in acrimony and outrage on the part of the girl's family, who suddenly find their daughter taken from them without their knowledge or permission. Sometimes at this stage the parents will intervene to take the girl back. The couple either remains in hiding with relatives elsewhere or, if the girl's family succeeds in getting her back, she might run off again until her parents finally are induced, by promises of handsome marriage payments, to accept the situation.

An incident during my first years of fieldwork dramatized this when a girl eloped from the clan section in which I was living. Her relatives managed to find her and they forcibly brought her back. Because she threatened to run away again, they set up a post in the central thoroughfare in front of the clan's houses (and directly in front of mine), where the whole village could witness what was going on, and tied the girl by her arms and legs to the post. She stood there for hours in the burning sun. Finally, the groom's relatives managed to mobilize their resources; toward evening they appeared walking slowly up the plaza from their own clan ward, each person bearing a tree branch festooned with dozens of Australian banknotes and valuable feather decorations. After being paraded up the center of the village, these flamboyant "money trees" were duly presented as peace offerings to the girl's relatives. The girl was then released from her public humiliation, although not handed over to her prospective groom until further payments were assured. The bride's relatives were extremely angry because they considered the boy's people to be an indigent lot who would never be able to raise a decent marriage payment. Thus it was only through the dramatic gesture of the money trees that the groom and his clan prevailed.

This was an extreme case, and I never witnessed another similar performance. Nevertheless, this single "social drama" (Turner 1957) strikingly illustrated the conflict of interests and emotions aroused in the social act of marriage: the righteous anger of the family whose daughter had been "stolen" from them; the peace offerings of the groom's kin who were anxious to prove that they were respectable people ready to pay for what they had taken; the girl, humiliated and punished for deserting her kin without their knowledge and without concern for their rights; and, finally, the vindication of her action by the groom's relatives' public demonstration of their esteem for her. The dynamic of the situation is clear: outrage and anger of those who lost a valuable member of their group, appeasement and placation by those who gained a valuable new member.

Although marriage usually begins in a situation where the bride's relatives' anger must be assuaged by suitably generous gifts, the groom's relatives have the advantage because they are in possession of the bride. It is usually several years before the major portion of the marriage payments are complete. Not surprisingly, in these circumstances quarrels and tensions are ever present, yet, as is usual for Mekeo, these are rarely aired openly. Ostensibly, relationships between in-laws are expected to be close and amicable. In addition to the marriage payments, and payments at the birth of children, the husband is personally obligated to provide labor at feasts held by his wife's descent group. The brothers-in-law (*ipa gava*), the men married to women born of the clan, play a key role in the mortuary ceremonies. Certain tasks can be performed only by them: they must dig the grave and, later, build a fence around it. The wives of the men of the clan cook and prepare food while the clan members, men and women, mourn the deceased. These obligations are taken very seriously and although men often complain of the time involved, they do not dare shirk them (see also Hau'ofa 1981:150–51).

Mekeo are reluctant to give up their daughters to other cultural groups because foreign spouses cannot be depended on to provide essential labor.

Since most Mekeo villages are large and comprise several descent groups, many marriages take place within the community, a factor that no doubt makes the *ipa gava* obligations somewhat less onerous. Mekeo villages are not far distant from one another, and people are expected to attend feasts regardless of the inconvenience. These obligations create frequent occasions when affines must interact and, generally speaking, a friendly, joking atmosphere prevails. It is considered appropriate for the *ipa gava* to "play" (*opua*), even at the mortuary ceremonies, as this is thought to help cheer up the mourners. Occasionally, special feasts are held by a clan to fete its *ipa gava*. Hau'ofa (1981:130ff.) has thoroughly documented the underlying hostility that surfaces in the humiliating nature of the accompanying *opua*, in which, for example, the *ipa gava* may be presented with huge amounts of cooked meat which they are forced to eat in public until they vomit. They then begin to eat again until every morsel has been consumed. Nevertheless, tensions are never allowed to erupt into open violence.[9] On an individual level, brothers-in-law are often close friends and helpers who are on good terms. As in most Melanesian societies, marriage involves ongoing exchanges and obligations over the lifetime of the couple.

Although women leave their natal group on marriage to live with and work for their husband's descent group, they maintain close ties with their own agnates (see also Hau'ofa 1981:130). They attend their clan's feasts with their husbands, not to work but to be waited on by their clan brothers' wives. On their deaths, their bodies are taken to their own clan for mourning and burial, and their clan performs the death feasts. Women visit their agnates frequently and can always find refuge there if they are ill-treated by husbands or in-laws. Parents always seem happy to care for and raise their daughters' children, even though they accept the father's clan's rights to them. In the close interaction that takes place between brothers-in-law, men ensure their sisters are properly treated and will rebuke a husband if the wife seems ill, tired, or overworked. When husband or wife dies, the in-laws supervise the mourning period of the surviving spouse—a period that demands segregation from society, or confinement in the case of widows, for a year or more. Spouses are rarely held directly responsible for a partner's death, yet the relatives of the deceased almost always take the attitude that the surviving spouse was somehow negligent. Should the bereaved spouse fail to display appropriate grief or be lax in observing the strict mourning procedures, the in-laws complain loudly in public and seek covert revenge if sufficiently provoked (see also Hau'ofa 1981:151–52).

Leadership and Ritual Specialization

The complexity of Mekeo leadership and ritual specialization has been described by several ethnographers (Seligman 1910; Belshaw 1951; Stephen

1974; Hau'ofa 1981; Mosko 1985). "Peace chiefs," "war chiefs," "senior peace chiefs," "junior peace chiefs," "peace sorcerers," "war sorcerers," various "chief's functionaries," and lesser ritual experts, such as "prayer men," have been identified. The terms *chief* and *sorcerer* have been commonly employed ever since Seligman's research was published in 1910, but I have nevertheless decided to avoid them here. Seligman presumably based his usage on the ethnographic writings of the missionaries of the Catholic Mission of the Sacred Heart (Sacré Coeur), from whom he obtained most of his information about the Mekeo. I have come to the conclusion this long-standing terminology is misleading, making the task of accurate ethnographic description more difficult than necessary. "Chief" implies a functional, political role that is largely inappropriate in this cultural context. "Sorcerer" has a specific anthropological usage (i.e., a person attributed with ritual death-dealing powers), which is confusing since many other persons besides "peace sorcerers" and "war sorcerers" are attributed with such powers. Furthermore, the term has negative connotations of a subtly misleading kind (Stephen 1987b).

A literal translation of Mekeo terms conveys more vividly the meanings attached to different roles and will promote an appreciation of their nuances; indeed, it provides a useful way to begin to describe the different leadership roles. Students of Mekeo culture are fortunate to have the Mekeo-French dictionary compiled in the 1920s and 1930s by Father Desnoes, a priest of the Sacred Heart mission. Although never published, Desnoes's two-volume typewritten manuscript (1941) is a remarkable work of scholarship, providing, in its large number of entries and meticulous investigations of meanings and usage, a vast compendium of Mekeo culture. I have found it of the greatest value as an independent check on my own understanding and as a means of deepening my knowledge of the language: I have already referred to its authority and shall have frequent occasion to do so throughout this book.

The two most prominent roles are that of *lopia* and *ugauga*—"chief" and "sorcerer," respectively. According to Desnoes (1941:627), the word *lopia* means "chief, dignity or position of a chief (chef, dignité de chef)." Its second meaning he notes as "good, handsome (bon, beau)" as an adjective; "goodness, kindness (bonté)" as a subject; and "well, properly (bien, comme il faut)" as a verbal suffix. The word *lopia* is not, however, except in abbreviated form, used alone to refer to a leader or chief; rather, one says *lopia auga*, "he is a chief," or *oi lopia aumu*, "you are a chief." *Au* is the word for man, with the suffix *ga* indicating its relationship to the preceding word. Thus *lopia auga* is a man of *lopia*, and *lopia* is used in the sense of good, kind, benevolent— which is, as people will tell you, exactly what the *lopia auga* must be. I can think of no single English word precisely capturing all the connotations of *lopia*, but "a man of kindness" comes close. *Lopia* is often used as an adverb to mean "correctly," "properly"; thus I would ask people whether I had spoken correctly or pronounced something properly and they would reply, if it were correct, "*Lo* [you] *ifa* [spoke] *lopiani.*" One refers to people doing or making things properly thusly: "*Ke* [they] *kapaisa* [made it] *lopiani.*"[10]

The first meaning of the term *ugauga* listed in Desnoes's "Mekeo Dictionary" (1941:1018) is "sorcerer, sorcery" (sorcier, sorcellerie). The second listed meaning is "sad, dejected" (triste, abattu). I have sometimes heard the term used in ordinary speech to mean "lament" or "groan with sorrow" (*e ugauga ugauga*—the repetition of the word produces an onomatopoeic representation of lamentation). As Desnoes indicates, the word by itself may indicate "sorcery" or "sorcerer," but when one wants to specify "sorcerer," one says *ugauga auga*—a man of *ugauga*. Thus he is, literally, "a man of sorrow." The term has a double meaning when used in this way, since the *ugauga* causes sorrow to others by inflicting disease or death upon them, but at the same time he, himself, must be in a state of mourning. The ritually active *ugauga*, a veritable man of sorrow, is almost always a widower; his sombre dress and isolation from society are in general imposed on widowers.

In addition to the *lopia* and the *ugauga*, there are also the *iso*, the war leader, and the *faia*, the specialist in war sorcery. These offices have usually been translated as "war chief" and "war sorcerer," respectively, implying a correspondence and a neat opposition between the pairs that is not accurate. *Iso* literally means "spear"; thus we have "the man of the spear" (*iso auga*). *Faia* is the name of a particular kind of ritual used to bring about death by violent means, including accidents such as falls, attacks by wild animals, and deaths in battle. *Faia* also means "cinnamon bark," a substance used ritually for its properties in attracting spirit presences. The *faia auga* might thus be literally rendered as "man of cinnamon bark." The same pattern is followed in the terms that describe the *lopia*'s important functionaries (see also Hau'ofa 1981): the "man of the knife" (*aiva auga*) and "the man of the string" (*uve auga*), whose job it is to assist the *lopia* at feasts by cutting and dividing the meat presented to the guests (see also Hau'ofa 1981:207). There are, in addition, as I noted when discussing the structure of descent groups, senior (*fa'aniau*) and junior (*eke*) *lopia*, and senior and junior *iso*.

One can discern in this variety of roles four distinct kinds of major functionaries: *lopia*, *ugauga*, *iso*, and *faia*. Within each speciality, there might also be found senior (*fa'aniau*) and junior (*eke*) lines. Customarily, the *lopia*, the man of kindness, took precedence and had effective control over the other three. The man of the spear could involve the clan in battle only with the agreement of the man of kindness, who also acted as peacemaker. The man of sorrow punished only at the direction or with the permission of the man of kindness, who ensured that only miscreants, not the law abiding, were victims. The rituals of the man of cinnamon bark determined which of his own men would die in battle; he acted in consultation with the man of kindness, *not* the man of the spear, so as to spare as many as possible and to see that troublemakers rather than righteous men fell in battle. My informants stressed that the *iso auga* did not control the *faia*, he merely led his clan into battle. The rituals of the *faia* of the two opposing sides determined which side won. The role of the *faia* in relation to the *iso* is thus not directly comparable to the relationship of the *ugauga* to the *lopia*.[11] Instead, all three roles—*iso, faia,* and *ugauga*—were in principle subordinate to the *lopia*. One of my most expert informants demonstrated this graphically by holding up his right hand and pointing to the long middle finger, saying "This is the *lopia*." Then using his left hand, he clasped his other shorter fingers around the middle finger and said, "These are *iso, faia, ugauga;* they assist him, they stand beside the *lopia*."

In the past, a reciprocal feasting relationship existed between the man of the spear and the man of kindness. When the *lopia* attended feasts held by the heads of other descent groups, he would share the meat and food presented to him with his spear man. Likewise, when the spear man attended feasts held by the spear men of other descent groups, he would share the meat he received with his *lopia*. As already noted, only the senior man of kindness can perform the death ceremonies. In a sense, death links the four roles: the spear man's actions lead to death in battle, as do the ritual actions of the cinnamon bark man, while the man of sorrow brings death in peacetime. It remains to the man of kindness to perform the ceremonies that bring the period of mourning to an end and restore normal social life following the disruption of death.

The senior *lopia*, we have seen, heads the senior section of his clan, while the *iso, ugauga,* and *faia* are members of junior sections and lines. Thus the man of kindness is the benevolent elder brother, using his seniority and authority to direct the actions of his younger brothers. He is at the apex, the middle finger of the hand, ensuring the proper maintenance of the social order. Although warfare ceased prior to 1900 (Stephen 1974), the titles and special ritual knowledge associated with both the *iso* and the *faia* were maintained.[12] Men of the spear continued to install their eldest sons in their place and the rituals of *faia* sorcery were passed on to the appropriate heirs, but there were no longer special functions associated with war. Spear men do not today carry spears or lead their men into battle, nor have they done so for three or four generations; they now act as lineage heads, as junior men of kindness despite their warrior heritage. *Faia* sorcery, formerly used to determine who died in battle, could be employed for other kinds of violent deaths; its practitioners are thus regarded as little different from the *ugauga*. When identifying the important men of the community, people often refer separately to the *lopia aui*, the *iso aui*, the *faia aui* and the *ugauga aui*, but throughout the entire period of my fieldwork, the major division in function and symbolism was between the *lopia* and the *ugauga* (as is indicated by Hau'ofa's [1981] research).

Although there is a significant relationship between leadership roles and the structuring of the descent group, there is no simple one-to-one correlation between them. The threefold structuring of sections of many large clans does not directly correlate with the fourfold division of *lopia, ugauga, iso,* and *faia*.

Every village-based clan has its own *lopia,* or it must be allied with another clan that does, but only a few clans have their own *ugauga.* Both are said to be essential to the social order, but people explain that any *lopia* can call upon the services of any *ugauga,* regardless of his descent group membership. Large village-based clans, however, usually do have an *ugauga* lineage or one allied with them, and they usually have an Iso section and a man of the spear heading it. Cinnamon bark men are found much more rarely, and few clans, even large ones, can boast them. Just as the man of kindness can call upon any man of sorrow when need be, so he can enlist the ritual assistance of a cinnamon bark man. Precisely how this operated in times of war is not entirely clear.

It is difficult to reconstruct with confidence the nature of leadership and ritual specialization prior to pacification since it is beyond the reach of living memory. Just as it is hard to identify precisely what today represents the survival of earlier forms and what represents changes brought about by pacification and colonial rule. One might object that the word *lopia* is sometimes used in conjunction with the other three terms, and thus one may hear of *iso lopia, faia lopia,* and *ugauga lopia,* suggesting that the term *lopia* means simply "chief" or "leader." It is my conviction that these combinations are anomalous usages—contradictions in terms developed in the necessary process of communicating to government and mission the indigenous cultural forms. Different kinds of leaders or chiefs were easily comprehensible to the external authorities, more subtle distinctions were not. Thus it has become common for Mekeo themselves, especially when explaining their culture to outsiders, to use the term *lopia* in a sense sometimes shorn of its primary meaning of benevolence and kindness. Hau'ofa (1981:190) makes the identical point. But regardless of its primary meaning, there can be little doubt, given the detailed descriptions of other ethnographers as well as myself, when the word *lopia* (or *lopia auga*) is used by itself, my translation "the man of kindness" is appropriate. The man of kindness and the man of sorrow have more than merely social or political functions; they have a symbolic significance encapsulating on many levels Mekeo understanding of themselves and their world. In the next chapter I will explore further the complex "evocational fields" (to use Sperber's [1975] concept), surrounding these key symbols (Ortner 1973).[13]

Although the effects of external influence are not the focus of this study, it is impossible to describe Mekeo culture without reference to them. Since the late nineteenth century, there has been continuous contact and interaction with missionaries, government officers, traders, adventurers and travelers, and several ethnographers (see Seligman 1910; Egidi 1912; Williamson 1913; Guis 1936; Belshaw 1951; Stephen 1974; Hau'ofa 1981; Mosko 1985). The first government station was established in the region, on land belonging to Aipeana village, in 1890. The same year, the Catholic Mission of the Sacred Heart, already established on Yule Island, set up their first stations inland. Within less than a decade, the entire Mekeo region was reported to be well under government control; tribal warfare had ceased and the Catholic mission could count a large number of converts in every Mekeo community (Stephen 1974). The first village schools were set up by the Sacred Heart missionaries even before they built their churches (Dupeyrat 1935). My oldest informants all attended school for two or three years. Elders would often roar with laughter when recounting their school days to me, declaring all they ever learned was to say their prayers! Nevertheless, thanks to the devoted efforts of the Catholic mission in the pre-war years, in the late 1960s many middle-aged and older people could read and write their own language and speak adequate English. Some had achieved full literacy in English, had become teachers, and had even trained for the priesthood.

Prior to the Second World War, the region was a quiet colonial backwater. There were few European settlers or enterprises in the immediate vicinity, although many young men did seek occasional work as laborers on European plantations in the Nara and Kabadi region to the east. The well-intentioned but unfortunately clumsy efforts of Sir Hubert Murray's regime to promote in-digenous economic development through the introduction of "Native Tax" and village plantation schemes did much to strain relationships between the Mekeo and the colonial government but little to improve the economy. It was not until the war, when every able-bodied man was conscripted to provide labor for the Bulldog and Kokoda trails, that the narrow horizons of village life opened up onto a wider world. The war brought new experiences and new hopes and expectations to the Mekeo, and new policies for economic and social development to the Australian colonial administration (Stephen 1974).

The pace of life for Mekeo changed dramatically after the war, as it did for many Papuans. Whereas previously men worked on nearby plantations to raise their tax money, now they traveled to Port Moresby to find employment as laborers and domestic servants; others went for secondary or technical education or to the Catholic mission schools on Yule Island. Soon it became the norm for young men to spend the time before marriage away from the village. In the villages, too, there were new opportunities: government-sponsored programs for rice growing and for village cooperatives in the 1950s and, in the 1960s, various government-assisted plans for individual economic enterprises (Stephen 1974). Villagers were discovering an easy and reliable source of cash by marketing their locally grown betel (areca) nuts in the town. The growth of Port Moresby itself, increasing opportunities for education, and the begin-nings of policy to localize government appointments meant that by the early 1960s there were many better jobs than laboring and domestic service available to Papua New Guineans. The success of mission and government educational policies was becoming evident by the late 1960s. When I began fieldwork, everyone under the age of thirty could speak fluent English, and most could read and write simple English. Girls, as well as boys, were undertaking sec-ondary schooling and were training to become nurses and teachers. The government-sponsored programs for economic development in the 1950s and 1960s were admittedly a disappointment on both sides, yet there were achievements. Individuals and small groups set up small retail stores, bought tractors and motor vehicles, and experimented with various ventures to earn cash. The 1960s saw political change in the establishment of local government councils and the beginning of elections for a national assembly. The pace of change continued to accelerate over the next two decades.

Despite the many external influences over the last century, Mekeo culture retains a richness and coherence of its own—a fact Hau'ofa emphasizes (1981:3–5, 20–25). These are no pure, primeval, untouched primitive people; Mekeo are well aware of the existence of a wider world. Their culture and society has had to adapt to many foreign influences and demands. Much of what one assumes to be "traditional" culture turns out to be, in fact, a creative adaptation of introduced influences (for example, the distinctive and stylish male dress). Culture is not, as we always seem to need to remind ourselves, a static entity, but a continuously adaptive process that is learned and created anew in the development and maturation of each individual culture bearer (Herdt 1989a:27–30). The puzzle is not how cultures change, since change is inevitable, but rather how cultures retain identity in change. That, however, is not the question explored in this book. It is the coherence of Mekeo culture, as I knew it in the 1960s, 1970s, and early 1980s, that concerns me. The visible ordering of Mekeo society I have described is not a historical reconstruction of what things were like in some hypothetical "traditional" past, but what I observed. Perhaps even more striking is the fact that this harmony has been achieved in the face of so much external pressure for change. Life in a Mekeo village is not merely orderly and harmonious, it is curiously self-contained. Surrounded by the natural abundance afforded by fertile gardens and land, the people are confidently assured of their material well-being, and they continue to find meaningful a way of life very different from that which they know lies just beyond their villages. Undoubtedly Mekeo culture has and is changing, as do all cultures, but it continues to be *their* culture, with its own inherent order and style.

2

Manifest and Concealed

Everything in the Mekeo view is understood to have a visible and a concealed aspect. That which is visible, open, in plain sight, easy to comprehend is termed *ofakae*. That which is hidden from view, not available to ordinary perception, or secret, is termed *ogevake*. All phenomena are regarded as having both a manifest, *ofakae*, and a concealed, *ogevake*, aspect. *Ogevake* does not necessarily indicate something totally unknown, but rather something known to someone but kept concealed, or something well known to all but not spoken about openly. *Ogevake kapa*, a hidden or secret matter, is only done or talked about covertly. Thus, for example, everyone knows adultery occurs, but it is *ogevake kapa*—something done in secret and not, except in unfortunate circumstances, brought into the public arena. Condemned by the public moral code because it threatens the harmony of social relationships, it is nevertheless part of human existence; as long as it is kept concealed it does not threaten the surface harmony of society. Distinguishing between *ofakae* and *ogevake* is, however, no easy matter for an outsider. One may assume because everyone knows something that it must be *ofakae*, but I soon discovered this was not so. For example, all Mekeo suspect that many men of kindness employ destructive rituals of various kinds without the intermediary services of the man of sorrow. Yet such suspicions are *ogevake kapa*, and are not mentioned openly. Conversely, when one is told something is secret, such as ''sorcery,'' one assumes that whatever is learned about it must be *ogevake*. Yet when I would attempt to confirm this supposedly esoteric information with a range of other people, I often found that everyone knows of it: it is public knowledge about secret things.

Closely associated with *ofakae* and *ogevake,* manifest and concealed, are notions of exterior and interior, *afe* and *alo.* Everything has an outside, which is plain to see and publicly accessible, and an inside obscured from view. What is displayed outside may be very different from what is contained inside; indeed, Mekeo expect it to be so. Light (*eaea*) and darkness (*umu*) and day (*kina*) and night (*gapi*) are further associations linked to outside and inside, manifest and concealed. What is plainly visible is well-lit and bright, revealed in the clear light of day. But at night, in darkness, things are obscured, just as things may be concealed inside something. Things outside, in clear view, are easy to understand (*ofakae*); things inside, concealed, are difficult to understand (*pigi*). Desnoes (1941:811) gives as one example of the use of *ofakae* and *pigi:* "Oi malami e pigi; lai malamai ofa = kaegai [Your language is difficult, ours is easy]."

Every manifest phenomenon has a concealed inside which does not immediately meet the eye. Identifying these different levels is crucial to understanding all aspects of Mekeo culture, but deciding where the divisions are is tricky. An obvious duality exists in the public symbolism of the man of kindness and the man of sorrow, yet a little deeper look reveals that the manifest realm of social relationships has its own dark interior quite separate from the invisible, dangerous spirit realm. To explore the concepts of *ofakae* and *ogevake* I will begin by examining the public roles of the man of kindness and the man of sorrow to reveal some of the complexities lying beneath this apparently simple dualism. I will then pursue the divisions expressed in the outside and inside of the human person, and in the outside and the inside of physical bodies.

Manifest Symbols of the Social and Cosmic Order: The Man of Kindness and the Man of Sorrow

Even a superficial acquaintance with a Mekeo community discloses the existence of the man of kindness and the man of sorrow. I did not spend more than a few hours visiting the area before someone had explained their functions to me. Mekeo possess a well-established ideology about the way their society operates—or should operate—and they are eager to impress it upon even the casual visitor. So forceful is the articulation of this ideal order that one finds it difficult somehow to discriminate between what one is told and what one can actually observe (a tendency noticeable also in Hau'ofa's writing, especially 1971, and of which he himself is very much aware, 1981:2). When I first heard about, and observed, the role of the man of kindness, it was as a white stranger being welcomed at his *ufu,* which was itself a concrete expression of his generosity and largesse. It was thus I first met my most memorable informants and friends. At the time, I was collecting oral histories concerning the first European explorers, missionaries, and government officials who entered the area in the 1880s and 1890s. The elders always had plenty of stories of the past to relate, but they also took the opportunity to explain to me something of the importance of the men of kindness. They would regale me with monologues enumerating the functions and significance of the role (years later I heard them delivered as public speeches accompanying the installation of a new man of kindness and on other public occasions as well). Although not fixed in structure to any great degree, these homilies were evidently formalized public statements of the duties and obligations of the office and were known to all present. Those gathered around would nod and murmur approvingly as each point was made, their familiarity with the speeches revealed as they spoke the words softly along with the speaker.

Discussions with the elders usually began by one of them explaining to me that the supervision of the building and maintenance of the *ufu* itself were key responsibilities of the man of kindness. It was of concern to the whole clan since here hospitality and prestations of food were offered by the man of kindness on behalf of his clan. Here the men of the clan met to discuss matters and socialize; here visitors were given food and shelter. Even if the *lopia* himself was not present, it was the duty of his clansmen to provide hospitality in his name. Generosity (*gavegave*), the elders stressed, was one of the most important virtues of the man of kindness, and it was in the clan meeting house that he must publicly demonstrate it. (*Gavegave* also means kind, benevolent.) Here generosity lacks the competitive edge it has in many Melanesian societies; Mekeo do not give to shame rivals (as, for example, do the Siuai; see Oliver 1955; Lindstrom 1984).[1]

People never seemed to tire of enumerating the functions of the man of kindness; I needed only to display a little interest to be showered with further details. Not only did Mekeo enjoy explaining their worldview to an outsider, they perhaps felt a need for its constant reiteration (since such, of course, is a way of bringing it into being). The *lopia's* responsibilities, the homilies would continue, are to look after (*ima*) his people, to be available on the *ufu* to talk with them and advise them in everyday matters, to hold the death feasts, to make peace. He must be generous, merciful, and benevolent, his conduct a model for all to emulate. In his dealings with others he "must think of peace not war"; he neither lies nor holds grudges as do ordinary folk. He is merciful and forgiving with his own people. His special insignia is the *uma pa'o*, a chest ornament made of pig's tusks, and he carries a ritually potent limepot (*faoga*) and lime stick (*lekeleke*). His house must be built next to his *ufu* and sited with its axis parallel to the village plaza, distinguishing it from the dwellings of ordinary folk (*ulalu aui*), which face the plaza, and it is constructed with materials that were traditionally not permitted others. The firstborn son must fill the position of *lopia;* he is prepared for this task from childhood by never being allowed to eat the *uma faga*, a ritually significant portion of pork fat and skin, which only the *lopia* himself may cut up at feasts.

Genealogies of every descent group in Inawi indicate that men of kindness are in fact usually the most senior descendants of the most senior patrilineage of their descent group (see also Hau'ofa 1981:209ff.). Although the position of *lopia* is determined by birth, the son of a *lopia* must be properly installed in the position to perform its functions. A large, expensive feast is necessary to do this. A father usually holds such a feast for his son in his own lifetime because if he died without doing so, the clan would be left with no one capable of performing the death feasts.

The elders impressed upon me the duty of ordinary people to respect the man of kindness, obey his word, and provide him with pigs and labor for his feasts. Should they fail to do so, or should they disturb the social order with stealing, adultery, assault, or murder, he will see they are punished by calling upon the man of sorrow to take action against them. The man of kindness does not himself punish his own kin. This is left to the man of sorrow, who is expected to act in concert with the man of kindness and at his command. His position, too, is hereditary, though not all descent groups have a man of sorrow in their ranks. Because of the highly dangerous ritual activities in which he engages, he, in contrast to the man of kindness, must live apart from the rest of the community. One elder summed up these ideals for me with great succinctness: "*Lopia* means in our language one who is kind and good and does not cause harm or sorrow. *Ugauga* is the one who can cause harm and sorrow."

Such, in brief, is the ideal social order Mekeo articulate for the outsider and recite to themselves on public occasions. In these public statements, the role of the man of kindness is more elaborated. The man of sorrow is depicted primarily as his henchman, as the punitive force that backs the man of kindness's benevolent authority. People commonly explain in English that the *ugauga* is like the *lopia*'s "policeman" (for an identical observation see Hau'ofa 1981:250).

This ideal social order is reinforced in highly visible forms of symbolic public expression. Explicit statements about the roles of *lopia* and *ugauga* are realized in their performance and actions at social gatherings, in particular the feasts (*gaku*) and food distributions that must be held periodically by each localized descent group. Mekeo group activities are usually marked by the presentation of food and drink to participants by a host. This ranges from an informal work party of neighbors and kin helping to repair a house, in which case the house owner must provide appropriate hospitality, to large feasts held by the whole clan section in the name of its *lopia*. Generosity (*gavegave*) is a social virtue at all levels, and the man of kindness displays it on a grand scale. The most frequent occasions presided over by him are the death ceremonies. His responsibility is to organize and plan the feasts, ensuring they are carried out correctly. The feasts begin with the feeding of the in-laws who dig the grave and build a fence around it, and end with the termination of mourning, *umu pua*, which can be several months to a year or more after the death. The termination of mourning is the largest of several observances, requiring the most effort to gather the necessary food, including pigs, an effort which is the duty of all the clan (i.e., the localized village segment of the clan), and of the close relatives of the deceased in particular. People assert that one of the most important things the man of kindness does for his people is to hold the death feasts, especially the termination of mourning, which frees relatives of the deceased from various restrictions and privations, and allows the whole community to resume normal life.

The feasts and food gifts organized by the men of kindness are complex affairs, with important social and political ramifications that have been discussed at length by others (Seligman 1910; Hau'ofa 1981). Mosko (1985) has identified multiple layers of symbolic significance in similar ceremonies held by Bush Mekeo. At present, I am concerned only with the most overt level of symbolism: as public spectacles dramatizing the role of the men of kindness. (Later chapters will explore deeper levels of meaning in the death rituals.) At these ceremonies the ethnographer—and the community as a whole—observes the men of kindness and the men of sorrow in their most public, most highly visible, and most impressive roles. These occasions, as Hau'ofa points out (1981:148), also vividly express the social ideal of agnatic solidarity that should prevail between members of descent groups.

At all feasts held in his name, the man of kindness plays the part of genial host. He sits, surrounded by his clansmen, in the center of the meeting house, welcoming guests as they arrive and bidding them to sit down on the mats spread out before them. While he converses with the guests, his assistants bring betel nut for the guests to chew. Betel nut is considered to be a mark *par excellence* of hospitality, and a prescribed etiquette surrounds its presentation. Other assistants, clansmen of the officiating man of kindness, bring cooked food and drink for the guests. The guests include the heads and members of the descent groups that make up the village and those of certain descent groups from other villages that have special ties with the officiating head, including the *ufu apie* (chapter 1), who are the major recipients of meat and vegetables at feasts. The men of kindness and other important men assume their positions at the meeting house in a dignified manner and sit conversing among themselves and with their host while refreshments are served.

The careful distribution of food to the guests, according to their relationship to the host group and their rank, is literally of vital concern, for failure to perform this correctly is expected to lead to deaths in the host group from *ugauga* sorcery (see also Hau'ofa 1981:279). It is the host *lopia*'s responsibility, in consultation with the knowledgeable men and elders of his clan, to see the distribution is carried out properly (*lopiani*). The actual serving, dividing, and arranging of food consumed on the spot by the guests, and the uncooked food they take home with them, is done by the *lopia*'s assistants. He himself is left free to talk with his guests and his advisers; but only he can cut up the special segment of fat and skin taken from the back of the pig—the *uma faga*. This one office he must perform himself.

The presence of the men of sorrow is also mandatory at important public feasts, their function being to observe that appropriate etiquette is followed and that each guest receives his proper due—and subsequently to take ritual action if any mistakes are made. The man of sorrow of the officiating clan (or one associated with it) will be present, as will those associated with the guest descent groups. The men of sorrow, however, do not sit with the other guests and participants; they stand on the periphery of the village watching the proceedings or sit at the back of the meeting house, segregated from the other important men (they enter from ladders at the rear, while other visitors enter from the front). They do nothing but watch and receive their gifts of food, but they hardly go unnoticed. They are clad entirely in black or very dark blue (both regarded as *umu,* the color of cinders, and charcoal, and death). Emaciated as a consequence of their ritual fasting, their eyes glitter in deep, skull-like sockets; they are usually middle-aged or older. Faces impassive, they move like wraiths. Even to an outsider from a different culture, these aloof skeletal figures dressed in black exert a cold menace—images that might be drawn from nightmares in any culture! It is no surprise they are believed to haunt graveyards and to be in constant communion with the spirits of the dead; Hau'ofa (1981:242) observes that an interpreter once commented to him in English that they were "devils." Ordinary men and women make no attempt to disguise their fear of these dark presences and do their best to avoid coming anywhere near them.

The silent, forbidding forms of the men of sorrow are a stark contrast against the gaily colored clothing, flowers, and decorations worn by the rest of the crowd—bright red and brilliant yellow predominate—and the atmosphere of celebration, bustle, and talk surrounding the man of kindness. He also wears bright colors and may decorate himself lavishly with flowers and shell ornaments. He is expected to be strong and well-nourished in body and, ideally, tall and robust; he is a big man (*au akaikia*) in every respect. Whereas a pot-bellied man (*kolukolu*) is ridiculed, a well-built person, male or female, is expected to be muscular and fleshy (*faga e alogai*). Just as the *lopia* represents the ideal of social behavior, so he should physically embody the ideal. Someone deformed or incapacitated could not become a man of kindness, so it was often said; the position would pass to his younger brother or another suitable candidate. A man of kindness must also be married. In direct contrast, the man of sorrow is a widower (*oaoae*) or, if he is married, he must live apart from his wife. His black accoutrements are the mark of his widower's status; his starved body is the result of fasting that symbolizes his grief. He wears the black feathers of the wild cassowary and a neck ornament (*kiki fua*) representing the wattles of the cassowary. In keeping with his role as the focus of human sociability, the man of kindness decorates himself with a large chest-pendant of domestic pigs' tusks, polished and glistening, as mark of his status.

These contrasts are sharply defined in the drama of public feasts and the overt presentation of self and body and are very visible indications of function and significance. The contrasts are underlined by the positions in the layout of the village settlement appointed to the man of kindness and the man of sorrow. The social centrality of the man of kindness is represented by the very space he occupies. A Mekeo village, as I have noted, is arranged on a rectangular plan, with a clear central space many yards wide and several hundred yards in length. The clan meeting house, where the man of kindness presides, should (and usually does) directly face the central thoroughfare. His appointed place on the *ufu* is next to the central front post, the *opogo,* to which he is often figuratively likened (see also Hau'ofa 1981:201). His domestic dwelling is built close to the *ufu* and thus to the central space of the village. Both his ritual and his ordinary domestic life is located in, or near, the most open and visible part of the village.

In appropriate contrast, men of sorrow live, or should live, away from the village. They are supposed to have special houses (*fauapi*) built in the bush, where they store their dangerous implements and potions and where their dread rituals are undertaken (see also Hau'ofa 1981:59–60). In fact, the *ugauga* known to me lived in small widowers' houses (*gove*) on the edge of the village, where they were isolated from the domestic dwellings but were not entirely out of view. During my first period of fieldwork, only one man of sorrow lived outside the village, in a small settlement with his sons and their families; this could not be properly described as a *fauapi,* which should be built in the bush away from all human society. People always insisted, however, that *fauapi* were still maintained and the fact that one never saw them simply proved the point that the men of sorrow always operated in the utmost secrecy. Whether these bush retreats exist,[2] the man of sorrow's actual location, on the margin of human habitation, is a highly visible contrast to the centrality of the man of kindness. When a man of sorrow visits the village, he must not traverse the main thoroughfare, the *pagua inaega,* but must use only the paths at the back of the village where the cleared space merges into surrounding bush. In my experience, they did in fact usually keep to the periphery and surrounding bush, always entering the *ufu* from the rear, and seeming to appear and disappear on public occasions without one ever being certain when they arrived or left.

The segregation of the man of sorrow from the rest of society is necessary because of the powers that he invokes and that emanate from him. He deals with the spirits of the dead (*isage*) as well as other spirit beings—entities considered so dangerous that he alone who has the ritual knowledge and who rigorously prepares himself, can withstand contact with them. The man of sorrow is said to become like a spirit of the dead (*isage*), and his physical appearance in public, as I have just described, dramatically conveys this. The powers he invokes come from the spirit realm, but they are under the control of the man of kindness; that is, at least, according to the stated ideal. As is ideal, the man of sorrow usually remains excluded from and unseen by society, except at feasts held by the man of kindness, when he appears at the man of kindness's command and as the recipient of his largesse—a public enactment of the stated ideal.

I have so far only touched upon some of the rich symbolism surrounding *lopia* and *ugauga,* since I am attempting here to describe the first, most visible, layer. The *lopia* and *ugauga* express not only a division of social authority but also a cosmological duality signifying the opposing of the realm of the living to the realm of the spirits and the dead—not just "culture versus nature." In their overt symbolism, the man of kindness and the man of sorrow represent an opposition between the visible, safe, domestic domain of human sociability and the dark, invisible, dangerous realm of spirit forces. Together, they mediate this cosmic duality, with the *lopia* overtly controlling the use in human society of destructive powers the *ugauga* invokes from the spirit realm. So far, my information concerning the roles of the man of kindness and the man of sorrow is virtually identical to Hau'ofa's (1971, 1981) descriptions; indeed, I might simply have referred to his work, except that I considered it necessary to show that my own independently collected data and observations revealed the same picture (see also Stephen 1974, 1979b).

The Harmonious Outside of Society

The role of the man of kindness in its manifest symbolism represents, obviously and redundantly, the harmony and goodwill that ideally should prevail in human society. The relationship with his clansmen is described in terms of mutual familial ties of affection and obligation. Clansmen are referred to as his *aga akina,* his elder and younger brothers. He must look after (*ima*) and take tender care of them, especially by holding the death feasts and by seeing that peace and harmony prevail in the social order. In turn, clansmen must provide him with the pigs and vegetables needed for his feasts and heed his word (*aina ke logonia*). Members of the same descent group are united by fraternal closeness, affection, and mutual help. Since descent group members share residential and garden land, they live and work together. And although daily tasks and gardening are carried out at the level of the individual household, there is the inevitable constant interaction with those who are close neighbors as well as close kin. Many concerns, marriages and deaths in particular, draw clansmen together in cooperative effort. Within the same village, the different descent groups ideally, and usually in fact, interact harmoniously—at least on the surface. Not only do they share the same village settlement, but generations of intermarriage result in close ties of affinity and descent that link the whole community. When a death occurs, everyone experiences a sense of loss.

In these large communities overt violence is rare or very short-lived (Hau'ofa 1981:66ff. confirms this impression for Beipa village). When it does break out, usually in a domestic context, it is quickly stopped by other household members and neighbors, who physically separate the protagonists and take them off in separate directions, talking soothingly to them until they have calmed down. Violence between groups within the same community is rare, and I have never witnessed an occurrence. Violent clashes with other communities are also rare and are likely to attract the attention of external law enforcing agencies before they progress very far. The introduction of alcohol into village life, a problem by the 1980s, has led to some increased brawling, particularly between young men, at rugby matches and dances, but on the whole it rarely gets out of hand. The feasts of the men of kindness are dignified affairs, even when enlivened by traditional dancing, which is orderly and graceful despite the highly spectacular effects achieved with colorful costumes and body painting. Indeed, the deportment and self-presentation of villagers on all occasions is, as I have noted, smooth, measured and controlled.

At this point I need to return to the symbolism of the spatial layout of the village settlement and explore it a little further. The man of kindness is visibly located in the center of human society, whereas the man of sorrow is located beyond its periphery, where human habitation gives way to the bush and its nonhuman denizens. Surrounding the central space are the domestic houses (e'a) occupied by married couples, children, and unmarried or widowed women. Beyond them, at the edge of the village settlement are found the habitations (gove) of the widowers and bachelors, both of whom are suspected of having dealings with the man of sorrow, who (in theory) is located in his fauapi in the bush beyond. These men are the peripheral members of society, those without women who are seeking to enter or re-enter adult society by acquiring wives. Progression from the central village space to the margins of social space represents a movement from what is socially open, clear, and public (ofakae) to what is increasingly more concealed (ogevake). As Mosko (1985:21) shows for the Bush Mekeo, the cleared space which the village occupies is considered outside space, in contrast to the space covered and obstructed (kupu) by the surrounding bush (kupu), which is regarded as inside space. When one enters the village, one is said to come out (pealai) from the bush, just as one comes out (pealai) of one's house. That is to say, one emerges from a concealed inside into the visible outside. Thus, in the Mekeo view, when moving in the opposite direction, from the central plaza to the boundary of the settlement, one gradually moves from visible outside to concealed inside.

The central space of the village is the most public place in the village, where one is exposed to the scrutiny of all. In the glaring heat of day, this large central space dazzles with light. People find it more comfortable to walk between the rows of houses or at the back of the village, which is partially shaded by shrubs and trees, than to venture into the merciless brightness of the pagua inaega. Hau'ofa (1981:74) notes that when going about their daily tasks, villagers tend to take these other paths, feeling that the central space is just too public and exposed. I often wondered why, in such a torrid climate, there were not more trees planted to shade the village center and the houses. When I asked about this, people just shrugged their shoulders and replied they abhorred the thought of their houses being overhung (i.e., hidden) by growth that would rot their timbers and thatched roofs. I was also puzzled by the fact that feasts were always held during the very hottest part of the day when the sun was at its height, a time when one might expect that people would prefer to rest quietly in the shade. Instead, everyone was anxious that proceedings were completed during daylight; one could sit talking and gossiping as long as one liked into the evening on the *ufu,* but the important tasks, such as the food distribution, the burial, or the handing over of the knife to the new man of kindness, had to be completed before it was dark. For a long time I saw no particular significance in the fact that the meeting houses are always open structures, without walls. It is now obvious to me that anyone sitting in the *ufu* is in plain sight of the whole village. Ideally, the man of kindness should be in the ufu at all times, available to talk with his people and be consulted by them; in other words, he should always be visible, his presence always manifest (*ofakae*).

The association of the central space of the village, the meeting houses, and the men of kindness with openness, daylight, and visibility is evident. The *lopia*'s position in society is not simply central, it must be manifest. The importance of feasts being held in daylight is indicated by the other meanings of the term for sun, *kina.* This word also means "day" and "appear," and it forms the root of *pakina,* meaning "to make visible, to explain, to make clear." The actions of the man of kindness must be visible; they must be seen by all and understood by all. For this reason the central space of the village is kept clear; it cannot be in shadow or obscured (*kupu*) by trees or shrubs (*kupu*). The overt role of the man of kindness becomes an unmistakable representation of the smooth, bright, clearly visible public face of society. He must be as sharply defined as possible from the shadowy, obscure world inhabited by the man of sorrow. Whereas visibility, openness, and clarity characterize the actions of the former, the latter conceals himself in the bush, away from human society, communicating there in solitude with the dangerous powers of the spirit realm. The man of sorrow goes abroad at night, invisible under the cover of darkness; secrecy, silence, and stealth are his habitual modes.

Lying between the bright center of open public space and the surrounding darkness of the obscuring bush is the domestic space inhabited by ordinary folk. The houses are close together, throwing shadow on the paths between them. What goes on behind the walls of dwellings is not visible, but concealed (*ogevake*). In general, people sit, eat, and entertain visitors on open verandas and clearly visible platforms; the interior of the house is used only for private activities such as sleeping and sex. Valuables, money and, in particular, stores of feather and shell ornaments are stored in the interior of houses, and people are always careful to keep their stocks of such items secret.[3] Potentially dangerous ritual objects and relics may also be stored in secret inside. One rarely has reason to enter the interior of another's house because visitors are always entertained on the open verandas. The concealed interiors of domestic houses are assumed to hide things, such as anger. If one remains inside the house—that is, away from the view of others—Mekeo assume one is angry and avoiding other people. A refusal to go to the *ufu* on public occasions is a clear demonstration of social avoidance and, implicitly, anger (see also Hau'ofa 1981:284).

I have now left the brightly lit arena of visible sociability associated with the man of kindness and have entered the more shadowy region of the concealed (*ogevake*) as it pertains to ordinary folk. It is to this middle region—still a far cry from the secret world of the man of sorrow—that I now turn.

The Concealed Inside of Human Society

People are fond of saying, "Ah! That is just what he says with his mouth (*akegai*). But what he is really thinking inside himself (*alogai*) we do not know." They are only too well aware that beneath the ideally smooth, unruffled surface of social harmony run currents of powerful and destructive emotions—jealousy, anger, greed, desire, fear. Discerning these invisible currents constantly occupies people's thoughts and private conversations. What is done and said openly is one thing, but every overt action is presumed to have another side. At the same time, Mekeo admit they are careful not to reveal their inner thoughts and desires. Hau'ofa puts it aptly: "Nothing is accepted at face value. The watch word is *apie apie:* there are two sides to everything (1981:217)."

In confidence people often disclosed to me intense fears and suspicions of others including, indeed especially, close kin, agnates, and even their clan *lopia,* the man of kindness himself. People's anxieties centered around the very persons with whom they were supposed to have the most harmonious and supportive relationships. It should be emphasized that my intention here is not to provide an exhaustive description of the nature of social conflict and tension, but to illustrate people's explicit recognition of the darker inside of human society.

A brief anecdote will show how my attention was drawn to this darker inside. Only a few weeks after I began my first fieldwork in the region, the death of an important and much beloved old man occurred. He was the younger brother (an actual sibling) of a senior man of kindness. On the day of the funeral ceremonies this man of kindness sat by himself on the veranda of his house, looking in no way distressed or as if he were mourning. I wondered why he had not gone to the *ufu* with the other people. I soon heard the rumors that it was he, the man of kindness and the elder brother of the deceased, who was responsible for the death. New to the culture, and thus far exposed only to the public ideals, I was shocked. Everyone extolled the virtues of the dead man and there seemed to have been no possible reason for punishing him, and surely, I protested, the man of kindness would not kill his own brother. My friends smiled at this naiveté, replying that in the case of "sorcery," one looked to one's own brother first! Nor was it necessary to involve an intermediary; most people seemed to believe that the man of kindness had deployed his own ritual powers to bring about the death.

His action, sitting in full view on his veranda showing no sign of grief while the rest of the village buried his brother, seemed highly provocative, and I wondered to what dramatic denouement these events might lead; however, I waited in vain. As I was to find in all subsequent deaths attributed to ritual powers—as most deaths are—there were no open accusations, no public attempts to identify, by divination or other means, the protagonist. Although in some cases, such as this one, there may be some agreement in the rumors concerning who is responsible and why, this is by no means always so. I usually found that people, depending upon the closeness of their relationship to the deceased and various other factors, tended to give different explanations and suspect different agents. Those close to the deceased might interpret the death as the result of jealousy (*pikupa*), while others might point to some misdemeanor committed by the deceased in the past. People's views change over time, so that an explanation for a death shortly after it occurs may be quite different from one given by the same person several months or years later. Nor do people deny this; they admit that in retrospect events may be seen differently, and perhaps more clearly. The fact is since no public decision or action is ever taken on such matters, they remain forever a matter of speculation and are not forgotten. Action may be taken against the suspected culprits via covert counterrituals, but these are *ogevake kapa,* concealed things, to which only the very few people directly involved are privy.

Years later, long after the death of this prominent man of kindness, his own son told me in confidence that he believed his father was responsible for his uncle's death, and that he could not forgive him for this. Indeed, people were inclined to explain the old man's death as ritual punishment for killing his brother, whom everyone in the community loved. The motive for the first killing was said to be jealousy: it was reason enough that the younger brother had been more liked and respected for the elder to want to do away with him. It should be added that both men at the time of their deaths were in their sixties or early seventies, and that the second death took place some years after the first. I was to hear several more versions from different people of these deaths; remarkably, in strictly confidential conversations with me, more than one person actually claimed responsibility for the second death, that of the man of kindness.

Despite the ideal of close agnatic solidarity, a man first looks to his own brother as the agent of sorcery. Despite public assertions that the *lopia* looks after and protects his clansmen and does not himself wield destructive powers, people covertly admit they always suspect him along with the man of sorrow. This dark side of close relationships is the theme of the most important Mekeo myth, that of A'aisa, the founder of the existing social order. A'aisa and his younger brother, Isapini, quarreled over trivial matters and then killed each other's sons, Isapini employing the rituals of *mefu*,[4] A'aisa the rituals of *ugauga*. Because of A'aisa's actions, so it is said, people today still kill their brothers with lethal rituals because of jealousy (see also Hau'ofa 1981). Everyone knows this is so because it is inherent in the order of things established by A'aisa. This dark aspect of human relationships exists and cannot be avoided. Mekeo do not, however, celebrate or welcome its presence. What is celebrated and emphasized in collective symbolism and the public rituals of the men of kindness and the men of sorrow is the *other* face of human society, where peace and harmony prevail.

When I first began fieldwork, I was impressed by Marwick's (1964, 1965) notion that accusations of sorcery/witchcraft might provide, if carefully recorded and tabulated, a useful guide to the direction of social tensions and strain within a particular social structure. Yet despite my determined efforts to trace the events following all deaths in the community, I found Marwick's suggestion of little practical use because for Mekeo it was not a matter of open accusations and collective identification of a culprit, but rather, as I have explained, of covert suspicions and fears. Trends in suspicions and fears were certainly discernible, but if they indicated social structural strains, then these were in the very bastions of social order: the agnatic descent groups and their hereditary leaders, the men of kindness.

In general, people suspected those who were close to them, both in relationship and in physical space, of employing mystical means to harm and kill them. They did not expect ritual attacks as a result of unprovoked malice. It was those persons who they had in some way injured or had given some good cause for resentment that they suspected. If one reneges on an obligation to someone, fails to give someone their due, or arouses the anger or jealousy of kin, then sickness, misfortune, or death are the expected consequence. Of the eight deaths occurring in the community during my 1969–1971 fieldwork, I recorded the attributions of seven, all of which were believed to involve lethal rituals used by, or on behalf of, a close agnatic or affinal relative of the deceased (Stephen 1974). Hau'ofa (1981:269ff.) records a similar pattern in Beipa village and further observes the extent to which people were inclined to see their own clan heads, the men of kindness, as implicated.

Throughout my first period of fieldwork, when specifically investigating social change, I was barraged with rumors concerning the opposition of the descent group leaders to social change and, in particular, to the schemes for economic development endorsed by the colonial government in the 1960s and 1970s. The deaths of several people closely related to those initiating or prominently engaged in the new business ventures that took place during these decades were rumored to be consequences of the disapproval of the men of kindness, and the failure of most business ventures was seen as further proof of this opposition (Stephen 1974). Interviews with business leaders in several villages revealed the underlying suspicion, jealousy, and fear surrounding the activities of the men of kindness and the men of sorrow. Aspiring entrepreneurs confessed anxieties concerning the jealousy of neighbors and kin but, above all, emphasized fears of these "important men."

All but the most trifling injuries and illness are also likely to be attributed to mystical harm exerted by human agents. For example, an educated young man visiting his parents after working away from the village made a mistake in distributing presents to his relatives. He gave two "uncles" (agnates of his father's generation), who had donated money to send him to school, better presents than two other more senior agnates, who had not contributed to his schooling. As a result of this breach of etiquette, his father explained to me, the boy's sister, who lives in the village with her parents, suffered a very painful and debilitating abscess on the leg which was not cured until the offended relatives were paid. Even such an apparently trivial matter can be the focus of much anxiety and concern, although, once again, none of this reaches the public forum.

In-laws are often suspected of wanting to do harm, especially when the exchanges of wealth accompanying a marriage have not been completed. Thus, if a woman loses a baby or fails to conceive, her father or brothers are likely to be thought by the husband to be responsible. An elderly woman, a neighbor during my 1980s fieldwork, was childless because, it was said, when her bride wealth was distributed, the head of the clan section did not receive his due and was outraged. Many similar cases could be related.

People often observe: "You can do as you like (*oi ifomu*), no one forces you to do anything. But if you fail to do the correct thing, you will suffer."

Mekeo seem endlessly preoccupied with people's rights and dues and how these relate to seniority, kin relationships, marriage ties, and many other factors. I have referred to the distribution of food at chiefs' feasts and how even a seemingly small breach of etiquette is thought justification for a sorcery death. The same ethic applies at a more domestic level. People are forever discussing and commenting on the failure of others to perform their social duties and obligations properly. For example, to go out hunting and shoot a wild pig and not give it to the man of kindness if a feast is imminent is a very serious matter. It is not only the men of kindness who have rights over others, however. Everyone, according to gender, age, and social position, have their rights and can be expected to be angry if not given their due. Wives are not usually suspected of complicity in ritual attacks on their husbands (men are likely to suspect their own close agnates), but if a man, as was common in the past, spends most of his time away from his wife and sleeps in the *ufu*, leaving her alone, then she might deal with this neglect by putting ritually poisonous substances in his food. The web of rights and dues is endlessly complex to the outsider, but for Mekeo, this is the very stuff of social life and all adults seem to relish its intricacies.[5]

Mekeo personal relationships are inevitably fraught with these tensions. Yet people do manage to interact on a day-to-day basis and few or none of these tensions are revealed. Consider the following example. My research assistant and interpreter during my first fieldwork, an educated young man who spoke fluent English, informed me one day that the man with whom he had earlier been conversing at the clan meeting house was in fact responsible for killing his (the speaker's) small daughter. Startled by this, I asked what he meant. He replied that his small daughter died as a result of this man hiring a man of sorrow to kill her, and thus punish, him, the father. I was left speechless by his matter-of-fact manner and his ability to sit chatting amicably—as I had just seen him do—with someone he believed killed his child.[6] That was when I was new to the culture: I grew to expect such disclosures.

A few more examples will help illustrate how pervasive such attitudes are. In the neighborhood immediate to where I lived in 1980, a young married man and his wife attributed the deaths of two of their small children to the anger of the wife's brother over bride wealth payments. Yet the husband had an ostensibly close and friendly relationship with his brother-in-law: they often hunted and made gardens together and frequently visited each other. Another middle-aged married man, who had been seriously ill for two or three years but could get no relief for his suffering despite many visits to the hospital in Port Moresby and to private European medical practitioners, believed his father, a man of sorrow, was slowly killing him because of long-standing tensions between them (see chapter 14). Yet there was no overt hostility between them. Another neighbor believed the death of his small daughter was due to his daring to put an iron roof on his house instead of the traditional thatch (a breach of the *lopia*'s rights to certain building materials). Yet he continued to attend feasts held by his clan head, as indeed he must if he was not to give up all social life or leave the village. People well known to me were involved in these cases, but no doubt similar examples could be found in every household in the village. These attitudes are an integral part of the fabric of society—of its concealed inside.

The Outside and Inside of the Person

It must be emphasized that *ogevake* matters are never discussed openly; they are the subject of endless rumor, intrigue, and covert discussion. My information about the darker side of social relationships always came from conversations and comments made in strict confidence to me, and at the time I did not discriminate sufficiently between what might be said openly in a public context and what might be said in confidence to an intimate. During my 1969–1971 fieldwork I rarely had one-to-one interviews during which no other person was present, but I often talked with people at their homes, or in their gardens, with only their spouse and children present. As an outsider, who had no political or other vested interest in these affairs, I think people often regarded me as someone with whom they could discuss some of their inner thoughts without risking the repercussions that could develop should these thoughts be revealed to those embroiled in the events. People did not discuss such intimate concerns as their sexual life, but then I did not ask them to; topics such as sorcery, the opposition of the men of kindness to individual ambition, and rumors surrounding recent deaths and illness in the community were discussed at length, with little or no prompting on my part. Thus I did not realize these matters were "concealed things." In other words, I constructed my picture of social relationships with little sensitivity to the actual level of discourse in which people engaged.

What was said and done openly and what might be said and done in secret were carefully separated. Each, however, was regarded as an independent, real, and valid domain. My own cultural preconceptions obscured this. Westerners tend to assume a single "truth," finding pride, perhaps naively, in openness: "What you see is what you get." If something is kept out of sight, it is assumed that it must represent the "real" significance; the rest is just facade. Consequently, I believed that what people told me in confidence was the "truth" and that public action and speech were merely intended to screen the underlying "reality." In contrast, in the Mekeo view there is not a single truth, but multiple "truths." Both levels of social interaction—the manifest and the concealed—exist. One is not a disguise to hide the other. Surfaces can be kept smooth and controlled, and Mekeo succeed well at this. Some men of kindness are suspected, indeed firmly believed, to act covertly in ways that conflict with the public ideal. This does not, in the Mekeo view, mean their manifest role is a sham. People *do* maintain a smooth controlled surface to social interaction; the man of kindness *does* act generously and benevolently for all to see.

As an outsider, new to the culture, it was easy to be dazzled by the dual aspect of cultural symbols, their capacity to provide both "models of" and "models for" society, so that one is mistaken for the other (Geertz 1975b). The efficacy of a symbol, as Mekeo themselves seem to appreciate, lies not in its accuracy as a reflection of an existing order but in its power to create such an order in the minds of participants and—we need to remind ourselves—the eyes of the observer.[7]

It is tempting, but misleading, to gloss *ofakae* (manifest) and *ogevake* (concealed) as "public" and "private." These Western concepts contrast collective versus individual interests within different legal spheres of action (Moore 1984). What is "private" is of no concern to the public sphere, it is the domain of individual responsibility and specific kinds of rights; these legalistic connotations are entirely at odds with the meanings of *ofakae* and *ogevake*. Both refer to modes of perception and of knowledge, not legal and political rights. Although *ogevake* does not indicate "private" in the sense of personal or pertaining to a single individual, much that Westerners would term "private" falls under this heading, such as sexuality and the elimination of bodily wastes. Yet Mekeo also regard as *ogevake* those matters that have vital concern for the group as a whole and that cannot logically be included in our category of "private." Two examples are the social tensions underlying the surface of social harmony, and those actions of the men of kindness that are decidedly less than kind.

We can now begin to discern two parts of the Mekeo person and self which, at first glance, might appear equivalent to our divisions of a public and private self. I have described how the self Mekeo present in public to others is very different from that revealed to intimates in confidence. Even if one is burdened by the conviction that a neighbor is responsible for a child's death, one masks one's feelings in public and treats the culprit civilly when met. If the root cause of a child's illness is the anger of a brother-in-law, one still maintains friendly relations with him, at least on the surface. Perhaps a wife is angry with her spouse; he does not openly challenge her, but secretly disposes of the food she brings him. One strives to be controlled and inscrutable, allowing no one the advantage of knowing what is really in one's mind. At the same time, one is aware that other people likewise dissemble.[8]

Mekeo, I think, do not experience a public and a private self, as we do, but rather an outside and an inside to the self. The outside is what other people can see; the inside is kept hidden from others and is known only to one's self. This is implied in what I have written so far, but the language the Mekeo use to refer to these aspects further supports my case. When people speak of their inner thoughts and feelings, they speak of what is *alouai*—"inside myself." Whereas Westerners would say, "We do not know what is in his mind," Mekeo say, literally, "We do not know what he thinks inside himself" (*alogai*). People speak of sadness and mental suffering as *alou ekieki*, literally, "my inside hurting," and of happiness as *alou egama*, literally, "my inside growing or beginning." One's external presence (or absence) is referred to by the term for eyes and, more generally, for face—*maa(ga)*. Desnoes's "Mekeo Dictionary" (1941:634) defines the term as "eye, face, figure, appearance (*oeil; visage, figure, apparence*)." A person's absence, according to Desnoes (1941:635), is expressed as *maaga e afu;* and "in his absence" as *maaga oapugai*. An expression common in my own experience, "he told me," translates as *maauai e ifa*, or "he said it to my face." *Maagai* means, generally, "in the presence of," "in front of" such and such a person. It is to one's face that public, social interactions take place. One's face can, of course, be carefully composed or disguised to express whatever is socially appropriate. What others see of one's face (i.e., of one's overt social presence) is not, however, simply a matter of show, but is of crucial importance. It is surely of significance here, given the emphasis on visibility in the concept of *ofakae*, that what is stressed is the organ, or location, of *sight*.

The Beautiful Surface and the
Dangerous Interior of the Body

Some of the subtle distinctions involved in the concepts of manifest (*ofakae*) and concealed (*ogevake*) can perhaps be brought into clearer relief by considering them as they apply to the outside and the inside of the body.[9]

Handsome faces and bodies are much admired, and careful attention is given to the presentation and decoration of the body surface. The very ugly, the physically weak, and the ill-formed may be openly ridiculed and are likely to find it impossible to marry. Take, for example, the comment (overheard on my veranda coming from the neighboring house) of a pretty, young married woman, who was at the time chafing under her mother-in-law's iron rule, to a skinny, elderly bachelor with one wall eye, as he passed by: "Oh! It's only you. I thought it was some scrawny old fowl scratching around the house!" To the best of my knowledge, there was nothing behind this remark other than the young woman's desire to vent her spleen on someone or something weaker and socially even less important than herself. Taunts and insults from nubile girls concerning the appearance of young bachelors, and the tragic consequences that follow, are the recurring theme of myth, as are the comical difficulties experienced by the ugly and ill-favored in finding a bride. Ufa, an owl of unusually grotesque appearance, is the central character of a whole series of such tales.

Physical beauty is stressed as a key element in erotic attraction. There exists an elaborate corpus of love ritual directed primarily to making a person beautiful in the eyes of the opposite sex. The term to describe such rituals, *pakai,* meaning literally "to decorate" or "make beautiful," indicates this intent. As observed in chapter 1, men are considered more in need of ritual aid in seeking lovers or spouses than women, who are said to be intrinsically desirable. Males thus ordinarily devote more care and attention to grooming and self-decoration. On the special occasions celebrated with traditional dancing (*geva*), participating girls and women decorate themselves splendidly with flowers and traditional valuables such as shells, dogs' teeth, and feathers, paint their faces with intricate geometrical designs, and wear gaily patterned grass skirts; yet, even so, they cannot compete with the principal male dancers, who are crowned with magnificent feather headdresses several feet high.

Women are not thought less beautiful than men. Mekeo ideas of beauty in general are modeled on female rather than male physical characteristics. The myth of Kulua the frog, who was so ugly he was unable to find a bride until he persuaded his sister, Kopi, to masquerade as a young man in his stead, is persuasive here. It is only when the young man, Kulua, takes on the attractive appearance of a girl (the sister does the courting by day; the brother replaces her and makes love to his bride at night, in the dark) that he is successful in finding a mate. Mekeo ideals of beauty place emphasis on a smooth, light, shining, hairless face and body. A hairy face or body is said to be repellent, and many insults are based on accusations of having a hairy mouth, or worse, hairy genitals. Both sexes are said to shave the pudenda. The association of a smooth hairless face with feminine beauty is clearly indicated in the entry under *papie*, "woman," in Desnoes's "Mekeo Dictionary" (1941:922):

> *[A]u lopiaga, ake ae pui=pui, ake papiega.* Est un bel homme, il n'a pas de barbe: il a un menton comme une femme. [He is a handsome man, he has no beard: he has a chin like a woman.]

Light, smooth skins, free of blemishes or marks are favored and on special occasions may be rubbed with turmeric and coconut oil to enhance their appearance. Very dark skins or those disfigured with skin diseases are disliked. Cleanliness is also stressed. Except for those under ritual restrictions, or the sick and elderly, most people bathe every day, and young people make much use of scented soaps and powders. Sweet-smelling herbs, plants, and flowers feature prominently in love ritual; perfumes, including store-bought European scents, are considered powerful agents in making oneself attractive to the opposite sex, although, again, it is usually men who employ them. Light, bright, gay colors in clothing and decoration are preferred by both sexes. Dark colors are disliked as they represent mourning and death and are worn only by widows and widowers and those in mourning for close relatives—and, of course, the men of sorrow.

The word *velo*, usually translated into English as "good," has a range of associations that are aesthetic, sensuous, and functional rather than moral. The connotations of *velo* and its opposite, *apala*, reveal the characteristics of beauty that in Mekeo eyes are preferred. A handsome man is *au velo*. Love songs serenade the beloved with *oi papie velomu*, "you beautiful woman." Desnoes (1941) lists the meanings of *velo* as "pretty, beautiful, straight (*joli, beau, droit*)." It is used with the further sense of "smooth" (i.e., not rough). When people speak of *tsiapu* (clothes) *velo*, they refer to clothes of bright colors; *tsiapu apala* refer to the dark clothes worn for mourning. Alternatively, *tsiapu velo* might refer to a soft, smooth fabric and *tsiapu apala* to a rough, coarse fabric. A smooth, straight road is *keaga velo;* a rough, winding, or boggy track is *keaga apala. Apala* conveys "rough," "ugly," "dark," "of little significance." "Poor fellow" is rendered in Mekeo *au apala*, as is the familiar and affectionate "old man." *Apala* also indicates difficulty and dangerousness. If a particular plant is referred to emphatically as *apala*, it means it is poisonous. If a particular ritual is described as *apala*, it is dangerous for the practitioner to undertake. In contrast to all the things represented as *apala* are those that Mekeo regard as beautiful: softness, smoothness, clearness, cleanness, bright, gay colors, sweet smells, and graceful movements.

Where Westerners assert that "beauty is only skin deep," Mekeo might say that only skin—and surface—has the capacity to be beautiful. There is always the realization that the soft, smooth, clean, bright surface conceals other things not beautiful. The skin or surface, by its very nature, conceals what it contains (cf. A. J. Strathern 1977). There is also a marked sense of the potential for deliberate disguise. Facial and body painting on special occasions is done to make the person beautiful and sexually attractive, but people also draw attention to its advantages in disguising the appearance, and even the identity, of a person. A plain or ugly face can be transformed by skillful painting and the accompanying rituals. Transformed in his mask of beauty, Mekeo say, a man who has a powerful love ritual at his disposal can seduce any girl or woman he likes, without her realizing who he is (see also Hau'ofa 1981:301). Disguise and transformation is especially the forte of the man of sorrow (see chapter 12); he is said to be able to disguise his appearance, and even make himself invisible. The important point is that surfaces can be controlled by being smoothed, painted and decorated to be made beautiful. What those surfaces conceal cannot so easily be brought under control.

From within the beautiful and beguiling body issue dirty, repugnant, and highly dangerous substances (cf. Kakar 1982 and the Western notion of the body as a ''dirt factory''). Any bodily excretion—sweat, tears, spittle, urine, faeces, sexual fluids, blood, pus, mucus—is considered dirty and dangerous, both to those who come into contact with such substances and to those who excrete them. All these excreted substances, plus any part of body substance separated from the body—hair, nail clippings, dirt or skin scraped from the body, teeth, even clothing that has been worn and not washed—are all termed *faga ofuga,* ''dirt of the body'' (literally ''skin,'' but skin is used to refer to the body as a whole, that is, its exterior). Thus what comes from inside the body is regarded as the dirt of its outside. Contact with another person's body dirt is not simply regarded as repugnant, it is believed to cause sickness and even death; it is something that, if undertaken voluntarily, indicates a special degree of care and self-sacrifice on the part of that person. People speak of the way in which parents who care for an infant must themselves be soiled with the infant's constant excretions, an aspect of parental care for which, it is said, offspring should be ever grateful. Those who nurse the sick and the old and helpless run the risk of endangering their own health by this intimate contact with the patient's body dirt. People illustrate their love and concern for an old parent by detailing how they wiped their rheumy eyes, dressed their sores, and took care of their most intimate needs without complaint. Spouses and lovers are said to exchange body dirt during sexual contact. One's offspring may be referred to, disparagingly, as merely one's ''body dirt.''

Although all body dirt is considered dangerous, blood of all kinds is considered the most contaminating. Blood, fluids, and tissue evacuated in childbirth, menstrual blood, and all blood excreted during illness or as a result of wounds and accidents is regarded as especially contaminating and ritually powerful. The body substance of the dead is regarded as more dangerous than that of living persons. Once dead, the whole body, including the exterior, becomes body dirt. At funerals, the close relatives of the deceased, who must wash and prepare the body for burial, and those who deliberately stroke, embrace, and touch the body to demonstrate their grief, are considered to be contaminated by this contact. The mourners take special measures to cleanse themselves; they must fast and must not prepare or cook food for others, and they take particular care not to introduce the body dirt on their hands into their own bodies.

Body dirt of all kinds is dangerous to the person from whom it originates, and it is ritually powerful in the sense that it can be employed to harm the person concerned. Possession of the body dirt of a dead person is believed to give power over the spirit of the deceased, and it can then be directed to kill that person's living relatives. Consequently, people ensure that they carefully dispose of the remains of the dead and their own body dirt, particularly faeces, blood of any kind, and the fluids and issues evacuated in childbirth. As I shall discuss later (part III), body substance provides the basis of all kinds of esoteric ritual, not just of the destructive techniques.

This fear of contamination is not primarily marked by gender differences, as one might expect from the studies of many Papua New Guinea societies. There is no special emphasis on the contaminating influence of female substances on males, but rather on the danger of all bodily substances regardless of the gender of the persons concerned. Nor is it the case, as for example among Wogeo islanders (Hogbin 1970), that the sexual secretions of one sex are considered to be especially inimical to the other. There are no elaborate prophylactic measures comparable to those of the Wogeo to protect male and female against the dangers of normal sexual contact. Yet, the sexual act certainly is thought to hold potential danger since a partner may take the opportunity to obtain covertly some of one's body substance and use it against one, either in destructive rituals or in love ritual.[10] There are various restrictions on sexual contact appropriate to each sex which must be observed during a person's reproductive life. These include the *megomego* procedures for women which follow childbirth, a postpartum taboo on sex between the parents until, ideally, the child is walking, and the necessity for males involved in certain rituals to abstain from sex for the duration of these activities. Menstrual blood, although contaminating like all body substance, is not regarded with special horror by men, nor is sexual intercourse during menstruation, although it is said to be avoided. Although neither gender is considered especially threatened by the bodily secretions of the other, females lose more body substance—and more vital body substance—than do males. Males do not usually excrete blood, whereas women frequently do, in menstruation and childbirth; thus women suffer greater danger of having their body substance expropriated and used against them.

Beneath its smooth, clean, and beautiful exterior, the interior of the human body is considered an unstable flux of substances moving in and out of its orifices. At one level, social interaction could be analyzed, in the manner Mosko (1985) has described for Bush Mekeo culture, as the means of managing flows of substance between bodies in the continuing processes of digestion, elimination, conception, birth, and death. But to describe Mekeo society thus would be to represent it in a way foreign to the way in which Mekeo themselves usually speak of their social world.[11] The inside of the human body and its dirty, dangerous products belong to the domain of "concealed things." Mekeo prefer to focus their attention on the bright, open aspects of society, typified by the central plaza, where the man of kindness displays his largesse and people openly participate in the enjoyment of communal feasting in celebration of the social reciprocities that link them. They do not draw attention to the individual who removes himself from the throng to squat hidden in the bush on the periphery of the settlement and there privately eliminate his bodily wastes, nor to the dark figure who may crouch hidden (i'ovake) there, waiting for the chance to obtain his victim's body dirt. Love and sexual attraction are aroused by handsome faces, beautifully decorated graceful bodies, music and dance, and glistening, oiled, and perfumed skins; that lovers also exchange body dirt is the concern of the man of sorrow, whose interest is with the ritual potency of these secretions.

Concepts concerning body substance are obviously significant in defining the boundaries of self. Mekeo are acutely aware that their own bodies are vulnerable to contamination from the bodily substances of others and to the danger of being attacked via expropriations of their own body substance. This knowledge is available to all; it is the precise details of how such processes operate and how they may be ritually manipulated that constitute esoteric information. The inside and outside of the body is not just a metaphor for the inside and outside of society (Douglas 1970), it is a separate, primary experiential realm for the person through which his or her existence as a person is both realized and threatened. Indeed, this intense concern with the inside of the body and its products reflects Mekeo awareness of self as a separate physical entity that must be defended and protected from too close a contact with others.[12] These issues will be taken up in detail in later chapters.

Reading Hau'ofa's (1981) ethnography helped me clarify my own ideas concerning the complex dualities of Mekeo epistemology. Hau'ofa stresses the double-sidedness of all phenomena in the Mekeo view. His ethnography is keenly sensitive to the undercurrents of tension that underlie the surface social order, and he richly documents many examples. In fact, his data are very similar to mine up to this point, although our interpretations differ somewhat. For Hau'ofa, the two sides to social relationships are indicative of the "ambivalence" underlying all aspects of Mekeo culture—an ambivalence that is handled, he argues, by the division of all aspects of authority into "good" and "bad." Yet what strikes me is the degree to which this ambivalence is a matter of conscious awareness for Mekeo. Their cultural forms do not so much act as defense mechanisms that protect consciousness from the awareness of underlying conflict, rather they serve to emphasize and bring into awareness the existence of conflicting emotions and desires. Mekeo are keenly aware of the conflict of love and hate in close relationships, and they do not attempt to deny the existence of negative emotions in themselves. They aim neither to stifle nor repress them, but attempt only to restrict their manifest expression. Were Mekeo not so disconcertingly in touch with the interior disorder this surface harmony masks, their concern with surface control could well be interpreted as a classic obsessional defence. I emphasize again that Western cultural assumptions tend to blur understanding here. For us there must be one truth— the rest is sham. Not so for the Mekeo; their culture forces them to confront their own emotional conflicts in dealing with one another, and they can accept the contradictions in consciousness.

A further problem, in my opinion, is introduced by Hau'ofa's use of the terms *good, bad,* and *evil* (words that have no doubt gained currency among Mekeo in their attempts to translate indigenous concepts to the Catholic missionaries). More appropriate categories are *ofakae* and *ogevake*—"manifest" and "concealed." *Ogevake* is not necessarily "bad," nor *ofakae* necessarily "good." I have pointed to the fallacy of attributing purely moral implications to the term *apala,* the word usually translated into English as "bad." Concealed things are not necessarily bad, since one's inner thoughts, desires, and emotions are usually concealed. What is bad is to express one's inner thoughts and desires openly and thus reveal the inside of one's self. Mekeo are primarily concerned with ensuring that actions are appropriate to the particular domain in which the actions occur; thus, manifest and concealed cannot be confused or mixed, they must be kept scrupulously apart.

Not surprisingly, during my initial fieldwork I was often plagued by the uneasy feeling that I could not penetrate beyond the surface of Mekeo culture. I felt that much more was going on than I could ever fully access. This may be a common experience for the outsider to any new culture.[13] So much is happening that is simply opaque, and no one thinks to explain, or really can explain, these circumstances, often because what the outsider needs to know is part of implicit, not explicit, cultural knowledge (LeVine 1984). Concealment, disguise, and trickery are key concerns for Mekeo—indeed, they are motifs intricately woven throughout the design of their culture. It was not simply that people were hiding things from me, the outsider, they were forever attempting to conceal their actions, thoughts, and desires from one another.

3

From Visible Things: Fieldwork 1969–1971

My initial fieldwork yielded no lack of information concerning the spirit realm and the activities of the man of sorrow, but what was available to me then, although I was not aware of it at the time, were only the manifest, visible aspects. I knew, of course, of the essential duality of the Mekeo worldview, but I did not fully appreciate its implications. What I have described as the "concealed inside" of social relations soon emerged in the context of everyday conversation and events. I was inclined, however, to interpret this information as the "truth" about social interaction, rather than understanding that both surface harmony and concealed aggressions were, in the Mekeo view, two necessary aspects of the same phenomenon. Furthermore, the symbolic opposition of the roles of the men of kindness and the men of sorrow constituted in itself such a neat duality that I did not think to question what might lie behind it.

My goal then, of course, was not to acquire esoteric knowledge nor to penetrate the secrets of the mysterious activities of the men of sorrow. I went to Mekeo originally to study culture change as a result of colonial rule. Mekeo appealed to me for various reasons. Its experience of European contact reached back into the nineteenth century, yet it had attracted little attention from other scholars, apart from an ethnographic survey by Seligman (1910) in the early 1900s, and in contrast with the Highlands and many other regions of Papua New Guinea, it had a reputation for conservatism and antiwhite sentiment. When I began fieldwork for my Ph.D., my research proposal was for a study combining conventional historical archival research with ethnographic fieldwork and oral history to build up a picture of local attitudes to colonial rule and social change.[1] Since no extensive ethnographic research had been carried out since Seligman's, my first task was basic ethnographic investigation. Shortly after I began, Epeli Hau'ofa also decided to work in Mekeo; he proposed an analysis of the present society as he knew I was working on social change, but this did not obviate the need for me to establish an ethnographic basis upon which to examine social and cultural change. My first phase of fieldwork was characterized by the usual activities and methods of field ethnographers. I, with helpers, mapped the village and surrounds, took a detailed household census, collected genealogies, observed and participated in public feasting and exchanges, observed work parties, meetings, and other group activities, took photographs, went to the gardens, sat and watched the passing ebb and flow of everyday life, and interviewed people on many diverse topics.

With the hindsight afforded by later fieldwork, I now realize that when I left Mekeo in December 1971 I had not penetrated beyond the manifest face of the spirit realm as represented in the public symbolism. What I wrote and published prior to my 1980s fieldwork (Stephen 1974, 1977, 1979b, 1979c) reflects this limited perspective.[2] Before I can begin to describe concealed aspects, it is necessary to outline the information that was openly available to me concerning the spirit realm and the man of sorrow. It needs to be kept firmly in mind that what is said on one level may turn out to be quite the contrary at another level, and that all of this information had to be re-assessed in view of what I learned later. I present in this chapter the public layer as I first encountered it, the *ofakae* aspect of things pertaining to the spirit realm and of people's interactions with it.

The Manifest Face of the Spirit Realm

"Ordinary people don't know about such things, only the men of sorrow (*ugauga aui*) know, and what they know, they won't tell." This was a common response throughout my initial fieldwork to almost any specific question about the spirit realm and people's interaction with it. More sophisticated people might counter enquiries a little differently, replying: "What we believe is really the same as what the missionaries preach, only we say A'aisa created us and you say God."

Friends were likely to respond by launching into a lengthy discussion of the rumored activities and practices of the men of sorrow. Here I encountered a range of levels of discourse. The first level represents the openly acknowledged and symbolically represented order of things. The second represents the attempts of more educated people to justify their beliefs to a European. The third, which I originally mistook for genuine information about esoteric matters, was essentially lay speculation and gossip about esoteric matters. What the man of sorrow is reputed to do is by no means exactly how he operates, but that, of course, serves to protect the exclusiveness of his knowledge (Lindstrom 1984;

Luhrmann 1989). Despite their differences, these responses represented a consistent view of the spirit world as a realm of dangerous power mediated only by the man of sorrow; thus they reiterated the public symbolism.

My enquiries about the spirit world in general were often treated as indirect requests for information concerning the secrets of the man of sorrow. No ordinary person, I was assured, ever tried to interact with or call upon the assistance of the spirits. Furthermore, the spirits themselves had no dealings with the living unless they were conjured by a man of sorrow to attack or injure someone. One elder explained: "The spirits [*isage*] are like [hunting] dogs; they just sit and watch and do nothing until the man of sorrow [*ugauga*] calls them to attack someone."

The spirit entities most often referred to were the dead (*isage*). This category includes the recent dead, distant ancestors, and the heroes and other powerful beings who are the subjects of the myths (*isonioni*). I sometimes heard accounts of people being frightened by the appearance of the ghost of someone recently dead. Occasionally friends remarked to me how they awoke feeling heavy and lethargic because of the presence of spirits of the dead around their houses, noting that in the past the bodies of the dead were buried under houses and that, no doubt, some remains were still to be found there. Men who were in the habit of going hunting by themselves at night claimed they occasionally encountered animals and reptiles in the bush whose strange appearance or behavior clearly revealed they were *isage*. Some confessed they were too frightened to go hunting alone because of the possibility of such encounters. Although no serious harm was expected, most people preferred not to take the risk. More direct contact with the remains of the dead, such as handling a corpse before burial or inadvertently uncovering old bones when digging a new grave, could bring serious illness or even death if proper precautions were not taken.

I heard nothing about the spirits of the dead, or ancestors, protecting, helping, or bringing benefits to the living. The spirit world seemed to be the province of the dead, whose powers were inimical to the living. Although people referred to many kinds of ritual in addition to the lethal *ugauga* of the man of sorrow, these rituals were also presented in a negative light and treated with the same secrecy. In confidence people might comment that such and such a person possessed a charm or spell for hunting, gardening, or for good luck in love or gambling, as was evidenced by their success in these activities. But I was given the impression such minor powers were in no way comparable with the rites of the man of sorrow and required no significant involvement with spirit forces. Major rituals for hunting, for war, for gardening, for love and courting, for controlling the weather, and for a host of other purposes were said to be in the hands of certain powerful men, who were usually not specifically identified. Yet since such rituals were never performed in public, they were not easily observed or accessible. I found it was just as impossible to collect the spells and other elements of these rituals as it was to uncover the secrets of *ugauga*. The precise relationship between these minor and major rituals and *ugauga* sorcery itself was also impossible to determine. But certainly the impression given was that ''sorcery'' was essentially different in kind from other esoteric rituals, an impression equally conveyed by Hau'ofa (1981: 218ff.). A few men of kindness were reputed to possess rituals for hunting and for weather control, but the most powerful experts, those with the greatest number of rituals available to them, were always said to be the men of sorrow.

I could not, moreover, discern a division in powers that placed productive and beneficent rituals in the hands of the man of kindness while confining destructive rituals to the man of sorrow. My most reliable sources of information always insisted that although a few men of kindness did possess major ritual knowledge, such was not inherent in the position, but extrinsic to it. Many men of kindness had no such powers, they pointed out. Furthermore, when people referred to the men of kindness employing ritual it was invariably in a negative context. For example, one might be rumored to be withholding the rain to punish the village, another might be punishing his people by withholding game. Yet when the rain fell as expected, or people were successful in the hunt, no one attributed this to the positive action of a man of kindness, or to any ritual expert. It was only if there occurred some unexpected or unusual dearth, or excessive abundance, that people acknowledged such influence. Unlike those New Guinea cultures where ritual is understood to be essential to all aspects of human existence, and where the fertility and abundance of the natural world is seen to depend on it (e.g., the Garia, see Lawrence 1984), Mekeo seemed to take the natural, material world for granted and saw ritual efficacy at work only in situations where the normal, expected order of things was changed, or perverted, in some way.

In addition to the dead, the other spirit beings most often mentioned were the *faifai*. These water spirits, I was told, inhabit the river, creeks, pools, and swamps, and are important in rituals to bring rain and fish. They might also be summoned by certain powerful men to inflict illness and death on human victims. Unlike the *isage,* they are nonhuman in origin. They are said to resemble people with straight long hair, white skins, and pale eyes (revealing their underwater origin) or to take the form of aquatic creatures such as crocodiles, pythons, large fish, tortoises, and lizards. The physical appearance of Europeans is often compared with the *faifai,* and when the first Europeans arrived in the region they were initially taken to be *faifai* spirits (Stephen 1974). People emphasized that encounters with these beings, like encounters with spirits of the dead, were potentially dangerous and even fatal, depending on the degree of contact; only ritual experts dared to traffic with them. I could find out little more about the *faifai* and could not identify any real-life situations in which their influence was mentioned in explanation. Perhaps the English term *fairies,* which is sometimes used to translate the Mekeo term, combined with my failure to find out much about *faifai*, led me to conclude the water spirits were the stuff of more whimsical fantasy and of little practical importance in people's lives. This assumption proved totally off the mark; I later discovered they played a highly significant role, especially as the agents of major and minor sickness (see chapters 6, 8, 10, 11).

The elders sometimes responded to my requests for information about the spirit world by telling me myths. They always stressed, however, they could tell me only the public versions; there were also esoteric versions known exclusively to the men of sorrow. The most important of these myths were those that dealt with the exploits of A'aisa, the myth hero (an account of the key episodes is given in chapter 1). The "really powerful" versions were said to be the special property of the men of sorrow, but even ordinary people were familiar with the outline of A'aisa's story. When explicating various aspects of their culture and social organization, ordinary men and women, as well as knowledgeable elders, often referred to the precedents laid down by A'aisa (see also Hau'ofa 1981:77ff.). A'aisa's actions provide the origin of many of the key features of the culture—a classic "social charter" in Malinowski's (1974) terms. It was A'aisa himself who initiated the existing social order, creating the positions of the men of kindness (*lopia aui*), the men of the spear (*iso aui*), the men of the cinnamon bark (*faia aui*), and the men of sorrow (*ugauga aui*). It was A'aisa who conferred the rituals associated with these roles, and it is he who is said to be the source of the most important esoteric knowledge. It was A'aisa, who by his quarrel with his younger brother, Isapini, initiated jealousy (*pikupa*) in human relationships and the lethal rituals of *ugauga* to implement revenge. It was the actions of A'aisa that brought death into human existence, and it was none other than A'aisa who initiated the death feasts—but here I am beginning to enter the penumbra of esoteric knowledge (chapter 15).[3]

Although the social charter aspect of the A'aisa story was obvious enough to me, its significance in terms of people's understanding of the spirit world and the cosmic order was less self-evident. The Mekeo have other myths, or narratives, but these appeared to be little more than explanatory folktales. For instance, there is the tale of how the dog became the enemy of the other animals, of how the river came to be, of how the fishing trap originated—ostensibly innocuous folk tales recited merely for entertainment. Subsequently I discovered they too were the vehicles of important ritual knowledge (chapter 9). But at this time I had access only to the public versions. The A'aisa myth alone was acknowledged to have serious import, yet this import was never clearly explained.

When I tried to obtain an exegesis of these various narratives, the usual laconic response prevailed: "Only the men of sorrow know more, and they won't tell you what they know!" Sometimes a man of sorrow himself would portentously announce that he would recite a myth unknown to ordinary folk.

He might tell how A'aisa gave death to the people, or how A'aisa journeyed with the body of his dead son, or how he made wallabies (which are, indeed, key episodes of the myths, see chapter 15). But commentary was never offered, nor could I extract any, nor were these versions significantly different from those told by laypersons. Faced with another dead end, I tried to focus my questions on A'aisa, only to encounter a different impasse. Invariably, my questions were met, by ordinary people and knowledgeable elders alike, with a comparison of A'aisa with the Christian God. Countless times I heard people declare: "You whites say 'Deo' [the Catholic mission translation for God], we say 'A'aisa.' It's the same!"

Christian Influence

Since its establishment in the region in the late nineteenth century, the Catholic Mission of the Sacred Heart has had continuous and pervasive influence on the Mekeo (Dupeyrat 1935; Stephen 1974; Hau'ofa 1981). The nature and extent of this influence is a complex topic beyond the scope of my study, yet it is evident that in attempting to understand conceptions of the spirit realm, we must take into account the fact that Mekeo have been exposed to the teachings and rituals of Catholicism for over a century. Even the oldest people have grown up in a community wherein everyone is at least a nominal Catholic and where schools, other educational facilities, and medical and health services have been provided (almost exclusively until the postwar years) by the Catholic mission. Yet despite the very visible presence of the mission, my first impressions were that Mekeo Christianity was little more than skin deep, except in the case of a well-educated, younger minority (Stephen 1974).

Inawi village has its own church, built at one end of the village in a fenced yard, along with the mission-run village primary school and a small house where the parish priest lodges overnight on his frequent visits from Beipa, the mission headquarters. The church is a large, shabby, but rather charming structure built of sawn timber. The inside is adorned with elaborate painted statues, now a little faded and chipped, of religious figures imported many years ago from Italy or Spain; they stand benignly in their niches, framed by traditional geometric designs fashioned by village artists. Except for the altar and its furnishings, the interior is bare; the congregation always sits on the floor, men on one side, women on the other. Attendance at church services and prayers was always sparse on those days when the parish priest was not officiating: a few elderly people, some young girls, a handful of school children the teacher managed to round up. A much larger, enthusiastic congregation arrived when the parish priest was in attendance. People demonstrated the greatest fondness and personal respect for their European parish priest, who had been in the region for nearly thirty years.

Yet, Christianity as a faith or a way of life seemed to me to be far less in evidence. In the first place, it was apparent that the influence of Christian teachings had had little or no impact on people's beliefs in the efficacy of sorcery and other esoteric ritual. Nor had it destroyed Mekeo belief in the existence of A'aisa, the traditional culture hero. As Hau'ofa (1981:21–22) observes, the Catholics, unlike many Protestant missionaries, favored no deliberate policy of attacking traditional culture, but rather attempted to work in cooperation with, and through, traditional authorities. There was no attempt to confront or condemn the men of sorrow themselves. Such policies no doubt served to underline a sense that Christian teachings and traditional beliefs were not necessarily inimical or mutually exclusive (Stephen 1974). During my first fieldwork, people's most extensive statements to me about the spirit world were framed as comparisons with Christian beliefs. For example:

"The missionaries say that if we do wrong, God will punish us; our ancestors said if we do wrong, A'aisa is watching us and we will be punished. The missionaries say that when we die our souls will go to God in Heaven; our ancestors said that when we die our spirits will go to A'aisa's place, Kariko."

A'aisa is sometimes identified as God the Father; his younger brother, Isapini, is likened to Jesus. Many similar comparisons are made, varying according to the education and experience of the speaker. There are no obvious divisions along the lines of "Christians" and "Pagans," as in some Papua New Guinea communities (e.g., Lawrence 1964; Burridge 1960; Tuzin 1989). Indeed virtually all Mekeo regard themselves as Christians and Catholics. Even a man of sorrow might wear a crucifix around his neck and attend church services. A man of sorrow once asked me during my early fieldwork whether it was true, as the missionaries told him, that his father and grandfathers were now in hell, with horns growing out of their heads, in punishment for their actions. Years later I asked the same man if he did not attend church services because he lacked faith in Christian teachings. He replied that his activities as a man of sorrow precluded him from taking communion without first confessing his sins, and this he had not done. Whenever he was ready to make contrition, he could do so—but he was in no hurry. This attitude typifies many who do not dismiss or oppose Christianity, but who seem to treat it as largely irrelevant.

My later fieldwork brought a new appreciation of how deep the influence of Christian teachings has been on people's minds, hearts, and imaginations (see chapters 6 and 8). There are many well-educated, devout Catholics, particularly among the younger people. There are also many older people, with little formal education, who regard themselves as devoted Christians and are regular churchgoers and staunch supporters of the Catholic mission, yet their intellectual grasp of Christian dogma is slight. In the case of this second and larger group, a god of love and forgiveness seems absent from their understanding. Christian figures are treated as sources of ritual efficacy to bring healing and to bring help in love and other mundane activities, rather than as symbols of forgiveness and redemption. Although people equate A'aisa with God, the similarities are not persuasive. The A'aisa of the myths is not a creator, nor do any but the men of sorrow "pray" to him. He is a trickster who deceives and punishes all who cross him, not a forgiving savior. I do not want to enter into the complex theoretical arguments concerning the nature of "conversion" and of syncretism of belief. There are evidently many different layers to Mekeo "Christianity," just as Mekeo today have many different levels of education, both secular and religious, and many varied kinds of experience of life beyond their village communities.

For the majority of people discussed in these pages, the teachings of Christianity and indigenous beliefs in the spirit realm seem to co-exist without conflict. Or rather, as I will show, they have become inextricably interwoven. Yet it is true that whatever changes—and innumerable subtle modifications—Christianity may have brought, A'aisa and the cosmic order he initiated continue to dominate the Mekeo worldview. My concern is not to identify a hypothetical "pure" system of "traditional" beliefs, but to provide an ethnography of lived and living experience in a culture that has been exposed to a century of European influence.

Lay Speculation Concerning "Sorcery"

"Sorcery" was a topic ordinary people were keen to discuss with me, although always in confidence. They readily explained that the men of sorrow possessed esoteric knowledge and rituals to control the spirits of the dead, and even to invoke powerful beings such as A'aisa himself. The spirit realm was said to be infused with heat, *isapu* (the same word is used for the heat of the sun or of fire). Not only were the spirits possessed of this heat, so too were relics of the dead such as bones, teeth, or dried flesh and organs. The man of sorrow constructed his deadly charms by combining such relics with various potent substances, thus generating *isapu* (see also Hau'ofa 1981:219–222). He deployed special stones (*kepo*) infused with this heat and by means of them, in conjunction with powerful spells (*mega*), he could summon the spirits to kill or inflict sickness on his victims. Certain kinds of sorcery required the victim's leavings—his urine, faeces, spittle, or similar; other techniques did not. The man of sorrow robbed bodies from graves in order to take the parts of the flesh and organs that gave him power over the spirit of the dead person. All serious illness and death was caused by the man of sorrow, and the spirits never attacked nor harmed the living unless they were called upon by him, so it was always said.

The powers invoked by the man of sorrow are so strong and so dangerous that he must take care that he himself does not fall victim. Not only must the practitioner be instructed in the correct rituals and incantations but he must undergo a severe regime of fasting, isolation, and sexual abstinence referred to as *gope* (see also Hau'ofa 1981:234–243). Over a period of several months he thus prepares his body for the task. Many cautionary tales were told of men of sorrow who failed to do so.

As a result of his ritual regime and preparation, and as a consequence of the powerful relics and substances he keeps with him, the man of sorrow's very physical person was said to become charged with destructive power (see also Hau'ofa 1981:234). When he appears on public occasions, he is believed to be carrying powerful charms on his person which affect anyone who is not likewise ritually prepared, and everyone takes good care to keep as far away as possible. An educated young man told me how he had been accidently "hit" by a man of sorrow's powers. He was on the way to the gardens when he suddenly saw a man of sorrow from his village, one who was well known to him, appear at the side of the track. He told him to say nothing and go at once to his place in the bush and wait there until he returned. Terrified, the young man ran as fast as his legs would carry him and collapsed in a faint when he reached the designated place. He recalled being seized by terrible pains in all his limbs and the overwhelming fear that he was about to die. Finally, the man of sorrow returned, gave him some medicines, said spells over him, and told him to rest. Later he explained he was on his way to attack a victim, carrying the lethal charm, when the young man had met him on the track and was struck down instead of the intended victim. My informant was convinced that had he not been treated immediately, he would have died. Others told similar tales of terrifying encounters with *ugauga*.

It is said that when a person is affected by the powers of the man of sorrow, as a result of either some accidental contact or a deliberate attack, only the assailant can cure his victim (see also Hau'ofa 1981:243) (I later discovered this is not quite accurate). Relatives of the victim must seek the man of sorrow out in the hope of buying him off. They might simply approach the one they suspect or they might consult a diviner. All this must take place, however, in strictest secrecy; one would never learn, unless one were closely related to the victim, which man of sorrow or which diviner was consulted (Hau'ofa 1981:245 also stresses the absolute privacy in which such matters are negotiated). I could not even get my friends to give me the names of those people who operated as diviners. They would sidestep my questions and mutter about people in "other villages" one could approach. Rumors about illness and deaths, about payments made to the men of sorrow, about secret consultations with diviners were in profusion—but of visible social action there was very little.

Different destructive techniques were lumped together as "sorcery" (*ugauga*). Likewise, no distinctions were drawn between different kinds of practitioners. In private gossip the man of sorrow's public role as the legitimate holder of destructive powers used at the behest of the man of kindness seemed to dissolve into a kind of universal bogeyman, ever ready to attack others out of pure malice. Most people seemed to doubt whether the man of kindness was strong enough to control him and suspected that the man of sorrow killed merely for personal motives such as revenge or payment. Nevertheless, in discussing actual cases, people usually did interpret death or serious illness as the consequence of wrongdoing on the part of the sufferer (see also Hau'ofa 1981:269ff.). The community as a whole seemed ever anxious and aware of the dangerous powers in the hands of senior and high-ranking men, powers, moreover, that could be bought if one were wealthy enough.

I assumed—naively as it turned out—that what friends told me in confidence about sorcery constituted esoteric knowledge. I took this information for an accurate general description of the activities of the man of sorrow, even though the precise details of his rituals were unknown, or withheld. In fact, what I have just described constitutes little more than gossip about what the man of sorrow is believed to do. There was a rich vein of such discourse readily available to the outsider; one might occupy oneself for hours on end, as indeed I did, listening to it. Nor did the real experts betray anything to me that might alter laymen's conceptions. Although these general descriptions were by no means entirely inaccurate, they were subtly misleading (chapter 13).

Despite all the gossip and speculation about sorcery I listened to throughout my first phase of fieldwork, and despite many discussions with men of sorrow themselves, I never felt I grasped people's real understandings concerning the spirit world or their relations with it. Yet to be any more insistent might have risked losing what cooperation I had. Mekeo presented me with a very consistent and articulate view of a powerful but negatively charged spirit realm which could be used by a few powerful men for primarily destructive, punitive purposes. This realm was one of which ordinary people knew little or nothing, being concerned only with avoiding contact with it at all costs. All the information I collected served only to reinforce the public symbolism described earlier. If my efforts to gain a more nuanced picture seem clumsy and ineffectual, that impression can be countered by pointing out that Hau'ofa's (1975, 1981) comprehensive research in neighboring communities adds more detail, but no great differences to the general outline sketched here.[4]

Encountering the Men of Knowledge

Ironic as it may seem, during my initial fieldwork I had befriended the very persons who knew all there was to know about hidden things, and who might have told me everything I wanted to know. Since these early encounters paved the way for subsequent dialogues, it is worth recounting some of the more outstanding.

Perhaps my favorite was a gentle old man in his seventies, whom I will call Luke (I follow the practice of referring to people by commonly used baptismal

Luke

names, but not their own). Luke was short and thin, with a wiry muscularity. He dressed in shabby shorts and shirts, or sometimes the traditional male attire of a belt and perineal band, paying none of the attention to his appearance that most other men, even of his age, affected. His scanty hair was grey and receding from a broad, high forehead. His face, striking in its keen intelligence and alertness, was dominated by a dignified Roman nose, with deep lines on either side leading to a straight, determined mouth. His eyes were penetrating, with none of the opaqueness characteristic of old age. Despite his small stature and careless dress, he was a commanding presence. He always appeared to me an incarnation of that fabled creature, the ''primitive philosopher.'' Not only was he a mine of information on any topic but he took delight in explaining and systematizing this knowledge. Whereas others would impatiently brush aside my attempts to point out inconsistencies, Luke would pause, cock his head to one side and, fixing me with that penetrating and pleased look a professor gives the student who asks an unusually intelligent question, he would carefully examine my objection. When at last satisfied I had indeed identified some inconsistency, he would sit rubbing his chin and nodding his head, mulling over the problem in the manner of all devoted scholars until he reached a solution. His capacity to counter my objections with answers based on logical inconsistencies never failed to amaze me.

These conversations had to take place through an interpreter, as the intricacies of our discussions were far beyond my halting attempts in Mekeo. Even my interpreter came to look forward to the sessions with Luke, and he often asked him questions of his own which I could not have thought of without an insider's knowledge. The young man who served as my main interpreter was fluent in English and highly intelligent; he had secondary schooling and had worked in Port Moresby for the government for some years before deciding to return to the village to marry and settle down. He evidently had never before had the opportunity to hear his culture expounded in such clear and detailed terms. He took almost as much pleasure as I did in Luke's expositions and, given his education and work experience, he savored my attempts as a European to build some bridge between Mekeo and my own cultural concepts. Luke was now too old for hard physical labor, and he spent most of his time just sitting on the veranda of his little house, rocking in his hammock. Often he would dandle his two-year-old grandson on his knee while we talked. Luke always had time, and our discussions soon became a regular feature of my routine: not a week passed without several hours with him. Even so, his fund of stories, myths, clan histories, and personal reminiscences seemed inexhaustible.

Luke possessed that sine qua non of knowledge in an oral culture, a remarkable memory, and he was greatly admired for it. People would often comment that whereas they usually forgot things, Luke retained everything he was ever told. But he impressed me above all with a moral dignity, a benevolent and idealistic view of human society and the world at large as defined by his cultural perspective, which he never tired of explaining. It was from Luke, especially, that I learned about the role of the man of kindness and its moral force. A member of the *lopia*'s lineage, Luke's widely respected knowledge and venerable age made him an invaluable adviser. He was the community's authority concerning its relationship with the colonial government, and in our discussions Luke presented a forceful and consistent account of events within the framework of an ideal moral order (Stephen 1974; 1977). His view was by no means idiosyncratic, but it was the most articulate and comprehensive. Luke was respected and admired by the community as a whole. I never heard ill of him, and in this culture of endless covert suspicions and intrigue, that alone was remarkable. Nor did he speak ill of others. In his gentle wisdom, he seemed to embody the ideals he expounded.

Ironically, Luke emerges in retrospect as the most enigmatic of all, simply because I subsequently heard nothing to alter this idealistic view. I later discovered a darker side to the reputation of every other prominent man in the community (chapter 9). So much was my understanding of things changed by this, that I am now convinced Luke's almost saintly public persona was only part of the picture, and perhaps to some extent the construct of my own idealizations.

An equally outstanding, although very different, character was George, [*George*] reputedly the oldest man in the village and a highly respected man of kindness. He was a huge, rollicking man, although never a buffoon. He would rock with laughter at his own jokes and have fun with the younger men as they sat together in the clan meeting house without for a moment compromising his dignity. Well into his seventies at the time, his bulky physique was still muscular. He always appeared in public with his fine head of hair teased up into the great halo favored by Mekeo men and as stylishly dressed as any of the younger ''dandies.'' There was nothing harsh or forbidding in his manner, yet his straight back, huge frame, broad impassive face, and authoritative tone of voice all conveyed a man used to receiving deference.

George was expected, as clan leader and elder, to spend much of his time deliberating with his kinsmen and with the other senior men. He almost always found time to talk to me, and like Luke, he enjoyed our discussions. He was full of humorous tales of youthful exploits, of how he and his comrades hoodwinked patrol officers and other colonial officials. He told of the gruelling mountain patrols young Mekeo men were conscripted for in the 1920s and 1930s (Stephen 1974). The hungry porters would surreptitiously eat the supplies in the boxes they carried, then fill them with stones before handing over to the mountain carriers, so that the white patrol officer did not notice the loss until later. He described the community's experiences of the Second World War and of his exploits as a village constable (Stephen 1974, 1979c). I asked whether during his term of office he ever was struck or beaten by white officials. Drawing himself up to his full impressive height, he roared, ''No, they would not dare, for if they did I would have hit them back!'' One can imagine only a foolhardy patrol officer would attempt it. In addition to his position as a junior man of kindness (*lopia eke*), George was a rain expert, a role involving special ritual powers to invoke and control the water spirits, the *faifai;* the real significance of these powers only became clear to me years later (chapter 9).

From the time I arrived in the village, the topic of sorcery seemed to arise at every juncture. No death took place in the community that was not attributed to it; people constantly explained their actions in terms of fears of it. I was forever being warned by ordinary people not to spend time in the company of those elders who possessed dangerous ritual knowledge. They were impressed not a jot by my assertions that Europeans were unaffected by sorcery. Everyone could recall stories of Europeans, including government officers and Catholic priests and nuns, who had suffered from sorcery. Even if I lacked the good sense to take care of myself, they scolded, I should think of my friends and neighbors before encouraging such dangerous persons to visit. Should they or their families become sick, neighbors warned, I would be to blame. For my part, I was, of course, eager to talk with the men of sorrow. Very early in my fieldwork, I was introduced to a famous man of sorrow visiting from another village. A small, skinny figure clad in a cast-off European suit jacket and torn shorts, with scanty hair wrapped in a dirty scarf, he nevertheless conveyed a remarkable, chilling presence. Fixing me with stony black eyes like those of a snake, he held out his hand for me to shake, muttering something as he did so which sounded like a threat or a challenge. Those present quickly translated for me: ''I can kill you, if I wanted to, just by taking your hand.'' I took his hand and attempted to return his glance firmly. I had little doubt he meant exactly what he said.

The community's solicitousness on my behalf was both touching and rather irritating. I wanted to be taken more seriously and treated less like some vulnerable creature requiring constant protection. I would have preferred to forget I was a young white woman, usually on my own, in a strange and physically harsh environment, but people were ever mindful of these circumstances. They expressed concern lest my fair skin get burned in the sun, bitten by insects, or scratched by thorns and grasses in the bush; the women marveled at my tender feet—softer than their hands, they exclaimed—and my apparent uselessness for the hard physical work that they performed every day in their gardens. They worried lest I should get sick, or that poison might be put in my food when I visited other places. I was never, during this period, allowed to go anywhere outside the village without an escort, even for a walk. There was general consternation when I insisted on sleeping in a house by myself as it was feared young men might attempt to break into the house at night to rape me. The family that built my house for me were thus saddled, I later realized, with responsibility for my safety. But the attitude of protective concern was pervasive. When my husband was with me, people relaxed a little, but then there was concern for both of us. The prevailing belief that we, as Europeans, were fragile, vulnerable and in need of special care never wavered.

Yet the villagers were very indulgent and tolerant of whatever we did; we were never upbraided for social gaffes, which we were undoubtedly forever committing unaware. Wherever we went, we were made to feel welcome. Apart from the insistence that I be accompanied when I went outside the village (neither was my husband allowed beyond village boundaries by himself), there were no restrictions placed on me as a woman, and I was always graciously welcomed at the clan meeting houses, which are male preserves. I even visited male elders and widowers at their bachelor's houses (*gove*), but I was warned by ordinary people that this was dangerous as I might be exposed to the influence of the powerful ritual objects and relics stored in such places. The elders, with their amused but good-natured tolerance of my questioning and curiosity—indeed, of my odd and curious presence—typified the response of the community as a whole. In short, I was treated much like a child, a creature who, being ignorant and vulnerable, cannot be expected to take responsibility for its social actions, who has yet to assume a position where it has social obligations of its own. Its actions are the responsibility of mature others; it must be protected against its own ignorance and weakness, yet at the same time allowed to explore and learn (cf. Schneider 1968:9). Culturally, of course, I *was* a child—just learning to speak.

Three men of sorrow were among those who became my best sources of information and, I suppose, my protectors as well: Augustine, Opu, and Aisaga. Neither Luke nor the more flamboyant George (despite his knowledge of *faifai* ritual) were identified as men of sorrow. The oldest of the three, Augustine, was a positively mischievous character. He was in his late sixties or early seventies and seemed to delight in scandalizing and terrifying my neighbors by visiting my house to talk with me. He would make it as visible a public spectacle as he could, limping arthritically across the open space of the village, his dusty black widower's garb clutched around him like the feathers of an old blackbird (the image has a special aptness that I discovered later: such feathers are used in the secret medicines prepared for death-dealing rituals). Women and children scattered, and men withdrew at a more dignified pace. He would chuckle at this hasty retreat and settle down to talk. He also loved to invite me to have ''tea'' with him on the veranda of his little bachelor's house; in his youth he had worked as a cook for Europeans and had learned to bake bread, scones, and other delicacies. He built a special oven in the village, but no one seemed to want to eat food prepared by *his* hands except foolish Europeans like myself (men of sorrow are believed to be constantly handling ritually dangerous objects and substances, and they thus contaminate anything they touch).

Augustine was a maddening, but wonderful source of information on ritual matters. He would never answer the questions I put to him, instead veering off willfully onto whatever topic happened to take his fancy. In this way I often learned much more than I would have dared to ask for directly. It is only now I have any appreciation of what an ordeal these sessions were for my interpreter, who had not only to eat the old man's food but absorb the dangerous information that Augustine occasionally let slip. Years later I discovered that after I left, the interpreter had to kill a large pig and present riches to Augustine as a payment for what was revealed during these sessions.

Another man of sorrow, Opu, lived in a bachelor's house built close to the back of my house, where I could hear him everyday coughing painfully. Opu was a rather pathetic figure—just how pathetic I did not fully understand—but he always conducted himself with scrupulous dignity. His illness and ritual privations had reduced him to skin and bone; even so, he always contrived to present a neat, controlled appearance. Appropriate to his widower's status, he wore a severe, plain black *rami*, tightened around his wasted body with a broad black leather belt, black mourning arm bands, and a necklace of black beads. His hair, which I suspected (correctly) he dyed black, was always carefully combed up into a neat halo above his strangely wizened face. He would sit straight-backed and alert; his voice was always firm and dignified, yet his small black eyes and the sagging flesh around them betrayed his suffering. It was common knowledge that Opu was dying of tuberculosis because of his laxity in observing the ritual regime (*gope*) necessary for practicing men of sorrow. Opu, it was rumored, had slept with his wife at a time when he was handling the lethal objects and potions used in *ugauga* sorcery. His carelessness, it was said, first killed his wife and now, more slowly, was killing him.

I never heard his side of the story, but years later, after his death, one of Opu's sons told me his father believed that he and his wife were poisoned. Thus it appears Opu did not himself accept responsibility for the fate that had befallen him, or perhaps simply could not admit it. But certainly as far as the rest of the community was concerned, he had only himself to blame, and no one, not even his close agnates, had much sympathy for him. I assumed, naively, that his relatives looked after him, at least to the extent of providing his food, since his wife was dead and he was sick. Occasionally I would send him a plate of food, particularly if I had been presented with food at some public gathering. John, my husband, who always rose early before the rest of the village was awake, got into the habit when he was there of taking over a cup of coffee to Opu, the only other person awake at that early hour. We had no idea this might be the only refreshment he would receive for days on end. Later I learned that none of his relatives were prepared to take responsibility for him, and he depended on what little might come his way when food was shared at his lineage meeting house. His three sons were looked after by other families, but the boys were either too young to be of any help to him or were away at school. Ignored by his relatives, feared and avoided by the rest of the village because of his ritual knowledge, Opu sat alone on his veranda day after day, but he never complained to us or revealed his situation. Throughout this first period of fieldwork, despite all the time I spent interviewing the elders, no one offered or agreed to tell me a single spell (*mega*). It was Opu who imparted the first, and only, spell I was able to record then. In fact, he told my husband. It was a hunting spell for catching birds in nets. No doubt the hot cup of coffee brought to him on many mornings in the lonely hours just before dawn was appreciated.

A totally different presence was Aisaga, who was to play a leading role during my subsequent period of fieldwork and who is a key figure in the chapters that follow. He was the lineage head of the clan section in which I resided and one of the most renowned men of sorrow in the whole Mekeo region. Aisaga was the clan's war leader, but he had passed on this position to his eldest son, who was a married man in his thirties. The knowledge of *ugauga* sorcery was also part of Aisaga's birthright, and he had assumed this role when he was widowed some seven or so years earlier. He lived away from the village, which was appropriate for a practicing man of sorrow, although two of his adult sons and their families lived with him. Nevertheless, the fact that he lived outside the community undoubtedly added to the fear in which he was held, and allowed him to stage-manage his appearances to great effect. On Sundays, when lineage members gathered to share food and converse, or on any important public occasion held by his clan, Aisaga would suddenly materialize in the gloom at the back of the meeting house (*ufu*), the part reserved for widowers and men of sorrow. One never saw him arrive, or leave; he was simply there one moment and gone the next. He rarely spoke but sat silent and aloof from the rest of the group, who took care not to sit too close to him. If he did speak, it was in a quiet and extremely dignified manner, and everything stopped until he had finished.

Tall and bone-thin, Aisaga always appeared in the village carefully dressed in black. His hair was usually bound up in a widower's snood, his haughty, aristocratic face composed into a frozen mask of bony planes and hollow cheeks. Long sinewy arms and legs were tightly bound at various points with mourning bands, emphasizing the way in which his ritual fasting and privation had stripped every last ounce of spare flesh from his tall frame, giving it a curious elegance. The light, yellowish tone of his skin was also the result of his ritual privations. Holding himself perfectly straight and motionless, he would sit for hours, his remote black eyes seemingly not focused on the common conviviality and social hubbub before him. I really could not have guessed his age, for his face seemed as timeless and immobile as an ancient Egyptian sculpture (years later I learned that the adept aims to convert vulnerable flesh into imperishable stone).[5] I knew he had adult, almost middle-aged sons and daughters, and so I assumed him to be well into his sixties. The mission's records gave his birth date as 1917; he was thus then only in his fifties. Aisaga was indeed an awe-inspiring and impressive figure, a living symbol of his culture's traditions of sacred and temporal power.

Away from the village, however, this imposing public persona was put aside, and a more relaxed, although still forceful presence emerged. When we first visited Aisaga's farm, as he had invited John and myself to do, we were greeted by a shouted welcome from a tall figure clad in blue jeans and perched halfway up a tree, repairing a high fence around the property. This proved to be none other than Aisaga himself. With his usually impassive countenance wreathed in smiles and his grizzled unruly hair flying about his face, he was unrecognizable as the spectral black-clad figure that appeared on public occasions. He led us around his property, showed us the family residence where his sons and their wives and children lived, and then took us to his own small bachelor's house, built at some distance from the main settlement, where we were to have tea with him. Aisaga seemed pleased we had taken the trouble to visit him and talked with us in a jovial and relaxed manner. The same cannot be said of the interpreter I persuaded to come with us, the same one that was brave enough to endure the visits with old Augustine. The interpreter was tense and wary and not at all reassured by Aisaga's friendly manner. Later he asked if I had noticed the round objects hanging from a chain suspended over a small fire on Aisaga's veranda. These, he averred, were the lethal charms used to ensorcell Aisaga's victims.

As head of the lineage on whose land my house was built, Aisaga had at least some degree of responsibility for me. At first there had been arguments over this land between Aisaga and the man who built the house for me, who was his classificatory younger brother. Fortunately these troubles were soon ironed out. While my house was being built, I lived in a small house belonging to the Catholic mission next to the village church, which was isolated from the rest of the village in its own compound. People were concerned about my safety here, as I insisted on sleeping by myself at night. Later I was told Aisaga had announced to the village that while I stayed in the mission house he would himself patrol the bush at the back of the compound each night, spear in hand. Whether he actually did so, he had publicly announced I was under his protection. Perhaps this was the reason he appeared so concerned when early in 1971 my husband broke his leg in a motorbike accident.

The accident occurred a few hundred yards from the Catholic Mission Hospital near Beipa village, about three miles distant. John was carried to the hospital, where he was visited that evening by Aisaga, who came in the dark, his face grim and his axe over his shoulder. The Mekeo nurses fled as he approached, leaving him alone with the patient; he stood at the foot of bed, muttered a few words and then left. He may have felt the accident was some reflection on his own reputation, since he had publicly declared us to be under his protection.

I did not receive news of the accident until the evening, and as the news spread about the village there was much concern. Our friends were upset, but they indicated we had brought this misfortune on our own heads by willfully ignoring their warnings. It was not implied that harm had been done to us deliberately; simply being in the company of ritually potent elders such as Augustine and Aisaga involved danger. Now we would have to learn from our hard experience, our friends implied, and suffer the consequences—a recurring theme in this culture.

The leg fracture was a bad one, right through the knee-joint, but after surgery in Australia and three months of recuperation, John returned with me to Mekeo with the leg mended. Everyone was delighted and surprised to see us both. In the rough circumstances of village life, in a torrid tropical climate where infection quickly takes hold, comparatively simple injuries such as a broken limb can lead to amputation and death (see chapter 8 for a tragic example). Friends confessed they had not expected to see John again. I really cannot say what they thought when we continued just as we had before the accident. At this time I had only three months in which to finish my fieldwork, so I increased the time spent interviewing the elders. I now began to visit them on my own without interpreters. Only a few days prior to our final departure, a ''breakthrough'' occurred. Throughout the whole time of my fieldwork I heard about, but had never seen, the dangerous objects and relics supposedly used by the men of sorrow. It was impossible to be shown such things, I was always told, because the danger involved to me was simply too great. Many people believed that inadvertent exposure to such objects caused the motorbike accident. So I had no way of knowing whether they existed or were simply part of a fantasy system surrounding what the men of sorrow were supposed to do.[6] At the last minute, Aisaga decided to show us some of these potent things.

During my last months in Mekeo in 1971, Aisaga frequently visited us in the village, usually bringing a present of eggs, which he knew Europeans appreciated. I spent many hours talking with him, and he told me myths (although never the esoteric versions) and stories of the past. I asked about sorcery, but only in general terms. At last he suggested that John and I visit him at his farm, but this time without an interpreter (by now we could communicate a little in Mekeo). He awaited us on the veranda of his bachelor's house. This time there was no tea. Almost as soon as we settled ourselves, he disappeared into the dark interior of the little house and emerged with a metal box. He opened it and proceeded to unwrap the contents, which proved to be packets of all kinds of unidentifiable dried substances and other small objects. He explained each in turn but my vocabulary was not up to this; all I could understand was that these were substances used in hunting charms. From another box he extracted and unwrapped various stones of different colors and shapes. He handled these more circumspectly, not touching them directly but using the bark cloth in which they had been wrapped to manipulate them. Others he moved around with sticks, avoiding direct contact. These, I assumed, must be the sorcery stones, but no, they also were for hunting. I pointed to the objects hanging over the fire that on a previous occasion my interpreter had assumed were containers of sorcery substances—these were also for hunting.

More stones and mysterious substances were brought out. I began to get confused; I tried to take notes but there was too much that was new and unknown. At last the boxes were repacked and put away. He got up to leave the house and motioned us to follow. He led us around while he dug up several more boxes from various places on the property where they were buried. These he took back to the house, but before unpacking them, he donned a huge pair of black rubber industrial gloves! These objects he exposed to view, handling them as little as possible. There were stones, crystals, human and animal teeth, and other things impossible to identify. Here, he explained, were the objects used for sorcery (*ugauga*), plus many kinds of disease infliction. Finally, he produced two complete human jaw bones: the skulls of his elder brother and sister, he said, who had died in their youth, while he was still a child. We were most carefully instructed not to reveal to anyone in the village what we had seen.

We got up to leave quite amazed by what had transpired and especially by the trust placed in us. As we walked along the track back to the village we began to laugh with relief that no mishap had occurred that might have given him excuse, or cause, to show us nothing more. If one of us had felt nauseous or become faint in the heat or had a bad headache—never unlikely occurrences in this climate—then we would have seen nothing since this would have beyond doubt demonstrated our weakness. He certainly had us keyed up, and, as always, he had carefully stage-managed his performance, or so it seemed. Just as we emerged from the bush track onto the main path leading to the village, we were literally nearly bowled over, although Aisaga could not have stage-managed this. To our utter astonishment, we were confronted by a galloping, riderless white horse that seemed to appear from nowhere and thundered at full speed down the jungle path. I swear I had not read a word of Jung at the time![7] Nor had we ever seen a horse in the vicinity before; it must have escaped from the Catholic mission station, three miles away. But let not rationality deny the aptness of this image of unleased power.

Only a few days remained until our departure. Toward the end of our stay, old George had taken to visiting us almost every day to ask when we were leaving. One morning he arrived very early; John was already up and sitting on the veranda, but I was still inside the house. Assuming I was asleep, they began to talk softly so as not to wake me. I could hardly believe my ears when I heard the conversation progressing comfortably—in English! In all the time I had known George he never uttered more than a word or two of English in my presence. I always had to struggle to communicate in the little Mekeo I could muster, and our lengthy conversations depended on the aid of an interpreter. Somehow he had managed all this time to deceive me. Finally I burst out, "George, you tricked me!" A roar of laughter greeted the discovery of his duplicity. As I emerged indignantly from the house to confront him, George soothed me with promises that now I knew a little of their language, and when I returned the next time they would teach me to speak it correctly. He was quite delighted with himself for having kept up the joke so long.

Luke had perpetrated a similar, although not quite such an elaborate joke. Luke also spoke no English, yet one day toward the end of our stay, John passed by his veranda and waved hello to him to be greeted with "Good morning John, where are you going," in perfect English. Delighted by John's surprise, the old man later revealed he had spent days practicing with his English-speaking son to achieve the desired effect. Much Mekeo humor depends on such deception. A good trick is calculated to provoke mirth and is always appreciated, just as the plots of many myths and folktales pivot on trickery, disguise, and the humorous—and tragic—consequences of deception.

This humor had a double edge. For me the jokes underlined a serious point. Like any ethnographer, I was aware of the necessity to communicate with people in their own language, but my progress was not fast enough. As in areas where Pidgin provides an effective lingua franca, English was so widely spoken I could easily collect material in it alone. Old people spoke little or no English, but there were plenty of interpreters. Moreover, good interpreters were valuable informants themselves, capable of providing not only a translation but an independent commentary on the information elicited from others (cf. Crapanzano 1980 on the three-way dialogue an interpreter's presence creates in the ethnographic encounter). This, in fact, was one way to overcome the kind of deception George had so gleefully perpetrated. But George was hinting at something more. Despite all the hours over many months that I spent with the elders, I had not begun to tap what they really knew in terms of esoteric knowledge. From their point of view, I had obtained little or no information of any real value.

On the morning we left, people gathered around to say goodbye. The elders lined up with tears streaming down their cheeks, including the three stony-faced men of sorrow, Aisaga, Opu, and Augustine. It should be added weeping is an accepted expression of emotion on appropriate social occasions in this culture, but it was only the elders who wept—younger friends waved us off gaily. The old men had reason to be sad, they explained, because even if we returned, they would no longer be there to see us. I thought perhaps now they might regret holding out so long and revealing so little of the secret knowledge they knew I wanted. Perhaps this was why Aisaga had shown us the powerful objects.

4

To Hidden Things:
Fieldwork 1980–1982

Seven years later I returned to New Guinea in December of 1978 to look for a new field site. Since completing my Ph.D., I had developed a new research interest in dreams and other states of non-ordinary consciousness such as trance and possession, particularly as they occurred in situations of social change. Unfortunately, I had virtually no data from my Mekeo fieldwork, although the comparative literature indicated their prominence in many Melanesian cultures (Stephen 1979a). It seemed I would have to find a different culture more suited to my new interests. I made a brief return visit to Mekeo, however, mainly with the intention of saying goodbye to old friends. Unexpectedly, the topic of dreams aroused much interest, and in a few days of enquiry I gathered such rich material (Stephen 1981), that I wondered what several months might bring. Within a week or so my mind was made up, and I began to prepare for another extended field trip. Sadly, very few of the elders were left. That rollicking, rambunctious, larger-than-life character George was dead. His daughter and grandchildren took me to visit his grave in the village cemetery, which was marked by a small white cross. I presented a large portrait of him, dressed proudly in all his finery, to his son, Alex. I visited Luke's family, who told me they buried him with his favorite chair, the plastic folding couch I gave him when I left the village. Opu had long since succumbed to tuberculosis. Surprisingly, Augustine was one of the few who remained, but he was now very old and fragile. I went to see Aisaga's family to find out what had happened to him. It turned out that he was staying with a friend in a nearby village across the river. His sons said he would be delighted to see us again, and arranged a visit.

The rumor was that Aisaga had been virtually chased out of the village after his clansmen blamed him for a recent death attributed to sorcery. This seemed to point to ominous changes in the village and auger badly for my plans. Seven years before, it would have been unthinkable for public accusations or actions to be taken against a man like Aisaga. It was difficult to enquire tactfully into the circumstances surrounding his absence: it was brushed aside as of no consequence. His sons seemed not at all concerned by the situation, and I guessed there was another side to the story.

We found Aisaga not in humble exile as rumored, but feted as an honored guest by his second son's father-in-law, an old friend and fellow expert in esoteric matters. Aisaga was little changed: he had the same dignified presence, the same tall, spare frame. Perhaps he seemed a little more relaxed, a little more approachable than he had been on public occasions in his own village. My husband and I, too, were treated as honored guests: chickens were killed and an elaborate meal was served to us at the meeting house by Aisaga's hosts. While they bustled around serving endless refreshments, I took the opportunity to discuss my plans with Aisaga. In his usual impassive way he took in what was said, nodding briefly to my requests and occasionally conferring with his sons. The matter was quickly settled. Yes, they would build me a house, right next to his own small bachelor's house at the back of the village, and assist me as they could. Furthermore, Aisaga declared, he would teach me many things he had not told me before. But at this point he firmly admonished me: I must first learn the language well enough to converse on my own. If I really wanted to learn about esoteric matters, he emphasized, there could be no intermediaries—not even his sons. Despite his apparent willingness to help—I took him for a man of his word—I was not able to return for more than a year, although I kept in touch with the family by letter.

The Burden of the Gift

My return to Mekeo in October 1980 marked the beginning of a new phase of fieldwork. I returned to gain a deeper knowledge of Mekeo culture. This time I learned the language well enough to converse without interpreters and was able to draw upon the benefits of long-established relationships with old friends and informants. Anthropologists are well aware of the many benefits that accrue to fieldworkers from return visits. All these things contributed positively to my new investigations, and I now had available Hau'ofa's (1975) doctoral dissertation as well as research being done by other anthropologists, including Mosko (1985) who worked among the nearby and closely related Bush Mekeo, and Monsell-Davis (1981) who studied the coastal Roro people. My new perspective, while drawing on all these advantages, did not emerge from them solely. Rather, a shift of focus, from public representations and observable social behavior to the private, inner experience of individuals, altered my relationship and entire mode of interaction with the Mekeo. This focus on private experience also led me into the secrets of esoteric knowledge. My interest in dreams and similar subjective states did not arise from any psychological interest per se, but from my conviction that such experiences were given cultural prominence in Melanesia in general (Stephen 1979a). Admittedly these issues impinged on the preserves of psychological anthropology and cross-cultural psychiatry, but the cultural origins of my interests were paramount (cf. Shweder 1990).

Within the first few weeks of my arrival, three important things became evident. Firstly, Aisaga, as he had promised, was gradually revealing some of the secret rituals. Secondly, other people, some of whom were old friends, were displaying a knowledge of esoteric matters I never suspected they had. Thirdly, some old friends were beginning to avoid me, and several people, admittedly those who did not know me well, were rebuffing all attempts on my part to interview them. People were happy to discuss dreaming in general, beliefs about its significance, and dream symbols and interpretations, but when it came to their own dreams, particularly recent dreams, it was a different matter. Yet I had the impression people regarded dreams in a very positive light (Stephen 1981). The rules of the game had changed in rather puzzling ways.

I had myself been a public figure during my first stay in Mekeo. I observed groups, appeared on public occasions, and talked with people at the clan meeting houses. When I visited people in their homes, others were present, an interpreter at least, and neighbors would often gather around. Some people did confer with me privately at my house, but they always brought along a child or someone else. Matters that concerned me were, overall, public concerns. One can see a paradox in my initial fieldwork: people insisted only the men of kindness and men of sorrow were the proper sources of information on cultural matters, yet in the same breath, they would warn me of the dangers of contact with these powerful individuals (a danger subsequently realized, in their view, in my husband's motorbike accident). At that time, John often accompanied me. This time, except for the first three weeks when he helped me set up, I was by myself. Although I was a woman, people described this new house as a *gove,* a place occupied by unmarried males, either bachelors or widowers (no Mekeo woman would live in a house by herself, partly out of concern for her safety and partly in the interests of propriety). It was built at the back of the village next to Aisaga's *gove.* Since most dangerous esoteric rituals require celibacy and cannot be undertaken by sexually active persons without severe risk, the mere fact of my solitude may have had sinister implications. I appeared in public and participated in group activities less and less. When I tried to talk about dreams with groups of people they would instruct me to come and see them privately, or they would quickly change the subject. Most of my time was spent talking to single individuals in private. As my house was built on the outer periphery of the village, I kept to the village back streets. In other words, I gradually retreated from the public arena. The community assumed I was now concerned with matters that all preferred to keep concealed.

My isolation was not intentionally sought, it was inevitable as I pursued these new lines of enquiry. In the past, people expressed anxiety about my safety, now they seemed more concerned about their own! Many friends confessed they were frightened to visit me because my house was so close to Aisaga's *gove*. Dangerous spirit presences and powerful entities lurked there, they intimated. Others declared they had wanted to help with building my house, but they soon fell sick and could not continue because of the oppressive influence of the place. Some hinted they would prefer I did not visit them, as they felt uncomfortable because of my close association with Aisaga. These attitudes played against me in one way, but on the other hand, people relaxed their insistence that it was too dangerous for me to learn about esoteric ritual. My picture of who possessed ritual knowledge had to be completely reassessed. I found there was no lack of people able to tell me about esoteric matters, and I became bolder in what I asked. Esoteric information was proving more accessible than anticipated. Yet it was much more difficult than I realized to collect information from ordinary people on dreaming.

At this point in my narrative, I am struck by many parallels between the situation I found myself in and the description by Favret-Saada (1980) of her encounters with witchcraft in modern, rural France. She explains that the investigator is necessarily placed within the "discourse of witchcraft" or else fails to gain any genuine information. One must be "caught" to participate in the discourse, or, inevitably becomes "caught" if one persists in engaging in it. In my case, during my first fieldwork I had not set out specifically to investigate sorcery—it was but one of many topics I examined—and I did not press people to reveal their secrets. Nevertheless I spent a great deal of my time in the company of those possessed of esoteric knowledge. The result, in the community's eyes, was my husband's motorbike accident: we were "caught" as victims. Yet, against everyone's expectations, we survived this ordeal and resumed our investigations. Was this why Aisaga finally decided to show us his sorcery stones and relics? When I returned in 1980, it was evident right from the start I had assumed a different "position within the discourse" because I was no longer a vulnerable person who might be caught by the influence of others. At first, like Favret-Saada, I was unaware of the ways in which I was being situated within a practical context of action and interpretation. From this point on there could be no sitting on the sidelines, no clinical objectivity. In acquiring secret knowledge I was forced to take responsibility for my actions, like it or not. This resulted in not only unforeseen consequences, but painful ones.

In imparting their ritual knowledge, people assumed I wanted to use it. They gave what they considered to be effective command of the rituals. This was, in their eyes, a highly valuable gift. Everything I wanted to know was not, however, suddenly and freely given. Many refused to divulge their secrets. A few agreed to talk about their dreams and similar experiences, but stopped short of revealing the texts of spells and other key elements. No one carelessly disposed of their knowledge. People impressed upon me the value of what they imparted and the dangers and responsibilities it entailed. I did not pay for ritual secrets. In any case, a simple cash transaction is not what the transfer of knowledge is about; like any exchange in Melanesian societies, it is embedded in the complex values surrounding the ''gift,'' in Mauss's (1966) sense. Mekeo esoteric knowledge is not part of formal competitive gift exchange systems (as is the case in some Melanesian societies), it is transferred within a very limited context of close kin relationships and intimate personal ties. Ideally it is passed between close agnatic kin: from father, grandfather, or father's brother to son, grandson, or nephew. In practice it is the personal possession of an individual who may confer it on anyone he or she chooses, but this is usually a close relative or a personal friend. (The circumstances will be examined in more detail in later chapters.)

What of my position as a recipient of secret knowledge? In many respects I was, of course, totally anomalous. I was an outsider, white, and female. Although women can and do acquire secret knowledge (chapter 10), no Mekeo woman would have tried to seek information from so many different sources, but, then, nor would any man. My status gave me certain advantages. I was outside the network of kin obligations. Experts who gave their secrets did so pointing out they would not, in fact, have to fear competition from me since I would soon return to my own country. They did not expect me to pay for what I received in the same manner as a member of the community, although this is not to say that I was not obligated. The fact I was a woman also, I think, acted in my favor. In the absence of male heirs, Mekeo women are sometimes taught even the most lethal and destructive rituals, but it is not expected they will ever put them to use: females preserve the knowledge and eventually pass it on to men. No doubt people could not be sure what a white woman might do, and some observed pointedly that in parts of Eastern Papua some women become sorcerers. Yet I think most felt less anxious about placing these powers in my hands than in allowing them to a man. In short, as a woman, I could be seen as passive recipient rather than active instrument. It is not that I *could* not use these powers, but rather that people were more convinced of assurances I would not.

What did people expect or want for their gifts? No immediate or specific payment was expected, but according to the moral and psychological force of the gift, there was no question I was indebted. Perhaps this was gratification in itself, since Melanesians are usually relegated to a position of inferiority with respect to whites. As in Melanesia generally, generosity is highly valued by Mekeo. Yet there was another level of expectation.

People often hinted at some kind of revelation, some kind of disclosure on my part. Friends would ask me about their dead relatives: did I not see them in Port Moresby or in Australia? Once when I visited a Waima village on the coast, an old man directed a long, garbled monologue to me in which he exhorted me to tell my mother and all my relatives in Australia that we could all now come back as the European government had gone for good. Observing my confusion, Aisaga explained later that the old man thought I was the dead returned, Aisaga's dead daughter in fact, and that the mother to whom the old man referred was Aisaga's dead wife. I was to hear many rumors that I was Aisaga's dead daughter. A neighbor and friend from the time of my earliest fieldwork later confessed to me that her dreams revealed that I, my husband, and white friends who had visited me during fieldwork were all dead relatives returned (chapter 8). Yet this woman had spent several months in Australia staying with her diplomat son.

These fantasies about whites being relatives returned from the dead are quite at variance with people's own practical experience and observation. Mekeo are not isolated, naive people who have no way to explain the European presence. Their history of European contact goes back to the nineteenth century (Stephen 1974). Comparatively speaking, they have had excellent educational opportunities; many people have tertiary education, have traveled outside the country, and have intermarried with whites and other foreigners. The capital, Port Moresby, with its amenities, is easily available to villagers who have access to cash from the sale of betel nut and garden produce in town; many Mekeo own vehicles and operate trade stores and a variety of businesses. Why do these fantasies have conviction? I suggest it is not because Mekeo lack cognitive means or the practical experience to distinguish between fantasy and reality; rather, these beliefs hold a powerful attraction because they express a compelling *emotional* need. What lends so much conviction to these fantasies is the desire to place relationships with Europeans into a meaningful context. That is to say, when I (or any other European) present myself as a friend, if that friendship—our relationship as human beings—is to be real and meaningful, then I (and others) *should* behave like kin.[1] The fantasy is about what I, and others, *should* be, and the problem is to get us to recognize, to stop denying, this underlying kinship—the ties that bind us as human beings.

Almost every fieldworker in Papua New Guinea has had experiences similar to those just described, or at least has felt the pressure of people's unvoiced but portentous expectations. In some areas these are given open expression in the form of cultic beliefs, where the ethnographer may be hailed as the bringer of cargo or as a new messiah.[2] Under such circumstances, one cannot but be made aware of the emotional dilemma on which relationships must pivot. The ethnographer needs help and cooperation and needs to establish close working relationships with as many in the community as possible, yet all the while he or she cannot escape the realization that no matter what is done, it is impossible to fulfil people's hopes—it is impossible to give what they want in return, and they cannot understand that.

The dilemma is highlighted in communities engaged in messianic movements. A similar tension underlies all fieldwork in Melanesia, perhaps in all tribal societies. I cannot "prove" this; I can only offer my own experience.

People in small, face-to-face societies want to draw us as ethnographers into their networks of personal obligations, want to insist upon and count upon their interrelatedness with us because no other kind of relationship (of a positive kind) is valid in their eyes. We, on the other hand, enter a community, set out to establish friendships with people knowing full well that it is a temporary arrangement, indeed an artificial one, set up for specific purposes which have to do with the collection of objective data concerning an object of study. This depersonalization of the endeavor is incomprehensible to the objects of our study. Depersonalization or "bureaucratization," as Weber (1983) and many following him have argued, be it regrettable or not, is inherent to the processes shaping our modern Western culture. We are products of it. We live in a world where relationships with others, even where these operate on a face-to-face basis, are not necessarily or primarily based on personal ties. Our informants inhabit a different world. These points have been made by many others, and do not need laboring here. For us the relationship was set up to be terminated, much like the psychoanalytic transference. For Melanesians there can be no such termination: a personal relationship simply cannot be cut off—not unless something has destroyed it.

Perhaps because I have come and gone many times from Mekeo, I am particularly aware of people's implicit expectation that I *should* stay. Some readers will feel it is my own self-gratifying fantasy that people wanted me to stay. Perhaps so, but I do not think this is based in any way upon affection for me as an individual personality. It is not that they like or love *me* as a person, but rather that, having invested so much in me, I should not be able to avoid the obligations involved. Mekeo do not necessarily love their neighbors and kin (though of course they do love many); they are often extremely ambivalent in their attitudes to those close to them, as Hau'ofa (1981) has shown so well. Yet they are tied to the members of their community by bonds of obligation and reciprocity that last a lifetime and beyond, continuing in the lifetimes of their children and grandchildren. The relationships I established with the elders during my early fieldwork were later maintained and developed by their children. People asked me to stay—they would give me land to live on or to start a business, whatever I wanted. I have suggested that my position as an outsider in the community was an advantage in collecting esoteric knowledge since I would not remain in the community to use it. Yet, paradoxically, it seems in giving me their valuable gifts of knowledge, people hoped to persuade me to accept and recognize continuing ties to them. The more people gave, the greater this expectation. This, I think, was especially true of Aisaga, a true man of knowledge, who had more to give, and gave more, than anyone else. Just how burdensome these gifts became will emerge in part III, where the psychological conflicts inherent in the transmission of ritual knowledge are a major theme.

The pleasure of mutual recognition in the ethnographic encounter is balanced by the pain of not being able to meet the other's expectations. My study, like all ethnographies, is a product of this irreconcilable tension. Two things, however, might be seen to make it more painful and more difficult than most. In the first place, I was asking for valuable esoteric knowledge, which accentuated the problems involved in personal indebtedness, obligation, and impossible expectations. In the second, in probing inner experience and private fantasy, it might be argued I was evoking emotional responses more akin to the transference, and countertransference, relationships between patient and analyst than the (supposedly) more impersonal, distanced encounter between informant and ethnographer (Crapanzano 1980). (Clearly there is a great deal to be said concerning the difficulties of engaging with people's inner fantasy worlds—see Crapanzano 1980; Kracke 1981; LeVine 1981; Paul 1989; Herdt and Stoller 1990. I will return to these thorny issues in following chapters.) Many pitfalls had to be negotiated: the sensitivities of engaging in people's innermost experiences and the emotional responses, on both sides, that this elicits; the ethical dilemma in dealing with esoteric and intimate material; the problem of being faithful to scientific and scholarly accuracy while protecting people's privacy and exclusiveness of knowledge.

A Glimpse into the Hidden World

The nature of this new fieldwork, which did lead to new understandings of "hidden things," can perhaps best be illustrated by a series of events that took place within the first few weeks of my return in 1980. The narrative centers around the illness and subsequent death of a young married woman from complications in childbirth. It underlines the practical and ethical problems of getting access to "concealed things." The story does not lack inherent drama and pathos, yet its plot hinges upon a number of seemingly trivial occurrences. The events described will appear so ordinary and essentially mundane one might wonder why they were not available to me previously; I will return to this question.

There are two principal actors in this drama, both of whom played a leading role throughout this new phase of fieldwork. First there is Alex, son of the redoubtable George. I had not known Alex during my earlier fieldwork because he was employed as a carpenter away from the village; I met him briefly on my visit in 1978–79. He was to become one of my most helpful and valuable informants and friends when I returned. This, I believe, was not an accident, but the result of his determination to perpetuate the friendship his dead father had begun; Alex himself intimated this. On his own initiative, he came to see me very shortly after my arrival and offered to help in any way he could. He spoke passable English and was well acquainted with European ways from his several years of work experience. Also, he said, he could impart many things George had taught him about dreams and related matters. I assumed he was looking for a job as an interpreter and was delighted by the offer. As things turned out, I made little use of interpreters during this fieldwork; nevertheless, Alex was to prove an extremely valuable source of information on many things. A tall, angular man in his mid-forties, he had none of his formidable father's presence or bombast, although I often glimpsed the lineaments of the old man's features in his plain, intelligent face. He was quiet, good-humored, easy to get on with—almost a little diffident in manner. I found him thoroughly likeable and dependable, and I knew him to be well respected throughout the community. He had married a Highlands woman and they had several children, the eldest a girl of marriageable age. Although he was the second son, Alex had acquired much of his father's ritual knowledge because his elder brother was absent from the village. Alex returned to live at home before the death of his father, thus he became the recipient of ritual knowledge, which is the prerogative of the eldest son. No one spoke of him as a person versed in esoteric matters, and it was only as I got to know him that I discovered how well informed he was.

The man of sorrow, Aisaga, was the other person in a leading role. Throughout this new fieldwork, Aisaga and his family were my most important contacts, friends, and protectors. By building a house for me on their land, they effectively took responsibility for my safety and well-being. Aisaga specifically instructed family members to speak in front of me as one of them, and he took care to explain family quarrels and tensions to me. When other people came to consult on some important matter and I was there, he would prompt them, if they hesitated, to speak in confidence to both of us; he told people, in my presence, he was teaching me the traditions of secret knowledge. All this is not to assume I was privy to everything transpiring in his extended household, nor that I had access to all his confidential dealings, particularly with other ritual experts. Aisaga never let his right hand know what the left was doing; what I saw was what he intended me to see. Nevertheless, as a member of his extended household, I had access to much that previously was concealed.

I was now forever hearing that what I wanted to know were *ogevake kapa*—concealed things. Aisaga was determined to make this clear to me and to warn me of the difficulties and pitfalls of investigating what he knew were potentially dangerous areas. When I had approached him concerning a return visit, he had stressed that if I wanted to learn about sorcery and other esoteric matters, I would have to learn Mekeo well enough to dispense with interpreters. Once I made the decision to return for further fieldwork, I made a concerted effort to work with the extensive language material available from my earlier research. By the time I returned I could converse, very haltingly, with Aisaga. Pleased by my efforts, he took it upon himself, as his old friend George had promised, to teach me to speak "properly" (*lopiani*). This I am sure I never achieved, but in a few weeks I was much more proficient. All my conversations with Aisaga took place without interpreters. From the outset, I spent several hours each day talking with him, usually alone.

I have explained how I was treated much as a child during my first fieldwork. Most people dealt with me differently now; after all, I was nearly ten years older. Aisaga alone maintained a position of parental authority. He took responsibility for me, for what I did that offended or caused trouble for him and myself with others, and for actions of mine that put me in danger. Aisaga was well aware of my cultural naivety and did his best to prepare me. Dreams were connected with the spirit realm and with secret ritual knowledge but, equally significantly, they impinged upon that covert world of erotic attraction and tensions referred to earlier and the deep currents of suspicion, conflict, and intrigue in social relationships in general.

Shortly after I began my second fieldwork Aisaga asked whether I knew the names of the various parts of the body. He proceeded to point to his head, eyes, nose, and mouth, naming each part in turn. He pointed to his chest, remarking that for "you whites" (*oi naomi*) women's breasts (*oi papiemi u'umi*) are "ogevake kapa"—concealed things—but "not for us" (*lai la'i*). Then, as decorously as possible, he indicated and named more intimate parts, saying: "*Ogevake kapa*—concealed things, other people will not tell you because these are concealed things." He then proceeded to list a number of swearwords and obscene expressions, explaining that I would hear these words, but that everyone would be too embarrassed (*meagai*) to translate; each, not surprisingly, dwelt upon the genitals, male or female, or some form of copulation. In fact, thanks to Father Desnoes's "Mekeo Dictionary," I already had a knowledge of anatomical parts—and some swearwords!—but Aisaga was correct in observing no man would be likely to tell me such things. It was undoubtedly difficult even for him, and only the generation's difference in our ages and his sense of responsibility for my safety made it possible. Indeed, despite the fact that several women gave me spells and other esoteric knowledge (chapter 10), none ever offered such explanations. Aisaga further cautioned that since I would often be talking about concealed things to men on my own, I must take special care. Enumerating various subtle facial expressions and gestures by which a man might indicate erotic interest in a woman, he warned me to watch what I was offered to eat or drink in case someone should try to put love potions in my food. The problem was, he said, that most did not understand how to prepare the potions properly and might end up poisoning me by mistake! All Mekeo women, he said, knew to be wary of such things, but since I did not, he had to warn me. So, from the very beginning of my new fieldwork, I was alerted to the practical necessity of understanding and dealing with concealed things of many kinds.

The Narrative (October–November 1980)

On 31 October 1980, less than two weeks after my arrival in the village, Alex came to report a recent dream (I had explained as best I could to Alex and other people my interest in dreams and the importance of recording them shortly after they occurred). That morning he had fallen into a deep sleep after returning tired from an early trip to the garden. He dreamed that the men of his clan were decorating themselves and painting their faces for a traditional dance (*geva*). He, too, donned his feather headdress, took his hand-drum, and joined the other dancers from his clan, Reed, which included the women born into the clan (but now married to men of other descent groups). Both men and women went in a group to dance, drum, and sing in the middle of the village in front of the meeting house of the host clan, Breadfruit. There the dream ended.

Dreams, as I knew from previous brief investigations (Stephen 1981), were valued as predictions, particularly of sickness, death, and other imminent misfortune. They rarely literally depicted the future, but rather represented it in symbolic form that had to be interpreted to reveal the underlying message. I had no idea, however, what the symbolism of dancing meant, and when I asked Alex, he replied he was not sure. In retrospect, I realized he knew perfectly well: it predicted a death, either in his clan or in the clan hosting the dance. Perhaps it was his usual diffidence. In any case, when I suggested that we consult Aisaga, he readily agreed.

I could see Aisaga sitting alone, as usual, on his small veranda. Although now resident in the village, he lived in virtual seclusion, his family providing his food and other domestic needs but, otherwise, leaving him alone. Visitors were rare, and came on some specific errand. He appeared in public only on those occasions when his own subclan, of whom he was the most senior representative, officially offered hospitality at its meeting house. He never visited the meeting houses of other clans in the village, nor was he ever seen around the village or its environs. As one of the most renowned ritual experts in the whole region—and the sole surviving man of sorrow of the oldest living generation in his community—his very physical presence was believed dangerous to anyone who came into contact; people avoided him whenever possible, even his own family. It was necessary, however, that he be consulted in any important matter affecting his family or descent group. At some point in the following events Aisaga would have had to be consulted, but I think Alex would not have come to him so early were it not for my intervention.

After quickly jotting down Alex's dream, I led him over to see Aisaga. He was now in his mid-sixties, and his physical appearance was, as always, totally in keeping with his public role as a man of sorrow. Tall, skeletal, carefully dressed in black as befitted his status, he conveyed a sense of absolute self-possession and control. He received us and responded to our enquiries with his accustomed grave courtesy. Despite this, I noted that Alex seemed a little nervous and less than totally comfortable. Aisaga listened to what we had to say, then for some considerable time sat puffing quietly on his cigarette, his back held straight, his haughty face impassive, his eyes fixed somewhere in front of him. We sat in silence, and tension mounted—Aisaga stage-managed every situation for maximum effect. He had a deep, somewhat hoarse voice, and his usually brief and decisive statements were always punctuated by little dry coughs. At last he replied, gently, that as Alex himself no doubt realized, the dream was an omen of death, either for someone from Alex's clan or from the clan that had hosted the dance in the dream. For my benefit, he explained the dream was of a type known to everyone, wherein the images signify the opposite of what will occur in waking reality. Here the people decorating themselves for the joyous celebration of the dance would soon be donning black and mourning a death. Even though no one in Alex's clan was at that time close to death, the import of the dream was unmistakable. Aisaga advised Alex to tell his relatives about his dream and warn them to be careful, and to tell them to watch over one another for the next few weeks. If they took care, the dream might come to nothing (*la'i e mia*); otherwise, one of them would die. There we left the matter and went on to talk of other things.

It was two weeks before the subject of Alex's dream was raised again.[3] On the evening of November 15 I was sitting talking with Aisaga on his veranda with two of his teenage grandsons, whom he was chiding for never coming to spend time with him to learn about ritual matters. The boys were clearly uncomfortable and not much interested in what he had to say. Finally, in an apparent attempt to hold the boys' attention, Aisaga took out his equipment for divination and began to display the technique. I had not seen divination performed before, although I had often been told about it. Divination is not performed in public, and this was the only occasion I saw Aisaga actually divine while others, besides myself, were present. The equipment consisted of a medium-size cowrie shell (*logu*—this technique of divination is also termed *logu*) and what appeared to be a short stick, about the length and thickness of my index finger, wrapped in a strip of cloth. Aisaga muttered incantations under his breath (spells are never said out loud in case others overhear and thus learn them), blew on the shell and the stick, placed the shell on the uneven floor of split bamboo, and then, in one sure movement of his hand, held the stick vertically, touched it on the curved back of the cowrie shell, and removed his hand. Surprisingly, the stick remained as placed, standing upright vertically on the back of the shell. He waited a few moments, then repeated the procedure. He went through the same motions several times, and each time the stick remained standing, improbably balanced on its end on a curved surface. I, of course, was intrigued and wanted to know more—what was the stick and how did it stand up as it did?—but the two grandsons just sat and squirmed in miserable silence. Aisaga put down the shell and stick and began pulling the finger joints of both hands; this he repeated, but each time two joints refused to crack. (This is another form of divination know as *ima oge,* literally meaning ''hand pull.'')

At last, Aisaga gravely announced the divination indicated someone would shortly die. Just that day, Aisaga's eldest son's wife, Mary, had returned from Port Moresby with the news that her brother's wife, Ruth, was hospitalized and very ill following a difficult childbirth. Mary's *afakua* (male kinsmen of her descent group) had asked her to approach her father-in-law, Aisaga, to cure the sick woman. In response to her request, Aisaga decided to divine the outcome. The answer was quite plain: nothing would avail, Ruth would die. The two grandsons took off like startled rabbits after this announcement, leaving me to question Aisaga.

Aisaga extolled the reliability of the divination result. He explained that when he bespelled the shell and the "stick," he invoked the spirits of his fathers and grandfathers, asking them to come and answer his question. The stick was in fact a fragment of the arm bone of one of his ancestors. When he called upon the spirits, they responded by holding up the bone if the answer was yes, and letting it fall if it were no. Certainly the impression given in the performance was that something held up the bone. Likewise, when the answer was negative, no matter how many times the bone was placed upright on the shell, with apparently identical movements, it would fall. Possibly any slight of hand expert could produce a similar effect with a little experimentation, but the only audience usually present is the operator—deception seems pointless. Aisaga experienced the movements of the bone as controlled by something other than his own hand, which he interpreted as the action of the spirits.[4] The spirits of his ancestors had plainly foretold Ruth's death.

This placed Aisaga in a somewhat awkward position with regard to his daughter-in-law Mary and her relatives. He was convinced that no matter what he did, Ruth would die; yet if he refused to treat her, people might easily assume he wanted her dead and that his rituals were responsible for her present condition. It was not until the next day I realized Aisaga connected this case with the dream Alex reported two weeks before. Alex and I had been visiting a relative of his in another village, an expert in rain rituals. When we returned in the late afternoon, Aisaga called the two of us over to tell us of his divination. Alex had already surmised Ruth's illness might be the predicted misfortune. Ruth was a member of his own descent group, Reed clan, and she was married to a man from the other descent group indicated in the dream, Breadfruit clan. The fit with the dream symbolism was very neat, since the two clans in the dream would be the principal mourners for Ruth's death; moreover, there was an emphasis on the women of Alex's descent group dancing. Aisaga told Alex he had no doubt it was Ruth who would die. Up until this point, he considered the dream merely a warning of an eventuality that might be avoided, and no specific person was indicated; following the divination the outcome was a certainty. He instructed Alex to tell only his close relatives and explain that nothing could be done to avert the death. Although Alex might well have suspected Aisaga was the man of sorrow who inflicted the illness, it seems he accepted this denial of responsibility.

Two days passed before I heard anything further. The next day, November 19, I found Aisaga occupied for most of the morning talking to two visitors, an unusual occurrence. I did not like to intrude on the discussion, which was evidently a serious one. Later I learned the two visitors were men related to the sick woman (but not from her descent group). The news they brought was bad: Ruth had been fed intravenously for three weeks and the doctors in Port Moresby said it was a "village sickness" that did not respond to their treatment, so they were sending her home. The relatives had come to ask Aisaga to treat her. He explained to them, as he had to Alex, that he knew for certain Ruth would die and that it was impossible to cure her.

The next day, November 20, I spent the morning talking with Aisaga about other matters. About midday I was preparing to leave when he interrupted his flow of conversation to sneeze. He looked a little startled, then explained the sneeze was an omen. That particular kind of sneeze always signified death in the family; it did not indicate who would die, only that a death of some relative was imminent. Two or three hours later I heard the unmistakable sounds of lamentations shattering the sleepy stillness of the hot afternoon. Aisaga's omen about Ruth's death, it appeared, was right. Then I realized the wailing was much too close to be that of the relatives of the sick woman, who lived at the end of the village, several hundred yards distant. It turned out that a small child, the grandchild of one of the senior men of Aisaga's subclan, had died that afternoon while visiting another village with its mother; the body had just been brought home. Later that day, I rather unpleasantly pointed out to Aisaga that his omen had proved false. With his usual air of unruffled dignity, he replied that, on the contrary, the omen was correct. A member of his family had died, indeed one much more closely related to him than Ruth. He had merely failed to interpret it correctly because he was expecting Ruth's, not the child's death.

The following morning, November 21, Aisaga was visited by his son-in-law Henry, who was concerned about the death of the previous day. The clansmen of the father believed the mother's clan had made the child sick because of dissatisfaction over marriage payments. They had recently approached Henry, as one of the mother's kinsmen, to cure it. Now that the child was dead, Henry and his kin were likely to be thought responsible. Henry, it should be added, was not a man of sorrow, but there are other ritual means used by people to kill the offspring of the marriages of their children (see chapter 9). The accusers were Aisaga's own clansmen. He advised Henry not to worry, observing that younger men had gone about things improperly when more senior men, such as himself, should have been consulted. Implicating his own clansmen, he then suggested to Henry it might be the father's side who, dissatisfied with the behavior of their daughter-in-law, had killed the infant.

Henry was also worried about a nightmare his wife, Ann, had two nights before. In the dream she was seized by someone she could not see clearly—a sort of hazy form—and then felt a terrible pain inside her. She woke up screaming, and her cries roused her husband. The pain grew worse and finally she collapsed (*mae afu*); toward morning she revived and started to feel better.

Aisaga connected this experience not to the death of the child, but as a sign of the deteriorating condition of the sick woman, Ruth, who was still in Port Moresby. To avoid further unpleasant visitations, Aisaga gave Henry a protective charm to place in his house. He explained Ruth must now be very close to death because her spirit (*lalauga*) had already left her body and had returned to the village to trouble her relatives (she was related in different ways to both Henry and his wife). This explanation seemed even more appropriate when that evening we learned Ruth had just arrived from Port Moresby and been taken to the Catholic mission hospital at Beipa, about three miles away.

On the morning of November 23, I learned from Aisaga that Ruth had been brought to the village overnight from the mission hospital. The relatives were now determined to bring in traditional curers, since all else had failed. A man of sorrow from Inawae village, about four miles away, was undertaking her treatment and there seemed to be some optimism that she was responding. Aisaga, however, was quietly scathing in his comments to me: "Does this man think he is God that he can raise the dead? The woman has been sick for several weeks and has been unable to eat for two. The time for spells and medicines is when the illness has just begun, not when it has gone on for a long time." Late in the afternoon we saw a truck driving out of the village with another well-known man of sorrow from a different neighboring village, Aipeana, on board. Aisaga must now have felt the growing resentment and suspicion among his own family and other relatives, but he still steadfastly refused to treat Ruth.

Convinced Ruth would die, and having expected the death for some days, Aisaga decided to determine precisely when it would occur. Early on the morning of November 24, before anyone else was up, he performed another divination. He told me of the result later. I am not certain whether he informed anyone else, but I doubt it. This divination established beyond doubt, in his view, that Ruth would die that very day. He explained that one could ask precise questions of the spirits through divination, provided they could be answered by a simple affirmative or negative (unlike omens such as the sneeze, which only indicated an unspecified death). He asked the spirits would Ruth (naming her) die that day; if the answer was yes, the bone would stand up on the back of the shell. Each time he tried it, the spirits held up the bone. We spent some time discussing divination and I asked him to teach me the technique. He agreed, but after sitting in silence for sometime he seemed to change his mind. Perhaps to distract me, he suggested I go down to the opposite end of the village, where Ruth's relatives had gathered, to see for myself what was going on.

I was a little discomforted by this suggestion. Would people suspect Aisaga had sent me to find out what was going on? Certainly they knew I would relay whatever they told me to him. Already, after little more than a month in the field, I found old friends avoiding me. When I went to see them, they would explain they were too frightened to visit me. Other things had changed since my first fieldwork in the early 1970s when there were still several old men alive who were renowned as ritual experts. Now Aisaga alone remained, and consequently every serious illness and death in the village was likely to be laid at his door. To make the situation more touchy, whereas in the past most young men had gone to work in Port Moresby and other towns before settling down to marriage and village life, employment was now becoming scarce and many youths hung around the village with little or nothing to keep them occupied. Even worse, heavy drinking had become commonplace on public occasions and, as a result, the controls that formerly operated on public behavior were often dissolved in the volume of alcohol so eagerly consumed. A group of angry relatives would never in the past dare to confront a man of sorrow suspected of causing a death. Yet only eighteen months before, after a death in the village, an angry mob that included Aisaga's own clansmen converged on his house, threatening to kill him. They were driven off by Aisaga and his three adult sons, who confronted them with loaded shotguns. It was this incident that led Aisaga to seek refuge in a neighboring village, where I had visited him in January 1979.

I had to tread carefully. Aisaga was in an awkward position, and I did not want meddling on my part to exacerbate things. He, however, assured me no one would object to my presence and that his daughter-in-law Mary was there with the other relatives. He had apparently changed his mind about telling me the divination spell and intended to get rid of me (politely) before I pressed him further, so I thought I might as well go along with his suggestion.

When I reached the other end of the village I discovered a miserable huddle of relatives, mainly women; the men were digging a grave in the cemetery nearby. Had Aisaga's prediction already been realized? The grave was not for Ruth, but for her infant. The Catholic mission hospital at Beipa had been caring for the baby, but it died that morning. I talked with a few people; they seemed to think that the mother was improving as a result of the efforts of the Inawae man of sorrow. Following Aisaga's instructions, I enquired if there had been any dreams concerning the sick woman, although I had little confidence in receiving a truthful answer. I accepted the response that there were none as polite refusal to divulge further information (when Mekeo do not want to discuss something, they often simply deny any knowledge of it). I then learned that the man of sorrow had just arrived to visit the patient. Noticing my friend Alex on the sidelines talking with someone who seemed familiar, although I could not place him immediately, I went over to join them.

Alex hailed me in his usual cheerful, friendly manner, then turned to the man beside him, introducing him as Aufe, who had come to "say spells" for the sick woman. I then recognized Aufe, whom I had met several years before in Port Moresby through other Mekeo living in town; he had given me excellent information on sorcery and other matters. The eldest son of a man of sorrow, he had proved a most knowledgeable and cooperative informant. So this was the expert called in to cure the patient! Now in his late forties, Aufe was a small, wry man with a quietly confident manner. He explained that since we had last met, he had returned to the village to live and, as his father had died some years ago, he now acted in his stead. We chatted for a while, then he said he must go to see the sick woman. I asked if I could accompany him, and he agreed readily enough.

Alex led the way. To my eyes, the scene that met us was a surrealistic one. The house where the patient lay was a rickety shanty built very high off the ground; we had to climb several steep ladders to reach it. It was partly roofed by a few rusted sheets of corrugated iron but lacked walls; new tablecloths and sheets had been strung up, providing an ineffectual barrier against the harsh morning sun. The unconscious woman lay motionless on an old mattress on the bare floor; her body was covered with a clean sheet, a handkerchief placed over her mouth. Her eyes were turned up, exposing the whites under swollen, half-shut eyelids; the only sign of life was her stertorous breathing. A woman sat beside her, keeping watch; she brushed flies away from Ruth's masklike face, occasionally wiping the slightly drooling mouth. Aufe approached and asked various questions: had Ruth moved, been able to eat or drink, or responded to anything at all? The attendant tried unsuccessfully to rouse Ruth, shaking her by the shoulders and calling her by name, gently slapping her cheeks. Next she tried to force open the patient's mouth with a spoon but the jaws remained locked. Aufe asked about her breathing and whether she was still coughing up froth. Finally he whispered a spell over a cup of water. The attendant took it and attempted to force a teaspoon of water through Ruth's clenched teeth. The consultation was over in a few minutes.

While waiting for a truck to take him home, Aufe discussed the case with Alex and me. Our conversation was in English, which Alex and Aufe speak fluently. (No one else approached us.) Ruth, he said, was much better than when they brought her from the mission hospital. She was coughing up a great deal of white froth and breathing with difficulty because it blocked her throat and lungs. He had said spells to get rid of the froth, it had subsided, and now her breathing was much easier. But she was still not eating or drinking. The role of the man of sorrow, Aufe remarked to me, was "like a business." He comes to try to help the sick person, and the relatives pay him for his efforts. Before his father died, Aufe continued, he taught him all his knowledge. Some younger people like himself were still learning the ritual necessary to be a man of sorrow. The man of sorrow helped his people, just as the European doctor, and both were rewarded for their services. His remarks were made with evident simplicity and sincerity.

After Aufe left, I spent a little while longer with Alex. He shared the view Ruth was improving, and I did not have the heart to press him about his dream omen. I knew Aisaga would be interested to hear the news, and I was keen to hear his response, especially in view of his conviction that Ruth would die that very day. Aisaga was not in the least put out, remaining adamant the death would occur sometime that day. I told him of the baby, venturing this was what his divination indicated. He coldly dismissed my suggestion. The spirits had answered him quite specifically that Ruth herself would die. Then he asked if anyone had any dreams to relate. I admitted I heard of none. "Exactly," said he, "that is because she is very near death; if she was recovering someone would have dreamed." People would be happy to relate any favorable dreams, of course. Aisaga took this to be further indication Ruth was past help. When someone is seriously ill, people pay close attention to their dreams in the hope of receiving some sign of the patient's recovery.

Despite Aisaga's pronouncements, I heard no further news that day. I went to bed wondering how he would explain the failure of his divination; he seemed so adamant and so dismissive of my suggestion that the baby, not Ruth, was indicated. The next morning, November 25, I was met by Aisaga's youngest son with the news Ruth died during the night. She expired before the new day dawned, as Aisaga predicted. They buried her that afternoon. I was told the relatives painted her face and clad her body in gaily colored grass skirts and shell ornaments, as if for a traditional dance (*geva*), so that she might lie in state on the clan meeting house while the community mourned her. The remains of young, handsome people such as Ruth are often treated in this way, I was told, but I had never seen it done before because I had attended only the funerals of old people and small children.

There is little more to relate. That afternoon, prior to the funeral, Aisaga was visited by two friends, one a man of sorrow from another village, who had come to discuss an important event. Their descent group was shortly to install a new man of kindness. Aisaga was invited to attend and to play a leading role by supervising the activities of the men of sorrow, who must ensure traditional etiquette is properly observed on such an important occasion. While Aisaga was occupied with his visitors, most of his extended household attended the funeral. As brothers-in-law (*ipa gava*) to the clan of the dead woman, two of his sons had to help dig the grave and build a fence for it while their wives joined the other mourners. In the evening the family returned, worn out from the emotion of the day. Mary, the wife of Aisaga's eldest son, was unable to sleep that night because of troubling visions. Each time she closed her eyes, she saw a procession of horrible apparitions with huge teeth, distorted faces, and bulging eyes, and she would cry out in fright. Discussing these visions the following morning, I asked Mary if she was dreaming, but she insisted she was not dreaming—the images passed in front of her "just as if they were figures on a movie screen." She had no idea who or what these horrible apparitions were, they were just spirits (*isage*). Mary could tell me no more, but when I asked Aisaga, he identified them as Aisomo and Kopomo, A'aisa's companions (*A'aisa ega papiau*). When you saw them, he said, it was a sign that an epidemic might soon break out in the village; they also came when anyone died. His visitors of the previous day, he said, heard the voices of these spirits as they entered the village. When a death took place it was usual for the relatives of the deceased to have such experiences, he explained.

Following the emotion-charged funeral, the atmosphere in the village became less tense. I wondered whether there would yet be repercussions, but whatever the gossip or rumors were, they did not reach me. A brief incident two days later revealed that circumspection on my part was still advisable. On the evening of November 27, a young man, known in the community as a loutish and disreputable type, came to my house. He was drunk and rambling incoherently. Angry about the death of Ruth, whom he claimed was related to him, he accused me of teaching some special rituals to Aisaga, and threatened me with violence if I did not reveal them to him so he could get even with Aisaga. Looking around him wildly, he confessed he feared to come to my place and dared to now only because he was so drunk. Seeing it was useless to reason with him, I left my house and went over to Aisaga's veranda, inviting him to come and talk there. Aisaga summoned one of his sons, and the drunk was quickly persuaded to leave quietly. Aisaga appeared worried and said he would keep watch during the night to make sure the youth did not return. But this, fortunately, was the end of the matter—at least as far as any public, overt action was involved.

This narrative highlights several issues to be examined in greater detail in subsequent chapters. It is evident my prior understandings of the spirit realm and its relationship to human society were being seriously challenged. Although stated ideals and public symbolism (described in the opening chapters) declare that only the man of sorrow has any dealings with the spirit realm, it emerges that everyone—ritual experts and ordinary people alike—is aware of participating in a close, even intimate, contact with the realm of spirit powers through dreams, waking visions, and similar experiences. Furthermore, the roles actually played by persons identified as the men of sorrow now begin to emerge in a rather different light. Ideally, the man of sorrow's sole function is to punish social miscreants with sickness and death—a punitive role underlined in the public symbolism, but here a different aspect comes to the fore. Aisaga is identified as a man of sorrow, yet in the events just recounted he does no harm to anyone, nor is he asked to do so. In fact, he is called upon to provide information, advice, and help. During my early fieldwork I often observed things that made the men of kindness seem less than kind, but never before had I witnessed anything suggesting a less-than-malevolent side to the man of sorrow.

The importance of healing as an aspect of the man of sorrow's activities is indicated—this is yet another anomaly in view of the manifest ideal. According to the descriptions people usually give of sorcery, it is the cause of all serious illness and death. The man of sorrow is not represented as a healer but is said simply to destroy the lethal charms he used to attack the victim, who then recovers. Hau'ofa's (1981:245–249) discussion of the curative powers of sorcerers also emphasizes that he who inflicts a disease is the one who must cure it. From this perspective, the man of sorrow is attributed with powers to nullify the effects of his own destructive actions, but is not regarded as someone who alleviates pain and suffering in general. The distinction may seem a subtle one, but I think it significant.[5] Here in practice we find a different picture: Aufe does not present himself as Ruth's attacker, and Aisaga refuses to treat her, not because someone else is responsible but because his divination revealed that no one could save her. I was to discover in many other similar situations that healing was not necessarily performed by the assailant, and that many illnesses were not in fact attributed to deliberate human agency.

In contrast to some small interior New Guinea groups where the whole community participates in spirit seances and healing rituals, such as the Gebusi (Knauft 1985), the Kaluli (Schieffelin 1977), the Daribi (Wagner 1972), the Samo (Shaw 1990), and the Sambia (Herdt 1989b), Mekeo do not perform healing in public nor is it the focus of group participation. Hau'ofa's (1981:245) observations in different Mekeo communities confirm this.

Sick people, like angry people, remain inside their houses, and as I have noted, the interior of domestic houses is not a space any person other than the occupants usually enters. When someone is seriously ill, other people, relatives and neighbors, do not gather in close physical proximity to the patient; they gather outside on verandas or on open platforms built under the house. Only one or two close relatives will actually sit by the patient and attend to his or her physical needs. This is partly due to fears of the dangerous effects of contact with another person's body wastes and substance. A very sick person is usually separated and isolated from the rest of the community, as was Ruth, who lay in an empty room with only one attendant while relatives and friends with doleful faces sat at a distance outside.

Likewise, in taking ritual action to help the sick person, no public participation is involved. One or two of the very closest relatives of the patient, perhaps in consultation with their lineage head, decide upon a course of action, but whatever is done is done in secret. Gossip circulates, of course, and when a man of sorrow from another village visits, no one is in doubt as to the significance. In fact, a visit such as that made by Aufe is unusual; more often the man of sorrow does not have direct contact with his patient. One or two relatives approach him alone (oapugai), and if he agrees to treat the patient he will simply send bespelled potions and medicines via these intermediaries. Such was the case when Aisaga treated the sick. Apart from his own children and grandchildren, who usually were brought to him in person, he simply sent bespelled medicines to the patient (see chapter 14).

My close association with Aisaga now gave me access to the cases he treated, and I also was able to observe a few instances of the healer/diviner Josephina (see chapter 10) in action. But often what transpired was so minimal and covert that had it not been drawn to my attention. I might not have noticed. A subsequent covert drama of inner experience, which I describe in part III, more than compensated for this paucity of overt action.

Ruth's case was unique in all my field experience in that I was able to observe a man of sorrow from a different village treat a sick person. No other opportunity occurred during my 1980s fieldwork. A combination of circumstances made this opportunity possible: I knew Alex, who was the senior member of the lineage responsible for initiating action on behalf of Ruth; the man of sorrow called upon was also someone well known to me; I managed, quite fortuitously, to arrive on the scene just as the pair of them—alone—were preparing to visit Ruth; and I was rude enough to ask if I could accompany them. No Mekeo would have done that. Both men were accustomed to European ways, having spent several years working in urban centers, but even so, they may have been just too startled to refuse. What surprises me, in retrospect, is that I dared to ask. There was something almost indecent about my intrusion; I had no right to be there as Aufe examined and treated his patient. These were ''concealed things,'' and not for public view—mine or anyone else's. Recall that of all the anxious relatives, neighbors, and friends waiting while Ruth's baby was buried, only one, Alex (the lineage head and close agnatic relative of the sick woman), had accompanied Aufe to see Ruth, who was attended by a single female relative. Even when we returned outside after visiting the patient and stood talking, not a single person approached or sought to question us about her condition. Neither Alex not Aufe displayed any embarrassment at my action (but consider here how one dissembles one's inner feelings in this culture). I did not attempt to repeat this performance. Dealing with concealed things was never easy or comfortable.

The concealed nature of all the key events described is evident. It is in individual, inner experiences, such as dreams and visions, that the hidden world of spirit powers becomes closest to tangible reality for everyone. It is in secret rituals, witnessed by very few—indeed, usually by no one except the practitioner himself—that the ritual expert attempts to mediate and influence spirit powers. A nightmare, a spell muttered into a cup of water, private consultations, whispered confidences—either such things had previously seemed of absolutely no consequence whatsoever, too trivial to record, or I simply had not had access to them. I will put aside for now the problem of the relationship between the public, manifest aspects of the spirit realm and the hidden things my new investigations were uncovering. Not until the end of part III, when more evidence has been presented, will it be possible to deal with this question.

5

A Distinctive Mode
of Imagination

The neatness of fit described in the previous chapter between the dreams, the omens, the divination rituals, and the actual events that culminated in Ruth's death may appear disquieting or deliberately provocative. It seems to challenge the rational, scientific explanatory system to which Westerners adhere. Such is not my intention. I do not share the Mekeo view that the spirits of the dead (or any other spirit entity) communicate in dreams and other omens, can be contacted or controlled through ritual, or indeed even exist. Yet I accept the *experiential* reality of such occurrences for those people who report them. And my observation of events, as illustrated here, was that people were usually able to relate their experiences most persuasively to concrete occurrences. From the external observer's viewpoint, Alex's dream might well seem no more than a simple form of superstitious belief. Placed in context, however, the dream imagery and waking reality weave together powerfully, taking on a compelling configuration. In Alex's dream, the young woman, dressed for celebration, danced with the happy throng of her clanspeople in front of the clan *ufu*. The dream imagery hauntingly prefigures the reality of her dead body, dressed in all her dancing finery, laid out in state on the *ufu*, surrounded by her weeping relatives. A single instance such as this might easily be dismissed, but I encountered many more. We should not be too ready to dismiss the possibility that dreams, divination, omens, and other fleeting intuitions may be subtle ways of bringing people in touch with valuable information and understandings not always available to public discursive formulation.[1]

The bulk of this study is concerned with the ways in which particular Mekeo persons pay attention to, attempt to guide, and put to conscious use their dreams and waking visions, which are probably mixed inextricably with daydreams and reverie—what from a psychoanalytic perspective would be regarded as the products of unconscious fantasy. The problem is this: How are we to deal with this kind of material without imposing our external interpretative frameworks and without losing sensitivity to the positive value that members of the culture place on such experience? Equally undesirable is the alternate path—giving in to our own unconscious credulity and gullible desire for wonders, as Freud (1933) has so pointedly warned against. Before proceeding with our ethnographic exploration of Mekeo inner worlds, guidelines need to be developed for dealing with the difficulties of interpretation that lie ahead. I offer the idea of "autonomous imagination" (Stephen 1989a) as a theoretical orientation to the problems posed by my unusual data; it has in fact largely grown out of the data itself. It is neither "proved" nor established by the material presented here; my intention is merely to show how the ethnography calls for such an interpretative framework and is, in turn, clarified by it.

A Special Kind of Symbolic Thought

Barth (1987) has argued that cosmological beliefs in Melanesian cultures can best be understood not as symbolic reflections of social relationships, as so many ethnographies have striven to show, but rather as complex structures of thought serving to link and orient the self to the external world. He examines a number of Mountain Ok groups to demonstrate that the differences cannot be meaningfully understood, let alone explained, by variations in social organization and relationships. In identifying the self as the locus and reference point of Melanesian cosmological symbols, Barth makes a daring move for a scholar who identifies himself as a social anthropologist. Even more daring is the direction this departure points: the realization we are dealing not only with symbolism directed to the self, but a mode of symbolic thought that does not operate according to logical structures or semantic codes:

> Given the high cultural valuation, especially in secret ritual, of modes of association which we in our culture allow only exceptionally gifted artists, Ok cosmology is built on descriptions governed by criteria of aptness of imagery, and generalization by assimilation or condensation. The resultant tradition of knowledge has its own dignity and force, very imperfectly captured by a narrowly "cerebral" and abstract interpretation. Its main strength lies in how it directs and molds the person's subjective experience, and thus creates emotions and sensibilities that are harmonious with a vast structure of percepts and events in nature. (Barth 1987:73)

Barth squarely faces the challenge to recognize in the symbolism of myth, ritual, and cosmological belief a mode of thought operating primarily in the realm of the emotional and the affective, a mode which, as he points out, bears close resemblance to the psychoanalytic concept of primary process thinking.

Noy's (1969) revision of the orthodox concept of primary process thinking, which Barth takes up, raises several interesting issues. Noy proposes, in contrast to the Freudian view, that the primary process continues to develop in the individual alongside other cognitive capacities. What distinguishes it from these other forms of cognition, according to Noy, is its comparative immunity to feedback from sensory perception and incoming information. Its function is to relate things (external objects) to the self in terms of their affective qualities. He argues that the infant begins life by relating to everything in pleasure-pain terms: asking what is it for and what it does before ever wondering what it *is*. In contrast, language and secondary process thinking direct the growing child's attention to communicating with others and to understanding things as objects within an external relational system. With the development of these capacities, entities become apprehended as abstractions; that is, mental representations of these entities are not limited to how they relate to the experiences of self. The primary process, Noy argues, operates to create a sense of self as a continuity across time and change.

In a later formulation (1979), Noy suggests that form in art relates to the artist's ability to provide a resolution of inner conflicts and an integration of the different parts of the self. He writes of the fragmentation of the self and of the difficulty of creating a unified sense of identity:

> The never-ending efforts of the ego to arrange its disparate and contradictory motives, ideas, and emotions into some pattern of order and inner harmony is the prerequisite for safe-guarding its self-identity and maintaining the integration of the self vis-à-vis the object and outer reality. The search for the best formulae to accomplish this task is therefore a universal human endeavor common to all people.
>
> The creative artist belongs to the small group of human beings, which also includes creative scientists, philosophers, and originators of religions and ideologies, who are endowed with the talent to supply the needed formulae. (1979: 251)

Up to this point I agree, but I doubt Noy's idea that art achieves its effect by communicating across three "censor barriers":

> The problem of the creative artist is how to find the best form to transmit the meaning inherent in the work of art from its origin in the deepest layer of the artist's mind to its final destiny, the deepest layer of the mind of the consumer. Along the route there are three censor stations that the artist must cross: his own inner defences and controls; the surface protective barrier of the perceptual apparatus of the consumer; and the inner defences and controls of the consumer. What is called "good form" in art is that form which succeeds in getting the artist's message across these three censor stations with minimal resistance and minimal distortion of the original meanings. . . . The second censor is the only

one exclusive to art. The crucial problem of any art creation is how to cross the superficial defences of the perceptual apparatus, a precondition for its message being admitted into the deeper layers of the mind. (1979:238)

This implies that symbolism is primarily a disguise and that the aim of art is to hide a deeper meaning from consciousness. I would think, rather, that art seeks to represent that which cannot be expressed in abstract language and thought. Noy fails to capture the autonomous nature of this process—the sense that, although it creates the self, it seems to be separate from it, more powerful, more mysterious. One has the sense of controlling and purposefully using "secondary process thought"—normal, waking cognition. One is invaded, caught up in a separate reality, when "primary process" emerges. It is alien to the conscious self. Even those who experience it in a most positive fashion feel it to be something outside the self (Stephen 1989a).

Noy describes his as an ego psychology approach. The position he takes seems to bring him close to Jung's (1967) theory of the integrative function of unconscious fantasy, although Noy would perhaps deny this. Ego psychology, of whatever persuasion, moves in the direction of meanings constructed by ego rather than drives and instincts, but in doing so tends to lose sight of what lies outside consciousness. Everything begins to look so reasonable in terms of the ego's goals. And here, I think, is the danger of losing Barth's point that we must recognize another form of symbolic thinking—one that cannot be reduced to logical structures and oppositions or semantic codes.

In Barth's view Mountain Ok cosmological thinking not only relates to the self and provides its orientation to the world and society, the symbols themselves arise out of the individual creativity of the ritual expert. Circumstances require that the ritual savant must retain in memory for many years, without the opportunity to rehearse or compare, the "score" of the ritual performance. This, Barth points out, results in ritual symbols being subjected to extensive reworking within the private fantasy system and primary process thinking of the savant. Thus, over time, ritual meanings and practices may easily diverge to form different traditions. This process of changing, improvising, and inventing cultural symbols, Barth shows, is grounded in the subjective meanings, affects, and desires of the individual expert who must act as a repository of ritual knowledge.

In contrast to earlier, more static views of neatly constructed symbolic systems, the emergent, generative capacity of cultural symbols is now an important theme in anthropology (Sahlins 1981; Valeri 1985; Clifford and Marcus 1986; Wagner 1975). But in the work of structuralist theorists such as Sahlins or Valeri, and in the different model developed by Wagner, one sees replication of earlier assumptions of a formal logic underlying symbolic transformations. Thus symbols change, are transposed, reinvented, or "obviated," but always according to some uncoverable, inherent formal logic. Barth's advocation of the subjective self of emotion and desire as the locus of change firmly breaks with this tradition.

Noy's revisions, as drawn upon by Barth, move beyond the orthodox psychoanalytic view of primary process as inferior and maladaptive and directed only at infantile hallucinatory wish fulfillment (Rycroft 1972). Yet to accept his formulation still ties interpretations to a framework wherein symbolism is regarded as disguise, cultural symbols are regarded as id disguises writ large, and a generally negative view of this mode of thinking prevails. Even for Noy, works of art consist of expression, disguised in artistic form, of deeper levels of the mind (i.e., the id). We still are limited to ego's struggles to resolve the varying demands of id, superego, and reality, although primary process, according to Noy, is the means used by the ego in constructing an integrated sense of self.[2]

Obeyesekere's (1981:169) concept of "hypnomantic consciousness" offers another view. He proposes that a special kind of consciousness emerges in ecstasy, trance, or dream vision that has a creative capacity to "generate subjective imagery and cultural meaning." In his studies of Sri Lankan ecstatics, Obeyesekere demonstrates the role of hypnomantic consciousness in religious and cultural innovation. He identifies two linked processes, "objectification," the expression of private emotions in a public idiom (77), and "subjectification," the reverse process whereby cultural ideas are used to justify the introduction of innovative acts and meanings (123). Obeyesekere stresses the creative and positive nature of fantasy in non-Western cultures, suggesting that in the West its use has probably been distorted by the performance principle (166–167). Like Noy, with his revision of primary process thinking, Obeyesekere's ideas have been developed largely within a psychoanalytic context, although he adds anthropological and cross-cultural insights. Certainly Obeyesekere (1981:191–192) goes further than Noy in recognizing the creative role of fantasy as a mode able to transcend its infantile beginnings:

> These pieces from the unconscious are molded into a different form that transcends their origin. The wellspring of the prophet's creativity is no different from that of the painter, the poet, and the scientist. This essay sprang from my fantasy, but the essay itself is not a fantasy, since the original fantasy was mediated through my discipline and my critical faculties into its present form. So it is with us all. Our informants have other ways and models for transforming fantasy into a creative product.

These arguments are well put, and I might almost be content to stop there, yet I feel Obeyesekere does not take the case for a special kind of imagination quite far enough.

Other proposals from within anthropology for new attention to the creative role of fantasy come from Kracke (1987) and Price-Williams (1987). Kracke, like Barth, follows Noy's revised concept of primary process thinking, demonstrating the intimate relationship between dream and myth and the unique mode of imagery thought both employ. In his essay on "waking dreams" in the same collection (Tedlock 1987b), Price-Williams takes up the nineteenth-century concept of the "mytho-poetic function" of the unconscious, the capacity observed by early investigators of the unconscious to produce fantasies and narratives with evident mythic characteristics and themes. It was a capacity observable in the outpourings of spiritualistic mediums, would-be religious prophets, and mystics. For Jung and his followers, exploring the "mytho-poetic function" became a central concern, but it was largely passed over by Freud and his tradition (Ellenberger 1970), and Jung's theories have attracted little serious interest from anthropologists. In a recent review of psychoanalytic anthropology, Paul (1989:183–184) points to an emerging interest in more positive approaches to fantasy, but makes no reference to Jung. It is evident, however, that if creative aspects of fantasy and imagination in cultural production are to become a new focus of anthropological investigation, as indicated in the work of Barth, Obeyesekere, Kracke, Price-Williams, and others (Tedlock 1987a; Basso 1987; Herdt 1987; Herdt and Stephen 1989; Ewing 1990a), then Jung's opus cannot be ignored.[3]

I am not implying a rediscovery of Jungian psychology of the unconscious is all that is needed to solve our problems. Throughout this book I attempt to weave between psychoanalytic theory and other views of fantasy and creativity. My approach is perhaps excessively pragmatic, but given the state of our theoretical understandings of such matters, I believe it necessary to use ethnographic observations as the touchstone and to draw upon whatever models, theories, insights, and guiding metaphors are available. I will not hesitate to draw upon the work of Freud, Jung, and others, including Laing's (1965) theories of schizophrenia, and various information processing models of mind, as it suits me and where these ideas seem to speak to the cultural forms I attempt to interpret. I do not, however, advocate merely an undisciplined eclecticism.

Autonomous Imagination

As a more flexible and open-ended framework for investigation, Herdt and I (Stephen and Herdt 1989) have proposed the concept of "autonomous imagination." We describe it as autonomous to distinguish it from the imagination that operates in ordinary waking consciousness and to stress its autonomy from a person's conscious devising. Barth (1987), Obeyesekere (1981), Kracke (1987) and Price-Williams (1987) have, in their different ways, pointed to the positive and creative role of fantasy in the production of cultural symbols and meanings. Autonomous imagination goes somewhat further in identifying certain significant characteristics of this distinctive imaginative mode. Furthermore, the concept does not depend upon theories that assume the existence of an "unconscious mind," although neither does it discount such theories.

To briefly summarize, "autonomous imagination" posits the existence in the mind of a continuous stream of imagery thought that operates mostly outside consciousness and beyond conscious control. Although not usually available to consciousness, it can spontaneously enter consciousness in dreams, and sometimes in waking visions, and is experienced as taking place independently of a person's conscious invention or will. With special training, a person may learn to bring the stream of imagery into consciousness and direct its unfolding, as is found in the controlled trances of shamanism and meditative practises, in hypnosis, Jungian "active imagination," and numerous Western psychotherapeutic techniques. Certain important qualities not only clearly distinguish it from modes of thought operating in ordinary consciousness but also suggest capacities beyond those usually available in consciousness cognition. It is distinctive in: a) being more freely and richly inventive than ordinary thought processes, b) emerging into consciousness as vivid, hallucinatory imagery, and c) possessing a different kind of access to memory. Another significant feature is its special sensitivity and responsiveness to external (cultural) environmental cues and direction, which enable communication to and from deeper levels of self without the person's conscious awareness. It also has the capacity to communicate from, and back to, levels of mental and bodily processes beyond conscious control.

As a way of summarizing arguments presented in more detail elsewhere (Stephen 1989a, 1989c), I will discuss these five characteristics of autonomous imagination.

A Vivid Exteriorization of Inner Imagery

This feature of autonomous imagination is most simply illustrated by the dream. In dreaming, mental imagery is registered by the dreamer as an external and autonomous reality, one she or he had no part in making. It is only on waking that one returns to one's cultural epistemology and can sigh with relief, "Ah, it was only a dream." Mekeo, and others, might sigh more deeply, and ponder on a deeper significance that Westerners so easily dismiss. The same vividness of internally generated imagery taking over, and replacing, external reality may also occur in waking states. But, whereas dreams are expected during sleep (indeed the laboratory studies of sleep have demonstrated clearly that dreaming takes place in regularly occurring phases throughout the night in all persons; see Jones 1976; Cohen 1979), "waking dreams" (Price-Williams 1987) are much less usual and occur under special circumstances. Waking dreams (visions or hallucinations) arise spontaneously, as laboratory studies have established, in situations of sensory deprivation, when incoming sensory data and stimuli are reduced to a minimum (Siegel and West 1975;

Bowers and Meichenbaum 1984). Waking dreams may occur under natural conditions, as when a driver travels long distances at night on a monotonously straight highway or a sailor is alone at sea, or may be deliberately induced, when a laboratory subject is isolated by a gazenfield device or a hermit meditates in his cave.

A mounting body of experimental data on hypnosis has revealed that far from being asleep (as the term *hypnosis* implies) the hypnotic subject is awake (or can be instructed to be awake and active), but is engrossed in powerfully realized inner imagery (E. R. Hilgard 1977; Barber 1979; Fromm and Shor 1979a; J. Hilgard 1979; Bowers 1976, Sheehan 1979; Sheehan and McConkey 1982). The subject may even be quite aware that the image she or he perceives is internally generated, yet it has such a compelling presence it not merely appears to exist in external reality, it can actually block reality out. This is most persuasively demonstrated in the use of hypnotic imagery to overcome pain in dental and other surgical procedures (Sarbin and Slagle 1979). A similar imperviousness to pain and the fear of physical injury can be observed in many shamanic feats, such as fire-walking, piercing the body with skewers and knifes, and other ordeals (Eliade 1972; Obeyesekere 1981). My point is that in these various situations, inner imagery is so powerfully realized it shuts out external events entirely, even when they involve intense physical pain and danger.

However research attempts to account for it, it seems beyond doubt that the mind is possessed of a special capacity to produce internally generated imagery that can intrude into consciousness and be experienced as external reality. Of course, psychoanalysis would have no argument with that. The question is whether such a capacity represents an inferior, regressed mode of thought emerging only under situations of psychic conflict, or whether it should be understood as a potentially creative and constructive capacity, more akin to a talent than a symptom of psychic disturbance.

A Greater Freedom and Richness of Inventiveness

Earlier investigations into hypnosis tended to stress the suggestibility and dependency of the successful hypnotic subject, thus seeing in hypnosis a regression to primary process thinking. Only some people, it was found, had the capacity to become deeply hypnotized. There has, however, been a growing trend in the research literature over the last several years that stresses the active and constructive role the subject plays. Many researchers have stressed the imaginative capacities of good hypnotic subjects rather than their psychological dependency or propensity for regression (Barber, Spanos, and Chaves 1974; Bowers 1976; E. R. Hilgard 1977; Barber 1979; Orne 1979; Sheehan and McConkey 1982). Indeed the question seemed to be: Was hypnosis no more than a special kind of imaginative performance? Hypnosis may well involve the engagement of a special kind of imagination—but the emphasis should certainly be on "special." It is no ordinary imagination, in the sense of wishful thinking or daydreaming, that would enable me to persuade myself that "this doesn't hurt" when the surgeon is cutting into my tissues with his scalpel. Under such circumstances, most of us, I think, would prefer some kind of chemical anesthesia. My point is not that pain cannot be blocked by imagination, but that a special kind of imagination is required—one most of us do not command at will, at least not without special training.

Hypnosis research has revealed complex fictional narratives produced by "good" hypnotic subjects in so-called "age-regression" experiences (E. R. Hilgard 1977). In these sessions the subject is instructed to return to various points in her or his childhood, sometimes taking the sequence right back to supposed intrauterine events. Initial experiments suggested that real-life memories, forgotten or repressed, were being captured. Later investigations (E. R. Hilgard 1977:46–59; Sheehan and McConkey 1982:150), however, proved that real-life memories (confirmed by others, parents, teachers, etc.) were being interwoven with fictitious events, but in a manner highly persuasive to both the experimenter and the subject. Subjects had no awareness of inventing or making up the childhood experiences—it was as if they had in fact been transported back in time to being a two-year-old or even a babe in the womb. Likewise, various notorious reincarnation experiences elicited under hypnosis (E. R. Hilgard 1977:51ff.), for example the Bridey Murphy case (Bernstein 1965), have been demonstrated to be unconscious fictions produced by subjects out of long-forgotten readings and childhood experience. The crucial point here, however, is not the fact of fabrication but the circumstances that a) the fiction was created outside the conscious awareness of the fabricator, and b) the fiction was so cleverly and convincingly structured, and composed of such rich, lifelike detail, that even skeptical researchers were convinced by them. Evidently some people have available to them, under hypnosis, a creative capacity far greater than deliberate inventiveness allows.

Similar phenomena have been observed in cases of multiple personality and in Western mediumistic seances, as well as in the trances and spirit possessions of tribal cultures (Ellenberger 1970; E. R. Hilgard 1977). In cases of multiple personality, a secondary personality may emerge that appears more mature, better informed, and more intelligent than the "normal" personality of the patient (E. R. Hilgard 1977:27, 40, 136; Jung 1977:89–90). Three or more personalities may emerge at different times, each with their own supposed experiences and memories, dramatically demonstrating the mind's capacity to weave complex fictions outside conscious awareness. Although much of the pronouncements made in spiritualist seances are of a trivial or inferior nature, it is well known that some mediums in their trance states have written musical scores, poetry, novels, and works of occult philosophy, all supposedly under the guidance of some dead genius or master (Ellenberger 1970; E. R. Hilgard 1977). It was this apparently effortless creativity evinced in many dissociated states that prompted early investigators of the unconscious like Flournoy to write of the "mytho-poetic" function of the unconscious mind (Ellenberger 1970).

It is not necessary to point to such rare, and apparently abnormal, states to identify the special creativity of autonomous imagination. Many novelists, artists, poets, and musicians attest to the autonomous nature of the creative processes they command. Many artists do not so much fashion, devise, or deliberately invent a work of art as somehow discover it ready-made: the novel or the story is said to "write itself" as if the author were but the mouthpiece or pen through which some "other" communicated, much like the spiritualistic medium. (For discussion of the use creative artists make of dreams see Rothenberg 1979:40–50; Rycroft 1979; Ullman and Zimmerman 1979:8–9.) For those of us who painfully struggle to shape our arguments and refine our concepts in order to produce anything in writing, such creativity indeed appears magical and a little difficult to take seriously. Yet we have only to look to our own dream experience to appreciate that even the most rational and prosaic of us is capable of spinning amazing fantasy fictions in dreams that we would find impossible to produce in waking consciousness. Many dream researchers (French and Fromm 1964; Greenberg 1970; Pearlman 1970; Krippner and Hughes 1970; Hadfield 1974:113–116; Jones 1976:164–171; Cartwright 1978; Cohen 1979; Ullman and Zimmerman 1979; Rothenberg 1979:35–40; Hunt 1989) regard dreaming as a special kind of imaginative process with creative and adaptive potential, but the facility of narrative inventiveness we possess in dreams compared with our conscious thought processes is self-evident.

This special imaginative capacity glimpsed fleetingly in dreams would appear to exist in all of us. But only certain individuals, such as the creative artist or Barth's Mountain Ok savant, are able to draw upon it in consciousness. I should stress, however, that although all artistic creativity may to some extent draw upon a subliminal stream of autonomous imagination, there is clearly a vast difference between states of mind wherein the artist or creative thinker controls and deploys in consciousness a train of thought and those states where the artist, like the shaman or spirit medium, seems to become merely a mouthpiece or vehicle for some more powerful "other." It is only in these latter cases of "artistic possession" where another, self-alien (although not necessarily negative) force seems to take over, one that I would identify as manifesting the full characteristics of autonomous imagining.

A More Extensive Access to Memory

In producing its narratives, autonomous imagination draws upon memories and information unavailable to conscious thought. This can be evidenced on the basis of the dream alone, wherein recent happenings (the Freudian "day residue") may be combined with long-forgotten childhood memories and other material. It has been particularly well documented in the hypnosis research, which has shown that even though the supposed memories elicited under hypnosis do not all represent real events, forgotten and repressed material may in fact be uncovered (E. R. Hilgard 1977:46–48, 51–59; Sheehan and Mc-Conkey 1982:150). Indeed, it is this facility to tap material of which the subject has no conscious recollection whatsoever that has been used to explain the supposed "reincarnation" experiences.

One of the most striking instances of this more extensive access to memory is provided by hypnotic therapeutic techniques in which past memories of some traumatic event causing disturbance to the patient is altered, thus removing the symptoms associated with it (E. R. Hilgard 1977:44–46). The procedure involves getting the patient to "re-live" the traumatic event under hypnosis while the therapist suggests a different, more positive outcome. The "script" of the memory is changed by the therapist's suggestions, and only the new, positive version is retained.

A Heightened Responsiveness to External Suggestion

The hypnotic techniques just described point to ways in which autonomous imagination takes up suggestions or direction coming from the environmental context, bypasses conscious awareness, and communicates to a deeper level of the mind which is, in this instance, long-term memory storage. The patient outside of the hypnotic state is not aware that the memory has been manipulated in any way; he or she is simply aware of a change in symptoms and attitude.

Although the stream of imagery thought arises spontaneously without conscious will or intent being involved, once it emerges into consciousness it is especially responsive to external cues. On the one hand, the person involved in the flow of imagery perceives it as an external reality, yet on the other, he or she may participate in its unfolding in an active way. Furthermore, the nature of the imagery, and the direction it takes, may be shaped by external circumstances, yet still without the participant's awareness. From an experiential perspective, this imagery is as real, vivid, and external as physical reality. Again, this is perhaps most clearly illustrated by the hypnosis research. According to hypnosis researcher Bowers (1976:108):

> Hypnotic subjects are not actively trying, in any ordinary sense, to behave purposefully in accordance with . . . hypnotic suggestions. Instead, suggested events are experienced as *happening to them* in ways that would require active effort to resist.

When the subject is told his or her arm is getting lighter and lighter, the arm is felt to rise of its own accord. Likewise, when told that a long-lost friend is in the room, the hypnotic subject sees the friend as a flesh and blood reality.

The hypnotist's suggestion becomes not so much a command as a description of what is happening to the subject. Undoubtedly, as researchers point out, the subject is actively cooperating with the train of thought being suggested by the hypnotist, yet at the same time, the imagery generated becomes entirely compelling (Sheehan and McConkey 1982). How and why the hypnotist's suggestion activates this flow of imagery remains a matter of conjecture, but the phenomenon itself is well established. In various types of Western therapeutic techniques involving visualization and directed imagery (reviewed by Singer and Pope 1978), such as "autogenic training," a person can be instructed to provide a cue or command for him or herself intended to generate specific kinds of imagery, thus employing a form of auto- or self-hypnosis. The intention, as in situations where a hypnotist provides the suggestion, is to generate imagery that the person perceives as being as real as that provided by the physical senses. In all these examples, imagery not the creation of the conscious self can be brought into consciousness by means of an external suggestion or cue.

A similar process can be observed in shamanic trance, spirit mediumship, and possession, where the shaman, in the appropriate ritual context, can visualize and impersonate spirit presences or undertake epic journeys to the spirit world (Eliade 1972; Peters and Price-Williams 1980; Noll 1985). In these circumstances cultural context and expectations suggest the nature of the imagery, but there is no reason to doubt that the shaman's conviction in the reality of the entities he meets is any less vivid and powerful than that of the Western hypnotic subject. An apparent contradiction emerges here. In hypnosis autonomous imagination is highly amenable to suggestion, yet in many forms of trance the subject seems totally self-absorbed and impervious to the outside world. In all cases, the subject's attention is intensely focused on the unfolding of inner imagery, and his or her consciousness is oblivious to the external context. It is the stream of autonomous imagery that takes up a suggested or an expected scenario and creates it as its own image-world.

Various differences in the conscious control and recall are possessed by different kinds of practitioners. The shaman may be "possessed" or totally invaded by some spirit presence and after the performance will have no memory of what took place; he or she may converse with the spirits, even involving the audience, and may be fully aware of all that transpires during the seance. On the other hand, a person having no control over the situation at all may be possessed by a spirit, in which case the occurrence is likely to be interpreted as an affliction or illness or the onset of a shamanic vocation.

We can distinguish between situations wherein external cues communicate to inner process of imagery thought—with the conscious "I" merely the witness of what arises—and those where there is a spontaneous entry into consciousness of inner imagery, as in dreams, waking dreams, multiple personalities, and uncontrolled spirit possession. In these latter contexts, inner imagery enters consciousness communicating either to the conscious self (the dream), or an external audience (multiple personality, spirit possession), things of which the conscious "I" has no knowledge.

Psychological studies have demonstrated the suggestibility prevailing in altered states of consciousness, and in hypnosis in particular (Shor 1965; Ludwig 1969; Bowers 1976:85–109; Sheehan and McConkey 1982:7; Peters and Price-Williams 1983). Underlining the same point, anthropological studies have revealed the influence of culture in shaping the form taken by alternate states of consciousness, including drug-induced states. Even dreams can be influenced by external conditions and cultural expectations (Watkins 1984: 21–24; Cartwright 1978:46–49; Tart 1969b). All this strongly suggests that a two-way communication operates: from inner self to the external world, and from external world to inner self, via the medium of autonomous imagery.

Communicating to Mind and Body Outside Conscious Control

This special imaginative mode can affect psychological and somatic processes beyond volitional control. Such a capacity is evidently related to the two-way communication just described. The hypnosis research again provides the most telling evidence. Hypnotic therapies have proved to be anything but panaceas for all ills, and only some patients are able to enter the deep hypnosis required for more complex tasks. Nevertheless, there is a large body of carefully monitored experimental research (reviewed by Sarbin and Slagle 1979; see also Bowers 1976:21–40, 140–152; E. R. Hilgard 1977:44–46, 58–59) to demonstrate the effectiveness of hypnosis in influencing and controlling a range of physical and psychological symptoms. The reasons for its effectiveness are still not understood, despite the amount of research devoted to it, but its effectiveness in many contexts is beyond dispute. Various kinds of imagery techniques, including behavior modification, are widely used in Western therapies (reviewed by Singer and Pope 1978a, 1978b).

The ability of the hypnotist to control pain through hypnosis is matched by the shaman and the spirit medium. Demonstrations such as fire-walking, piercing the body with spikes and knives, and hanging from metal hooks are commonly part of the shaman's or mystic's performance (Peters and Price-Williams 1980; Obeyesekere 1981). Accelerated healing is also often claimed, as the physical damage to the body caused by these feats is said to heal almost immediately. My point here, I should stress, is not that such phenomena are "simply auto-hypnosis," since the nature of hypnosis itself is equally a puzzle. In both the Western context of experimentation with hypnosis and anthropological studies of cross-cultural uses of altered states of consciousness, there is a similar use of internal imagery to control physiological processes normally outside any person's conscious control. Finally, there exists a pervasive association in Western and other cultures of dreams, visions, trances, and possession with healing, both as symptoms and as the means of restoring body and psyche to health (Eliade 1972; Kiev 1964; Bourguignon 1973, 1976; Moerman 1979; Stephen 1979a; Kakar 1982; Peters and Price-Williams 1983).

The question remains: what might be the origin (physiological, psychological) and function of this distinctive mode of imagination? It does not necessarily have to arise from, or be linked to, the Freudian id, although it may well be. An important function, I have suggested (Stephen 1989c), may be related to the building up of emotional and affective schema in the individual. I do not, however, propose the "unconscious," in either a Freudian or a Jungian sense, as its source. Instead, one might consider an information processing model of mind which proposes that a stream of imagery occupied with internal sources of information operates continuously alongside other cognitive processes that must deal with incoming sensory stimuli from the external world. Experimental psychological studies of sleep and dreams (Cartwright 1969: 369–370, 1978:66; Cohen 1979), of waking fantasy (Singer 1974:188–200; Singer and Pope 1978a), and of sensory deprivation (Siegel and West 1975; Bowers and Meichenbaum 1984), neurophysiological studies of brain functioning (Dimond 1972; Springer and Deutsch 1981; Corballis 1983), studies of drug-induced hallucinations and alternate states of consciousness (West 1975), and various cognitive theories of mental processing all, in their different ways, point to the existence of such a stream (or streams) of imagery.[4]

Since it emerges under conditions of high cortical arousal combined with low sensory input (Singer 1974; West 1975; Cartwright 1978), the process (or processes) must have some identifiable neurophysiological basis. Its functions presumably relate to information processing procedures of the brain, possibly, as I have suggested, connected to the storage and creation of affective patterns of memory. There is no necessity to argue that it arises, as does the psychoanalytic theory of primary process, out of the infant's capacity to hallucinate the satisfaction of unfulfilled needs, since this only begs the question of the origination of the process. Nor is it necessary to argue that the process serves only the interests of the id in achieving disguised satisfaction of forbidden wishes. Instead, one can presume it exists in all human beings as a part of the basic information processing procedures of the mind (and is grounded in the normal neurophysiological functioning of the brain itself). My intent is not to do away with the insights of depth psychology—far from it. My point is simply that the existence of a unique kind of imagination can be posited on other, independent grounds, which in fact lends support to the findings of depth psychology. As is evident from previous chapters, my intent is not to squeeze or force the ethnography of subjective states into a rigid mold but rather to create a dialogue between general models and rich specifics.

For those who find such models of mind objectionably mechanistic, may I emphasize they are but that: models. One can of course approach what I call "autonomous imagination" on the basis of its phenomenology without seeking its origin or functions within the mind. Indeed, understanding of the nature of the mind remains so elusive that one might be better off avoiding such questions. Yet, for my part, I find it intriguing and instructive that experimental psychology of the last two to three decades can provide a more positive view of mental phenomena that have long been regarded as pathological both in scientific and popular Western culture.

In this discussion I have drawn primarily upon hypnosis research. It is the most extensive and most rigorous body of experimental research relating to the topic conducted in laboratory conditions that employs a self-consciously scientific methodology. Yet this research confirms much of what can be observed in the cross-cultural findings of anthropology on alternate states of consciousness, spirit possession, shamanism, and similar phenomena. What the anthropological studies particularly underline is the very high value put upon such modes of thought in other cultures, where dreams, visions, trance, and possession are perceived as providing access to creative and transformative powers. If Western anthropologists are prepared to take cognizance of the features of autonomous imagination I have just outlined, we may begin to realize why, as the anthropological record so abundantly shows, other cultures greatly value and seek to engage it.

If we accept the existence of a powerful and creative imagination operating outside conscious awareness, then its significance in the generation of modifications, innovations, and variations on cultural themes becomes obvious. Let me briefly return to Barth's (1987) Mountain Ok savant, who must re-create the pinnacle ritual performance of his culture every ten to fifteen years. How does he achieve this feat? It is not accomplished simply by accurately retrieving the ritual "text" from memory or by forgetting some and improvising other parts ad hoc—rather, it is a subtle process of combination that involves personal memory and feelings and desires—primary process intertwined with memory. If we think in terms of autonomous imagining rather than primary process, then we can understand that the savant is able, in waking or sleeping dreams or merely deep reverie, to access a powerfully inventive mode of thought that presents to him images, symbols, and narratives far richer than his conscious devising. These are effortlessly woven out of cultural information stored in memory and inner feelings and desires, none of which is likely to be fully available to the savant's consciousness except in this new, largely autonomous synthesis. Thus the savant does not consciously invent or improvise, but rather finds revealed to his conscious self a vision of sacred realities much in the manner of the creative artist, as Barth himself argues.

At this point I again encounter the difficulty that not all, but only specific, states of creativity involve autonomous imagining. Barth does not discuss the Baktaman savant's mode of experience, and this was probably not available to direct observation by the ethnographer. Nevertheless, it is evident the savant does not view his cosmological revelations as his personal creation; he does not regard himself as the author of these ideas in the same way that I am aware of being the author of this book, despite the many important contributions others have made to its ideas and presentation. In this crucial sense, the Baktaman savant seeks a re-creation and revelation of cosmological truths from outside himself, from a source much more powerful and mysterious.

Noy's (1969, 1979) concept of primary process thinking stops short of fully recognizing the powerfulness of the imaginative mode I describe here. From the perspective of autonomous imagination, we can understand that cosmological beliefs, myth, and ritual draw upon a spontaneous capacity first to generate new symbolic forms, or variations on existing ones, and second to use these forms to communicate to deeper levels of self. It is an emergent capacity in all human beings, but some (shamans, ritual experts, and other mediators of the "Sacred Other" in tribal cultures, and some artists, writers, and musicians in Western cultures) have greater access to it and an ability to harness it to conscious ends. Perhaps I claim too much for autonomous imagination, perhaps too little. Yet there are substantial grounds to indicate that such a distinctive imagination exists, and that it does possess important capacities not usually available to ordinary consciousness. Only our Western cultural discomfort with the irrational, I suspect, prevents us from giving it closer attention.

Part II

Dreaming and the Hidden Self

[D]reaming is a longer and more lucid wakefulness. Dreaming is knowing. In addition to diurnal learning arises another, necessarily rebellious form of learning, beyond the law.

Octavio Paz, *The Siren and the Seashell*

6

Dreams

Dreams proved to be my entrée to Mekeo understandings of concealed aspects of the spirit world, yet dreams are not unequivocally regarded in a positive light by Mekeo, nor did dreams provide a simple "open sesame." Dreams are as puzzling, subtle, and elusive a phenomenon for Mekeo as they are for us—indeed perhaps far more so—and are not lightly disclosed, even to intimates. They are *ogevake kapa* in all the senses so far identified: they are concerned with concealed personal actions, thoughts, and desires; they disclose information about the hidden world of spirit forces; and they provide a medium whereby the possessors of esoteric ritual knowledge achieve their ends. Investigating dreams, like all concealed things, was difficult: I had to tread warily in this sensitive territory.

Since dreaming provides the major evidential basis for my discussion of Mekeo inner experience, it is necessary to examine various aspects of dreaming as closely as possible. Only careful attention to what might at first appear unnecessary detail will enable the reader to enter these inner worlds and to gain some sense of their richness. Here, at least, I can aim for Geertz's (1975c) "thick description," even if I never quite achieve it. I do not offer an exhaustive coverage of the topic; discussion focuses on certain specific issues that have direct relevance to my arguments concerning magic and the self. This and the following two chapters deal with what dreaming reveals of Mekeo understandings of the self and its components, of the nature of consciousness and different levels of "reality," and of how dreams are used as a means of gaining self-knowledge. Throughout part II I will focus on ordinary men and women. The experience of ritual experts must wait until part III, since it can only be properly evaluated against a broad context of understanding and usage.

Collecting Dream Reports

A not uncommon response to my questions about recent dreams was an irritated or angry exclamation: "I'm not sick! Why should I be dreaming?" Continuous dreaming, I learned, is considered by Mekeo to be not only unusual but undesirable, indeed unhealthy, unless one is deliberately inducing it by ritual means. Initially I had planned to collect data allowing a content analysis of dreams (Hall and Van de Castle 1966) for a significant section of the population, comparing gender, age groups, social status, and other factors (see Gregor 1981 for an ethnographic use of content analysis). People's reluctance to reveal dreams as they occurred finally persuaded me to drop such an approach. The retrospective "dream histories" Mekeo related were not likely to provide accurate data about what they were in fact dreaming at a particular time and thus would not be comparable with data collected elsewhere. Yet to have persisted with my attempts to collect reports of dreams every day from a wide sample of the community would have destroyed all rapport.[1] Although I tried to explain what I was doing, most people became annoyed and defensive when I questioned them day after day. Only sick people, I was told, dream every night, or those who ritually induce dreaming; so why bother ordinary, healthy folk? My insistent enquires implied things I never intended: either that people were sickly and abnormal or that they were, against their express denials, covert ritual experts. Those who did not know me well would usually look surprised, if not a little scandalized, when I attempted to probe about their dreams. It was soon impressed upon me that dreams were regarded as dangerous knowledge— long before I fully understood why.[2]

Many people, both lay persons and ritual experts, did tell me about their dreams, but it was on their terms, not mine. Invariably, a time and a location where we could talk privately was suggested. Few would come to my house. This may partly have been because of anxiety concerning the proximity to Aisaga, but I suspect they were not only more certain of privacy in their own surroundings but also felt more in control of the situation. They usually designated a time when other members of the household were absent and neighbors were not likely to be around, such as mid-morning after adults had left for the gardens and children had gone to school. If I arrived too early, an uncomfortable wait ensued until everyone else left.

Not only was the setting usually determined, so also was the nature and direction of discussion. Any interview is a dialogue shaped by both participants (Crapanzano 1980; Herdt and Stoller 1990), yet I was struck at the time by the impression that people had carefully prepared in their minds what they were going to say. This impression was heightened in retrospect, when I listened to the tape-recordings (despite people's concern for privacy, very few made any objections to sessions being recorded). Occasionally, the discussion took an unexpected turn, and someone would let more slip than was perhaps intended, but most had a specific story to tell. Little or no prompting was required to get them started, and apart from my occasional requests for clarification, interviews would often proceed virtually as monologues. Only when things began to slow down did I intervene to elicit additional information. Discussion usually began along the lines of:

"So you want to talk about dreams?"

"Yes. I would like you to tell me about any dreams you have had, any important dreams or dreams that came true [e gama]."

This would be sufficient to launch into the account. Undoubtedly people did try to give the information they understood me to want, yet my sense is of having to make do with what they were prepared to give. This consisted in the main of narratives of past dreams as related to actual waking experience. Most people had several examples to relate and some proved to have extensive dream memories. Interviews often ran for three hours or more at one sitting.

Characteristically, the report of the dream would be fairly brief, centering around a single episode or motif, and would be followed by a longer explanation of its meaning and how it was borne out in subsequent waking events. Dreams occurring many years previously were often included, as well as more recent ones. Sometimes sequences and recurring dreams were described. The overt purpose of these dream histories was to demonstrate to me (the eliciter) the ways in which a particular person's dreams afforded knowledge of things hidden from waking awareness.

People described the examples that they were able to fashion into a personally meaningful account. They did not, or would only reluctantly, relate dreams they could not understand. Recent examples, where the link with waking events was yet to be realized, were thus not readily disclosed. The exceptions were dreams wherein past experience clearly demonstrated the probable outcome. Alex's dream of dancing is a classic instance. Not only is this symbolic equation of death with dancing a widely recognized symbolic reversal, I later discovered that Alex recalled a whole series of recurring dreams incorporating the same motif.

In many instances the interviews led into discussions—and revelations—of ritual secrets. I was aware of a link between dreaming and esoteric ritual, but at first did not appreciate the two were so closely interwoven. I suspect some people refused to discuss dreaming with me for this reason. Requests for information on the topic brought me unexpected rebuffs, but also an equally unexpected harvest of esoteric knowledge. In this manner I discovered another side to many old friends whom I had no idea possessed ritual knowledge (chapters 9, 11). Ritual experts have the means to enhance and control dreaming to specific ends. Yet even the ordinary person who cares to pay attention to dreams may find a natural capacity to perceive hidden things. Dreaming thus can be regarded as a skill which ritual increases. The last time I talked with wily old Augustine, the man of sorrow (who was still alive when I returned in

December 1978–February 1979), he observed: "Ah! Dreaming is another *ikifa*. I didn't tell you about that."

The word *ikifa,* which I have elsewhere (Stephen 1981) translated not quite accurately as "power," is used to refer to ritual knowledge and, in a more general sense, to any learned skill (chapter 9). Dreaming is *ikifa* in both these senses. Thus in telling their dreams even ordinary people were demonstrating a special skill and saw themselves as imparting valuable knowledge to me. They were not, in their view, looking to me for relief from symptoms, problems, or inner conflicts.

Their stance placed me in a position rather different from that of many recent anthropological investigators of dreams who seem to find themselves negotiated into a therapeutic role, even if they do not consciously set out with such in mind (e.g., Crapanzano 1980; LeVine 1981; Kracke 1981, 1987; Herdt 1987). The discussions that provided my information were not in any sense clinical interviews (cf. Herdt and Stoller 1990), but were simply the kind of personal interaction ethnographers usually employ. Certain parallels could be drawn with a psychotherapeutic context, yet the differences should also be recognized. There was no shared understanding of a therapeutic encounter, no claim to a clinician's role of authority, no expectation of relief from suffering. I do not have psychiatric training nor training in clinical psychology; I was not there to "treat" people nor even to help resolve their emotional conflicts in some informal way. Nor would people have accepted me in this guise had I so presented myself. In their view, they were telling me about things that I did not understand and they did. Those who felt insecure about dream and fantasy experiences simply would not discuss them. Furthermore, I did not try to intervene, challenge, or guide people's self-revelations in any therapeutic way; my aim was just to get them talking, and to listen. Nor did I encourage them to explore their subjectivity more deeply or in new ways, as Herdt and Stoller (1990) achieve in their interviewing on Sambia erotics and subjectivity.

Yet it is true that I asked people to discuss their inner lives—the products, in the view of Western anthropology, of unconscious fantasy intermixed with conscious interpretation—and that I was probing and entering into Mekeo imaginative worlds. In doing so, complex emotional valences were set up between myself and informants. The psychoanalytic tradition would suggest, even to those who do not accept all its premises, that when a person engages in a dialogue with another concerning his or her fantasies, memories, and secret desires, a particularly emotionally charged relationship is likely to emerge. "Transference," "counter-transference," or what you will, this dialogue takes on a dynamic apart from the conscious intent of the participants (Paul 1989: 178–181). These issues underlie all the material discussed here but will come to the fore in part III, "The Sorrows of Knowledge."

Perhaps the temptation for the ethnographer to change roles and become the healer is ever present. Having learned to negotiate the cultural terrain of the other, the observer desires to "enlighten" the observed. Crapanzano's (1980) portrait of Tuhami, the Moroccan tile maker and teller of tales, pivots on such a dilemma. Enchanted as he was by Tuhami, Crapanzano nevertheless feels the need to end their dialogue by providing some "cure." Yet why divest Tuhami of the rich fabric of fantasy he uses to swathe the ugly banalities of his life? I can understand Crapanzano's desire to reciprocate, to ease his own sense of what I referred to earlier as the "burden of the gift." I might have wished to do the same, but any "cures" I proffered would have been gratuitous, since Mekeo believed they were benefiting me.

Are ethnographic investigators of dreams drawn into a therapeutic role by the dynamics of the transference relationship and the informant's dependency needs, or by the interviewer's personal fantasies of power? Kilbourne (1981b: 310) writes of Moroccan dream interpreters and their clients as being engaged in a system of shared fantasy which "encourages both interpreter and dreamer to assume the roles and to aspire to the ideals of 'good' father and 'good' child respectively (regression in the service of the super-ego/ego ideal)."

I suggest that the ethnographer, particularly if not trained in psychoanalytic techniques, also may succumb unconsciously to a similar kind of complicity. On the other hand, no matter how professional their command of theory and technique, psychoanalytically oriented researchers are directed by an assumption that dreams are by their nature not understood by the dreamer. They are thus inevitably placed in a position of superior knowledge and power, not only to determine the dream's meaning but also to use that knowledge to assist the dreamer in dealing with his or her unconscious conflicts (this was Crapanzano's dilemma).

All this makes it difficult to deal with the cultural validity of dreaming as a mode of self-knowledge. Anthropologists have, of course, long recognized the importance of dreams in many cultures as channels of knowledge and power, as Kilbourne (1981a) notes. Yet only rarely have they rejected the position of the analyst eliciting information from a dreamer who is presumed to be ignorant of its real import in favor of the more humble stance of a student learning to fathom dream secrets from those who understand them.[3] Tedlock's (1981, 1987a) work is notable here, as is Basso's (1987); both eschew any assumptions about the "real" nature of dreaming and seek to understand how particular cultures not only conceptualize but actually use it to construct culturally valid knowledge. I am not suggesting anthropology lacks sensitive studies of dreaming in cultural context, but I am pointing to the curious dynamic of power that emerges in so many studies where the ethnographer engages individuals in reporting their dreams.[4]

Mekeo presumably did gain particular kinds of satisfaction, both conscious and unconscious, from telling me what they did (cf. LeVine 1981). Our discussions perhaps provided a means to reveal self in a context not otherwise allowed in this culture (Herdt 1987). Mekeo expend much effort in disguising their inner feelings from one another; it is perhaps a relief, even a pleasure, to have an opportunity to disclose private thoughts and emotions to someone who is not in a position to use the knowledge in any practical way.[5] I have described the careful and deliberate manner in which dreams were discussed with me. As I shall disclose, a similar guardedness prevails in all Mekeo dream communications. Tedlock, in drawing attention to the naivety of dealing with dreams as if they were discrete "objects," argues that dream reporting can better be understood as a "psychodynamic communicative process" (Tedlock 1987a). In such a situation, the ethnographer's role is shifted from analyst to "listener." This is the role I see myself taking; the listener is, of course, not an objective recording machine, but a participant in the communicative process.

The Part of Self That Dreams

If one were to ask what a dream is in the abstract, Mekeo would most likely reply that dreams are omens. They warn of impending misfortune, danger, illness and, especially, death. This view is clearly illustrated by Alex's dream of dancing in front of the *ufu*. Omens of death were the most common and frequently reported of all dreams I recorded. Everyone from teenagers to elders, laypersons and ritual experts, men and women, claimed to have had dreams accurately predicting the deaths of close relatives and other people in the community. People often remarked that they knew their dreams were true because of their many accurate premonitions of death. Sometimes they would add that it was the spirits (*isage*) of their dead relatives that gave them these messages. Beyond the fact that dreams are warnings and that many dream messages come true, people did not have much to say. Detailed information emerged only in the context of discussing and interpreting actual examples. What I describe here represents not an emic description but an outsider observer's synthetic view of some of the principles underlying Mekeo dream discourse.

Dreaming, or dreams—the same word, *nipi,* is used for the verbal and noun forms—takes place when, during sleep, a person's *lalauga* leaves his or her body (*imauga*). The term *lalauga* is variously translated by Mekeo, largely following the Catholic mission translations, as "spirit" or "soul." Both renditions are inappropriate and misleading in subtle ways. Since the *lalauga* is the part of the self that acts in the dream, I shall begin by translating it as the "dream-self." Dreaming (*nipi*) is caused by the activity of the dream-self (*lalauga*) when separated from the physical body (*imauga*) and is later recalled in waking thought. One speaks of "I," the waking conscious self, as performing or undertaking the dreaming—*lau la nipi.* That is to say, dreaming is a state experienced by "I," but it is a state caused by the action of my dream-self in leaving my body. Thus it conveys the sense that one part of the self is able somehow to observe the actions and desires of another part of the self.

The term *lalauga* can be used in two subtly different senses. It may describe an image or likeness of something, that is, a reflection in a mirror or water, a photograph, a portrait, or a dream image. Or it may indicate the aspect of a person's self that acts in a dream. I shall refer to these two different meanings as the "dream-image" and the "dream-self," respectively. It is usually assumed when the dream-image of a particular person appears in a dream that this indicates his or her dream-self. It is not merely a likeness, but signifies some part of the person's actual being. According to Desnoes (1941:596), *lalauga* may mean "soul," "shadow," "portrait," and "drawing." It has the further meaning of a ghost or apparition perceived in waking consciousness. What links these various connotations is the notion of a nonmaterial, bodiless entity. That is to say, a *lalauga* can be seen (either in waking or dreaming consciousness) but has no material substance. Most important, it does not refer to images held in the mind but to images external to the mind perceiving them. A shadow, a reflection, a picture of something—these are entities perceived in the external world; they are separate from the images we create in our heads. So too are dream images different from the thoughts we consciously hold in our minds. Mekeo sometimes say that particular dreams may be merely the result of one's waking thoughts and concerns and thus have no significance whatsoever. But usually they stress the given, external quality of the imagery. Take, for instance, the following observation by a woman who claimed to have received important dream insights concerning her husband's desire for another woman:

"Now when I dreamed that, the next morning I told my husband, 'Well that did not come out of my conscious thoughts (*opouai*). Inside myself I was not thinking bad things. But it was a dream. You were cheating on me, but it was a dream!' "

The clarity with which the dreamer is able to distinguish between the imagery of her dream and her own internal processes of conscious thought is exemplary but typical. Another example from the same woman illustrates how dream images and waking reality are carefully separated, even when the two seem to merge into a single experience.

Dream of a Plane Bringing Store Goods

"Another dream—I dreamed this about a year ago. At night I went to sleep and I dreamed of a plane flying overhead. My elder brother, his dream-self, was setting up a tradestore here. My younger brother was living in Lae; his dream-self was bringing store goods in the plane to give to my elder brother to set up the tradestore. His dream-self had loaded the goods into the plane and it was flying here at night. At night the plane—I was dreaming it—the plane was flying here in the night. It came at night—those two old houses, we were sleeping there. It was bringing the store goods—bags of flour, rice, and sugar, biscuits and other goods—so my elder brother could make a store here.

"I could hear the noise of the plane—I was dreaming—I heard the noise of the plane coming. I wanted to go and carry the goods from the plane, so I got up [wakes up], and I sat a while, and then a plane came flying over the house. I could hear the noise of two planes. Then I woke up our widow and told her, 'Get up! I was dreaming about a plane coming and now a real plane [palai ko'a] is flying overhead. I was dreaming about a plane coming with store goods for my brother to make a trade store, and now I can hear the noise of a real plane!'

"Then the plane was circling around above the house and I called out to my husband, 'Do you hear the noise of the planes?'"

In this example, the dreamer is so struck by the coinciding of her dream of a plane with her waking perception of planes flying overhead that she rouses two other people to confirm it. Her need to "reality-test" and her description of waking to the noise of a "real" plane is little different from the way Westernees might recount a similar experience. For her, as for us, reality is what takes place in waking experience and can be confirmed by others. The images of the dream are of a different order from waking perceptions of the material world. In fact, I would suggest Mekeo culture provides a means of discriminating more finely than we do in ordinary speech between these different orders of experience. We would say, "I was dreaming that I heard a plane and then I woke up and heard the sound of real planes," without indicating what aspect or part of "I" was involved, thus implying an identical self in two different states of awareness (dreaming and waking). In contrast, Mekeo discriminate not only between two different states of awareness, but between two different aspects of self involved. The dreamer observed: "I was dreaming and I heard the noise of the plane. Then I—my bodily self [imau(u)]—got up and I heard the noise of a plane."

Here she contrasts her two selves: her dream-self (understood by the context) and her bodily self, which is stated specifically. Her bodily self is the "I," which inhabits the waking world of material entities, "real" planes, and other, physical, embodied people. Her dream-self, a bodiless image perceived by her and others in dreams, inhabits a world of imagery without material substance. People sometimes say that the spirits of their dead relatives "cause them to dream" (panipia) or that spirits visit them in dreams, but the encounter, regardless of its nature, takes place between the dream-self of the dreamer and the dream-selves of the entities appearing in the dream. It is evident that bodily reality constitutes the center of this dreamer's concerns. The nonmaterial world of dream imagery is important to her, as to other Mekeo, only because it holds significant insights into what is to take place in her waking existence.[6]

Interpreting Dreams

There exists no elaborate typology of dreams that people can reel off for the ethnographer. Important distinctions concerning different types emerge only in practice, in the interpreting of specific instances. Although dreams may, in rare cases, literally depict in their imagery the outcome of future events, most are regarded as veiled or distorted representations. They are said to contain a significance or link (*oko*) for which the waking mind must search (*kapuleisa*). Like figurative, metaphorical, and veiled speech, dream-imagery is referred to as *palapole*, a term Desnoes (1941:909) translates as "conundrum," "riddle," "trick." The message carried by the dream must be unraveled or decoded to uncover its meaning. What the waking self can recall of the dream cannot be taken at face value (recall Hau'ofa's 1981:217 observation that Mekeo are inclined to take *nothing* at face value).

A relationship is assumed between the dream imagery and the events it reflects in the dream realm, and a link is assumed between these events and subsequent occurrences in the waking world, but the precise nature of this linkage constitutes the puzzle. It may be one of reversal, or opposites, as in Alex's dream of death being omened by dancing and celebration. Alternatively, it may be of similarity; for example, to dream of losing a tooth signifies the death of a close relative. Alex told me of a dream he had some years before, of losing an eye tooth, which was shortly followed by the illness and death of his infant son. A connection may be established simply on the basis of the dreamer's past experience. Thus Alex claimed that for many years he had a series of dreams in which a dead sweetheart would appear and he would talk with her. Though the dead girl did not directly indicate who would die, a death would subsequently occur in the part of the village where, in the dream, Alex encountered her. Dreams of falling—from trees, bridges, or other heights—are interpreted as indicating sickness, injury, or some misfortune for the dreamer. Dreams of departing on a journey and returning signify illness and recovery, while to depart and not to return indicates death.

Many such dream symbols are widely known to everyone and it is easy initially to gain the impression that dream interpretation is in essence a matter of knowing an extensive repertoire of symbolic equivalents. In practice, successful dream interpretation proves to be much more complex and fluid. To begin, the dream one assumes to be a symbolic representation may turn out to be a literal depiction of waking events. One must also take into account the personal circumstances of the dreamer—age, sex, current concerns, ritual status—and the context of external circumstances involving other people in which the dream occurs. The person's past dream experience must also be taken into account, since this serves, as in the case of Alex's recurring dreams of his dead sweetheart, to establish personal dream equivalences. All of these considerations will affect differently the way in which the dream-imagery should be read.

Given all this, one might expect that Mekeo dreamers have virtually free rein to draw whatever meaning suits their conscious purposes. Yet it becomes clear in the texts and interpretations people give of actual examples that certain implicit expectations concerning the information carried by dreams serve to limit in practice the meanings assigned to them. Regardless of the actual surface content, interpretations of the underlying dream message are almost always related to one or more of the following:

1. Warnings of sickness, injury, or death for the dreamer or another person(s).

2. Omens of recovery from sickness for self or others.

3. Visits to the land of the dead or to the water spirits' abodes.

4. Encounters with spirit beings, including spirits of the dead, the water spirits, the myth people, and Christian figures (God, Jesus, the Virgin Mary, and the saints).

5. Revelations of ritual knowledge, including medicines and spells.

6. Indications of the future success or failure of various enterprises, including love affairs.

7. Omens concerning the outcome of rituals.

Ordinary persons and ritual experts alike interpret their dreams in these ways, with the difference only that since experts are constantly performing rituals of various kinds, the majority of their dreams are interpreted as indicators of the success or failure of their endeavors, and thus fall into the last category.

The manifest content of the dream (as reported to me) may, but often does not, contain imagery literally representing the themes listed. Rather people seem to *expect* their dreams to relate to these matters and read them accordingly. In the case of omens of death, sickness, and recovery, the surface content rarely literally depicts the future. Thus people did not dream of the deaths of their relatives and loved ones, but they had many dreams that they consciously interpreted to signify such events. Alex's dream of dancing, of losing a tooth, and of talking with his dead sweetheart are classic examples. Similarly, dream imagery interpreted to mean recovery from illness usually bore only a metaphorical resemblance to the message it was believed to contain. For example, a married woman dreamed that two girls returned two lost umbrellas to her, indicating the recovery of her two sick children. If the manifest content of the dream actually depicts a known person's death, then it is read symbolically or metaphorically to refer not to a person, but to an animal. It might foretell the killing of a domestic pig or of a game animal in hunting.

Dreams interpreted as visits to the land of the dead—and many ordinary people laid claim to such experiences—tend to lie halfway between a literal and a metaphorical reading. Any dream of journeying to an unknown and beautiful place is regarded as a visit to the spirit world. The place may be a traditional Papuan village or a European city, or some amazing, brightly colored landscape. The individual variations are many, but to see a mysterious foreign place, particularly a large, populous European city, in a dream is always interpreted in this way. The dreamer may encounter the dream-selves of other living people (indicating their imminent death), the dream-selves of the dead, or the dream-selves of spirit beings such as A'aisa and the myth people (though this is rare for laypersons). More commonly, ordinary persons encounter Christian figures such as Saint Peter, God, or Jesus. The inhabitants of the strange city may be Europeans. Often the place is entirely deserted, or the dreamer may hear voices but be unable to see the inhabitants.

A significant variation on this type of dream is one wherein the dream-self visits places under water. Such dreams were perhaps even more widely reported. Dream imagery relating to events on, in, or under water, whether river, ocean, swamps, or lakes, is interpreted as relating to the *faifai* water spirits. A great many Mekeo dreams begin with the dreamer diving down under water. This is always an indication of visiting the *faifai*'s abode, and whatever beings are encountered there will be interpreted as *faifai* spirits. Such dreams are almost all related to sickness and recovery since the *faifai* spirits are believed to capture and strike the dream-selves of human beings thus causing illness and death. A great many ritually induced dreams, as well as the spontaneous dreams of ordinary folk, involve the *faifai* spirits or at least the watery elements that cause the dreams to be interpreted as dreams of the *faifai*. The precise significance of the imagery will vary according to the various circumstances previously mentioned. Since water spirits are believed to assume the form of people with white skins and straight hair, a European appearing in a dream might signify a water spirit or alternatively a spirit of the dead. Only dream-images of Europeans personally known to the dreamer would be regarded as representing themselves. The importance of the *faifai* in the dreams of both ordinary people and ritual experts totally confounded my earlier assumption (chapter 3) that they played only a trivial part in the cosmic order.

These dreams of visiting the land of the dead or the underwater abodes of the *faifai* spirits tend in some examples to merge with encounters with spirit beings, which I have listed as the fourth recurring theme. In many examples, encounters with specific spirit entities occur without the motif of a journey. One's dream-self may simply meet with a dead relative, a water spirit, or some other being without a particular place being indicated or else in some familiar location such as the village, its environs, in the gardens, or the bush. Such a meeting may constitute an omen—as in Alex's dream rendezvous with his departed lover—or provide other kinds of information.

Often a dream encounter with a dead relative or with a water spirit involves the acquiring of ritual knowledge. Once again, Alex provides us with an excellent example. He volunteered the following (reported in English) during one of our first discussions on dreaming:

"A recent dream—I was sailing in a steamer when I saw a person coming and he gave me a thing [charm] for rain [rituals]. He said it was a stone for rain magic. He told me, 'When you put it in the water, rain will come. Or when you put it near the fire, the sun will get hot.' He gave me that stone and then I was just thinking—and then I saw my dead father. That person [the giver of the stone] *was* my father. Then I woke up with a start. But there was nothing in my hand. So I don't know the truth about it."

After recounting several other recent dreams, he told of how he once had a ritual medicine (*fu'a*) revealed in a dream and that later, in waking reality, he came across the plant in the bush and used it as he had been instructed—and found it highly effective. But he was not certain what the dream about his father giving him the stone signified. It should be recalled that his father, the redoubtable George, was in fact a renowned rain expert.

Similar examples were recalled by many people. A particularly striking one was provided by the grandson of another powerful adept. He recalled that after his grandfather's death, his spirit returned in a dream to finish teaching some important spells that he had not had time to fully impart while alive. Via this dream instruction, the grandson now felt himself to be fully possessed of the appropriate knowledge. The *faifai* spirits are also often claimed as the source of dream revelations of ritual knowledge, not only by ritual experts but laypersons as well. It is evident in such cases, as indicated in Alex's dream of the rain stone, that the manifest dream imagery is taken as a literal communication of specific information, unlike the more symbolic dream omens of death and sickness.

Christian figures—the Madonna, the saints, Jesus, and God—feature in many reported dreams, although usually those of laypersons rather than of ritual experts. Many people claimed to have visited heaven or hell in their dreams. When such images appear they are taken to be literal representations and not symbolic of something else. Mekeo have been exposed to more than a century of Catholic mission influence and most people are at least nominal Catholics, yet it always seemed to me that their Christianity was no more than a veneer (chapter 3). The prominence of Christian symbols and motifs in dreams forced me to a new realization of the extent to which the mission's teachings have in fact deeply penetrated people's inner lives. Nevertheless, Mekeo have appropriated these powerful images in their own way. Many who regarded themselves as devout Catholics claimed that when worried or troubled over something, such as illness in the family, they would pray and then receive help in the form of dreams. This is a practice not, of course, approved of by the Church, and one wherein prayer and Christian images of power are being used in the manner of indigenous spells and ritual. Even in the case of individuals who are not notably devout or even practicing Christians, Christian symbolism may abound. What stands out in general is the prominence of Christian spirit entities in the manifest content of reported dreams, images which, in the dreamer's estimation, bring help, healing, and power, just as do other denizens of the hidden realm (see chapter 8).

All kinds of information may be revealed in dreams via direct communication with spirit beings (as in the example of the grandfather who returns to complete his transmission of important spells) or, alternatively, indicated metaphorically by the dream imagery. One may receive a warning of a fight in the village, see the face of one's future bride, learn who has stolen produce from one's gardens, discover that one's partner or neighbor is engaging in clandestine love affairs, learn that kin, neighbors, or friends harbor ill will against one, or be reassured that a loan application to the bank will be approved! People extract all manner of information from their dreams, ranging from the sublime to the very trivial. Yet even ordinary folk who pay no particular attention to their dreams, indeed would ignore them altogether if they could, are well aware that dreaming involves them in an intimate and continuing interaction with the mysterious hidden world of spirit forces. Anyone may claim to know what heaven looks like, to have direct conversations with God, to converse with the dead, or to receive magical instruction from a *faifai* spirit. The general patterns outlined here are exemplified in the dream histories sampled in chapter 8. What separates the layperson from the ritual expert, as I shall show in part III, is that the latter possesses the means to induce and guide dreaming to specific ends, while the former experiences his or her dreams as mainly spontaneous and uncontrolled.

Overall, Mekeo dream interpretation is highly flexible and can be understood fully only as it operates in practice. This flexibility no doubt serves to defend belief in the link between the dream reality and waking reality, since lack of correlation between the two can be explained merely as failure to fathom the true import of the dream. What is more fixed are the matters to which dreams are expected to relate: death, sickness, and healing; encounters with spirit beings; misfortune or success in various enterprises; omens concerning the outcome of rituals; revelation of ritual knowledge; and erotic matters. In practice, most dreams are read as metaphorical statements (cf. Wagner 1972) relating to one of these concerns, although any future trend may be reflected.[7]

Tedlock (1981) describes many similar principles operating in several Mesoamerican dream theories. She points out that in addition to "intratextual" analysis, Quiché dream interpretation involves what she terms "contextual" and "intertextual" levels. Her arguments are equally applicable to Mekeo dreaming. Like the Quiché, Mekeo are highly attentive to the personal circumstances and events of the dreamer's life—the contextual level—and equally to the relationship of the dream to other dreams (of the same person or those of other people occurring at the same time), as well as to information drawn from—the intertextual level—alternative sources such as divination and omens (as was clearly illustrated in the narrative of chapter 4; see also part III). Indeed, it is only in relation to these other contexts that the dream can be said to take on meaning at all. The dream histories Mekeo presented to me illustrate the desire to create such a context. Tedlock's arguments concerning the multiple levels at which indigenous interpretative systems operate underlines the importance of observing what people do with their dreams in practice. Normative statements abstracted from practice are likely to lead to oversimplification and trivialization. By focusing only on the intratextual level, psychoanalytically inclined anthropologists re-enforce the view that cultural defenses are operating against real insight in the dreamer's inner conflicts.[8] Exploring other levels of interpretation may reveal a rather different picture (chapter 8).

The Dangers of Dreaming

Although Mekeo regard dreaming positively as a source of valuable knowledge and insight into hidden things, like all phenomena it has a double aspect. It is also dangerous, not only because the knowledge it brings may be potentially harmful, but because *the very act involves risk to the dreamer.*

One who is dreaming is especially vulnerable to the influence and control of other forces and other persons. More specifically, one's dream-self is open to such influence and thus becomes the means whereby one's bodily self can be subjected to the control of others or can be ultimately destroyed. The actions performed by or on the dream-self in the dream realm are instrumental in nature; they have a crucial effect on waking reality. The close linking of dreams with sickness and death has already been indicated, but what has yet to be examined is the belief that sickness actually originates within the dream-self and only subsequently affects the bodily self. The man of sorrow, Aisaga, who has extensive knowledge of healing, explained this most succinctly: "The dream-self [*lalauga*] is the origin [*gome,* literally "root"] of sickness."

Minor illness may be regarded as merely the result of fatigue or overeating, but lasting indisposition is indicative of some mishap to the dream-self. Similarly interpreted are injuries Westerners would regard as accidental, such as a fall or cutting one's self with a knife. Any serious damage to the bodily self, either through illness or injury, does not arise initially from the internal processes or external actions of the body, but from prior actions of the dream-self. Only gradually is the body affected. Aisaga often emphasized in treating sickness that it was important to take action before the disease took too firm a hold. Once it was established little could be done, hence his derisive comments on a rival man of sorrow who was "trying to raise the dead" (chapter 4). The task of the healer is to persuade the dream-self to return before the body suffers serious damage. Sickness is believed to be caused by the actions of the dream-self when it becomes separated from the bodily self. If the dream-self suffers any kind of misfortune or commits some foolish or dangerous action the consequences will be suffered by the bodily self. In this respect, no injury or illness occurs purely by chance, it is prefigured in that other aspect of self.

When the dream-self leaves the body it is exposed to many potential dangers. It encounters the dream-selves of other living people, of the dead, and of spirit beings such as the water spirits, all of which may try to influence, control, or destroy it. If a person's dream-self accepts food offered by dead relatives, or their embraces, or agrees to leave with them on some journey, the bodily self will wither and perish; if it refuses, no harm will be done. Dreams resulting in injury to the bodily self need not be overtly unpleasant. For example, the dream-self may fall under the thrall of a handsome water-spirit lover; meanwhile one's bodily self falls sick. The dream-self is unpredictable, capricious; it may do foolish or risky things of its own accord; on the other hand, it may respond positively, and thus escape injury.

If the dream-self does not leave the body (i.e., if the person does not dream), then all the potential dangers of the other realm are avoided. In a healthy, normal state, the dream-self is not separated from the bodily self, even during sleep. Something must intervene to drive it out. In this sense, dreaming is an abnormal and vulnerable state. This is the reason why some people responded to my questions with a vehement denial, "I'm not sick! Why should I be dreaming!"

The dream-self may leave the body as the result of some desire unknown to, or in conflict with, the waking self; for example, longing to be with a dead spouse. The spirits may, of their own accord, make people dream (*isage e panipia*). If one is not soliciting it through ritual means, continuous dreaming is reason for concern. Either the dream-self is willfully putting the body at risk, or else some more powerful entity—spirit or human—is responsible. To further complicate matters, one's own dreaming is not the sole testimony—so too are the dreams of others. I may feel secure in the knowledge that no dreams disturbed my sleep, but others with better recall may have seen things hidden from me. People can ignore the dream warnings of others, but these premonitions may prove to be accurate.

Serious illness or accidents are usually attributed to some external agency acting upon the dream-self: a spirit being or force encountered in the dream realm, the dream-self of a ritual expert, or spirit beings directed by a human agent to attack the victim. The dreamer, of course, can only recall the escapades of the other self; she or he is helpless to alter its foolish or dangerous actions. Although people talk much about sickness being caused by sorcery and by the malice of the men of sorrow, when explanations are sought in specific contexts the answers are rather different. The water spirits are much more commonly invoked in these circumstances, and most instances attributed to them were not thought to be caused by human intervention. Another frequent explanation of illness is accidental contact with the powerful relics and substances used in various esoteric rituals.

Particular types of sickness or misfortune, such as snakebite, are considered indisputable evidence of ritual attack. Early in 1981, a man was bitten by a snake while in his gardens picking betel nut; he survived but was seriously ill for some time. During his illness, one of my friends related a dream concerning the incident. In it he saw a well-known man of sorrow shaking a spear in the direction of the house of the sick man. Having divulged this, he whispered that he saw clearly the face of the assailant and it was none other than my mentor Aisaga! No further explanation was necessary since the dream was a classic type: the throwing of the spear represented the snake sent to dispatch the victim. Since Aisaga is a renowned man of sorrow, it was no surprise he was identified; what amazed me was that my friend admitted this to me. I am not sure of his motives.

Sick people usually report dreams of being chased, beaten, and attacked, particularly by men from the mountains to the north, and of being chased by large animals, including cattle, horses, and cassowaries. The former are interpreted as attacks by spirits (or as a result of accidental contact with relics used in attracting the presence of the spirits). The latter are regarded as indications the dreamer is under attack by a man of sorrow. Cassowaries are particularly associated with the men of sorrow (chapter 2), but, it seems by extension, so are all large dangerous animals. A middle-aged man, who was ill at the time, recounted the following nightmares.

Dream of Being Chased by Cattle

"I dreamed about cattle. They came from Aipeana village, four of them. My dream-self was on the road when it saw them come out [of the bush]. When I saw the cattle I was frightened, I thought they were going to gore me. So I wanted to go into the bush beside the road so I could hide myself and get away. But there was a barricade there, I tried to bang my head against it, I kept banging my head against it, but I couldn't get past—then I woke up with a start. When I woke up my head was aching badly. Every day I dream like that."

Dream of Being Stabbed by Mountain People

"Lots of Kovio men were threatening to stab me with knifes. They wanted to kill me and they took their knifes and came to attack me. I took my knife and I frightened them off. Then they went off down the road, then they warned me and came and stabbed me with their knifes. They stabbed me in the back, they stabbed me in the front, they stabbed me many times—then I woke up with a start. That's what I dreamed, now I feel sick, my body is aching, my back is aching. The Kovio men were small, but they took their knifes and wanted to stab me. I took a big knife and frightened them off, then I tried to run. [Kovio people are small in stature compared with Mekeo, and this dreamer is a tall, strong man.] I ran but they came out farther down the road and stabbed me."

These dreams show the dream-self of the sick man is always wandering off from his bodily self and suffering attack by dangerous entities. His dream-self acts in a weak and ineffectual manner; it tries to defend itself, but cannot and ends up injured and frightened. Had the dream-self succeeded in driving off the mountain men, or escaping over the barricade from the cattle, then recovery would be indicated. But these dreams promise only continued suffering. Since cattle, horses, and cassowaries are well-known dream representations of the men of sorrow, and the savage mountain men representations of the angry spirits (*isage*) he controls (not the spirits of dead ancestors, but of enemies whose physical remains were taken in battle and given to the men of sorrow who then summon them to attack victims), the dreams indicate the sick man is being attacked via, or has been accidently exposed to, *ugauga* sorcery. This, however, is no more than he already knows.

It is intriguing that Freud observed that the dreams of anxious people were full of similar imagery of being attacked, beaten, and chased (1900; 1916b). Furthermore, the association of the paternal image with large and dangerous animals in childhood dreams is well established in the psychoanalytic literature (Freud 1979). Possibly in these Mekeo dreams of sickness and sorcery, patterns of dream imagery grounded in more universal human experience are given a specific cultural significance. The figure of the man of sorrow thus may become invested with the repressed fears and anxieties of childhood. His association with the powerful and punishing father is a dominant theme (see chapter 14, and also Stephen 1987b).[9]

These two dreams of sickness emphasize the closeness of the link between the dream-self and the physical body. The dream-self of the sick man is being stabbed, so he wakes with his body aching from the pain of the blows. His dream-self is threatened and he tries to escape, but can only bang his head against a barricade; when he wakes, his head throbs with pain. He is thus aware of two levels of suffering which are somehow interwoven: the sufferings of his other self when dreaming, the pains in his body when awake. To alleviate his sufferings, his dream-self must be brought back. In other words, the dream level of suffering must be stopped before the physical pain can be removed; this is the healer's task. The ritual use of dreams will be examined in part III; my intention here is merely to illustrate people's conviction that the actions of their dream-selves can be influenced through ritual implemented by others. Nightmares and anxiety dreams convince Mekeo that a part of self lying outside conscious awareness can be damaged, even destroyed, by others. Perhaps even this is not strong enough—I might say more accurately that people experience every illness and indisposition of the body as proof that I/me may be divided against myself by the ritual actions of others.

This sense of vulnerability owing to the divisibility of the self is underlined not only in physical ill health but in any circumstances where one's conscious will seems deflected from its proper tasks. Some, although not all, erotic dreams fall into this category. In referring to erotic dreams as a group or class, keep in mind that many dreams with overtly erotic imagery may be thought to relate to entirely different matters, while others with nothing to explicitly suggest it may be interpreted symbolically as relating to sexual conquest. The personal circumstances of the dreamer together with the context of events in which the dream takes place will determine the interpretation.

The dreamer's gender is probably the most important consideration. Since cultural convention asserts that the sexuality of females is muted (chapters 1 and 2), one might expect that girls and women experience erotic dreams as the result of cultural repression. Men claimed females were troubled by frequent erotic dreams but would never disclose them. Unmarried girls in particular are supposed to dream as a result of youths employing charms and spells to win their affections. If a girl (or a married woman) dreams of a particular lover, then, it is said, she will no longer resist his advances in waking reality. That is to say, once her dream-self has been won, her bodily self will soon be overcome by desire. A woman's only defence is to say nothing, for to admit to dreaming of a particular man would be tantamount to accepting him. Not surprisingly, I found that women were in fact reluctant to discuss these matters, except in general, and that they never spontaneously recounted their own erotic dreams. Women confessed their fear of men who were known to possess major love rituals, and they agreed that if such a man desired a woman, it would be impossible for her to resist. But no one actually confided personal details. In such a situation, the woman might simply give in, or she might alert her parents, or her husband if she were married, in the hope that the importunate lover might be persuaded to desist, or protective charms might be used to counteract his rituals.

In an essay on Arapesh dreams, Tuzin (1975) argues that the cultural system of dream interpretation operates to shield the dreamer's ego from guilt concerning overt eroticism since, in common with Mekeo views, such dreams are attributed to the influence of love ritual. In the Mekeo context, however, the dreamer in no way avoids the consequences. A Mekeo woman's dream is likely to be attributed to rituals directed against her conscious will, but a part of herself, her dream-self, is implicated. It is true she does not have conscious control over this aspect of self; nevertheless, she must bear the consequences of its actions. How she handles information concerning the desires of her other self is something she is accountable for; no Mekeo woman would be likely simply to ignore erotic dreams, and only the naive would consider them harmless.

In contrast to women, the overtly erotic dreams of males are usually interpreted as the result of implementing love rituals. Although only a few men possess knowledge of the major rituals, minor charms are known to many, and more potent charms can be acquired for a price from experts. A man who dreams of seducing a girl or woman is convinced he will shortly succeed in possessing her. In circumstances where a man is not currently interested in pursuing a woman, an overtly erotic dream might be interpreted symbolically to indicate good fortune in other kinds of affairs: luck in gambling, or in any business or enterprise in which the dreamer is currently engaged. In particular, dreams of sexual congress symbolize success in hunting. A man performing hunting rituals expects to dream of pursuing women, indicating his success in catching game. Conversely, in the standardized code of Mekeo dream symbols, to shoot or spear a bird or animal, particularly a female one, indicates success in love (this dream symbolism seems widespread across cultures; even in Western culture we speak of Cupid and his arrows and the wounds of love). In the Mekeo view, the secret, of course, is to learn how one's own dream symbols respond to context and circumstance in imaging the future: the astute man learns to judge whether on waking his success will lie in hunting game or pursuing women.

Dreams of water spirit lovers are common to both sexes and have the same consequences—the sickness, even destruction, of the bodily self. Similarly, dreams of erotic contact with the dead—merely touching them or eating the food offered by them—are interpreted for both sexes as a danger to the bodily self. Only dreams of living persons known to the dreamer vary in significance according to the dreamer's gender. The implication here is that dreams concerning human lovers are not seen to conflict with the conscious desires of males, whereas they are thought to be incompatible in the case of females. When the desires of the dream-self are in direct conflict with the conscious interests of the dreamer—as in instances indicating sickness or injury—the dream-self is believed to be under the sway of ritual influence exerted by another.

Indeed, the crucial point here is that any action of the dream-self subverting the dreamer's conscious desires are likely to be interpreted as the result of ritual intervention. The dream-self, once separated from the bodily self, is not only especially susceptible to other entities in the dream realm, it is not bound by the conventions and fears that dominate the waking I/me. This is doubly disturbing since I have no say in what my capricious dream-self does, and often not even any direct knowledge of it.

The dangers of dreaming are profound. Little wonder dreams are sometimes regarded with abhorrence—that dreaming is, as one man exclaimed, "like sorcery" (see chapter 8). People often speak of those "who have the power to change your mind"; they refer to specialists, like Aisaga, who possess major rituals. It is via the dream-self that such powerful individuals are believed to mold one's desires and behavior against one's conscious will. For the ordinary person, who lacks the means to exert conscious control over it, that other part of self can be the source of an especially insidious vulnerability.[10]

Self, the Cosmic Order, and Dreaming

My investigations into dreaming revealed three absolutely crucial things of which I had previously been entirely unaware and of which I had certainly not anticipated; nor would I have been likely to discover these things were it not for my new interest in dreams. In the first place, dreaming reveals the existence of a deeper layer of self beyond conscious awareness. Second, as will emerge even more forcefully in the discussion of ritually induced dreaming, it is this other layer of self that is both the agent of ritual action and the subject upon which it acts. Third, the whole cosmological order is predicated upon the existence of two interpenetrating modes of existence, one a physical, material, embodied world, the other a realm of powerful, transformative images without physical substance. Both the living and the dead, humans and spirits, exist in both modes of being (although, as will be seen later, not equally).

Finding suitable English terms to refer to these two states is awkward. One cannot, for example, refer to the "Seen" and the "Unseen" (like Schieffelin 1977), since both are, or can become, visible. Lawrence's (1964) "empirical" and "non-empirical" will not serve either since both realms are vividly experienced. For Mekeo, as I understand it, two states of being or "reality" are involved: one which involves an embodied existence, the other an existence without corporeal substance. To avoid complex circumlocutions, I will refer to these realms of corporeal and non-corporeal entities as the "embodied" and "disembodied" worlds.

I paid no attention to dreaming during my early fieldwork; there were too many other things of more obvious importance to be investigated. Ironically, I ignored the very key I lacked. Yet Mekeo dreams are not public matters available to all. Indeed, they are so much part of those things concealed by their very nature that after I realized their importance I found no easy access to them. Furthermore, Mekeo do not easily formulate ideas about dreaming in abstract terms. Its significance emerges only in praxis, from the careful examination of actual dream texts and their interpretation as reported by particular individuals. There is little to indicate to the outsider the role of dreams in Mekeo culture. Yet here I began to discover that what is private and concealed is absolutely crucial to understanding highly important aspects of the culture.

7

A Hidden Self

Dreaming is undoubtedly the context wherein the existence of another self, or part of self, emerges with greatest force and clarity. Yet it is not solely dreaming that provides evidence of the *lalauga*. Something of the other contexts in which this part of self operates must be understood to more fully appreciate its significance as a conceptualization of a part of self linked to, yet in many respects independent of, its other parts. Closer examination further emphasizes the inadequacy of such English translations as "spirit" or "soul" to capture its essence. Although it is evidently the part of self that interacts in the hidden world, it also has important consequences in social interactions and in everyday pragmatic situations. To identify *lalagua* as a soul or spirit distorts both these mundane qualities and its psychological salience. Mekeo conceptions of self are inevitably truncated and trivialized when separated from a consideration of the elusive self glimpsed in dreams—one which, I shall argue, might best be described as a "hidden self."

Other Contexts in Which the Hidden Self Appears

Consider the following comment from my friend Alex. I had just asked him whether he had heard about any dreams related to the recent death of a middle-aged woman (the discussion took place in English):

"No, I didn't hear any other. Oh yes, there was another one. Tom, he told me, from my clan. He was dreaming like that . . . no, not dreaming, but while he was sitting on the little veranda behind his house. He was sitting there and he thought he saw this Henry coming along—Henry, the husband of that [dead] woman. But he is not real, but Tom saw him coming—as if he were there. And after a few minutes, when he wanted to see him properly, then he couldn't see him again. Then we were sitting talking together about that. Is he [Henry] going to be in trouble [get sick] or what? Some were saying that the wife is already dead, so Henry he might die too. . . . We saw his *lalauga*—Henry's—we saw his *lalauga* going out. . . . So we are thinking, will Henry get sick or what?''

Alex makes clear the nature of this waking vision and its similarity to the dream omens of death. In fact, he starts off by describing it as a dream, but then specifies it was not. He has some difficulty in expressing himself in English, but the distinction is made easily in Mekeo; he would only have to say that Tom in his body (*imaugai*) saw the dream-self (*lalauga*) of Henry. Although we were speaking English, Alex uses the Mekeo term *lalauga* because he is unsure how to convey his meaning otherwise. When dreaming, one's own *lalauga* sees the *lalauga* of others. In waking, one's bodily self may sometimes see the *lalauga* of others. Imagery perceived in sleep dreams and in waking visions are all designated *lalauga*.

Waking visions, such as the brief encounter described by Alex, may over a period of time be merged with memories of sleep dreams (cf. Price-Williams 1987). This is especially likely since Mekeo belief gives no particular importance to them, and compared with sleep dreams, they play an insignificant role in ritual practice (the reasons for this will emerge in part III).

Just as excessive dreaming, unless ritually induced, is considered abnormal and unhealthy, so too are persistent waking visions. Two persons well known to me are subject to periodic episodes in which they claim to communicate with the spirits. Henrietta, an old lady in her late sixties, is notorious throughout the region for her claims, now extending over many years, to be in touch with the spirits and with the Christian God and saints. Many people observed she suffered ''headaches'' brought on by relics of the dead that her family persists in keeping in their house, which attract the spirits' presence; if the relics were removed, she would not be troubled in this way. But Henrietta herself takes a different view, believing she is the recipient of divine revelations.

A middle-aged married man, my neighbor during my first period of fieldwork, was subject to violent episodes, running amok through the village trying to spear anyone or anything he came across. I witnessed two such attacks and often discussed them with him. Ordinarily he is a quiet, heavy, lethargic man who does very little work, although he is pleasant enough in his manner and by no means unintelligent. Unlike Henrietta, he views his attacks as an illness. He explains that sometimes his head begins to ache badly, then he hears the spirits of his dead forefathers urging him to go out and spear anyone he can find. He confessed he used to keep relics of the dead in his house (he is the inheritor of some important esoteric knowledge, although not a practicing expert) and that when he got rid of these dangerous objects his attacks ceased. In the eyes of the community, both of these individuals are subject to temporary madness (*kania e kieki*);[1] at other times they are regarded no differently than anyone else, as both are respected, functioning, senior members of the community with adult children and numerous grandchildren.

When the imagery of the dream realm spontaneously invades waking consciousness and takes it over, Mekeo are convinced the person is sick. A brief or occasional intrusion is, however, no cause for alarm. Sometimes normal, healthy people may catch a glimpse of what is normally screened from waking perception. Ghosts of the recently dead and other various apparitions, all termed *lalauga,* occasionally appear to people, particularly when alone in the gardens or the bush. Following a death in the community, I usually heard reports, mostly secondhand, of people catching sight of the *lalauga* of the dead person in the gardens or on the road to the village. Such sightings are merely taken as evidence of the continued presence of the dead person around his or her former home. This is to be expected and does not cause fright or concern—people are perhaps only a little startled or saddened. More sinister apparitions might also be encountered. Occasionally, glimpses of foreign men of sorrow in the bush at the back of the village give cause for alarm, and people may be uncertain whether what they saw was a living man, a spirit (*isage*), or possibly A'aisa himself, the mythological founder of sorcery (see chapter 13 for examples). Encounters with the water spirits, *faifai,* are said to take place during waking states, although rarely. A few men claimed to have come across water spirits—usually beautiful women—in remote places in the bush and then to have fainted, or fallen into a stupor, later to recover and return home. None of these persons were well known to me and they would not agree to discuss their experiences. In any case, their claims were given no special significance by the rest of the community. Other waking visions of spirits—such as that experienced by Mary on the night of Ruth's funeral, when she saw horrible apparitions with huge fangs and broken necks (chapter 4)—are likewise given little attention, provided they are not persistent.

What these diverse examples reveal is that the *lalauga* of other persons and beings may appear to one in waking consciousness and, furthermore, that one's own *lalauga* can leave the body during waking consciousness. Both occurrences, however, are comparatively rare. In contrast, during sleep the *lalauga* frequently leaves, and returns, to the body.

The existence of the *lalauga* is revealed not only in such comparatively unusual states, but in the everyday well-being and effectiveness of one's bodily self. To a person knowledgeable in such matters, the actions of the *lalauga* are reflected in even minor indispositions, accidents, or merely a feeling of lethargy. Any split between conscious desire or will and the physical and mental energy to realize it might be described as owing to the action of one's *lalauga.* A diminution of energy, physical or mental, any faulty functioning of body and mind, is seen to result from a split between the two parts of oneself. To ensure the well-being of the bodily "I," the *lalauga* must not be allowed to wander off in pursuit of its own desires. Only the person who is always healthy and full of energy and enthusiasm for life need have no concern with his or her *lalauga* and pay it little mind.

Because he was instructing me in dangerous ritual knowledge, Aisaga took what seemed to me an excessively elaborate concern with my physical well-being: a slight headache, a runny nose, a disinclination to work, and he was anxiously looking for the cause. Any minor thing, he warned, might develop into something serious and should be treated as soon as it appeared. If I appeared a little clumsy, dropped things, or tripped, even though no serious mishap resulted, Aisaga would see my *lalauga* as the culprit. If I felt low on energy, cancelled my activities for the day, and kept to myself, my *lalauga* was the cause. Thus I was reminded at every turn of the significance of the actions of my *lalauga*.

Up until this point, I have been content to translate *lalauga* as "dream-image" and "dream-self." As our evidence mounts it becomes obvious that the *lalauga* is something more than a dream-self. It cannot be regarded simply as an animating principle, nor as the source of intelligence and consciousness, since the individual lives and experiences consciousness in its absence. There is a visible, bodily self (*imauga*) existing in a world of material objects perceived in waking experience, plus another part of self—a bodiless image (*lalauga*) inhabiting a world of noncorporeal imagery. This other self is truly a hidden self, since not only is it usually invisible to the waking perception of others, but is hidden even from one's own waking awareness, except to the extent that one can recall and accurately interpret one's dreams. Most important, it eludes one's conscious control and intentions.

Lalauga is almost impossible to translate because English lacks a "common sense" notion of a dual or multiple self.[2] Our sense of being a single entity, "I" or "one," dominates the language available to describe self. We do experience in ordinary, everyday life feelings of being divided against ourselves, of lacking the physical strength or moral courage to do what we would like to do. We talk of our bodies letting us down, or our emotions carrying us away. We lack "will-power," or "self-control," we feel "paralyzed" by indecision. Here is a unitary self, an "I," debilitated by weak or faulty appurtenances—a weak will, a feeble body, uncontrollable emotions—struggling with external forces. Mekeo, through the concept of the *lalauga,* are attuned to an inner struggle between the two parts of self. We need to look to psychological terminology and concepts for an appropriate equivalent. The division can be thought of in terms of conscious self and unconscious mind, ego and id (Stephen 1989b), or in nonpsychoanalytic terms, as divided streams of consciousness. Cosmological notions are involved; "soul" or "spirit" are the usual translations of what I am exploring, yet these terms are totally inadequate to capture the pragmatic psychological processes *lalagua* encompasses. Ironically, some Western psychologists such as James Hillman (1975) are currently attempting to put the "soul" back into our own overly rationalized and pathologized concepts of "psyche." (I will return shortly to what others have had to say about these comparative issues.)

Mekeo are firmly grounded in the physical reality of their waking existence, and their concern with the dream realm extends only to its links to waking experience. The "real" (*ko'a, ipauma*) world is that which is perceived, and acted upon, by the physical body and conscious thought. When one speaks of "I" (*lau*), one refers to one's conscious thoughts, emotions, feelings, and perceptions as located in the physical body. Mental activities—to think (*opo*), to know (*logo*), to understand (*kapuleisa*)—are all actions that "I" perform. Thinking is said to take place in the head (*kania*), and more specifically in the brain (*minoga*); this may be due to European influence, but it is the way people who speak no English describe their experience. To see (*isa*), to hear (*aina e logonia*), to smell (*foga e logonia*), and to touch (*afi opogaina*) are all capacities of the physical body, functions that "I" perform. Likewise, emotions are very specifically grounded in the physical body. For example, *guau e kupu* (literally, my "chest/stomach" is "closed/obstructed") indicates "I am angry"; *alou e kieki* (literally, "my inside hurts") means "I am sad"; *alou e gama* (literally, "my inside grows, or is reborn") means "I am happy."

"I/me" (*lau*), "myself" (*lau ifou*), and my waking thoughts and feelings are thus firmly located in my physical body. When I sleep, *lau la feu,* or when I fall unconscious, *la mae afu,* another part of myself which is not tied to my physical body emerges. Mekeo carefully distinguish between what they experience in their bodies (*imauga*), and what are the actions of their dream-selves (*lalauga*). The former constitute what Westerners describe as the perceptions of normal, waking consciousness, the latter what we classify in psychological terms as states of nonordinary consciousness.

For Mekeo, the sense of self, of existence as a thinking, feeling entity, is centered in conscious, waking experience. Yet there is also awareness of a part of one's self separable from consciousness and the physical body. This hidden aspect behaves almost like a totally independent entity. It can leave the body and operate in another mode of existence and achieve things impossible for the bodily self. Its actions can thwart the intentions, desires, and interests of the bodily self. Indeed, its existence does not depend on the body. People who assured me so earnestly that they knew nothing whatsoever of the spirit world were in fact well aware that, like it or not, every person, via that elusive other self, partly exists in the shadowy and perilous disembodied realm. The *lalauga* is a hidden self participating in a hidden world, and since there is no single word in English that captures its nuances, I shall refer to it as the "hidden self."

Negotiating the Multiple Layers of Self

It is time to gather up the several strands of my argument concerning Mekeo ideas of self. Putting aside for the moment the "hidden self," I will return to the divisions of manifest and concealed developed in part I. The bodily self (*imauga*) is composed of an inside and an outside, that is, what is visible and on the surface, and what is inside and concealed. These distinctions create at least four contrasting divisions of the self. There is the rigorously controlled surface/skin (*faga*) of the body structure and the concealed and contaminating interior substances (*faga ofuga*) of the body. There is the carefully presented public "face" (*maaga*) of social action, and the "inside self" (*alo*) of concealed thoughts and emotions.

A person must be able to negotiate all these levels in the ongoing processes of social relations. In defining I/me, in reflecting upon myself, and in representing myself to others, I must in Mekeo culture deal with these several interior and exterior layers. Social interaction, as I described in chapter 2, involves a sharp division between the "outside" and the "inside" self. Mekeo are much concerned with managing their public behavior in action and speech to conform to social ideals and expectations. Management of the physical body in smooth, controlled deportment, in the grooming, decoration, and dressing of the body, and in painting and disguising the body surface, all reflect the desire to present a physical presence that complies with the smooth mask required in public performance and action. Yet people are acutely aware that their own inner thoughts and emotions, and those of others, not only diverge from but may reverse social ideals.

The inside self provides the core layer, one might say, since it is here, inside the self (*alouai*), that the individual's desires, thoughts, and feelings are located; it is these thoughts and feelings that control, or strive to control, the public "face" and the body surface, "skin." There is, however, one part that is largely beyond conscious control: the interior of the body. What goes into and what comes out of the body is only to a limited extent a matter of choice (although we shall see in part III that the situation is different for ritual experts). What takes place within the body is not only uncontrollable but unknown to consciousness. People can, of course, restrict what they take into the body and carefully dispose of what comes out of it, and so they do, but the body interior with its mysterious processes of ingestion and elimination is a source of vulnerability. One may be destroyed by what goes into to it, or by what comes out of it. Via ingestion and elimination, what is other is incorporated into self, and what was self can be expropriated by others. I suggested earlier that this anxiety over the inside of the body and its products reflects anxiety concerning self-definition. (Fuller discussion of these points must be postponed until later when I take into account the effects of ritual practice on self-experience.)

The need to defend self in personal relationships clearly emerges in the constant emphasis on lies, jealousy, and shame. Quarrels, when they do break out in the village, resound with angry cries of "*Pifoge, pifoge!*" ("lies, lies!") Disguise and trickery (*fogefoge*) are a constant theme in humor, folktale, and myth. People think it is clever to deceive others, and expect others will treat them likewise. A'aisa, the mythological founder of the social order and originator of ritual knowledge, is the ultimate trickster; people often remark that A'aisa tricked the people (*papiau e foge'i*) and that is why the men of sorrow and others who inherited his secret knowledge still do so. What lies at the heart of this cultural play upon the theme of deception, I suggest, is the desire to defend self from other.

Most anthropological writing on deception and secrecy in Melanesia has concentrated on ritual contexts and its use in the exercise of political power by one social group (gender, age grade, senior versus junior) over another (Lindstrom 1984; Herdt 1982, 1984; Tuzin 1980). The psychological significance of deception has been little considered in an anthropological context (an exception being Luhrmann 1989). In the Mekeo case, this is not something that operates as much between groups as between individuals. The person who too openly reveals his or her feelings is considered naive. Mekeo contrive to be inscrutable, not transparent.

It can be no easy task to mark off even a psychological space that is not accessible to others in small face-to-face communities of only a few hundred people who are born and live out their lives together in constant close interaction. Physical privacy of any sort is almost impossible to achieve in these settings and everyone, effectively, knows everybody else's business. Deception alone provides the means of creating space. If one's thoughts and feelings are transparent and available to others, then they are not truly private, but are shared by others as well. One has no room for negotiation, bargaining, or surprise; if others already know your thoughts, they have the advantage and can deal with you when and how they choose. Mekeo use deception to gain the advantage over others (as did A'aisa, the mythological hero), to keep others guessing, and to defend oneself against the demands and manipulations of others. I can go even further and say that the Mekeo cultural elaboration of deceit as a key motif in social relationships reflects the anxieties of a cultural view of self that seems hard-pressed to defend its boundaries.

But if trickery and deceit serve to guard the "inside" self, they do so by erecting barriers that lead to misunderstanding and quarrels. The price of establishing the self's boundaries is social disharmony, a circumstance of which most Mekeo are only too well aware. People point out that in the myth of the origin of *ugauga* rituals, A'aisa deceived his brother Isapini by appearing to him in the form of a small boy, but was insulted when his brother failed to recognize him and treated him as a child. This apparently minor misunderstanding—caused by A'aisa own duplicity—leads to a bitter quarrel in which the brothers kill each other's sons.

Ofuege and *pikupa* (roughly "shame" and "jealousy") are the two most commonly offered explanations for social disharmony. Both are linked to deceit; both can be understood as forms of injury to I/me within a social relationship. *Pikupa* arises out of a sense that one has not been given one's due, that others are withholding things that should be shared. One therefore strives to ensure that relatives, friends, and allies receive their proper entitlement in all distributions of food, wealth, or goods. Failure to do so, whether at a clan feast, a distribution of bride wealth, or simply dividing up presents sent home by relatives working away from the village, can have serious repercussions. Furthermore, one should take care not to arouse *pikupa* by conspicuous wealth, success, or overly assertive behavior. To deprive someone else of their due, to make them feel deprived (*ulalu*), creates *pikupa*. Selfishness and greed on one person's part provokes the anger (*gua e kupu*) and *pikupa* of others. *Pikupa* is not simply unprovoked envy, but has its roots in the feeling that one is being deprived through the unjustifiable selfishness of others. The self has suffered damage in its relations with others, and in such a situation one is bound to seek revenge. Again, the A'aisa myth provides the prototype. As a young boy, A'aisa went hunting with the men and used his ritual knowledge to catch much game, which the bigger men then took from him, leaving nothing for him and his old mother. A'aisa eventually avenged himself by using trickery to seduce their wives.

Ofuege, on the other hand, arises out of a sense of the inner self being injured by exposure to public ridicule.[3] It is not necessarily associated with guilt, or with being caught out in some wrongdoing, as the word "shame" implies in English. Rather it is a matter of being publicly derided, whether that ridicule is merited or not. It is also, I think, a matter of the nature of the relationship with the person who exposes another. For example, personal insults concerning one's physical appearance, particularly from the opposite sex, are considered very shame inducing. Young men who are rejected with insults about their appearance by the girls they court are thought likely to seek revenge through ritual action. The young man who comes courting a girl is offering her an intimate relationship with him, a relationship the girl makes impossible by exposing her would-be lover to public derision. Many are the myths employing this situation as their starting point. In such cases, *ofuege* can be seen as the result of an attack on self-esteem.

Ofuege is also felt when things that should be kept well concealed and out of sight—*ogevake kapa*—are exposed to public view. There is a myth which explains why the dog cannot talk. At one time, Amue, the dog, could talk and lived with people as a member of the family. One day, Amue went to the gardens with his "mother" and "father" where he espied the two of them making love. Later, when they returned to the village, the dog told everyone what he had seen. Deeply shamed and angered by this, the man seized a log of wood and hit the dog over the muzzle, telling him he would never speak again. The dog's jaw was broken and from then on he could only howl and bark. Amue shamed the man not by revealing some wrong action, for example catching him in adultery, but simply by uncovering private sexual matters and thus making the couple an object of ridicule.

Pikupa and *ofuege* thus both grow out of a sense of injury to self in dealing with others. In a sense, they are the reverse of each other: *pikupa* is caused by others withholding what they should give to you, and *ofuege* is caused by others taking what rightfully belongs to you—your private thoughts and acts—and making them public. In either case self is diminished. In both cases the offense arises out of a highly developed sense of self and self-interest. As the A'aisa myth illustrates, even the closest social relationships are fraught with the divisive tensions of *pikupa* and *ofuege*—of self-interest versus relationship. In the Mekeo view, self is defined only at the expense of relationship. They see and expect no solution to this conflict: it is inherent in the nature of things, as imaged in their key myths and as evidenced in their everyday social interactions.

Mekeo spend much time commenting upon the negative aspects of social relationships, and of the fatal consequences of *pikupa* and *ofuege,* but they are, of course, aware that every person depends upon others. One cannot cut one's self off from kin, no matter what injury is felt. One must continue to interact with other people, even though social relationships inevitably pivot on mutual distrust. Mekeo attempt to shield self by keeping real thoughts and emotions concealed. At the same time, they know that others do the same, and that injuries to their self-esteem are easy to inflict unaware. In the midst of all this dissembling, suspicion, and distrust, the final irony may be that not only can one never really trust others, but that, in the end, neither can one trust one's self.

All the complicated negotiations among the several conscious layers of self must take place against the shadowy backdrop of the caprices of the hidden self. The inside self—that core of conscious awareness that Mekeo strive so hard to conceal from public view—may be exposed by the actions of the hidden self that are perceived by others. They may have secret knowledge about you—you can never be sure. One's dream-self appears in other people's dreams. If other people see your dream-self engaging in clandestine love affairs, or if your dream-self behaves in an abusive or aggressive way, this indicates a truth underlying your conscious motives and desires. Dreams may contain highly significant information about interpersonal relationships—but these dreams are likely to be kept secret. And just as people are expected to lie about their real intentions and motives, so too are they expected to lie about dreams. Were dreams and visions to be communicated freely, an endless web of fears and suspicions would be exposed. The hidden self adds layer upon layer to an already intricate pattern of conscious social deception and intrigue.

Communications Concerning the Hidden Self

Dreams are regarded as dangerous knowledge, to be handled with the greatest discretion, and collecting dream reports, particularly of current examples, is a task fraught with difficulty. Mekeo is no serendipitous dream-culture where the ethnographer may happily set out each morning to cull the night's fresh harvest of dreams from families sitting around their breakfast fires (cf. Gregor 1981). As well as being disclosures of self, Mekeo dreams also contain potentially explosive information concerning social relationships.

People do share dreams with others, but in a guarded way: certain dreams, at certain times, are shared with certain people. When a dream is communicated, it will be to one's spouse, one's children, or sometimes an intimate friend. A remarkable or disturbing instance is likely to be recounted in this intimate context immediately on waking. People seek confirmation and validation of their dream insights by sharing them with others, but are hesitant to reveal a dream omen more widely until proven accurate. In this way, a person gains the satisfaction of sharing dream experiences only with those who are prepared to be supportive and understanding.

In certain circumstances, dreams do become the subject of more public discussion. Occasionally when the men of the clan gather at their meeting house just to talk among themselves, someone may choose to reveal a recent dream that might have relevance to the group. Omens indicating success in hunting, for example, would be of interest if the clan were preparing to hold a feast. The group may decide on the probable meaning and advise the dreamer how to act upon it. Alex provided the following instance, which held more serious import:

"Hubert, of our clan, he had a dream about hunting. He was out hunting and shot two wild pigs and we [his clansmen] carried them back to the village. One of them was a village pig: we discovered that when we brought them home. But when he shot them in the bush, they appeared to be two wild pigs. Then the people of Palm clan said, 'Oh, why did you shoot our pig?' So there was nearly a big fight over this. That's what he, Hubert, dreamed. We [his clansmen] were thinking that this might mean that somebody might be killed in that place. They might shoot someone with a bow and arrow, or spear him—something like that. That's what we thought. Then also Hubert's [maternal] uncle is from Palm clan. So we told him, tell your uncle not to go to the garden or hunting in the bush for a few days [i.e., until the impending danger has passed]."

When dreams have relevance to others Mekeo feel a responsibility to warn the persons concerned, but the constant bearer of such tidings would soon become very unpopular indeed, and it is little wonder they are usually kept under cover.

There is another important consideration. Anyone who dares claim too much insight into hidden things is likely to arouse not only the anger and suspicion of ordinary people but also the jealousy of ritual experts. Anyone, except a well-seasoned adept, would be foolish to claim openly too much dream knowledge. In intimate relationships, however, such as between spouses and lovers, dreams or suspicions couched as dreams are said to play an important role. Revelations concerning love affairs, particularly of one's partner(s), are usually considered to point to the truth.

Among the Sambia, according to Herdt (1987), dreaming is communicated at public, private, and esoteric levels of discourse. My experience persuades me that, for Mekeo, dreams belong to a separate level of discourse. There is public discourse, confidential discourse, and secret esoteric discourse of ritual experts, but in addition there is a fourth level. Ordinary laypersons, who by definition are excluded from esoteric discourse, nevertheless have different frames of private discourse available to them. Herdt refers to some Sambia dreams as being so private that they are never, or very rarely indeed, told to others. My impression is that, in contrast to Sambia, Mekeo deliberately frame most dream (and related visionary) experience as separate from other kinds of personal experience. Mekeo describe their opinions, thoughts, hopes, ambitions, and fears at length, without ever mentioning dreaming. Over the various phases of my fieldwork I have had a great many such discussions with a wide range of people of different ages, gender, and social position. When the topic of dreaming is raised a very different interaction is set up, as I have described. Perhaps one could say that in confiding their inner thoughts, Mekeo express the self for which they take responsibility, the self they acknowledge as intentional—what we would call conscious will, or ego. This inside self, as has been described, is different from the carefully controlled and inscrutable public face, but it is also very different from the aspect revealed in dreams.

Comparative Perspectives

How does this Mekeo self of multiple layers and secret aspects compare with other formulations observed in similar cultures? Much recent anthropological writing has demonstrated that Western concepts of self and the individual are generally inappropriate when applied to other cultures, where different understandings prevail and where person and self are not discrete, bounded entities but rather are primarily defined in contexts of interpersonal relationships (Geertz 1984; Marriot 1976; L. Dumont 1965; Leenhardt 1979; M. Strathern 1988; White and Kirkpatrick 1985; Herdt and Stoller 1990). For Melanesia, Leenhardt's (1979) romantic view of the Canaque's diffuse mythic participation in the "other," both social and cosmic, has attracted new attention. Although Mekeo self-concepts certainly cannot be easily translated into Western terms, one important respect in which they seem somewhat anomalous is the degree of concern that centers on defining and defending self.

For Melanesia, Strathern (1988) has given a new and challenging form to the argument that the self is defined primarily in relationships in non-Western cultures. Yet as I read her account, I cannot help wondering how in all this complexity of relationship the Melanesian can have any sense of existing as an entity that possesses consciousness, will, and desire. Humans may look at themselves as the creations of social relations, economic forces, or as biologically determined organisms, but this is to treat people as objects, not as conscious, thinking, and acting agencies. I understand "self" precisely as a person's awareness of being such an agency. Clearly Strathern does not deny thoughts, emotions, and desires to Melanesians, since she attempts to present them as thinking, acting agents. Yet I fail to see of what or how this agent is constructed, or maintained, in the sequence of actions involving the relationships that she describes (Strathern 1988:268 ff.).

It is true that "the self," in the sense of "the individual," is a Western cultural construct, shaped over many centuries by complex historical processes unique to Western culture (Heller, Sosna, and Wellbery 1986; Lukes 1973; Greenblatt 1986; Davis 1986, Thomas 1971, Heelas and Locke 1971). Strathern rightly insists that our bounded, unitary self is a cultural achievement or, perhaps, aberration. Nevertheless, a self as a locus—however fluid, shifting, and divisible—of a person's thoughts, feelings, desires, and actions is, I have to assume, a necessary component of human consciousness. Animals possess consciousness; human beings surely possess self-consciousness. This is not to argue that self-concepts do not vary. Where the self begins and ends, and what pertains to it, are problems each culture answers differently (Herdt and Stephen 1989). Yet I think we must not let our confusion over what seems to *us* to be the highly fluid and divisible nature of other selves lead us to the conclusion that in the space between the social relationships that constitute the person there is nothing, or that the mistake is "to conceive of a center at all" (Strathern 1988:268–269). Surely there is a feeling, thinking, self-conscious human being there somewhere? One of the crucial existential problems for that human being is to define itself against, as well as in relation to, others.

Strathern criticizes Herdt's (1981, 1982, 1984) and similar studies of male initiation in New Guinea for putting at their center a Western notion of person and self, defined as clearly bounded and possessed of specific attributes. She passes over the intention of Herdt and his contributors to explore the self as a center of experiencing consciousness. Their task and achievement is in tracing how this experiential center of self is shaped by cultural means. Human beings—persons—can exist in social relationships only as they are able to think of, be conscious of, or desire such relationships. If Melanesians do conceive of person and self by the root metaphors Strathern proposes (or indeed by any other metaphors one might conjure), then they can do so only as thinking, self-reflective, self-conscious beings.

In explaining social relationships, Strathern (1988:269) may be satisfied to dispense with an "active agent at the creative or created center of relations." But in understanding the nature of self, one cannot dispense with the experiencing consciousness that is a human being. Explanations in terms of social relationships often seem contrived because social anthropology aims to explain everything in such terms. How people experience and understand their world are, by the very nature of the endeavor, put aside. Formerly, social anthropologists asserted one could only observe behavior, thus it was impossible to know what was in people's minds (D'Andrade 1984). The current emphasis on the person as a construct of social relationships seems to posit much the same position: that is, there is no subjectivity outside the relationship. By this move, social relationships are reestablished as the sole, valid focus of investigation.

Howard (1985) has warned against overreliance on the idea that personhood is inextricably woven into the fabric of social life, since Western culture also defines self in relationships. He poses this question (1985:414):

> [D]espite compelling evidence that most Pacific Islanders do not normally distinguish themselves as individualized entities in ordinary discourse, does this mean they do not have a clear conception of themselves as unique individuals?

He argues it would be better to look at how and to what degree self extends beyond the skin in all cultures instead of assuming a simplistic dichotomy between "them" and "us." Because of the very embeddedness of self in small-scale face-to-face societies, I think Western anthropologists also need to pay closer attention to how self is defended from others, a point raised by Roseman (1990:236–237).

It seems to me impossible to speak of "self-awareness" without examining how this is realized in the reported experience of real men and women. Work by McHugh (1989) and Ewing (1990b) draw attention to the important differences that emerge in views of self when moving from normative statements and cultural symbols to practical experience. McHugh points out that the now-influential views of Dumont and Marriot concerning the relational, divisible self in South Asian cultures were based upon normative and prescriptive statements elicited mainly from written texts. When one considers how such concepts are employed in practice in a particular culture, it is evident that cultural values concerning social embeddedness by no means preclude a firm experiential sense of being a separate individual. McHugh argues, correctly I believe, that the contrast between Western concepts of person and self have been overdrawn on the basis of cultural ideals, ignoring a commonality of human experience. Along similar lines, Ewing suggests the Western notion of a unitary self is likewise a cultural ideal, indeed one which is only achieved by ignoring the shifts, inconsistencies, and contradictions reflected in a person's ongoing process of self-representation. For Ewing, no self is a fixed, unambiguous, bounded entity, and self-identity is maintained only through an "illusion of wholeness." This much more subtle view of self, as a continuous process of shifting representations is as applicable to Western as to Asian and other cultures. Both McHugh and Ewing alert us to the fallacy of conflating norms with practice and thus exaggerating cultural differences.

The important corrective they offer might well be taken to heart by those who are inclined to doubt even the existence of an inner life for any but Western intellectuals! Clifford (1982:6) observes, "The notion of an 'inner' life is probably best understood as a fiction of fairly recent, and far from universal, application—even in the West." Of course it depends on what one means by an "inner" life, but are we to imagine that this pertains only to modern Western individuals? What of the many highly sophisticated philosophic and spiritual traditions of the East that are devoted to the development of inner awareness? Perhaps it would be more accurate, following Kakar's (1982:272) arguments, to say that it is the West which lacks sensitivity to inner states.

Here I touch upon the discrimination all cultures except modern, secular Western culture make between material and nonmaterial aspects of person and self. In probably all Melanesian cultures (see, e.g., Panoff 1968; Sørum 1980; Stephen 1989b; Lattas 1992), as in Mekeo, there is not one "true" self but rather many selves. "Self" and "other" are not the only considerations—the problem is that I/me encompasses more than one self and that there are multiple selves of others. If Mekeo selves are constituted in social relationships with living people, they are also constituted in interactions with entities of the disembodied world, which include the hidden selves of both the living and the dead. Indeed, it might well be said that the self defined in social relationships is an etic, not an emic, framework, since it suits our cultural construction of the world to assume only a social, embodied self. Most, if not all, tribal societies construe another or other parts.

In denying subjectivity to the "other" we seem to assume that because it takes different forms, and finds different areas of expression from that familiar in Western culture, it does not exist. For Mekeo, the hidden self revealed in dreams elicits a sensitivity to aspects of self outside conscious awareness and calls for a conscious attempt to deal with the implications of its actions and desires. Furthermore, the terminology used to describe dream states, dream imagery and the dream-self, provides a lucid and subtle description of different levels of subjective experience. Speculation about the hidden level of self creates a complex discourse of subjectivity for Mekeo—a discourse illustrated in the case studies presented in the following chapter.

8

Dreams and
Self-Knowledge

In contrast with earlier, more culture-bound views that the dream, being an intra-psychic event, contains only personal, idiosyncratic meanings, current anthropological approaches deal with dreams as communicative acts, and thus as cultural constructs involving shared understandings (reviewed in D'Andrade 1961; Bourguignon 1972; O'Nell 1976; Kennedy and Langness 1981; Kilbourne 1981a; Tedlock 1987a). My discussion reflects this more recent emphasis, but it is important not to overlook the role of Mekeo dreams as intra-personal communications. The question this chapter takes up is: How do actual people construe the selves they find in dreams and how do they put this knowledge to use—by integrating it, or failing to integrate it, with their conscious awareness of self? Four short case studies will be considered. All are of people well known to me during both phases of fieldwork; none are ritual experts. Their views are representative of ordinary, intelligent adults, and the dreams they report typify the general types of manifest content and interpretations outlined earlier.

Prominent in these accounts of ordinary men and women are circumstances and motifs which vividly draw to attention the fact that Mekeo culture in the late twentieth century is an amalgam of many indigenous and foreign influences. Over the last one hundred years or more it has had to absorb and modify a bewildering array of new ideas, new values, new desires, and new modes of behavior. The influence of Christianity, colonial rule, and secular education, and the impact of modernization and the cash economy have all left their mark on village life. Maria, one of the four dreamers, is a widow in her fifties and has spent several months in Australia visiting her diplomat son; she dreams of a spirit of the dead arriving in a helicopter! Joe, a middle-aged man, who has university-educated sons and liked to engage me in debates about "science," dreams of the afterlife as a place where sinners are put in European-style prisons. Andrew, a man in his seventies, claims he accepts what the mission teaches, that the dreams are just "thoughts," but then admits to a different view. Celestina, a married woman in her mid-thirties, prays to God that her dream-self will return safely from its adventures in the hidden world; in her dreams, the land of the dead is a great bustling city full of cars and trucks (a very common Mekeo dream-image). Christianity especially emerges as an important influence, as is apparent even in the small sample presented—these dreams are sufficient to indicate the pervasiveness of Christian beliefs. The Mekeo hidden world is populated not only by the spirits of the dead, the myth people, and the *faifai* spirits but also God, Jesus, the Virgin Mary, the Christian saints, and angels and devils. My early impressions were that Christianity had, at best, only an external influence on the culture (chapter 3); it was only when I began to investigate dreaming that I began to appreciate how deeply Christian teachings had been internalized. Christian imagery has been incorporated into the Mekeo imaginal world, and is now woven inextricably into preexisting mythic patterns.

The delicate task of identifying and unraveling the meanings given to this foreign imagery, and of deciding to what extent Mekeo consciousness has been altered by it, is beyond the scope of this study. I do not doubt that the expansion of the indigenous mythic symbolic realm has brought significant change, and that in the case of many highly educated and devout Mekeo Catholics a transformation in belief has occurred. Yet most village people, as exemplified by the following four case studies, engage with Christian dream imagery as they do with other spirit entities: as images of power capable of creating transformations in the dream realm and thus of events in the material world. Where Christian imagery is drawn upon, it is within a matrix of indigenous ideas concerning the nature of dreaming, the dream-self, and the link between the hidden and the embodied world. The point of this chapter is to describe how ordinary people, such as our four dreamers, use these concepts within a changed and changing world to reflect upon another part of self.

Celestina: Dreams of Death

Celestina is a quiet, self-possessed married woman in her mid-thirties. She has several children ranging in age from a baby of about eighteen months to a seventeen-year-old son. Her natal family is well known to me since her father is the acting man of kindness of the clan in which I lived during both phases of extended fieldwork. Her husband, Paul, often acted as my interpreter and field assistant during my early fieldwork. He has a few years secondary schooling and has spent time away from the village working for the government in minor clerical positions. Although a staunch supporter of the Catholic mission, his understanding of Christianity, like his wife's, is strongly colored by traditional beliefs. A handsome, intelligent couple, Paul and Celestina are well respected in the community.

Celestina is not only a prolific dreamer with a good memory, but in her view dreams provide important information about things screened from waking understanding. The examples she related to me were selected to demonstrate this. Our entire discussion was tape recorded; the dream texts given here were first transcribed by me in Mekeo and then translated into English.[1] She began with a dream that had occurred only two days previously of a house falling on her old mother and her brother's children. Although its import was yet to be realized in waking reality, she was in no doubt as to its significance—sickness and then recovery for those people who had managed to scramble out from under the fallen house. She went on to describe other past dreams that she believed had accurately predicted illness, recovery, or death for members of her family and herself. These were not merely simple omens but often provided both the means of identifying the cause of the illness and the means of healing it. The manifest content of the dreams varied considerably, yet Celestina related almost all to sickness, death, and healing. Her dream reports followed the standard form described in chapter 6 of a brief statement of the imagery of the dream followed by an explanation of how it related to subsequent waking events.

Celestina's confidence in her ability to read her dreams was matched by her courage in facing up to the disconcerting, indeed dangerous, exploits of her dream-self. In a long interview extending over several hours, she recounted a formidable dream history wherein her dream-self visited the land of the dead, brought back the dream-selves of her sick children from the underwater realm of the *faifai* spirits, obtained healing medicines from the *faifai,* and even heard God speak directly to it. Many of these dream adventures endangered her bodily self or caused it to suffer physical illness as the result of her dream-self being lured away by the spirits of the dead or tempted by water spirit lovers. This rich dream history is too long and complex to examine in full. I will focus on a selection of her dream premonitions of death, which featured prominently in her account.

Prior knowledge of the deaths of others, particularly of close kin, are the most frequent type of dream reported by Mekeo (chapter 6). Before considering Celestina's experiences, certain general points should be made. In the first place, it should be stressed that dream omens are not believed to cause the predicted death. The dreamer is not held to be responsible for the events taking place in the dream realm—not unless he or she has deliberately undertaken ritual action to these ends. Here, of course, is the rub. How is another person to know whether a reported dream is merely a spontaneously occurring omen—an unsolicited message from the spirit world—or the result of rituals deliberately undertaken? It was often said that people made covert threats in this manner, claiming that a dream omen was unsolicited, while hinting the opposite. It would depend, of course, on the person concerned; it would hardly be convincing coming from either someone who had no ritual knowledge or a woman, since women are not thought to implement destructive rituals. Even so, the reported omen might be taken as a hint concerning a third party's actions. Communicating dream information is a tricky matter. The cultural belief is that one *should* inform the persons concerned, because if forewarned of the impending danger they may be able to avoid it. Concern for one's kin and neighbors motivates telling the omen; at the same time, one cannot be certain whether others will interpret this as solicitude, or covert aggression.

Although one may well experience anxiety over whether to discuss a dream with others, the ordinary dreamer has no cause in cultural belief to feel responsibility or guilt for what is shown in the dream. Yet it is evident that omens of death bother most people, creating a degree of fear and anxiety that seemed to me disproportionate to the situation as consciously understood. Why should this be?

Mekeo are by no means unaware of ambivalence in close kin relationships: it is a key cultural theme (chapter 2). Although kin care for and support one another, they are also likely to end up destroying one another, just as the mythological brothers A'aisa and Isapini killed each others' sons. Yet while covert aggression is expected from kin, most people deny it in themselves. They tend to see others as the instigators of quarrels, and themselves as victims. Certain individuals, however, particularly men who possess important ritual knowledge, speak in private with little compunction of the ritual actions they have taken to harm or punish close kin (chapters 2 and 9). Individuals vary in the extent to which they recognize and accept their own negative feelings. Cultural values give explicit recognition to public affection, and covert aggression, in close relationships.

From a psychodynamic perspective, one might expect that those people who deny in consciousness their destructive wishes toward others might feel deeply troubled by dreams in which such wishes were expressed, particularly when the dream comes true. Omens of death cause many people to face what they readily recognize in others (owing to cultural belief) but do not wish to admit in themselves (owing to cultural ideals): their own aggressive desires toward others with whom they are close. Thus their emotional distress arises out of an inability to keep out of consciousness those desires incompatible with internalized cultural values (in Freudian terms, a failure, or threatened failure of repression).

Another important point to keep in mind is that most dreams of death are interpreted in consciousness to extract a message from their symbolism. The actual dream imagery, or manifest content, does not usually represent death in any direct way. For example, Celestina dreamed of herself and her brother emerging from two mosquito nets, while a third person, Mary, remained lying under the net. She interpreted this to signify death for the woman. If we take a Freudian view of the dream as a disguised death-wish directed toward Mary, then Celestina's interpretation seems to come close to exposing her own repressed aggression. Even though cultural belief denies her responsibility for the dream imagery, Celestina, in common with other people, finds it troubling. Yet had she made no conscious effort to understand, she might simply have forgotten it on waking.

Furthermore, as illustrated in the events surrounding Ruth's death (chapter 4), cultural values direct people to scrutinize all dreams, particularly in times of crisis. This must tend to focus attention on ambivalent feelings. I am not suggesting this is the primary factor in producing the dreams; rather, I think cultural expectations play an important role, particularly in deciding what is recalled and how it is interpreted. Once the dream is interpreted in consciousness and is fulfilled in waking reality when the person in question does indeed die, the dreamer's repressed aggressions threaten to enter conscious awareness, thus provoking fear and distress.

Celestina deals with such disquietening experiences by paying close attention to subsequent happenings. She described to me three instances of dreams that followed accurate omens of death in which the relatives concerned returned from the dead to take Celestina with them. The following occurred a few days after the death of Mary, whose demise was predicted in the dream of the three mosquito nets.

Dream of the Dead Returning

"Then I dreamed and her [Mary's] dream-self came back and wanted me to go with her. She came, she tried to force me. She said, 'Let's go together, I have been waiting for you to come.' She was dressed up for dancing, she had put flowers in her hair, and she had put on a very beautiful grass skirt. She came and said we would go together. I dreamed that. This is a different dream. Now she was dead, she had gone. I had the [other] dream, I told her about it, then she died. Now she was dead. But about a week after her death, she came back. Now I dreamed again, after she was dead. She came to me and told me, 'We must go together now. You told me, I went, and then I waited for you. But I waited and waited, but you didn't come. So now I've come for you.' I said to her, 'I will look after my children and raise them. Therefore we cannot go together.' Then she started to swear at me, 'You're a bloody fool [the English expression is used here], for what reason did you deceive me?' I just said, 'I must look after my children.' I refused to go with her.

"My dream-self refused to go; if I had gone with her, I would have died. So I told my husband, 'We must pray to God. My dream-self went but then it refused; I turned around and came back.' When I dream, I say the rosary, and we pray, and we are helped. My dreams come true [*e gama*]."

I know of no word in Mekeo for "guilt"; there may well be such a word but it is not a common one, as for example is the word for "shame" (*ofuege*), which one constantly hears. Yet in reading this dream report, I cannot escape the sense that it poignantly expresses Celestina's sense of guilt over the death of Mary, and at the same time, that it helps her to resolve this guilt.

My reading of the text is as follows, taking it simply as a narrative. The situation is stated plainly in the words and actions of the two protagonists—the dream-selves of Celestina and Mary. Mary insists that Celestina should come with her; she has been waiting for her, she looks attractive and inviting, has flowers in her hair, is dressed for a traditional dance. Celestina seems drawn by her, and then she holds back. Accompanying the dead does not appear horrible; rather, she seems to want to go, but at the last minute refuses. She says she must stay and look after her children, just as she might reject a pleasure outing because of the pressures of her family responsibilities. In other words, the dream presents a part of Celestina that acknowledges a desire to be with the dead woman but finally rejects this in favor of her competing desire to remain with her children. Mary then turns angry and abusive, accusing Celestina of lying to her and deceiving her, hinting that her claims on Celestina also have validity. Celestina must choose between these conflicting claims.

It is not stated directly that Celestina's first dream brought about Mary's death, but the link to that prior dream is made quite explicitly, first in Celestina's explanation of the circumstances of the dream, "I had that other dream, I told her about it and then she died." And then emphatically in Mary's statement in the dream, "We must go together now. *You told me, I went,* I waited for you." The accusation against Celestina is perfectly clear; she told Mary to leave (to die) and she did. Therefore Celestina must die too. Furthermore, Celestina's dream-self is almost prepared to accept the accusation and go with Mary, but at the last moment holds back. The dream puts the dead woman in the place, as it were, of Celestina's conscience (or super-ego?), accusing her of causing her relative's death. But Celestina's dream-self is finally able to reject this accusation by arguing that her obligations to the living must prevail. In my view, the dream narrative dramatizes an inner conflict between Celestina's feeling of responsibility for Mary's death and therefore the need to be punished—which is precisely what I understand the term "guilt" to mean.

In psychoanalytic terms, the dream report has probably been subjected to so much secondary revision that it is very difficult to place too much confidence in what represents the actual dream construction and Celestina's conscious rationalizations and amendments. As reported, the dream has a wishful construction about it, but one that serves the ego—the ultimate denial of guilt and a return to life. I have not attempted to essay a careful analysis of the latent content as I doubt that the nature of the text allows it. I think it is best to regard this dream report, and others discussed here, as fantasies constructed partly in and partly outside consciousness. An actual dream provides the basis upon which the person, in waking, reflects on, allowing him or her to reconstruct the dream events according to cultural guidelines and expectations.

The question of how far my reading departs from the understandings of Celestina herself must also be addressed. Roughly speaking, I take the position that the dream report is a story that one part of Celestina is telling to another part of herself. This is not so far from the Mekeo understanding, but the difference is that the dream narrative is seen to be an experience of another realm, the dream realm, by a part of the self, the dream-self, which is later recalled by the waking, bodily self. Do I read more into Celestina's narrative than does she? Undoubtedly so, yet I cannot believe that too much of what I see there entirely escapes her sharp intelligence.

Celestina does not speak, as we are tempted to do, of the repressed aggressive feelings provoked by her relative's death being directed into a self-destructive urge, since her culture does not provide her with such concepts. She does, however, explicitly recognize a conflict within herself between a desire to go with the dead and a desire to regain health and life. She is alerted to a self-destructive desire harbored by her dream-self which she knows has arisen out of the death of her relative. Furthermore, she recognizes the dangers this desire poses to her waking, bodily self.

In this dream there are no Gothic images of horror, no putrefying corpse reaching out with bony fingers from the grave, no ravening murderous ghost. Mary looks lovely, and she comes to persuade Celestina to go with her. Nothing worse eventuates than a minor quarrel when Celestina rejects her invitation. The surface content of the dream holds little or nothing that is terrifying or that even directly suggests death. Yet Celestina is in no doubt of the perils that this dream reveals. She urges her husband to pray with her to God that her dream-self will return. She evidently regards Christian prayer as instrumental in guiding the actions of the dream-self in the same way as traditional spells, a point to which I will shortly return.

Similar themes are evident in a second dream of the dead returning. The subject of this dream, Alice, was, like Mary, Celestina's clan sister (of the same lineage), and her death also had been revealed in a prior dream. Alice was a young unmarried girl who died some months after her leg was amputated because of a tropical ulcer. She appears as very large in the dream, presumably in contrast to her appearance just before her death; she was in fact physically small and delicate in build and must have been even more so in her final months. It is likely that Celestina, who is a tall, physically robust person, may often in fact have carried poor Alice, in the manner described in the dream, after the loss of her leg.

Dream of Carrying Alice Through the Village

"Another dream—I dreamed of the girl Alice. She died, then I had this dream. Her dream-self—she was dressed in beautiful clothes and her hair was down, she came—she looked beautiful, she was very big. Her dream-self came and wanted me to go with her. We left—my father and mother's house, I was there—and I came down the steps and we went. Then the girl's dream-self put her arms around my neck and I carried her on my back. She was bent over my back. I carried her until we came to Lopia Fa'a clan—there they had built a new platform—there is no platform there, but I am dreaming—and lots of people were gathered around this platform. Now the dream-selves of the people I saw there, now some of them have died. . . . Living people, they were not yet dead. There was a big crowd. Now the girl that I was carrying was getting very heavy. She was big, so she was heavy. So I said to her, 'Climb down here on to this platform, there are lots of people gathered so you can sit here.' I put her down at the steps and sat her down there, then I left and went home. Then I woke up.

"What I dream later happens, a death occurs. It turns out to be true. For many years I have dreamed like that."

As in the dream of Mary, Alice appears looking beautiful and invites Celestina's dream-self to go with her. Celestina must carry her—as presumably she did in waking life before the girl's death—but soon Alice becomes too heavy, for now she has become very large, and Celestina has to put her down. She sits her on a platform where there are gathered the dream-selves of many living people. Leaving Alice there, Celestina returns home. The first comment she makes about the dream is that it signified death for all those on the platform, a prediction, she claimed, that was fulfilled before a year had passed. But her own dream-self had once again escaped death.

The intention of the dead girl in the dream was, nevertheless, by no means lost on Celestina and was confirmed for her in an incident in real life occurring the very next day. She continued her account:

"The day after this dream, I and my husband went to pick betel nut and that [dead girl] grabbed me—my actual bodily self [*imauu maunina*]—around the throat and pulled. I might have died. I did not see her, but as we were walking through bamboo on our way to pick betel nut, I coughed and some rubbish [or an insect] fell into my mouth and stuck in my throat. I coughed and tried to spit it out, but I couldn't. I thought I would choke to death. My husband helped me. After a while I was alright. Then I thought, at night I dreamed and I saw that girl. I carried her on my back and she pulled on my throat. She wanted me to die. She wanted us to leave together, but I refused. I said I would not go—and now it happened. I might have choked to death, but I didn't. What she did to my throat in the dream [clasping her around the neck as she piggybacked her through the village], it had happened just like that. What I dreamed became true [ko'a]."

This mishap, which Celestina interprets as no accident, reiterates the dream threat to her—Alice wants her to die. Spirits of the dead are not supposed to behave in this way, attacking the living of their own accord, and I have not heard of a similar incident. It was only the preceding dream that led Celestina to give it this meaning. Nor does the manifest content of the dream contain images of death and vengeance. As in the previous dream, only Celestina's *conscious interpretation,* her linking of the dream-image of the girl's arms around her neck with the mishap in the bush the next day, provides gruesome import.

There is, it seems, an insistent voice in Celestina telling her that she should die—a voice she represents as that of the dead. Even though her dream-self rejects these accusations, in waking reality she is pursued by the dead determined to have their revenge. I see depicted in this dream narrative and its waking analogue another struggle between a punishing conscience (or superego?) and healthy instinct for life. Celestina does not possess these concepts, but what she is able to do is identify opposing forces in the dream realm that threaten her physical self. The dream, plus the incident in which she nearly chokes, alert her to aggression directed at herself.

The two dreams just discussed warned Celestina of the dangers of illness and death for her physical body if she were to dwell on her remorse toward the dead. A third dream occurred at a time when she was ill. It, also, is linked to the dead girl, Alice.

Dream of Going to the City of the Dead

"Another dream I had when I was sick—my dream-self went to the place of the dead. I saw a very good place. They [the spirits of the dead] lived really well. It was a wonderful town, with a great many people. It was a very happy place. I saw them—with white skins. There were lots of trucks and cars and other things in that place. It was like one of your [European] cities. I saw them there. I saw all those things, but I refused them. I would have to leave my family behind. Maria's daughter had died [Alice], a young unmarried girl, and I was wearing mourning for her at this time, but I had forgotten to put it on. So when they wanted us to enter that place, I said I would have to go back home and get the black clothes I wore for mourning. I said that, and then I came back to get the clothes.[2] Then I woke up.

"When I woke up, I said to myself, 'My dream-self went to the place of the dead and then came back. So I will pray so that my dream-self will return.' Then I told my husband, 'We should pray; my dream-self rejected the place of the dead and came back.' If I had entered that place, I would have died. But my dream-self refused it."

In this dream, as in the others, death appears desirable. The dead live in a wonderful, bustling city, and Celestina seems keen to join them until, at the last moment, she remembers she has not put on her mourning clothes for Alice and so returns home to fetch them. Her interpretation is that she will recover from her illness, since her dream-self did not enter the city of the dead. Once again, she and her husband pray together for her dream-self.

This dream, like the others, represents and then resolves a struggle between a desire to go with the dead and a desire to live. In the other two dreams, however, the dream-self is shown to be under strong external pressure from the dead to go with them. The self-destructive urge is represented as external to the self. In psychoanalytic terms, one might say Celestina's own unconscious aggressions have been displaced onto the dead, protecting her from conscious recognition of her own destructive urges. But in this third dream, neither the dead nor any other agency persuade or force the dream-self to leave; it is simply drawn of its own accord to the apparent delights offered by a great and beautiful city. On reflection, Celestina can hardly escape awareness that it is her own dream-self that seems bent on destruction. Of course, she is in fact sick when this dream takes place. The earlier dreams were, in her view, warnings of the consequences should she give into the demands of the dead, but now she has actually fallen ill. (Subsequent dreams reveal the means to cure herself.)

In my view, these dreams of death—a recurring theme of her "dream history"—reflect Celestina's deeply disturbing and conflicting emotions: her inner sense of responsibility, guilt, and the desire to be punished. Yet they also help her to come to terms with these conflicting emotions. They alert her to the self-destructive nature of her inner conflict; that much is explicit in her own interpretations. They also establish that her obligation to the dead is less important than her obligations to her living family. These may be things she could "rationalize" for herself, but the fact is the dream imagery provides the basis for conscious reflection. In her view, she can face this hidden part of herself and try to prevent it from causing harm to her bodily self. Or, to put it in psychodynamic terms, one might say she is able to prevent her guilt from hardening into a symptom and making her permanently ill.

A strong Christian influence is apparent in Celestina's prayers that her dream-self will return safely. She, like her husband, Paul, claimed that when they were worried about something, particularly an illness in the family, they would pray, usually to the Virgin Mary, for help and be rewarded by dreams in which the cause or a means to cure the illness was revealed. Although the prayers employed are Christian, the context of belief concerning sickness, the hidden self, and its relation to the body are not. In praying to God, Celestina hopes that like the *feuapi,* the dream healer/diviners, she can persuade her lost dream-self to return. She reported several other instances, also induced by Christian prayer, in which she dived down into the underwater abode of the *faifai* spirits to rescue the dream-selves of her sick children; these dreams were identical to those recounted by the traditional dream healers (see chapter 10). Celestina and her husband, in common with many villagers who regard themselves as good Catholics, have no compunction, indeed it would seem no understanding, as more educated and sophisticated Mekeo certainly do, that the Church disapproves of this magically instrumental use of prayer. It is significant, however, that those persons who possess traditional esoteric knowledge never claimed to use Christian prayer or to call upon the help of Christian figures. If Christian rituals may be used as a substitute by those who lack access to traditional knowledge, they have not become an alternate or competing basis of power for ritual experts.

One might perhaps wonder whether the easy applicability of Freudian models of guilt and repression to persons like Celestina, and others who will be introduced shortly, might not arise from the external context of culture change. Since it has long been argued that "guilt" is an artifact of Western culture, one might suspect that the guilt that arises from Celestina's dreams of the dead is the result of the mission's teachings. Had she been possessed of a highly developed and specific sense of guilt, and had this operated in situations where people unrelated or only distantly related to her were involved, I would have looked to this cause. But since her dreams metaphorically and indirectly symbolize what I identify as guilt, I am not so easily persuaded. Obeyesekere (1981:76–83), for example, discusses the symbolic representation of guilt in non-Western societies, while A. J. Strathern (1977) has argued against a simplistic division of shame and guilt applied to Melanesian cultures. Furthermore, one does not need to invoke Christian influence to explain worry and anxiety over dream omens concerning close relatives. The women in Celestina's dreams were her clan sisters of the same lineage. They were brought up together in the same ward of the village and, even after marriage, would return to their natal clan to participate in its group activities. According to traditional values, these women were tied to Celestina by the closest bonds of kinship and personal affection. Recognizing an underlying hostility toward them could only bring her pain.

Freudian concepts of ambivalence and repression can be applied to Celestina and others, I suggest, because of the way in which the concept of the hidden self enables Mekeo to articulate unconscious processes. Awareness of a hidden self unavailable to consciousness allows Mekeo to explore emotions and feelings they deny in consciousness, creating a subtle dialogue between the multiple parts of self. Even though Celestina did not always like what she found in her dreams, she had the courage to face up to them. My contention that she gained self-insight in this manner runs counter, of course, to the more orthodox psychoanalytic position that indigenous interpretative systems function as culturally constituted defense systems (Kilbourne 1981b).

Joe: "Dreams Are Like Sorcery"

Joe is a married man in his late fifties with adult sons and daughters. During my first fieldwork, he and his family were my neighbors and friends. During the years I was absent from the village, a long-standing quarrel between Aisaga, who was the head of his lineage, and Joe, a junior agnatic kinsman, had developed; as a result, I now had much less contact with him. I first knew him as a kind, honest, hard-working man, generally regarded in the community as a model of respectability, and a staunch supporter both of the Catholic mission and of the traditional authorities (who conventionally are not seen to be in conflict; see Stephen 1974). He was always ready to help out relatives and friends, and ever willing to contribute to any worthwhile community project. Although not naive, Joe was the kind of man likely to be imposed upon by others, so eager was he to please everyone. He had only a few years of primary education, but was always talking of the opportunities in education, business, and employment opening up for the new generation; his greatest hopes were to see his sons educated and successful. During the eight years that passed between the two periods of my fieldwork, his sons, along with many of the younger generation, did take up responsible professional positions, fulfilling his every ambition for them and bringing him considerable prosperity. Joe also changed a great deal in this time. Instead of finding happiness, he had become a troubled man. He now spent much of his time drinking, because, he explained, it was only when he drank that he could forget his worries and be happy.

I heard many rumors concerning Joe's rowdy, drunken behavior and of his insulting actions toward Aisaga and his family during these drinking bouts—behavior that was quite out of keeping with his former model character. While Aisaga's family was in mourning for the death of his younger daughter, at a time when the whole village should have observed bans on noisy gatherings and partying, Joe organized a beer party with his cronies and kept the village awake with their drunken singing and shouting. Such a breach of mourning restrictions, people pointed out, had been unthinkable in the past, and could be expected to bring retribution in the form of sorcery-inflicted illness or death for the miscreants. A powerful man like Aisaga was not likely to forget this painful personal insult, they added. Yet Joe persisted with his provocative behavior. His troubles stemmed largely from the fact that his adult sons were now seeking political influence and attempting to gain supporters throughout the region. All this landed Joe, a man without traditional status, in a situation where he appeared to be putting himself above men of higher rank, especially his "elder brother," Aisaga (see Stephen 1974 for similar examples). Aware of the "jealousy" (*pikupa*) his family's new wealth and influence aroused in the community in general, and of the dangers of retribution via sorcery, Joe's attempt to handle the situation by buying the support of cronies with free beer parties and forgetting his troubles in drink only served, of course, to make matters worse. Sadly, the realization of his ambitions for his sons had served to create conflicts with others, and conflict within himself. In contrast to his pleasant and kindly manner of former years, he was now alternatively truculent or querulous in his sober periods and, when drunk, abusive and raucous.

It was in fact a dream Joe spontaneously recounted in the early days of my first fieldwork, when I had no interest whatsoever in such matters, that subsequently alerted me to their possible significance in Mekeo culture. Yet, ironically, when I brought up the subject nearly a decade later, Joe began with the dismissive reply: ''I refuse to take any notice of dreams now. [*Pau nipi la umaka*].'' I was not a little started by his vehemence. But the reasons he gave are not what one might expect. Although he commented on the way that people lie about their dreams in order to intimidate others, the reason he gave for ignoring dreams was not that they are false, but that they come *true!* He exclaimed, ''We dream of people and then they die. Therefore I don't like it.'' On another occasion he observed, in tone of sheer disgust, ''Dreams are like sorcery!''

He related three dreams occurring many years before that had made a deep impression on him. The first two examples concerned the deaths of close relatives; they were unusual in that instead of representing the events in symbolic form, the dream imagery literally predicted waking reality. In one dream Joe saw the young wife of his classificatory brother (of the same clan) die in childbirth. Shortly afterward, the young woman died in just the manner pictured in his dream. Joe told me that he warned his kinsman of the dream but it was too late as the wife must have already been struck down by the men of sorrow when the dream took place. The second dream concerned the poisoning of Joe's classificatory uncle (of the same clan) by one of Joe's maternal uncles. Once again, the dream prediction was fulfilled. Joe was convinced of the identity of the murderer on the basis of his dream, but he did not dare reveal it to anyone else and simply tried to forget about it. He commented to me with much feeling: ''Well, that was a bad dream, I thought; so I didn't want to talk about it—then I forgot about it, but now I have told it to you. The dream happened. I dreamed someone died and then he really did die. It happened—just as I dreamed it!''

Both dreams occurred when he was a young, unmarried man, at least thirty years ago, yet it is evident they still trouble him. He makes an interesting contrast with Celestina. Joe's dreams of death are so repellent he resolves to ignore all dreams. Why the difference? Many people claim to have dream omens of the deaths of relatives and most express considerable anxiety about them. This is not explicable in terms of cultural belief, since the dream is not the cause, merely a premonition. I have argued from a Freudian perspective that anxiety results from bringing into consciousness a repressed desire for the death so depicted. Yet although people are made uneasy by such dreams, they do not usually attempt to block them out. Indeed, some pay the closest attention to them, like Celestina, and believe that such omens should be communicated to the persons concerned.

Joe, I think, finds it more difficult than most men in his culture to face his negative feelings toward others. He is a man who wants to be liked; he is noticeably more eager than most to please and to help others. People comment on this characteristic of his as unusual. He is, or was, open, almost ingenuous, in this most devious of cultures. He seems unable to manage his aggressive feelings by splitting his "outside" and "inside" self as many Mekeo delight in doing. His need to be liked (whatever its origin) and his dislike of dissembling require him to push out of conscious awareness his negative feelings toward others. His individual needs thus result in greater repression of aggression than is necessary for most Mekeo men. Consequently it is understandable that predicting the deaths of close kin is especially anxiety provoking for him.

Joe's dreams, furthermore, take a disturbing and unusual form according to Mekeo belief. They are *literal* representations of the death. Most people, like Alex and Celestina, have dreams that symbolize the death of a particular person; people assume, unless waking events indicate otherwise, that dreams are symbolic in form. If one dreams of death it is interpreted as a reference to hunting and killing animals. A telling example was provided by a woman whose husband's illness was causing the family much concern. She reported a dream in which her husband died, but to my surprise she indicated no concern, since the dream imagery was not a bad omen nor related to the husband at all—it signified the butchering of a family pig. (See also my dream, chapter 12). Joe's dreams are much more the classic nightmare where, according to Freud (1900), the dream censor fails in its disguise. Joe's dreams seem strange and unwarranted in their direct depiction of waking events.

Dreams, declared Joe, are like *ugauga* sorcery. Now, as it turns out, despite his amiable and respectable reputation in the past, he knows quite a lot about sorcery. At about the time these two dreams occurred, when he was still unmarried, he lived for a while with one of his agnatic kinsman, a highly renowned man of sorrow. Joe did not himself engage in *ugauga* sorcery, but he did perform various services such as preparing food, gathering medicines, and the like for the old man. It was then common for young unmarried men to act as cooks or servants to a man of sorrow in the hope of acquiring some knowledge of love rituals (see also Hau'ofa 1981). Joe is not a handsome man by his culture's standards: he has dark skin and rather lumpish, although amiable and intelligent, features, and he was totally bald by middle age. Baldness is such a great defect that some men resort to tradestore wigs. Perhaps as a young man he felt his physical unattractiveness would preclude winning a bride, and awareness of his physical unattractiveness may have made him more anxious to please, more eager to win favor. Another circumstance seems significant here: one dream depicts the death of his kinsman's wife in childbirth, an image suggesting jealousy of his clan brother of the same age who already had a wife and children.

Joe did not like to speak of his experience as an assistant to a man of sorrow, but he did, on my request, tell me a little about it. He always expressed abhorrence of anything to do with esoteric knowledge and the hidden world in general, hence his comment "Dreams are like sorcery" implied they were just as despicable. Perhaps—a third perhaps—Joe might even have been tempted to acquire some destructive rituals for himself. His repressed aggressions may have drawn him unconsciously to such a despised role. His two literal dreams of death expressed this desire with such intensity of emotion that some thirty years later he still spoke of them with horror. Evidently these two dreams disclosed an aspect of himself that moved with disturbing ease in the realm of spirit powers which he consciously so despised and feared.

A third dream, occurring a few years later, when he was married, demonstrated the same disquieting capacity. This was the dream Joe recounted to me during my first fieldwork and now, at my request, repeated.

A Dream of Heaven and Hell

"I had another dream, a long time ago (at least twenty years)—about my father-in-law. It happened about six months after his death. . . . He said, 'I have come to see you. For six months now God has been punishing me. Now the six months are up. I wanted to come and see you. I told God and so he sent me and I have come.' That's what he said to me. We talked for a while. He said, 'I have been making a garden, I have planted apples, pineapples, pears, lots of different food, tomatoes and onions, this is God's food I planted. I had to sleep in the garden to watch the crops. Devils came to steal the food so I had to guard it.' Then I said I wanted to go and see that place. 'Well, come,' he said.

"The two of us climbed down [from the house] and I stood behind him. Then like 'power' [the English word is used here] the two of us flew off; we flew until we came to the place he had spoken of and there we came down. We came down and then we went to his house, it was a fine house. We went up into it and I saw around inside it, then the two of us went to his garden, the place where he had planted apples, pears, pineapples, tomatoes, and onions. I saw that place, the garden bore very large, beautiful fruit. Then we the two of us started to come back. Then I could hear lots of voices, but I couldn't see anything. I asked my father-in-law if these were the voices of people from some village. 'No,' he said, 'It is the voices of the prisoners. It is the voices of people God is punishing. It is like the way the government gives prison sentences [to the living], some get life, some six months, some three months in prison. It's those people.'

"I said I wanted to see them so the two of us went and stood on the top of a hill—we stood on the top of the hill and looked down—then he gave me 'power' [the English word is used again here] and then I could see them. There were fine houses and lots of cars and trucks driving back and forth, well I saw lots of things! I saw them and I asked him, 'Those who are clearing the bush, who are cutting down really big trees, what are they doing?' He said, 'They are thieves and the men of sorrow; and people who have bad marriages—who marry another girl when they already have a wife—those people. Yes, those people God is punishing. They have to cut down the trees and when they finish, the tree stands up in its place again, and they have to cut it down again—that's their work. That's their punishment. And women who have bad marriages, they have to go collecting firewood; some just chop firewood, others have to pull out weeds—they pull out the weeds and then the weeds grow again and they have to keep pulling them out. That is their punishment.'[3] I asked, 'What about those who are driving the trucks and cars around the place?' 'Those ones have finished their prison terms,' he said, 'and now they can go out and travel around. And the carpenters who built those houses, their prison term is over and they have got out and because they know carpentry they have been given that work and they are building houses. But now it is time for us to go and for you to return,' he said. 'I must take you back and then come back here because God will come to inspect the place in the afternoon.'

"So we both went back to his house and then I stood behind him and followed him and we both flew until we reached home. I stopped in front of my house and began to climb the steps. He turned back and left. And then I woke up with a start. That is the end of the dream."

This dream is literally true in Joe's view. Its veracity is established by the other two dreams, both of which literally depicted the future and were confirmed by subsequent events. The truth it holds is not, however, a comfortable one since it denies the traditional and the Christian view of the afterlife. According to traditional belief the afterlife holds no punishments. Joe's dream asserts that humans will suffer punishment, yet not in the way the missionaries have taught. On waking, Joe wrote down his vision in Mekeo and pondered its meaning. He explained:

"That dream convinced me that there is only one place where God punishes people, the missionaries are not right. There is not hell, purgatory or limbo, but just one place where the sinners are put in prison and made to work. I believe in these dreams of mine. I dreamed my uncle died, and he died. And I dreamed that my elder brother's wife died, and she died. Then I had this dream—my dream-self [lalauu] went and saw that place. It saw it and then I said to myself that God's punishment and his prison originated here. But not punishment to our bodily selves [Ke imaua la'i]. But the punishment place for our lalaua [our nonbodily selves; in this context the natural translation is 'soul,' but it is evident that such a translation misses the link between the dream reality and the afterlife]. Then I worked it out [kapuleisa] that the government had read about this and therefore they had created prisons for our bodily selves [*imaua ketsipula*].''

The ancestors and the missionaries have lied! This is a very uncomfortable ''truth'' for a young man so eager to please all. Yet Joe was convinced by this vision above everything he had been taught to believe. One gains a glimpse here of a submerged rebellious streak in Joe that sets no store by the established authorities, whose rules and conventions he strives so hard to obey in his waking existence.

Mekeo cultural values, as I have observed, require that surfaces are always kept smooth. This involves conscious suppression, rather than repression, of emotion. But I have suggested that Joe's individual needs make conscious dealings with his aggressions toward close others difficult, hence he must push them out of consciousness. These long-denied desires are brought to the fore again in late middle-age, it seems, in his rowdy and insulting behavior during drinking bouts. A man who still wants to like and be liked by others, his new affluence places him in a situation wherein he is a target for the envy and criticism of his fellows no matter what he does. Furthermore, he is caught in a situation where his own position in his lineage combined with the ambitions of his adult sons make him the focus of a political struggle for power within the descent group, and within the community as a whole. His only escape is drinking. Ironically, it has the unintended, and for him unperceived, effect— although the whole community observes it with dismay—of giving free rein to that rebellious aspect of self. Yet it is a part of himself which, in sober waking consciousness, he so deeply despises and fears that he wants to block out all memory of dreaming. Joe is a troubled, confused man caught in a vicious circle only partly of his own making. From a Freudian perspective, one could understand his plight as the result of his repressed aggression being released by alcohol, thus temporarily bringing a sense of happiness and relief as repression is lifted, until the aggression is then turned on the self in renewed self-destructive behavior.

Whatever threads of Joe's personal experience I draw together to interpret his situation in the light of Western models, what is patently clear in terms of his own cultural beliefs is that in refusing to pay any attention to his dreams he is trying to cut himself off from an aspect of himself he wishes did not exist. His negative attitude is based in the truth his dreams hold about a part of himself he cannot face. Mekeo do not describe any psychic process which might be equated with the concept of repression, but they do explicitly recognize that the actions and desires of the dream-self may conflict with those of waking consciousness, and that the actions of the dream-self hold an inescapable truth. The most Joe can do is try to forget his dreams, to put them out of mind. But in doing so, he deprives himself of the one means Mekeo culture provides to him to come to terms with his inner battles.

Andrew: Dreams of a Dead Wife

A rather different position on dreaming was taken by Andrew, an elderly man in his seventies. Andrew is a senior man of kindness in a neighboring village and very knowledgeable in traditional ways. I met him when I first visited the Mekeo region in 1967, and he spoke then of the traditions of the man of kindness and of his own clan history. I met him many times in the years that followed, although I never came to know him well. His community is situated next to the central Catholic mission station for the area, and Andrew is widely known as a staunch supporter of the Church and a pillar both of traditional and Christian morality. The interview from which the following extracts are taken came about at the suggestion of, and with the assistance of, Michael, a church deacon. The interview, conducted in Mekeo, began with just the three of us, but three other people later joined us. This relatively public context, and the presence of Michael, naturally influenced and shaped the opinions expressed. Andrew began by providing a clear statement of the mission's teachings:

"Dreams are something like this. Just whatever we are thinking about at the time, whatever we are thinking a lot about, or whatever it is we desire, when we go to sleep our thought goes out and that becomes the dream. Our thought arises and becomes the dream and in the morning we tell it."

I questioned Andrew about claims that people receive ritual knowledge in dreams. He responded that some people did make such claims, but he dismissed them as false, intended merely to trick others. After spending some time complaining how people lie about their dreams in this way, Andrew unexpectedly said the following:

"A few days ago—Friday—Henry (his brother-in-law from Inawi village) came here and we went to Mass together. I told him that I had dreamed again and I wanted to tell him about it. I told him I had seen his sister [Andrew's dead wife]. She did not say anything to me, she just came and I saw her [in the dream]. When I have that dream a death follows in her village. When the dream-self of my wife comes and I see her like that, a death occurs in her village, so I told my brother-in-law about it."

At this stage in the discussion a third man joined us and recounted a recent dream about picking betel nut, a well-know omen of good fortune. To counter this, Andrew described a false dream warning he had been given referring to his own death:

"Some time ago Anna told me of a dream she had about an old *ufu* [clan meeting house] falling down. She said to me, 'Andrew, I had a dream about an old *ufu,* the central post [*opogo,* symbolically associated with the man of kindness] was cut right through and it fell and lay on the ground. Therefore I think that you must take care of your self because the dream indicates your death.' I replied, 'That was a dream and you have spoken well, but I will not try to take care of myself, for God only takes care of me and when he selects the time for my death, I will die.'''

His intent here is to discredit the idea that dreams provide accurate omens, since he is hale and hearty despite the prediction. Yet he had just mentioned that he, himself, regularly receives accurate omens of death through the dream appearances of his dead wife! The discussion continued, with two more people joining in, and Andrew occasionally interjecting a comment to the effect he did not value dreams, and therefore did not remember them.

As the discussion began to wind down, I returned to the topic of Andrew's dreams about his wife, asking if he dreamed of her often. He paused, remained silent for a few moments, and then replied very softly, and with much feeling:

"Yes, when my wife died I dreamed of her often. Everyday I thought of her and that thought became a dream. Lots of widowers have the same dreams. My wife died and now when her dream-self comes to me and I see her, a death occurs in her village. I told you about the one I had only a few days ago. She doesn't tell me a death will happen, it just happens after I have that dream. It has happened many times. [He gives a list of all the people who have died following these dreams. I then ask Andrew if he ever talked with his dead wife in his dreams.] Yes I often talked with her in dreams, but then she came and wanted to take my hand, but I refused to let her. Then she told me, 'I wanted to take your hand, but you refused so now I will go to my brothers' place.' So then we didn't talk together any more. I started to forget her."

It is evident from the tracking backward and forward in our conversation that Andrew far from dismisses the reality of his own dream experiences. While he is ready to agree in principle with the mission's teaching, he cannot escape the emotional impact of the dream encounters with his dead wife. Clearly, he views these as actual contacts with her dream-self and not merely his thoughts concerning her. Yet at the same time, I think he indicates that significant as these dreams are to him, he does not seek them. He accepts the fact that dreams are things to be eschewed, along with other traditional ritual, since they can be used to malicious and dangerous ends, but he does not deny their underlying truth. Andrew is evidently not burdened in the same way as is Joe by his dream experiences; he chooses to put them aside as something frowned upon by the Church, whose teachings in all things he tries to uphold.

Michael, the married deacon who arranged the interview with Andrew, is one of those comparatively few individuals who has a firm intellectual grasp of Christianity and whose training has led him to evaluate critically traditional beliefs in the light of Christian doctrine. He explained to me that his father, a man of Andrew's generation, had been an expert dream interpreter and healer but had declined to pass on his knowledge as he felt it incompatible with his son's Christian vocation. Michael observed of his father: "He believed in dreams very strongly; for him, they came true." Although Michael did not share this faith in dreams, he confessed that the old's man's insights could be disturbingly accurate:

"My father had a dream about a fight between Beipa and Aipeana villages. It was Sunday morning and we had just got up and he told this dream about all the people going out to fight pigs. And the pigs were fighting the men. And one man got up and killed one of the pigs. So my father said, 'Could be today, tomorrow or sometime this week, there will be big trouble. Not just in the same village, but between two villages. There is a land dispute between Ogofoina and Aivea clans, I am afraid a fight might break out between them.' Then straight after the second Mass, a fight did break out and a man was killed. Two fathers [European priests] stood in the middle of them, and the other clans came and stood in the way to separate those fighting. Then I saw for myself the dream happen. But as I told you, I don't really believe in dreams—now I'm just in the middle seeing both sides.

"My father told me, 'If you dream of killing another person, that means if you go to hunt you will kill a pig or some animal. But if you see pigs fighting that means there will be big fighting between men. Don't take it as animals that are going to fight, it's men that are going to fight.' I saw that with my own eyes and it's always been in my mind."

Michael expresses his position with admirable clarity—and honesty. He is a man in the middle, aware of both sides. He respects the truth his father perceived in dreams, yet he has committed himself to another belief. The way indicated by his secular and Christian education is the path he has chosen. He believes this a superior path, yet he does not despise the other. Unlike Andrew, who is an elderly man with no formal education, Michael does not look to his own dreams for self-knowledge, but he is sensitive to the insights others find in their own dreams.

Mission teaching and, more recently, secular education combine to challenge people's belief in the validity of dream experience. Yet the response has been not so much to question that mode of experience as to question the morality of employing dreaming as a means of perceiving the unknown. It is not that dreams are judged intrinsically false, but that people may use them unethically. The Fulagan Fijian nightmares studied by Herr (1981) make an intriguing contrast with these Mekeo dreams. According to Herr, Christian teachings have been so deeply internalized by Fulagans that to dream at all is regarded as engaging in the work of the devil. As a consequence, the therapeutic use of dreams, which Herr acknowledges is common in cultures with similar dream beliefs, has disappeared. Perhaps Joe's attitude that dreams are "like sorcery" comes close to the Fulagan view, but his extremely negative reaction is exceptional for Mekeo.

In my opinion, based on discussions with a wide range of people, few Mekeo are convinced that dreams are "merely thought" as Andrew maintained before he contradicted himself. Good Christians and well-educated people do not like to admit to beliefs they fear outsiders will ridicule, but in confidence they reveal a different side. A century of the mission's prohibitions may have succeeded in discouraging some people from attempting to learn how to use their dreams, as in the case of Michael and his father, but they have not destroyed conviction in the veracity of dream-acquired knowledge.

Maria: "What the Spirits Tell Me in Dreams Is True"

Indeed, the process of dreaming seems to aid some people in internalizing Christian symbols, as indicated in the next case study. Maria was my neighbor during my early fieldwork, and perhaps because she was a woman alone and I was most often on my own, she made an effort to befriend me. She would often visit, sitting for hours patiently attempting to converse with me, although I knew little Mekeo at the time and she knew even less English. Her husband had died some years before, leaving her to raise five small children. Dressed always in black, her hair shorn harshly close to her head, she was always lively and vivacious, her prematurely wrinkled face lit up by an intelligent smile. Small and thin, seemingly too delicate in build for the heavy labor expected of Mekeo women, she nevertheless managed to feed and care for her family. Sometimes she would bring her youngest daughter, Alice (the same Alice of Celestina's dreams), who was then a charmingly pretty girl of about twelve. Alice had her mother's delicate build and features and beautiful eyes, and was obviously highly intelligent, although rather shy. She and her younger brother, Henry, who had a face as angelic as his sister's, lived at home, while the three elder children were away at boarding school. The children could speak some English and we all became good friends. I enjoyed their company and felt comfortable with Maria, who from the beginning treated me as a friend and an equal. I usually found Mekeo, both men and women, unfailingly courteous, but there was something especially engaging and spontaneous about Maria's efforts to befriend me. I often found her first thing in the morning in close consultation with her neighbor, Bernadette. When I enquired, Maria told me they had been discussing her dreams of the night before, but having no interest in such matters then, I never pursued this.

When I returned in 1980, Maria's children were grown. Cute little Henry was a handsome young man about to complete high school. The eldest son had graduated from university, married, and was a member of the diplomatic service. He and his wife and children had spent two years in Australia, where Maria visited them for several weeks—a momentous experience for a woman in her fifties who had never been farther from her village than Port Moresby. Her eldest daughter was a trained nurse. The second son had married, and he and his wife were living in the village with Maria, which was a great help to her as she was now getting on in years. The youngest daughter, Alice, with all her promise of beauty and intelligence, was dead. After finishing primary school she went to boarding school. When about seventeen, she injured a leg during a high school sports match and the injury developed into a tropical ulcer. Despite medical treatment, the ulcer spread rapidly and the leg had to be amputated. Sent home to recuperate, her condition deteriorated, and within a short time she was dead.

Maria was no longer my neighbor, and I saw less of her. Because of the proximity of my new house to that of the man of sorrow, Aisaga, she avoided visiting me, insisting I come to her place. I soon discovered she, like so many of my Mekeo friends, was a remarkable dreamer. We had several long discussions concerning her past dreams, but, as was the case with most people, I was not able to collect her ongoing dreams. This may have partly been because of my failure to visit her regularly, but, as already explained, questioning people persistently only served to stir up suspicion. I could not do that and maintain co-operation. This, of course, emphasizes the danger of dream knowledge until it has been confirmed by waking events. People do confide recent dreams to intimates—Celestina told her husband, Maria told her neighbor and close friend, Bernadette, or else told her own children—but this close familial intimacy is not possible with a wide range of people. I was able to establish close ties with only Aisaga and his extended family. Nevertheless, Maria's dream history is of no little interest.

Following a now recognizable pattern, Maria began with a key dream which, in her view, validated the accuracy of information she derives from dreaming. It concerned a dream communication from her dead husband that was shortly afterward realized in waking reality. In the dream her husband told her that the Papua New Guinea army was about to make camp near the village, so she was to take vegetables and fruit from her garden and present it to the soldiers. As predicted, the soldiers arrived a few days later. Maria was convinced that one soldier who accepted her gifts of garden produce was none other than her dead husband. Similar communications from dead spouses are reported by many people. New widows and widowers especially, both of whom undergo severe and extended periods of mourning when they must be segregated from the rest of society (see also Hau'ofa 1981), admit to vivid dreams of their dead spouses.

The second dream directly concerned me, and my identity was not as a European visitor, but as a returned spirit of the dead. Maria's manner of relating this dream to me was quietly expectant, and the implication behind it was clear: since the first dream communication from the dead was proven beyond doubt in waking reality, this must have equal veracity.[4] She explained that this dream occurred after I gave her the news that a friend of mine from America was coming to visit me.

The Dead Returned as the Ethnographer

"Now I will tell you another dream—about one of our uncles, the brother of Bernadette's father. . . . That old man, the dead person, he came to talk to me. He came in a truck—or some thing that went around—like a plane but it went around—yes, a helicopter! He got out at my place and then he called to Bernadette and I. He told us, 'Bernadette, Maria, that person who has come to stay with you, her name is Frances.' He said that Bernadette's eldest sister, Frances, who was dead, was living here. 'And tomorrow, the girl that is coming from America, it is Catherine [another dead relative] who will come to your place. And a brother that teaches at the Mission school, Brother John, he is Bernadette's [deceased] elder brother.'

"That's what he told me. I said, 'I thought they were Europeans who had come to our place.' But he replied, 'No! Michele is really Frances, Bernadette's elder sister. And the one coming tomorrow from America to visit her, that is Catherine.'

"I did not tell other people about this dream, only Bernadette. Now you're asking about dreams, so I've told you. So then I was not sure if you were really Europeans [*nao ipaumi*] or the dead returned. But it was a dead person who told me these things.

"You see, my husband's words came true. The army people came. The place that he designated, there they made camp. You came here after that. And after you came, I dreamed. Then that old man told me those things."

I could hardly help but feel nonplused by this confession.[5] It was disconcerting to find the friendship that Maria had initiated, the rapport we had developed over years, was based upon a secret conviction I was a relative returned from the dead. How was I to respond to her expectations? I had asked her to discuss the intimate matters of her dreams in confidence; I could not suddenly dismiss these confidences. Since she had actually visited Australia during her son's stay, her belief seemed all the more remarkable and puzzling: surely she had seen for herself that flesh and blood people, not spirits, lived there? But of course the situation was not so simple—there are, in her view, real Europeans, and those such as myself who only appear to be Europeans. I was to encounter a similar response from many others. Maria must have observed my discomfort and my hesitation in answering. To my fumbling admission I could not understand what the dream meant because I was a living person born in Australia where my mother and father still lived, Maria merely nodded politely. She moved on to the next example, yet another that confirmed her view of things.

I have only her word that her dreams were realized in waking reality, but that is beside the point. What is significant is Maria's conviction, based on her own experience, that this dream-derived knowledge is accurate and true. Her examples are a little unusual in that they consist of direct and literal statements from the dead. This contrasts, for example, with Celestina's dreams, which were almost all symbolic, and with Joe's, which consisted of imagery literally depicting future events. Maria emphasizes that what she learns comes from the spirits of the dead, not ordinary people; she sees the source of her information as demonstration of its truth. The spirits of the dead are credited in Mekeo belief with knowledge of happenings in the dream realm, and thus of what is shaping the future of the embodied world.

Like Celestina, Maria describes a relationship with the spirit realm that comes very close to that of a ritual expert, yet she is not an expert, in either the eyes of the community or her own. She explicitly denies any traditional esoteric knowledge, although she claims to use Christian prayer in guiding her dreams to positive ends. The following example, given in another interview, shows how Christian symbols might be drawn upon to bring self-healing. She explained that she had been very sick for some time when this dream occurred. Her thigh was so painful that she could not work and could walk only with the aid of a stick. Her husband was still alive at that time, and he engaged a man of sorrow to cure her, but she refused his potions. Instead, she went to church and prayed to the Virgin Mary for relief from her suffering.

A Dream of Self-healing

"When I came home, I laid down and went to sleep. My dream-self went to a place in the bush, there was a very big sea there. My dream-self was standing in the water, up to my waist. And a snake came and bit my thigh. Then Jesus and his disciples appeared in a dingy; they were sailing about and then they took pity on me and they came and said, 'We will take you in the boat.' They took my arms and pulled me up into the boat. The snake that had wrapped itself around my leg fell off into the sea. They took me across to the other side and put me down there. There was a truck there and they put me in that truck and drove to the village. They stopped in front of my house and let me down. Then they all said goodbye to me, and I said goodbye to them. My husband was in the house and when he heard my voice he started to come out of the house, and I was about to climb up the steps—then I woke up with a start.

"Then the next day I started to feel better, and in a few days I could get around without the stick. My husband said to me, 'You refused to take the water bespelled by the men of sorrow but now, through your own prayers, Jesus has made you better.'"

I could not determine precisely the nature of her illness. Evidently it was not an injury to the leg, but presumably a boil or swelling such as that usually attributed to the water spirits. The sufferer depicts the pain as a snake wrapped around the afflicted part of the body. This is a culturally standardized representation, any snake found in water will be interpreted as a water spirit, whether in a dream, vision, or waking reality. Evidently a *faifai* water spirit is to blame for Maria's illness; the snake bites her and wraps around her leg as she is standing waist-deep in water. The dream does not merely identify the cause of the illness, it eliminates it. While she is stranded in a great sea struggling with the *faifai* snake, Jesus and his disciples come to her rescue.

The dream made a powerful impact on Maria, not only because it brought healing but also because it confirmed her determination to put her faith in the Christian God by praying to the Virgin Mary. It was after going to Church for prayers that she had this dream. Its imagery is shaped by the harsh reality of her bodily pain and her longing for relief. The incorporation of Christian symbols—Jesus as literal savior rescues Maria's dream-self from the water-spirit snake—serves to strengthen her faith in them, infusing them with the force of her own subjective desires. For Maria, Christian symbols in dreams literally bring healing and delivery from suffering.

A final example illustrates Maria's use of dreaming to come to terms with a different kind of pain—the grief of losing her child. In a second interview she told me of a dream occurring prior to the death of her daughter, Alice. It was a touching testimony to the conflicting emotions of a mother who was well aware her child faced an intolerable future, yet was desperate to keep her. The cruel reality was that Alice, if she lived, would have faced a life of total dependence on her relatives, with no hope of marriage and not even the possibility of making any useful contribution to the community. This is a culture where the brunt of subsistence labor falls to the women and girls; where prospective brides are admired more for their physical strength and capacity for hard work than anything else; where houses are built off the ground on stilts, all water must be carried in buckets from the river, firewood carried in great loads from the bush to do the daily cooking, and huge piles of vegetables harvested and carried home every day to feed the family. A girl with one leg, no matter how intelligent or how pretty, faces a bleak future. One can imagine Maria's despair. The wound might heal, but Alice's leg could not be replaced; even if Alice were to regain her health, she would remain a useless cripple.

Dream of a Daughter's Death

"I was staying at my son's house in Port Moresby at the time. One evening Alice said she had a lot of pain. I told my son. 'The child is suffering, it's no good, I had better take her home to the village tomorrow.' That night I went to sleep and I had a dream. He came—my [deceased] husband came to see me. He came to me and he told me, 'Maria, I am going to take Alice from you, she will look after me now. She will come and help me. You have Mary [the elder daughter] there with you, so I will take Alice from you. She can look after me. She will make my tea for me to drink, and help me. You have another daughter, she can look after you. I have one with me—a boy, Opu [who died as an infant]—so now the two of them will look after me. Opu came to me when he was small, now he is a teenage boy. Opu and Alice will look after me now. You have four children to look after you—Michael, Henry, John, and Mary—they will look after you. I will have two, Opu and Alice to look after me. So I will take her.'

"He said he would take Alice away from me so we quarrelled about it. I said, 'Please be generous, leave her, let her look after me. When I go out and then return home, she will make tea for me to drink. Mary is studying to be a nurse so she will be away from home, she won't be here to look after me. So please leave Alice here to look after me.' He threatened me, and then he took Alice and put her on his back and began to carry her away. I went behind him weeping and lamenting. He carried her to a truck and opened the door and put her in. Then he said to me, 'Maria, I will not give Alice back to you; you see I have taken her finally. You have your other daughter, I will have Alice.' He got in the truck and blew the horn and said goodbye, and told me to go back. The truck went off and I stood there weeping. 'He has taken her away for good,' I said to myself.

"In the morning I told my son, I wept and said, 'Your father has taken my Alice away, she won't stay with me. He took her away in a truck.' Then I told him to go and find a truck to take us to the village. She would die in the village, it couldn't be helped. He had taken her away, so nothing could be done now. She lived a few more days and then she died."

I have interpreted similar premonitionary dreams from Celestina and Joe on the basis of Freud's (1900, 1916b:187–190) arguments concerning the dreamer's ambivalence. This example, however, has more complex emotional valences: it is not so much an omen as a confirmation of what Maria already knew was inevitable. The narrative dramatizes the mother's conflict between keeping her child and letting her go, a tension finally resolved when the dead husband takes the child. The mother is left to face her grief. She awakens, not cured of her pain as in the dream of Jesus and the snake, but resigned to her loss and able to accept it.

Compared with Celestina and Joe, Maria's ambivalence seems much closer to the surface. The dream might express an unconscious wish for the girl to die so as to be rid of the burden she represents. Yet to hold on to her is just as selfish, perhaps more so, than letting go. In these circumstances, Maria's desire arises more out of selfish need to retain a love object than altruistic love of the child. The dream might thus be seen to stem from unconscious ambivalence melded with a more conscious awareness of emotional conflict.

The dream "tells" Maria a story with a clear message, a message, in her view, that comes from outside her own thoughts and emotions, bearing the authority of her dead husband. It thus has special conviction for her; we may all experience this sense of something more powerful showing a direction to us in our dreams. If Maria's dream arises out of id desires, its import is given a moral shape in consciousness. Reflecting on it enables her to come to an acceptance of what she could not previously face, losing her child. Moreover, there is recognition of a justness in this child going to her father, since Maria still has four other children. The dream does not arouse guilt, it resolves her guilt and her conflict. Of course, it is not the dream per se that achieves this, but rather the conscious meaning she gives to it.

She might, it is true, have sorted out her feelings without the aid of this dream; to an impartial observer it does little more than express what is only common sense.[6] In Maria's view, its message holds a very special kind of truth which merits further examination. It is not merely advice given by some other person, in which case, given Mekeo suspicions of the dissimulations of others, Maria might suspect some covert motive. Nor is it the product of merely her own (conscious) thought or desire, but of something that is beyond herself yet not contaminated by the interests of any living person. The message comes directly from her dead husband, who is not only the father of the child but a spirit being with supra-human knowledge. Through her dream, Maria gains direct access to this realm of power and knowledge; she does not have to rely on a diviner or on the incantations of a man of sorrow, she herself is able to draw upon it directly. Maria does not state it in so many words, but I think it is true to her belief to say that dreaming allows her to draw upon inner powers and strengths which help her to face the hardships of a difficult and lonely life.

Whether my interpretations of Maria's experience come near the truth, her own comments illustrate how dreams provide material for introspection and for defining and identifying her inner feelings. Furthermore, dreams prompt Maria to attend to her inner self. Maria and many other Mekeo use their dreams as a focus for inner dialogue, a dialogue that Westerners usually confine to an examination of thoughts and emotions in consciousness (unless, of course, they are engaged in some form of psychotherapy).

A final point to be considered is Maria's earlier history of visionary experience linked to Christian beliefs. As a young married woman, Maria claimed to have many waking visions in which she directly communicated with Jesus and God. She explained that the European nuns had remonstrated with her about these visions, urging her not to speak about them or seek to induce more. She could not understand why they were angry with her, but said that as a result her visions ceased. These events must have taken place sometime in the early 1950s after a prophetic movement led by a girl prophet, Philo, from an east Mekeo village, Inawaia, swept the region in 1940–1941 (Stephen 1974, 1977). Philo promised the overthrow of the powers of the men of sorrow and the establishment of God's will on earth, but the movement lasted only a few months before being forcibly put down by the colonial government after followers attacked the Catholic mission at Inawaia. With these events still fresh in their minds, missionaries were not likely to listen sympathetically to another young woman who claimed to have divine visions, and it is not surprising that they did their best to discourage Maria. She seemed hurt, as well as puzzled by their response, but her dreams subsequently took up the Christian symbols and themes that had previously occupied her waking visions. Maria is in many respects similar to Obeyesekere's (1981) Sri Lankan prophetesses. She seems to share their talent for transforming private passions into statements of public morality.

Dreaming as a Special Mode of Understanding

Some anthropologists (Hallpike 1979; Goody 1977), in contrasting Western notions of person and self with those of tribal cultures, argue that the latter lack the special contexts necessary to reflect upon the "purely private states" explored, for example, by Western novelists. This fact, Hallpike (1979:392) maintains, is evident to anyone "who studies published examples of oral literature . . . or texts from informants provided in ethnographers' monographs." What Western anthropologists should consider is that alternate contexts exist in tribal cultures and that dreaming is one of crucial significance. Several studies (Kracke 1981, 1987; Herdt 1987; Basso 1987; Tedlock 1987a; Ewing 1990a, 1990b) provide telling evidence to support this, suggesting that the examples discussed here are but part of a broader cross-cultural pattern.

The values and pressures of Christianity, millenarian aspirations, local politics, the wider context of power relationships in colonial and post-colonial regimes—all are indicated as forces operating on and in the private worlds of these dreamers. Dreams perhaps do more than merely reflect such changes. The "truth" held by a dream, Obeyesekere (1981) reminds us, is composed of a complex admixture of deep motivation, personal experience, and cultural belief. His study of Sri Lankan prophetesses[7] reveals how new symbolic forms with adaptive potential arise out of the individual's inner conflicts. Although Freudian insights have helped to identify their deep emotional roots, the dream accounts of Celestina, Joe, and Maria take personal instinctual conflicts and turn them into narratives with a wider ethical significance. Inner conflict may generate the need to seek new symbolic forms, but it does not necessarily follow that the imaginative processes employed are intrinsically inferior or maladaptive. These brief case studies point tantalizingly to the role of dreaming in internalizing foreign values and ideas, and in creating new cultural forms, but these are issues that cannot be pursued further here.

The key point of this discussion has been to show how reflection on dream experience is carefully developed and elaborated in Mekeo culture and put to good practical use to gain valid self-insight.[8] In this latter respect I depart from the views of those psychoanalytically inclined ethnographers who view indigenous interpretative systems as defenses shielding consciousness from the anxiety-provoking latent content of the dream (e.g., Kilbourne 1981b; Tuzin 1975). I suggested earlier that psychoanalytic approaches presuppose a particular position of authority in relation to the dream, making it difficult for the ethnographer to acknowledge that any valid knowledge might be achieved by the dreamer without the benefit of psychoanalytic guidance. Following Tedlock (1981), I have further argued that exclusive attention to the "intratextual level" of cultural dream codes and ignoring the "contextual" and "intertextual" levels perpetuate this attitude, stripping indigenous interpretative systems of their nuances and flexibility.

Psychoanalytic approaches thus tend to obscure positive and creative cultural uses of dreaming such as those found in the case studies. This material is consistent, however, with arguments outlined in chapter 5 concerning an autonomous form of imagination. Mekeo combine dreaming and dream interpretation in an ongoing process wherein the waking "I" reflects upon another aspect of self and upon the interweaving of imaginal and waking events. These reflections create a context for fantasy elaboration in consciousness, and their system of dream interpretation is loose enough to allow great freedom for individual improvisation. In my view, this becomes the means whereby persons like Celestina and Maria access the creative potential of autonomous imagination, guiding it partly in and partly outside of consciousness in the continual construction of self-identity.

For Mekeo, dreams are also a focus for conscious reflection on certain important existential questions. Dreams direct attention to a person's most intimate convictions and doubts, since they are understood to provide a deeper and different kind of insight than is available to the conscious self. It is not merely that dreams allow opportunity to deliberate such issues, they are believed to offer a means of knowing that penetrates to the heart of things. For Joe, Maria, Andrew, and Celestina, as for many Mekeo, dreams are a medium whereby the individual perceives a "truth" beyond any cultural tenet or imposed belief or "collective representation." Dreams do not lie outside culture in the sense that culture fails to shape or use them. Even so, they express the desires of an inner core of the self, which is surely what Freud told us. The case studies underline the subversive element in dreaming. Poet Octavio Paz (1976), pointing to a significance overriding cultural boundaries, describes dreaming as a "necessarily rebellious form of learning, beyond the law." In both these senses, dreams are a primary locus of awareness of a self composed of desires and passions which necessarily oppose the self to all "others."

For Mekeo who possess ritual knowledge, dreaming becomes the means to shape the hidden world to conscious ends. What for ordinary people may be disquieting or even terrifying glimpses of a different order of being are amplified by the ritual expert, especially the man of sorrow, into the means of accessing intense personal power. Yet it is important to understand that laypersons and adepts inhabit the same dream world; the difference lies only in the ability of the latter to control dream imagery.

1. A man of kindness (*lopia eke*) dressed for a feast (*gaku*) (1970).

2. (*above*) A man of sorrow
(*ugauga auga*) newly emerged from his
isolation after the period of mourning following
his wife's death. His pale skin and thin body
attest to the rigor of the *gope* regime
he has undertaken (1970).

3. (*below*) The distinctive male attire
favored in the late 1960s and 1970s.

4. (*opposite*) An old man dressed in
the traditional decorations of a
warrior (*iso auga*) (1971).

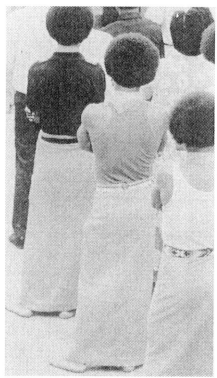

5. View down the village plaza (*pagua inaega*) from inside the meeting house (*ufu*) (1971).

6. Typical domestic houses lining the *pagua inaega*; to the back of them, the coconut palms and bush surrounding the settlement (1970).

7. On the periphery, where the cleared space of the village merges into the surrounding bush, is located the *gove* of a man of sorrow (1970).

8. The author talking with a man of sorrow at his *gove* (1982).

9. One of the community's most respected elders with his
small grandson (1971).

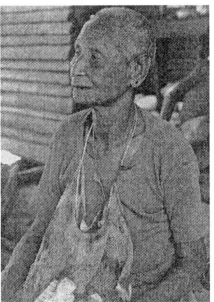

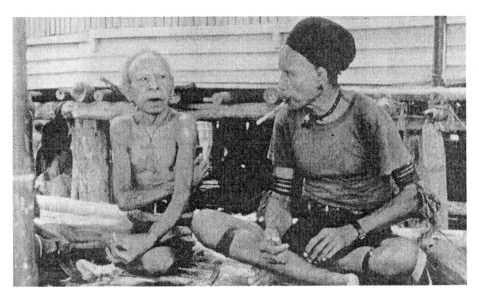

10. (*above, left*) A much feared elderly man of sorrow (1978).

11. (*above, right*) A venerable woman of knowledge (1981).

12. (*below*) Two men of sorrow conferring (1970).

13. (*above*) The men of sorrow at a feast for the installation
of a new man of kindness. They are watching proceedings from
the periphery and are well away from the crowd gathered
in the center of the village (1981).

14. (*opposite, above*) The riot of color, noise, and excitement at
the center of the village: dancers at a feast (1981).

15. (*opposite, below*) Lines of male
dancers beating drums (1981).

16. The handsome face of a young, unmarried
man (*o'oae*), painted and beautified for dancing (1981).

17. (*opposite, above*) Face of a married male (*au*) dancer (1981).

18. (*opposite, below*) Two young women
dressed for dancing (1981).

19, 20. Two men of sorrow (1971 and 1979).

Part III

The Sorrows of Knowledge

The magician is often compared to the rebel. The seduction his figure still exerts on us results from his having been the first to say no to the gods and yes to the human will. . . . Magic is a dangerous and sacrilegious enterprise, an affirmation of human power vis-à-vis the supernatural. Separated from the human herd, facing the gods, the magician is alone. His greatness and, almost always, his final sterility is rooted in that aloneness.

Octavio Paz, *The Bow and the Lyre*

9

The Traditions of
Secret Knowledge

Shortly after I began fieldwork in 1980, the man of sorrow (*ugauga auga*), Aisaga, asked why I wanted to learn *ugauga* sorcery. He assured me:

"If you want to kill someone, I can teach you many much easier, less burdensome rituals than *ugauga*. There are many other [ritual] ways. *Ugauga* is bad. You can't wash, you can't eat, you have to stay alone by yourself. I don't like to teach you that. There are heavy [*meau*] ways and there are light [*ilikae*] ways. I was taught both. They taught us [the senior descent line] both ways, but they taught only *ugauga* to our younger brothers [junior line of the lineage]. You don't have to use *ugauga* to kill, *ugauga* is used only if you want to make money."

He was as puzzled by my desire for *ugauga* sorcery as I was by his assertion it was unnecessary if all you wanted to do was kill someone. I understood the term to mean "sorcery," that is, death-dealing magic. Now I was discovering many rituals for bringing about death which were not *ugauga*. Furthermore, Aisaga possessed a rich and extensive repertoire, including constructive as well as destructive techniques, of which *ugauga* was but one. Mekeo esoteric knowledge is indeed *secret knowledge*—so carefully and jealously guarded that the very fact of possessing it is kept hidden, if possible. My understanding of it radically changed during my later fieldwork. Even experts do not know exactly what another expert knows, unless that person instructed them in the rite. What I had been told during my early fieldwork was not entirely inaccurate, yet it was sufficiently misleading and incomplete to obscure many things until I had direct experience of them. The degree of deliberate deception involved will become increasing clear as part III develops.

We are now ready to investigate more closely the nature of Mekeo esoteric knowledge and the ways in which it contributes to shaping a particular view of self and self-identity. This chapter begins by describing the corpus of knowledge and then examines the apparently, but in fact far from, simple question of who has access to what kinds of knowledge. Chapters 10 and 11 discuss four ritual experts (two women and two men), illustrating through descriptions of actual practice how their rituals shape inner experience, and then explain the variations existing among different practitioners and individuals. Chapters 12, 13 and 14 focus on a single individual, Aisaga, who exemplifies the all-powerful, invulnerable self developed by the man of sorrow. Although Aisaga represents the extreme opposite of an ordinary man or woman, the rituals of secret knowledge and the adept's interaction with the hidden world draw upon the potential that exists in every Mekeo self—one I have traced in laypersons such as Celestina and Maria. Finally, chapter 15 examines how these different potentials for the self are imaged in cultural symbolism and the cosmic ordering, and takes up the question of the apparent contradictions between individual experience and public representations.

The Corpus of Knowledge

In traditional anthropological parlance, Mekeo esoteric knowledge would be described as "magic." Like all the terms available to Western anthropologists to describe the belief systems of other cultures, the term "magic" carries with it a weight of extraneous cultural associations and intellectual baggage, much of which is inapplicable to Mekeo concepts and obscures Mekeo meanings. Nevertheless, the specific cultural beliefs involved fall into this general category, and are recognizable as similar in form and content to magic as described in other cultures, particularly in Melanesia.[1] For fear of injecting our inappropriate and rather prejudicial connotations, I avoid the term in reference to Mekeo beliefs and practices. The description presented here (see also Stephen 1987a) emerges from an examination and comparison of texts of spells, esoteric versions of myths, descriptions and observations of ritual techniques, and lists of ingredients, all collected during my 1980s fieldwork from several different experts, but all from one community. On this basis, I identify the general principles and underlying assumptions that order the system. Even ritual experts do not have a complete picture of the whole corpus: Individuals have knowledge of specific traditions; some may know only one or two, others dozens. There exists a potentially huge, diffuse body of traditions, with many local variants, of which only parts are known to any one individual. It is impossible to determine its full extent—without undertaking instruction, that is, from every ritual expert in the total population of the region!

The major fields of esoteric knowledge encompass a wide range of concerns: They include healing rites, the inflicting of sickness, injury and death, rites for hunting, gardening, fishing, war, rites for beauty, courting and seduction, weather control, and various forms of divination.[2] There are also charms for protection of self and property, for winning favor from others, and for gaining success in various tasks. Within each general field, there is not one but innumerable traditions. Thus under the general heading of love ritual—*pakai,* which means literally "to decorate or make beautiful"—there are rituals to make the practitioner beautiful or handsome, to make the desired partner dream of one, to prevent the girl or woman from crying out and revealing a seducer's presence, to make the desired woman anxious and unable to sleep from thoughts of the lover, to make a girl or woman mad with sexual desire, and various nasty forms of punishment to be used against those who reject a suitor's advances. The actual number of rites and charms is impossible to gauge. I have recorded dozens of ritual means intended just to make a man attractive to prospective lovers.

Each separate tradition, regardless of its nature or intent, is composed of the same basic elements. The implementation of a ritual involves the recitation of spells (*mega*) and the manipulation of special substances and objects (*fu'a*). Depending on the nature of the task, a prior regime involving dietary and other restrictions (*gope*) is necessary to prepare the practitioner. There is usually a myth (*isonioni*), at least in the case of major traditions, explaining the origin of the ritual and containing in its narrative other necessary information (i.e., the spells and ritual substances used). Some rituals require long and stringent preparation, incorporate lengthy spells and incantations, and employ large numbers of rare substances and highly dangerous objects, whereas others are much briefer and simpler; the basic structure, however, remains the same.

The myths, in their complete version, include all the essential information. Aisaga explained that when a ritual was taught to someone, all that had to be done was to recount the full version of the myth. The people who appear in the myth, whose names must be included, are the spirits called upon; the songs sung by them, which must be included, are the spells to be used; and the various objects, plants or animals employed by, or associated with, the main characters identify the special substances to be used. The myth is the vehicle for the transmission of secret knowledge. Which is why, of course, only abbreviated versions are told in public. What I assumed were merely simple explanatory folktales, such as "How the Dog Became the Enemy of the Other Animals" or "The Origin of the Fishing Trap" (chapter 3), now emerged in their esoteric forms as the explanations of important rituals—major rites for hunting in the former, fish-calling rituals in the latter. The same was true of the A'aisa myths: the complete versions provide the essential keys (i.e., the spells, objects, substances, and medicines) for all the rituals originated by A'aisa, including *ugauga* sorcery. Much more than just a social charter (cf. Hau'ofa 1981:77–83;106–109), Mekeo myths constitute a basic framework for the system of esoteric knowledge (cf. Young 1983).

The spells, substances, and objects employed in a particular rite are linked symbolically to its intention, usually constituting a simple or elaborate metaphorical statement of the desired outcome. A simple example: a plant sap that feels cold on the skin is used as a medicine to treat fever; the intention is that the body should become cool like the sap. The spell used in the rite calls upon cold streams and running water, again with the intention that the body of the patient should become cool like the water. In many instances, however, the link between the spells and medicines used and the intent of the ritual is established only through the myth. Thus a myth might explain that a particular plant is used in hunting rituals because it represents the transformed blood of a mythological hero, but in the absence of the myth there would be nothing to indicate its efficacy. I will postpone detailed discussion of these elements, and of the period of ritual preparation, until following chapters where their nature and function in actual use can be considered.

Within each general area of knowledge there are many separate traditions originating from different mythological heroes and possessed by different individuals. One person may know a particular ritual to inspire love in the beholder, another may know two, three, or more. There are various spells, medicines, and objects used to inspire admiration and desire that were originated by the major culture hero A'aisa. A'aisa, however, is not the only source of esoteric knowledge. Many other mythological heroes, whose exploits are recounted in the myths (*isonioni*), originated powerful love rituals; these include Foikale, Lainapa, Gava (the moon), Foame, and others. In addition, the exploits of other heroes, male and female, led to the origin of numerous love charms, spells, and potions; for example, Afugo and Agai originated rituals to induce incestuous desires, Afilako was a beautiful girl who became a plant that is used as a love charm, Goemau was a man who became a snake that is used as a medicine to induce sexual desire, Taitai and Piu are the planets Jupiter and Venus, who meet in the sky at a particular time of the year and are separated lovers, Lako Fagupi was a man with an enormously long penis, and Veke was a girl who dressed as a widower, then revealed herself as a beautiful girl, and the pool she washed in became the source of various potent medicines to arouse female desire. There are dozens of such tales, and many are identified with particular descent groups and families. For example, those associated with the girl Veke belong to Afai'i clan, because the place where she washed is on their land.

Hunting rituals also originated from different mythological heroes, some of whom are associated with particular descent groups, and are used for many different ends. There are varied rites for hunting with dogs, hunting with nets, hunting with baits, trapping birds and small animals, spearing pigs, spearing cassowaries, and hunting cuscus, and many others beside. There are, for example, numerous different spells and medicines just to make dogs fierce for hunting. There is A'aisa's ritual for dogs and for hunting, and there is A'aisa's brother, Isapini's, ritual for hunting. There is Foikale's hunting ritual, there is Ougo's (a giant pig), and similar rituals of other mythological figures (*isonioni papiau*) such as Oini, Piauviki and Alokene, Oiso'i Lauga, Omeome, and Niopiopi.

This proliferation of techniques and traditions is found in all types of ritual. There thus exists a vast body of secret ritual, parts of which are interrelated, and all of which operate on the same basic principles and methods but consist essentially of a great many separate traditions. Different areas of ritual are distinguished by Mekeo, although not necessarily as specifically named categories. For example, to enquire about rites for hunting, one could ask if a person knew any spells (*mega*) or medicines (*fu'a*) for hunting (*kapukapu*). Or one could ask more specifically for spells and medicines for dogs (*amue*), or cuscus (*ao*), or for trapping animals, and so on. Or even more specifically, one could ask whether a person knew *A'aisa ega amue* (A'aisa's ritual for dogs), or *Isapini ega uve* (Isapini's string). Each question (put to an appropriate expert) would elicit information concerning a particular kind of hunting ritual.

Collectively, all spells, medicines, and knowledge relating to esoteric ritual of all kinds are referred to as *ikifa.* One cannot, however, directly translate this term into English as "ritual" (or "magic"). Desnoes (1941:369) defines *ikifa* as an adjective and noun meaning: dexterous, skillful, clever, wise, learned; cleverness, wisdom, learning ("adroit, habile, sage, instruit; habileté, sagesse, instruction"). In my experience, it can be applied to any form of ability or instruction in a particular skill or task, but its use tends to imply knowledge of ritual—that is, of the required spells, myths, medicines, objects, and ritual actions. To call someone *ikifa auga,* literally, a wise or learned person, indicates that a person possesses important ritual knowledge. To *paikifa(nia)* a person is to impart a particular skill or knowledge, but again, this verbal form is especially used to refer to instruction in esoteric secrets. Furthermore, a person may know (*logo*) many things, yet not be regarded as *ikifa auga.* In fact one is said to know *ikifa;* thus *ikifa* refers to what is known, the skill or information itself, not the act of knowing. It might, for example, be said of an old man that he knew the customs (*kagakaga*) and many songs and stories, but was not *ikifa auga,* meaning that he did not possess major esoteric knowledge.

Ikifa as a general category includes knowledge and skills other than ritual ones, but all esoteric knowledge is referred to as *ikifa.* This indicates that ritual is regarded primarily as conferring a special kind of skill, adroitness, and cleverness not possessed by others. The *ikifa auga,* or *ikifa papiega,* is one who knows things not known to others and can do things others cannot do; his or her special knowledge is the source of unusual ability. *Ikifa* might be glossed as "special knowledge leading to special skills and effectiveness." It is not innate intelligence, for an individual may be intelligent but lack *ikifa.* It consists of specific instruction in some task. When Aisaga observed that I had shown the young girl who helped me with household tasks how to look after my European possessions, he said, "*Lo paikifania*" (You taught practical skills to her). He used exactly the same expression with reference to teaching me esoteric knowledge: *La paikifanio* (I taught esoteric skills to you). *Ikifa* is not knowledge per se, but knowledge of specific techniques to achieve a desired outcome, techniques not available generally. Although any practical skill which is learned might be described as *ikifa,* the essence, or quintessence, is ritual knowledge. The most valued, the most closely guarded, and the most difficult to acquire *ikifa* are the esoteric traditions of knowledge.

Whether the task is securing game for a feast, ensuring a large harvest in the gardens, killing one's enemies in war, finding a bride, ensuring a good rainfall for the crops, healing a sickness or injury, punishing those who flout social norms and obligations, or achieving success in almost any endeavor, there is a form of *ikifa* appropriate for the task. It is not, however, thought indispensable; rather, it is an additive, something that makes for the success and achievement of those who employ it. Ordinary people plant gardens without, go hunting without, find brides without *ikifa.* The fish come up the river, the rain falls, the sun shines, crops grow whether or not it is used. *Ikifa* is used to influence these happenings to suit the purposes of a particular individual. Thus an ordinary man out hunting may or may not find his quarry, but the *ikifa auga* will certainly bring back game, or prevent others from finding any, as he chooses. An ordinary man usually manages eventually to find a wife, but one knowledgeable in love charms will have numerous lovers. The ordinary man must hope that rain will fall at the right time, the man with *ikifa* can ensure it.

Ikifa does not consist of techniques to create anything, or bring anything new into being, but is the means by which humans can manipulate and control that which already exists. This is, of course, clearly implied in the sense of the word *ikifa,* as practical skill and ability. The Mekeo *ikifa auga* is believed able to do things ordinary people cannot, but he does not defy nature. The healer can heal the sick, he cannot raise the dead; charms and spells can bring rain, but not in the dry season; the expert in gardening ritual can ensure a good crop, but cannot turn stones into yams or sticks into bananas. The expert in love rites can make a woman desire a particular man, but he cannot materialize a flesh-and-blood woman out of air or turn a frog into a prince—although he can make an ugly man seem attractive.

Ikifa is very specific. It constitutes a certain ability directed to an individual task. When I refer to "an expert in love ritual" or "an expert in hunting rites," this does not indicate that such a person has generalized knowledge or powers, but that he possesses knowledge of one or more major rites such as catching pigs in nets, trapping birds, or making dogs fierce. People are not identified as "healers," "hunting experts," or "weather experts," but are known according to the specific rite(s) they possess. Here, however, the situation is complicated by the fact that the full extent of the *ikifa* a person commands is not usually made public, so not only the content, but the very fact of possessing it is concealed.

Since no one individual possesses the entire range of esoteric tradition, to outline with confidence an overall structure is virtually impossible. It is safer to start with the basic units and then observe how particular rites are acquired by particular individuals and in what combinations. Each unit, one might say, of *ikifa* consists of several related elements all directed to a specific end. Thus *ikifa* to make dogs fierce (*amue*, which means simply "dog"), or any other rite, consists of knowledge of a) a myth, b) a spell, c) medicines, d) special powerful objects, and e) the ritual preparation required of the practitioner. All these elements are related to the task of making dogs fierce, and they are linked together in the myth that explains their origin. Ideally, the practitioner should know each of the five elements, however, not all are necessary. If one knows all the elements, one does not need to recall the myth. In many instances no special preparation is required of the practitioner nor are any special objects necessary: the spell (*mega*) and medicines (*fu'a*) suffice. The minimal unit can be regarded as the *fu'a,* since a great many are used on their own in beauty and love ritual, treating minor illness or injury, protection, hunting, fishing, gardening, luck at cards, and many other things including injuring and even killing. Used in conjunction with appropriate spells, however, their ritual efficacy is considered much greater.

Evidently there are many levels and degrees of effectiveness. A simple ritual might involve no more than rubbing a special medicine on one's face to make one attractive to women. A stronger one might involve the use of a medicine in conjunction with spells. Some love ritual requires elaborate potions composed of many different substances that may be difficult and expensive or dangerous to acquire. Other love rituals can be as dangerous and exacting to perform as *ugauga* sorcery; these involve powerful spells and the use of highly noxious substances and require stringent and lengthy preparation on the part of the user. The same applies to all areas of esoteric ritual, whether ostensibly beneficent or destructive.

Contrary to the impression gained during my early fieldwork that sorcery, *ugauga*, constituted something inherently different from other types of ritual (an impression equally given by Hau'ofa 1981), later investigations revealed such was not the case, since the rituals of *ugauga* follow the same basic structure as all other rituals (Stephen 1987a). My accounts (1974, 1979b) of sorcery written prior to my 1980s fieldwork focused on the concept of *isapu,* as also do the accounts of Hau'ofa (1981:216ff.). It was *isapu* (which means heat, and refers both to the heat of the sun and the heat of fire) that people always mentioned when explaining how the men of sorrow's dread powers operated (chapter 3). Many could offer apparently quite sophisticated comparisons between the power of electricity and the operation of *isapu* (Stephen 1979b). Hau'ofa (1981:218) even refers to different kinds and degrees of *isapu,* as if the term were a gloss for "ritual power." Such is certainly the way it is used by laypeople attempting to explain their belief system to a European, as I found.

Isapu is an important element in *ugauga* sorcery, but not in all forms of ritual, including some of the most dangerous and destructive, such as those directed towards the *faifai* spirits. The proper element of the *faifai* spirits is water, not heat. The *faifai* expert does not attempt to generate *isapu* to summon the presence of the *faifai,* and the relics and medicines associated with the *faifai,* although potentially very dangerous to human beings, are not imbued with *isapu.*[3] But, of course, one would say naturally in English that such things are very "powerful." To use the term *isapu* as the equivalent of "ritual power" obscures many significant distinctions. It implies, incorrectly, that all major forms of ritual depend on it. It also suggests, misleadingly, that some impersonal force equivalent to *mana* is involved—a view, of course, that fits with many traditional views of the nature of magic (Codrington 1891; Malinowski 1974). *Isapu* is not, as I first thought, the general principle upon which the whole system of ritual belief pivots. Mekeo do not speak of a person possessing particular ritual "powers" (*isapu*), except when they are speaking English; they refer to someone knowing (*logonia*) a particular skill (*ikifa e logonia*).

Regardless of the intention of the ritual, the same basic elements—myth, spell, medicines, objects, and ritual regimen—are involved. What varies are the nature of the spirit beings invoked, the kinds and degree of potency of medicines required, the nature and potency of the necessary ritual objects and relics, and the rigor of the ritual regimen. All the elements are related, since the nature of medicines and relics depend upon which spirit presences are invoked, and the stringency of the practitioner's ritual regimen (*gope*) is determined by the relative potency of the ritual objects and relics. Some rituals require little or no preparation. *Ugauga* sorcery requires the most rigourous regimen (*gope*), yet there are also rituals to kill that require no *gope* whatsoever. Likewise, there are some hunting rituals which, because of the objects and relics they require, are so potent that the practitioner does injury to himself through constant use. Such are the rituals of Omeome, a lame boy; they are said to be very effective, but the expert who employs them eventually becomes lame—Aisaga attributed his own arthritic knee joints to this cause. (These are the "heavy" and "light" techniques mentioned by Aisaga and noted at the beginning of this chapter.) The heavy (*meau*) rituals are those which involve the use of highly (ritually) dangerous substances and objects, creating risk for the practitioner and the necessity for a rigorous *gope* regimen. "Light" (*ilikae*) rituals can achieve the same ends without the attendant risks. These heavy and light forms exist for all pursuits. I will address later the question of when the men of sorrow would choose to employ the heavy rituals. Distinctions between different types of ritual cannot be drawn on any simple basis such as sorcery versus productive techniques. This will become more evident in subsequent chapters as I examine the rituals in use.

Who Possesses Secret Knowledge?

Although public ideals and symbols assert that all important ritual knowledge is in the hands of the men of sorrow, in fact nearly everyone in the community possesses some minor rites, or at least fragments of them. The ideal applies only to the extent that certain men of sorrow, like Aisaga, do have the most extensive repertoires and the most intensive contacts with spirit world. There are many individuals, both men and women, in each community who are covertly identified as *ikifa aui,* "people of knowledge"—that is to say, people who know one, or possibly several, major esoteric traditions. The problem for the ethnographer is that these people are not so identified publicly, nor are they eager to reveal themselves. Nothing can be easily observed in everyday activities that would indicate the role of these individuals, but the community has a general idea of the kinds of traditions particular people are likely to command. This is because, in principle, acquisition is a matter of patrilineal inheritance. Many traditions, especially the major ones, are known to have a specific chain of transmission from the mythological founder. Particular descent groups and lineages within descent groups, located in particular villages, lay claim to specific traditions. For example, *ugauga* sorcery was first revealed by A'aisa, via his messenger Muki, to a man from Bebeo village. The descendants of this man thus represent the original line of transmission. Although seniority of transmission is acknowledged, it is of little practical consequence since, as people explain, the knowledge has long been shared among (*ke fake'i*) others, so that *ugauga* sorcery is now found everywhere. This applies generally to all types of ritual.

This transmission over time is bound up with the complex history of clan fission and migration that is recorded in oral tradition and reflected in the present pattern of local groupings (Seligman 1910; Belshaw 1951; Hau'ofa 1981; Stephen 1974). Clan histories tell of how the present descent groups originated from two, or sometimes four, original groups. As groups split, they established their own leaders, gradually acquiring their own esoteric traditions as circumstances allowed. It is not my intention here to attempt a reconstruction of the historical processes whereby the present structure of descent and local groups evolved or the divisions of ritual knowledge came about. There exists no single account in oral tradition, nor can one be satisfactorily constructed upon the basis of available evidence. Suffice to say there exists in principle the idea that esoteric traditions of all kinds were originally revealed to a few, and gradually acquired by others as the population increased, theoretically in definable chains of transmission. This division is thought to have taken place long ago, so that the present holders have inherited traditions owned by their lineage and family for many generations.

Although traditions are usually associated with particular descent groups, they are not available to all the members but are the personal property of a single individual, usually the most senior male representative of a lineage (although not necessarily the most senior lineage of the descent group). To preserve the line of inheritance the eldest son should inherit from his father, but since this is esoteric knowledge, performed and learned in private, a man might choose to pass certain things on to younger sons or completely ignore his eldest son. He may choose to teach his daughters or his wife, particularly if the rituals are of practical use to them—rituals such as gardening or healing spells—or if there are no male heirs. It is usually assumed the eldest son will inherit his father's knowledge, but in fact the community cannot be sure exactly how or to whom a man transfers his knowledge. In this way, over time, it is evident that despite the ideal of a single patrilineal line of inheritance, traditions are much more widely diffused.

Bits and pieces—a medicine, a spell, a myth—may be easily slipped as gifts to favorite younger sons or daughters, a grandchild, or a close friend, or exchanged in return for other knowledge—or even sold. People never part with knowledge lightly; it is a valuable personal asset. Old people use the threat of withholding their secrets, much as Westerners threaten to disinherit their heirs, to attempt to retain control over their offspring. In the end they may favor a more distant relative who cares for them in their old age. A dream diviner well known to me acquired the ritual from her mother-in-law, whom she nursed in her final illness. In the case of another female dream diviner, who inherited the ritual from her father, sons were passed over in her favor. Another woman was learning dream divination from her elderly mother. Indeed, women, to whom falls the care of elderly relatives, are in a good position to acquire knowledge since it may be passed on in gratitude.

Women of Knowledge

Women may acquire major rites of all kinds, and they pass it on to their sons and daughters as they see fit.[4] Ritual appropriate to female tasks, such as for gardening and certain kinds of fishing, as well as for many kinds of healing, and dream divination, are those rituals women are likely to perform for personal use. A woman would be unlikely to use on her own account hunting or war rituals, or *ugauga* sorcery or love ritual intended for male use,[5] but she might teach these to her husband, or sons, or brothers' sons. The woman is not merely a keeper of these traditions, they are her personal property and she may choose to withhold them from male heirs; if she teaches these rituals to another she will expect to be paid.

The importance of women in the transmission of traditions is indicated, for example, in the fact that Aisaga, who inherited many illustrious lines of major rituals according to the stipulated rules of seniority of patrilineal descent, nevertheless revealed that the source of much important knowledge had been a paternal grandmother. She was a Waima woman from the coast, but passed her knowledge on to her descendants in Mekeo. Another striking example was Alex's father, George. I had assumed, having never been told otherwise, that George's extensive powers as a rainmaker and controller of the *faifai* water spirits were acquired through the usual channels of agnatic inheritance, since George was the genealogically most senior member of his lineage. I later learned from Alex that George had acquired his major ritual powers from an elderly *woman,* his agnatic relative from another village, who took sick while visiting him and his family. She was too ill to return home and so revealed her secrets to George, who provided for her and looked after her until her death.

Nine women in the community, seven of whom I interviewed, had, or were identified as having, significant ritual knowledge. Margaret, a woman in her late thirties, was the wife of one of my neighbors. Her natal clan was in another village and her father (now deceased) was a renowned man of sorrow. She was never referred to as a knowledgeable person, yet it became clear in our discussions on dreams that she knew a good deal. Perhaps her father had taught her, or perhaps she had picked up certain information inadvertently—while collecting and preparing ritual medicines for his use, for instance. She was anxious to prevent others from finding out what she knew, especially the men of sorrow, whom she feared might take revenge if they realized she was privy to even minor secrets. Helen, an elderly married woman, was said to have an important hunting ritual for dogs. Since this rite consists primarily in feeding certain potions to the dogs and certain ritual restrictions on the practitioner, a woman may perform it, although men do the actual hunting.

Rebecca, another elderly woman, was said to possess, in addition to lesser traditions, rituals to make mosquitoes come in swarms to the village. This is a rite employed to wreak revenge on the community as a whole. (It seems remarkable to an outsider, who is continuously devoured by clouds of these pests, that they could possibly come in any greater numbers!) Grace, a woman in her sixties of great intelligence and force of character, was widely known to be a woman of knowledge. Her specialties included techniques for courting and gardening. Caroline and Denise, women in their fifties, practiced dream divination. Both were the wives of men who were important informants during my early fieldwork, yet at that time I knew nothing of their covert reputations as diviners. Janet, another dream diviner, was a middle-aged woman who learned the technique from her father. Finally, there was Josephina, a wonderful old lady in her seventies who truly merited the description *ikifa papiega,* a real woman of knowledge. She was undoubtedly the most respected female ritual expert in the community, best known for dream divination and healing, which she practiced for paying clients. Her daughter, Elizabeth, a middle-aged married woman, was being taught to take over the "practice." Both Janet and Josephina are described in detail in the next chapter.

Probably there are other women in the community who, unknown to me, have some significant ritual knowledge. Although I had long known the women just described, it was not until my 1980s fieldwork that I learned of their prowess. My new information came at first from Aisaga who, of course, was fully informed on all concealed things, but as other people began to accept my moving into in these shadowy areas, they too engaged me in a different discourse (Favret-Saada 1980). There are no simple criteria whereby any person can be judged a "specialist." Any of these nine women might termed an *ikifa papiega;* that is to say, each possesses techniques, and/or a depth of knowledge not generally available. Yet if one were to ask which of them were *ikifa papiega,* there would probably be considerable variation in opinion, and I think possibly only Grace and Josephina would be acknowledged by everyone. *Ikifa papiega* is merely as descriptive term, not a title, an office, or a clearly defined social role.

Everyone knew who practiced dream divination. Caroline, Denise, Josephina, Elizabeth, and Janet were all identified—here I must stress again that this was revealed covertly, never in public—as *feuapi* diviners. Dream divination and healing are the rituals women most regularly perform for payment. Since people, particularly infants and children, are always getting sick, the services of dream diviners are constantly in demand. When *feuapi* was first explained to me, people described it as a means of discovering the man of sorrow responsible for causing an illness (Hau'ofa 1981:244 describes it in the same manner). Later I learned that the role is confined neither to this, nor exclusively to matters involving *ugauga* sorcery. The dream diviner treats many minor illnesses and complaints, particularly of children. Where sorcery is divined, the *feuapi* merely advises the patient's relatives which men of sorrow to approach. In these cases, where relatives are desperate to find a cure, they are likely to pay the diviner a handsome fee. Cures of coughs and colds, sores and headaches, which are daily concerns, receive only modest payments and are usually performed frequently for kin and neighbors; clients from other villages are likely only in more serious cases.

The *feuapi* plays a significant ritual role in the community; the diviner's services as healer, in particular, are constantly called upon. Yet, no public ritual is enacted and there is no public acknowledgment of the role. No one openly admits to performing dream divination. Men too may be *feuapi,* but women are more often identified as such. This may be because the men who possess *feuapi* rituals are usually more renowned for other types of ritual. The *feuapi* diviner can be regarded as a ritual expert in the sense that she or he performs services for paying clients. Similarly, a woman widely regarded as an *ikifa papiega* is likely to obtain her covert reputation by using her rituals on the behalf of others. She might assist neighbors with a charm to help grow large yams, provide a potion to soothe skin rashes, bespell a sick child. The people she helps will be mostly relatives and neighbors, and only very small payments are involved. Nevertheless, both service and payment are valued.

That women are thought unlikely to employ destructive rituals stems partly from practical considerations. For example, it is unthinkable for a woman to isolate herself from the rest of the community as is necessary in *ugauga* sorcery. More significantly, such attitudes arise from deeply held cultural convictions that women's activities are productive in nature, not aggressive or destructive. Women, as I have noted, are valued as producers; they are kind-hearted, taking care of children, old people, and men. In comparison, males are considered selfish and hard-hearted—attitudes expressed by both genders. From both viewpoints, women have little need of secret knowledge for their own use, and only rites directed toward altruistic ends, such as healing and divination, are congenial to them.

Although women play a prominent role as dream healers and diviners, this is not an exclusively female domain, and in most other areas of ritual knowledge women are less prominent than men. Nor, as far as I have been able to determine, do women have any extensive body of traditions unknown to men. Furthermore, male ritual experts such as Aisaga are consulted about women's concerns: restrictions relating to pregnancy, the *megomego* procedures that follow the birth of a child, and complications relating to pregnancy and childbirth, as we saw in the case of Ruth (although men do not assist at births). Male experts such as Aisaga are also attributed with powers to inflict sterility, cause miscarriages, and control human reproduction and fertility in general. In short, many women possess significant esoteric knowledge and are regarded as ritual experts; nevertheless, the most renowned experts, with the greatest range and depth of knowledge, are men.[6]

Men of Knowledge

I have described the circumstances under which ritual traditions are acquired by others despite the ideal of patrilineal inheritance. Women play an important part, so also do younger sons: if the senior line dies out, or simply fails to preserve the knowledge, junior lines may perpetuate it. In consequence, the distribution of all traditions is much broader than Mekeo ideals admit. Many ordinary men, holding no significant seniority within the descent group, hold traditions of various kinds. In considering specific examples, as with the woman of knowledge, it is difficult to decide precisely when a man might be identified as an expert, since so many turn out to have covert reputations as such, and since it is so difficult to be sure who really knows what. Men are no more prepared than women to admit to knowing secret things.

Although I was only to discover it later, of those men who were my best informants during my early fieldwork, nearly all possessed one or more of the major secret traditions. The ward of the village where I lived comprised three allied clans totaling twenty-eight households and thus had approximately twenty-eight resident adult males.[7] Of these twenty-eight men, at least nine knew some notable esoteric lore. Two were men of kindness (*lopia aui*), one a war leader, and two were publicly recognized as men of sorrow (*ugauga aui*). The remaining four were ordinary men (*ulalu aui*) without special rank or status. In accordance with the public ideal, of these nine, only the two men of sorrow were openly identified as holders of secret knowledge.

Of the commoners (*ulalu aui*), one was reputed to have powerful love rituals, another knew spells for treating broken bones in addition to certain forms of war rituals, the third had in his youth spent some time as the assistant of a well-known man of sorrow (his senior agnatic kinsman) and thus acquired certain secrets, and the fourth owned techniques to cause infants to cry incessantly and waste away (*imoi ipapepepenia*). Only Henry, who had the ritual to kill babies, was paid by others to act on their behalf, and only he was considered an *ikifa auga,* or "man of knowledge." He was not, however, even covertly identified as a man of sorrow, despite the malignant nature of his powers.

Two of the three men of kindness in this ward held important traditions. One was in fact the brother of the deceased senior man of kindness of the dominant clan, which I will call Beach clan, and had for many years performed the office of *lopia* in the absence of the appropriate heir, who was working in Port Moresby. John, as I shall call him, was regarded, and functioned for all intents and purposes, as the senior man of kindness (*lopia fa'aniau*) of Beach clan. In his fifties when I began fieldwork, he was not publicly renowned for his ritual knowledge, yet over the years I was to discover he knew important rituals for hunting, for communicating with python spirits, and for calming people driven by the spirits of the dead to run amok. The junior man of kindness (*lopia eke*) of the second clan of the ward was a very charming, handsome man whose reputation for many love affairs was widely known. Appropriately, he turned out to be the possessor of a major tradition of love ritual; yet, although his reputation as a ladies' man was no secret, the fact he was a ritual expert was not disclosed until my return visit in the summer of 1979. Likewise, I was unaware that the war leader (*iso lopia*) of Beach clan possessed important hunting rituals, although since he was the eldest son of Aisaga, the renowned man of sorrow, I might have guessed as much. People, however, never referred to him as a man of knowledge, even during my second fieldwork. All of these three men were *ikifa aui,* men of knowledge, although they were never openly referred to as such. The two men publicly identified as men of sorrow were elderly widowers belonging to the war section of Beach clan. My mentor Aisaga was one; Opu, who died before my return visit, was the other (chapter 3).

The situation described here for one ward can be applied to the others. Many ordinary men have some significant secret knowledge. Important traditions tend to be held by the lineage heads of certain descent groups, and these include the men of kindness as well as men of sorrow; this point is best made by considering further examples.

Deadly Powers in the Hands
of the Men of Kindness

My old friend George was a junior man of kindness (*lopia eke*). I was aware all along of his reputation as a ritual expert, but it was not until years later, after his death, that I realized how formidable his powers were. He commanded rituals not only to bring rain, which is needed for crops to grow, but also to impose drought and cause famine; he could also bring torrential rains and floods to destroy gardens and the village. When several unusually dry seasons followed in a row just prior to and after George's death, people claimed he was angry with the community and thus had held back the rain to make them suffer. As a *faifai* expert, he could summon the fish to ascend the river, providing plentiful supplies for the community, or hold them back and create a dearth. His most feared power was his ability to direct the *faifai* spirits to inflict illness, and even death, on any person he chose.

Despite his jovial public persona, people were aware of his darker side and believed that he could, if angered, wreak disaster on the whole community and impose the most painful illness or death upon any individual who crossed him. Imagine my disbelief during my early fieldwork when one of my field assistants, David, privately confessed to me that he suffered a serious illness as a consequence of George's displeasure. At the time we were discussing the opposition of the men of kindness to business ventures undertaken by some of the more progressive individuals in the community, and I largely discounted David's accusation as typical of fears and rumors going around about the punishments inflicted on would-be entrepreneurs (Stephen 1974). Several years later, I talked with David about his dreams; he reported a series in which his dream-self was captured by the water spirits and, as a result, he became seriously ill. David's fears of George were not based on some vague rumor, I now appreciated, but grounded in the personal experience of dreams wherein night after night he was at the mercy of the *faifai* spirits. How did he recover from this illness, I asked? The answer clinched his point: he paid George to bespell him and retrieve his dream-self from the *faifai's* clutches. Such covert suspicions concerning George were common. He was regarded by the whole community as a formidable and dangerous ritual expert. Yet I was as well deceived on this account as I had been concerning his ability to speak English. How he would laugh at my double naivety if he were still alive to read this!

Four other lineage heads, all of the founding descent group of the village, Stone clan, proved to have similar reputations. Paul, a war leader of Stone clan, was an amiable old gentleman who had worked for the government for many years as an aid-post orderly. Like the other elders, he was a most cooperative and courteous informant on clan history and traditions. During my first period of fieldwork I spent many hours in discussions with him, and throughout that time I heard nothing to suggest that he possessed any sinister powers. When I approached him concerning the topic of dreams on my return in 1980, I was astonished to discover he not only knew, but claimed to use, lethal rituals against his own agnatic kin. He then proceeded to describe the techniques in detail to me with evident satisfaction! As with other old friends, my requests to discuss dreaming were interpreted by Paul as a veiled request for secret knowledge, to which he responded generously, drawing on his evidently rich fund.

The head of the junior section of Stone clan, Hubert, was publicly recognized as the hereditary holder of *faia* rituals. The term *faia* is used to refer to a wide range of spells, medicines, and ritual objects related to warfare, but in essence it is employed to cause people to be injured or killed in warfare, or in some other violent manner, for example, falling from a tree, being attacked by a wild animal such as a pig or cassowary or, nowadays, being involved in a road accident. Hubert was such a soft-spoken, frail and mild, but dignified old gentleman that nothing could seem more incongruous or inappropriate to his public persona. Since he lived permanently away from the village (owing to many serious tensions within his descent group caused by his marriage to a woman closely related to him), I heard little about his ritual prowess, and I never discussed the matter with him, except in the most general terms. When I questioned other well-informed people, such as Aisaga, about him, the un-equivocal reply was that the seemingly meek and mild Hubert was indeed a formidable man of knowledge who did not hesitate to implement his deadly techniques when required.

The most outstanding examples of clan heads commanding major rituals were found in the senior section of Stone clan—a fact so notorious I was aware of it even during my early fieldwork. This senior section had two claimants to the status of the man of kindness: one was the son of an adopted heir, the other was the son of a younger brother of the original line. People referred to the adoptive heir as the senior man of kindness (*lopia fa'aniau*) and the son of the younger brother as the junior man of kindness (*lopia eke*). The adoptive heir, like his father, people said, was lazy and not very intelligent. In contrast, Samuel, the representative of the original bloodline, a man in his sixties when I first arrived in the village, had a dignified presence and keen intelligence, and his reputation as a man of knowledge was no secret. Regarding himself as the rightful head of the Stone clan, Samuel had clearly prevailed over his sluggish and ineffectual rival, who was not only much younger, but lacked the wit to acquire esoteric knowledge even if it had been available to him.

Both Samuel and his brother were considered redoubtable adepts by the community. It was said Samuel was jealous of his brother's reputation and, when he died not long after I first arrived in the field, widespread rumor claimed that Samuel was responsible (this incident is described in chapter 2.) Samuel's reputation was known to me when I met him. Yet, like the others, he always appeared to be a kindly, mild-spoken old man, with a calm, dignified, and in no way forbidding, presence. He was an excellent source of information on clan histories and other matters, but he never discussed his ritual knowledge with me. He was dead by the time I returned in 1980. Even though throughout my early fieldwork I heard sinister rumors about certain men of kindness, it was nevertheless a jolt to discover a dark aspect to so many persons whom I thought I knew well, and whom I had accepted as fine examples of the public ideals. It was not easy to digest the fact that these kindly, affable elders were believed by the whole community to inflict illness, suffering, and death on their own people, and that they acknowledged their own powers. My 1980s fieldwork so changed my picture of Mekeo society that, in retrospect, the one who seems the most enigmatic is Luke, the "gentle philosopher" described in chapter 3, simply because I never had to reassess my idealistic view of him—which leaves me wondering why.

On Samuel's death, his eldest son, Richard, replaced him. Well educated and fluent in English, Richard had spent his life in increasingly important positions in government service. All the same, having reached late middle-age, he was steeped in the traditions of his own culture, and on his father's death he assumed his mantle as one of the foremost men of knowledge in the Mekeo region. Richard claimed, in fact, to have superior ritual knowledge since he had been directly taught not by his father but by his grandfather (this theme of rivalry between father and son in families where important secret traditions exist is a dominant one, and I will return to it). His grandfather, Richard explained, had command of all areas of ritual, including weather, hunting, gardening, love, war, healing, divination, *ugauga* sorcery, and various other destructive rituals.

To illustrate the extent and virulence of these ritual powers, Richard described a contest held between his grandfather and Aufo Afulo, an infamous man of sorrow from Eboa village. Aufo, it is said, extended a reign of terror over the whole region prior to the Second World War (see also Hau'ofa 1981:264–267). The story goes that Richard's grandfather challenged the notorious Aufo to see who could dispose of the most victims in the shortest time—a contest the man of kindness won! Whether true or not, this anecdote is striking. Deadly techniques are employed by a man of kindness merely to assert his own personal prestige as a man of knowledge. It must be emphasized that I am not dealing with tales told in public valorizing the exploits of one's forefathers, but a private communication, told in confidence.

According to Richard, his grandfather knew, and taught him, other lethal rituals in addition to *ugauga* sorcery that were superior to *ugauga* because they are much easier to implement and require no visible preparation and no isolation from the rest of the community. These other rituals have an added advantage: their perpetrator is impossible to identify through divination. Elder lines preserve these "light" (*ilikae*) rituals for themselves while passing onto their younger brothers the "heavy" (*meau*) practice of sorcery. If one compares the repertoires of the two foremost men of knowledge in this community—Richard, the man of kindness, and Aisaga, the man of sorrow—as I had the opportunity to do, they prove to be very similar in content and nature, a circumstance that the two experts recognize. The fact that a man of kindness might possess and actually implement death-dealing rituals is, of course, totally incompatible with the moral principles for which he stands. Such things are never discussed or admitted in public; nevertheless, everyone is aware of their concealed existence.[8]

Aisaga's status as a man of sorrow is worth considering in detail as it illustrates several points regarding the definition of the role. He often pointed out his proper status was that of war leader (*iso lopia*), even though he also knew, and had practiced for many years, *ugauga* sorcery. His clan, Beach clan, displays the threefold division favored by cultural convention and described in chapter 1: it consists of a senior, a junior, and a war section. This tripartite structure is conventionally explained by the circumstance that the founder of the group became the senior man of kindness, passing on to his younger brothers the positions of junior man of kindness and war leader; the descendants of the three brothers thus comprise the three sections. *Ugauga* sorcery, regardless of how it is believed to have been acquired, is associated with younger brothers and junior lines (see also Hau'ofa 1981:chapter 8). Ideally, senior lines retain the position of the man of kindness, while that of the man of sorrow is left to the juniors.

Aisaga belongs to the war section, which is the most junior of the three sections of Beach clan. Within his section, his is the most senior lineage. Just as the three sections of the larger group are said to originate from three brothers, so Aisaga's section is said to descend from three brothers—named individuals from whom the living members can trace their genealogical links. The senior brother, Aisaga's great-grandfather, was the war leader, and he is said to have passed onto his youngest brother the knowledge of *ugauga* sorcery, which then became the responsibility of the junior of the three lineages. Opu, the other man of sorrow, was a representative of this junior line. How did Aisaga, formerly a war leader, come to be regarded as a man of sorrow?

Aisaga installed his eldest son as war leader many years ago. Subsequently Aisaga's wife died. As a widower he was forced to live in seclusion outside society, and since he had inherited many major secret traditions, including *ugauga* sorcery, it was now expected by the community that he would become a practicing man of sorrow. When his period of mourning was over, he chose not to remarry but to remain in a state of ritual preparedness as a celibate widower. Thus he continued to be regarded by the community as a man of sorrow, while his son, Matthew, filled the role of war leader. When questioned about his dual role, Aisaga explained he inherited the position of war leader through his father and grandfather, but at the same time he was taught the many traditions of knowledge possessed by his family. While it was true that *ugauga* sorcery had been passed to the junior line, the knowledge was retained by his immediate forefathers to use when necessary. Even though his *akina* (classificatory younger brothers) inherited *ugauga* sorcery and rightfully practiced it, his own version of it, he asserted, was ascendent and more complete.

Aisaga's case makes it clear that while the roles of war leader and man of sorrow are incompatible in the sense that they cannot be undertaken simultaneously, there is no incongruity in one individual holding the ritual knowledge appropriate to both, and in playing each role at different times. Furthermore, it reveals that although seniors prefer to delegate the onerous *practice* of *ugauga* sorcery to younger brothers, they nevertheless are likely to retain the fullest versions of the traditions for themselves, thus ensuring that they keep the upper hand. It was to this fact, of course, that Aisaga alluded in his assurances that there were much easier and equally effective ways to kill than *ugauga*. This applies as well to the apparent anomaly wherein senior men of kindness, such as Samuel and Richard, of senior lines, covertly admit to possession of deadly rituals.

It might properly be objected that there is far less incongruity in a war leader possessing destructive rituals than a senior man of kindness. Aisaga himself often observed that when tribal warfare was banned by the colonial government, in the time of his grandfather and father, it was not difficult for them to adapt their rituals to peacetime. Besides, the war leaders had in their possession the human flesh and organs—relics of their war victims—which were the essential ingredients for *ugauga* sorcery. Evidently, since the role of war leader was primarily concerned with killing, the war leader might be seen to be more closely associated with the man of sorrow. (The difficulties of interpreting the war leader's role have already been raised; see chapter 1.) Since the late nineteenth century, the heads of war lineages, like Aisaga, have come to function in public as civilian leaders. Aisaga grew up learning the war rituals which were his heritage; yet, until he became a widower in late middle age, he had for more than twenty years played the benevolent role of family and lineage head.

What Distinguishes the Man of Sorrow from Other Ritual Experts?

I seem to have reached a point where any distinctions I might attempt to draw between the man of sorrow and other holders of major esoteric knowledge would be meaningless. Many people other than those identified as men of sorrow hold various kinds of death-dealing and destructive rituals, and they include commoners such as Henry with his techniques to kill infants. Moreover, it is especially the men of kindness of particular descent groups, such as George, Hubert, Paul, Samuel, and Richard, who are likely to have such rituals. Aisaga might play the role of clan head at one time and of a man of sorrow at another. It is evidently necessary to know the particular techniques termed *ugauga* in order to be a man of sorrow, but not all those individuals who know them are identified as *ugauga auga*. Indeed, women may possess the knowledge of *ugauga* but do not implement it. Furthermore, individuals identified as men of sorrow implement a wide range of other, nondestructive rituals.

It would, however, be false to conclude that there is no real difference in the roles of the man of sorrow and the man of kindness, or that nothing distinguishes the man of sorrow from other holders of deadly rituals. It is only when one is aware of the range of traditions, and who holds them, that one is in a position to determine the distinctive features (Schneider 1968) of the man of sorrow as a category. Evidently death-dealing ritual is not one, since there are many forms possessed by persons not identified as men of sorrow. It is ownership and implementation of a *particular* form, *ugauga,* which denotes the man of sorrow and furthermore, it is only the man of sorrow who is publicly acknowledged to have malignant powers. Paradoxically, although the real nature of his rituals are strictly secret, their practice is highly public. *Ugauga,* as Aisaga pointed out when trying to persuade me against learning it, involves a rigorous regime of seclusion, fasting, and deprivation, making it very evident to all whether one is implementing it. If a man continues to live with his wife and family, eats what he likes, and mixes as he pleases in society, no one will believe he is practicing *ugauga.* Furthermore, it is well known which clan, which lineages, and which individuals within those lineages are the hereditary holders. One cannot pretend to have knowledge of *ugauga* when everyone knows one has had no opportunity to acquire it. In short, the man of sorrow is not only publicly recognized to command ritual powers to kill, the very nature of his rituals ensures they cannot be implemented without the fact being public. It is now, I think, easier to understand more fully this seemingly paradoxical circumstance: in his public presence, the man of sorrow symbolizes the visible, manifest face of the spirit realm.

There is yet another aspect of the public nature of *ugauga* rituals to be considered, one foreshadowed in Aisaga's statement that one needed to employ *ugauga* rituals only if one wanted to make money. *Ugauga* rituals allow the practitioner to kill slowly. If he chooses, he can stop the process and restore the victim to health. *Ugauga* is a way to earn money, and one may inflict a sickness on someone purely to that end. Aisaga and others pointed out that the man of sorrow must be recompensed for the privations his rituals impose. Other people, including commoners and the men of kindness, may kill by ritual means, but only the man of sorrow is publicly attributed with responsibility for death, and he uses that attribution to extract payment and rewards. Exploring the ramifications of this will have to wait for later chapters.

I have attempted to demonstrate here the obfuscating effect of our categories "sorcerer" and "sorcery" in understanding the role of the man of sorrow, but it is not my intention to deny special meanings or significance to him—a significance that lies precisely in his visible, public status as the wielder of destructive ritual power.[9] What I have tried to show is that the overt symbolism surrounding the man of sorrow asserts a clear-cut division of ritual powers that is contradicted by what people know to be the situation on a less visible, deliberately concealed level.

10

Two Dream Diviners: Josephina and Janet

"Josephina, please explain to me: what is *feuapi?* Can I tape record this?"

I was sitting on a rickety bamboo veranda, shaded by the thatched roofs of overhanging houses, talking to an old lady in her seventies, a well-known dream healer and diviner (*feuapi*). The old lady's grandchildren set up an infernal racket as I began to record our conversation. She shooed them away, then turned to me with her small alert head cocked to one side and her wrinkled face smoothed into a thoughtful smile. After thinking a while she replied, in a calm, slightly husky voice:

"People are sick. . . . When people are sick, and when they bring money and riches[1] and give them to us, we bespell them. When I bespell them, then I lie down to sleep that night, and I go in search of their dream-selves. I go to the *faifai* water spirits' place; I go down into the water. They make ladders that go down. Other people don't see them, they don't know. When I sleep . . . when it's night, I see them and I go there. I go down [into the water] and I go along until I see the house where the person has been put. I ask, 'Has that one just come here?' 'Yes, that person came and now is staying here,' they reply. 'Well now give me that person, I want to take him away from here.' But if the water spirits refuse, I do not take the person. He stays there and I come back. The next morning the relatives of the sick person come to me and I tell them, 'His dream-self has gone and I saw it there. I saw it but I was not able to take it or bring it back. It is still there.' Then they go and get money and bring it, saying, 'Take this money and then bespell him.' When they bring money to give to me, I say the spells and that night I take the dream-self and I bring it back. Then I give it to the sick person saying, 'Last night I went and took hold of your dream-self and brought it and put it down in your place, then I went home. Then I woke up.' And the sick person replies, 'Now all is well, now I have recovered.' Yes, that is what we call *feuapi*.''

Josephina sends out her dream-self to search for and retrieve the lost dream-selves of her clients. Her descent into the water, encounters with the water spirits, and the restoring of the patient's dream-self are closely paralleled by adventures recounted earlier of ordinary persons like Celestina and Maria. The experiences of ritual experts differ not in kind, but in degree. What distinguishes Josephina is that she consciously directs the action of her dream-self and uses this ability on the behalf of fee-paying clients.

Although dreams and other subjective states provide access to the hidden realm for everyone, and even though every person participates in it to some degree, the ordinary person does not direct this interaction at will. Dreaming, brought about by the dream-self leaving the bodily self, occurs involuntarily, and the actions of the dream-self in the dream world are independent of the dreamer's waking desires. What happens there, and the subsequent effects on the bodily self, may be seen as positive and beneficial or as dangerous and destructive, depending on the actual circumstances and the attitude of the person concerned, but without ritual guidance she or he can neither determine nor escape the consequences. In contrast, the ritual expert possesses the means to influence dream events and to induce dreaming at will. The rituals of secret knowledge are, in fact, aimed precisely to this end.

My relationships with informants and the kind of problems posed by them have been raised earlier. Without going over the same ground again, certain issues should be restated. The information presented here is drawn primarily from ritual experts' verbal statements about their experiences and the practices they followed, statements such as that just quoted from Josephina. Usually, as on that occasion, secret traditions were transmitted in private conversations at some place selected by the instructor. No interpreters were used. This, of course, was to ensure that no third party acquired the knowledge. When Josephina finally agreed to tell me the spells and the medicines she employed in her rituals, she motioned me to follow her away from the house and we proceeded some way down a path leading into the bush before she was satisfied no one could possibly overhear us. Males had to manage the situation a little more carefully in the interests of propriety. It was necessary to find somewhere in public view so people could see what we were doing, but also to ensure others did not attempt to join the conversion. This was usually achieved by sending the family off to the garden for the day while we sat and talked alone on the veranda—the visible, public part of the family house. Neighbors and passers-by quickly recognized that they were not wanted. (Aisaga often insisted the old custom was never to reveal ritual knowledge after dark in case someone was hiding under the veranda or house.) Everyone in the community knew certain people were teaching me secret things, but no one except me knew exactly what.

Verbal transmission alone confers secret knowledge upon the recipient. Once one knows the appropriate spells and the special medicines and relics required for a particular rite, one is able to implement it. No instruction beyond this is essential. In the past, the rote learning of myths, lengthy spells, and complicated recipes of ingredients must have taken time. Young people acquired ritual secrets by attending senior relatives and gradually building up their knowledge, first perhaps by identifying and gathering the plants required for potions, later by being taught the myths and, finally, the spells. Only as they memorized each part would they progress to the next stage. Today, young people can write; those who persuade elders to identify medicines or recite the spells quickly copy them down in notebooks. Implementing the rite under the guidance of one's instructor is preferred. Josephina, for example, lived with a married daughter to whom she was teaching dream divining. The daughter had plenty of opportunity to practice under her mother's supervision, but this was not regarded as essential. A person who already has a wide understanding of the secret traditions—such as an established expert like Josephina or Aisaga— requires no prolonged period of training to acquire a new ritual. A verbal transmission of the information suffices, requiring only a brief visit of a few hours (or, at the most, a day or two) and a secret payment in return, or perhaps an exchange of ritual knowledge.

I did not pay people for information, regardless of whether they were laypersons or ritual experts. But when secret knowledge was involved, adepts impressed upon me that very valuable things were being bestowed, toward which I bore a weighty responsibility. The tension of people's expectations— the "burden of the gift"—was referred to earlier. There are limitations on what I can reveal. I find myself caught between a responsibility to preserve the confidentiality and trust of those who imparted their knowledge and a responsibility to scientific accuracy of reporting; somehow these conflicting demands must be accommodated. Mekeo esoteric knowledge is dangerous knowledge, not to be delivered into the hands of those who might use it heedlessly. In describing the experience of ritual experts, to ensure nobody can use the information to implement specific rituals, the actual texts of spells and the precise identity of the ritual substances and objects are not disclosed. This is hardly satisfactory from the point of view of a comprehensive cultural analysis but, accepting this necessary limitation, there is still much to be learned about the general nature of the rituals, their symbolism, and their influence on the adept's inner experience.

There are two main areas to examine: the kinds of experiences that ritual experts describe and how these experiences vary among ritual experts and in comparison with nonexperts; and how the elements of the rite—the spell, substances, and relics—influence these experiences. My intention is to show, through the statements of adepts themselves as far as possible, that the rituals of secret knowledge operate as a means of guiding and shaping inner experience. It is my intention to convey something of the character of each person and the circumstances under which she, or he, shared their knowledge. From this will gradually emerge the special—the unique—sense of self-identity possessed by the man or woman of knowledge. I begin with two women healers, Josephina and Janet.

A Woman of Knowledge: Josephina

Let us return to that tumbledown bamboo platform and wise Josephina. I had not met her during my early fieldwork, as she was then living in another village with one of her several married daughters, but her eldest son, Mark, and his family had been good friends. When I returned in December 1978–January 1979, Mark was very ill, his appearance changed to the extent that I did not recognize him until he spoke to me. He died before my next visit. Perhaps it was because of her son's friendship with me that Josephina and her daughter, Elizabeth, were so generous in sharing their knowledge. Mark, an elegant and charming man possessed of all the dandified good looks and rakish style Mekeo admire, had died in his prime and was still sadly missed by everyone. I only now discovered that he had been the possessor of important esoteric knowledge (see chapter 9). His blatant love affairs and seductions, the fruits of his ritual prowess, had aroused the anger of many and, as a result, the men of sorrow had been commissioned to do away with him, so it was rumored after his death.

Josephina was first introduced to me during my 1980s fieldwork by Maria, who had responded to my questions concerning women's ritual knowledge with the promise she would take me to see a real woman of knowledge. Our first meeting, as one might expect under the circumstances, was filled with the old lady's tearful recollections of her dead son. Yet even so, one could not help but be impressed by the dignity and commanding presence of this elderly mother and grandmother. In her mid-seventies, Josephina was still active and vigorous. When I arrived to talk with her I would often find she had already gone off to work in the gardens or had taken a load of vegetables to the coastal market or, if it were a Sunday, she might be visiting relatives in another village. She was small but straight, and possessed a special kind of beauty. It was evident that the dashing Mark had inherited his fine eyes, narrow-bridged, slightly aquiline nose, and sculptured cheekbones from his mother. My mentor, Aisaga, recalled that Josephina had been a great beauty in her youth and had been pursued by many men. Now in old age, her finely shaped head and her bronzed, deeply lined face recalled some ancient work of art glowing with the mellow patina of time. From a distance, her hair shaved close to her head (in the manner of elderly women), her slight person a bundle of drab blue widow's weeds, she might have been the old woman of the myths—the one who persuaded the young women to become flying foxes and leave their husbands while she became an old tortoise and sank into the river. At closer range one could observe the haughty carriage of her head, her penetrating eyes, and the calm confidence she commanded. She was unique, yet she was by no means the only elder of such outstanding dignity and wisdom. Many of the old people I encountered, such as the gentle philosopher Luke, rollicking George, and wily old Augustine, impressed me in a similar way.

This is a culture in which some people seem to become more fully realized, more imposing personalities in old age. A feeble, unimportant person might be the object of ridicule, but the man or woman who possesses important secret knowledge grows in stature and reputation with age. The very term used to refer to an old person, *apao(ga),* is indicative of respect. Josephina would appropriately be referred to or addressed directly as *papie apaoga,* meaning literally "woman old." The word *apao(ga)* has none of the negative value that is attached to the English term. Important men of the senior generation, for example, are politely referred to as such. English expressions of familiarity or contempt, such as "old man," "old fellow," and "poor fellow" are conveyed by the Mekeo expression *au apala,* literally "bad man." *Apaoga* connotes someone who is large, important, mature, or old, depending on context. A fine fat pig, ever an object of gratification and admiration in Melanesian cultures, is *uma apaoga,* a fine big building is described as *e'a apaoga,* a well-developed or mature unmarried girl is *ifiao apaoga.* The ancestors are referred to as the *papiau apaoi.* The term is used to mean the opposite of *kekele*—small, young, insignificant. These terms indicate Mekeo attitudes to age and youth. "Old" in the sense of "in the past," "formerly," "worn out" (e.g., clothes) is conveyed by the term *ufai(na).* It is used in opposition to *mama(ga),* "new." In this instance, it is not chronological age that is crucial, but whether something is used, familiar, and known (*ufaina*), or something novel and previously unknown (*mamaga*). This opposition of different associations, positive and negative, brought together in the English term "old" further reflects Mekeo attitudes to aging. Mekeo respect age not out of sentiment, but because the elders are considered to be more knowledgeable. They know more about the past, what the ancestors did, and about the correct observation of custom and tradition, but above all they have more effective command of the traditions of secret knowledge.

An old lady of such advanced years as Josephina is thought to have greater competence than younger practitioners of dream divining and healing. As a member of the most senior living generation, she is at least one step closer in the line of transmission from the mythological originator. Knowledge is believed to diminish a little with each generation, largely because the practitioner retains the final secrets until very close to death, often dying before they can be passed on (cf. Barth 1975). In addition, Josephina had demonstrated her ability to interact with the hidden world over a long time. Furthermore, as an old person, she is thought better able to bear whatever restrictions on fleshly pleasures her ritual practice necessitates. Josephina is accustomed to respect from all, including her own family, who have to treat her well if they expect to learn her ritual secrets, and grateful clients, who pay well for her services. This little old woman with her straight back and twinkling eyes is indeed a veritable *papie apaoga*, a highly respected personage.

Fortunately for me, Josephina and I got on well together, and I spent many hours in her company. Her alert mind is revealed in the following answers to my enquiries about dream healing, taken from our many conversations (which she allowed me to tape record). Josephina knew no English; I translate her actual wording as closely as possible, without rendering it too repetitious. Josephina continued her account of treating a patient thus:

''Perhaps the sick person's shoulders were very painful—a snake, a snake was crushing him. It had wrapped itself around and around him completely, and he just stayed like that. He tried to get free but he couldn't. I went with a knife—when I bespelled the sick person, I took a knife and put it beside me, and also I put it near the sick person while I bespelled him. I said the spells, and when they were finished I rubbed his skin [with the medicines] and then he went home. That night my dream-self, I got up and took that knife, and I went down [into the water] and searched. When I saw the snake I cut it up, I chopped it up. Then my dream-self made a fire and I put the chopped up parts of the snake on the fire and burned them.[2] Then I took the sick person's dream-self and I brought it back. When I brought it back, all was well. I rested a little and then I put it [the dream-self] into the sick person's body. When I had put it back, he was no longer sick. That night he slept soundly until morning. Then he came and told me, 'Tonight I was much better. I will not need to come again for you to bespell me.' But if people give me nothing then I will bespell them tomorrow and the next day and the next. But their pain will not cease until they bring something [payment] for me.''

Here Josephina describes the little that is visible to others of her rituals. The patient comes to her and is bespelled. This, as she explained later when she told me the spells, involved whispering the spells under her breath and then blowing onto a cup of water or tea which the patient then drinks. Next she takes certain leaves—these are the ritual medicines (*fu'a*)—which she first crushes up in her hand (so they cannot be identified by anyone else) and then rubs them on the skin of the patient. The wad of crushed leaves is placed aside with the knife she refers to and, later, when she lays down to sleep, both are put under her pillow. One day when I visited her, a small granddaughter was brought for her to bespell because the child was crying and fretful. Josephina's actions were so unobtrusive I might have missed it all. Muttering briefly, she blew upon the child, whom she had taken in her lap, and then quickly rubbed its limbs with some leaves she took out of her string bag. The child was then handed back to its mother without comment. This was not a serious case, but only a minor illness, Josephina explained. There would be no difficulty in retrieving the errant dream-self, unlike the serious case described above where she had to rescue the dream-self from the coils of a giant snake, or others where she had to fight off the water spirits who refused to relinquish the captive. Whether the case is serious or minor, the external actions performed to induce her dreams are little different. She did not explain why or how the spells and the medicines influenced her dreaming, she simply stated that dreaming follows the ritual.

Dealing with a serious illness occurs in two stages. First Josephina dreams to discover where the dream-self of the patient is; after locating it she knows how to proceed. The *faifai* water spirits figure prominently in her accounts. She talked about their villages which she visited under the water. In the past, she recalled, they used to have thatched houses but now, keeping up with the times, they have dwellings with cement steps and iron roofs! Sometimes they allow her to take the dream-self without any fuss, but often they refuse, sometimes insisting that the victim is now married to one of them and must stay there. Or else, as described above, she may find that a water spirit in the form of a python has seized the dream-self; then she must do battle to free it and destroy the spirit snake.

She also described the *apagapaga auni'i,* other spirits found in the bush. These spirits cause sickness by carrying the dream-selves of unsuspecting victims to the tops of the tall trees where these spirits live. The captured dream-self is stranded there and Josephina must climb the tree in a dream to rescue the victim. If these spirits, or the water spirits, are revealed in her dreams as the culprits, she can deal with them provided the patient or his relatives are prepared to pay her to undertake the risks involved. There is, however, a third eventuality in which neither she nor any other dream healer can retrieve the dream-self. If she finds the sick person's dream-self imprisoned in the house (*gove*)[3] of a man of sorrow, she is powerless to effect a cure. She explained:

"I tell people if it is water spirits or *apagapaga auni'i* who have taken them. But if it is the men of sorrow I am scared to say anything. Because they might get angry with me and kill me if I said anything. I go and see the dream-self in the house [*gove*] of the man of sorrow, but I don't tell the person this. When a man of sorrow has got their dream-self I just tell them to go to hospital and get treatment. But really I just refuse to do anything further—but if it is water spirits I can go and take their dream-selves from the water."

She later modified this, saying she would tell the patient she could do nothing for them and suggest they approach various men of sorrow in the hope of identifying the one responsible. She claimed that while she knew exactly where the dream-self was, she would never reveal the identity of the assailant for fear of her own life.

Feuapi, she made it clear, was a risky business. Her ability to locate the whereabouts of the lost dream-self could incur the wrath of the men of sorrow if she used it irresponsibly, and thus bring death upon herself or a member of her family. Nor were her encounters with the spirits without danger. I asked her: "When you try to rescue the dream-self of the sick person and you see the spirits fighting to keep it, or a huge snake wrapped around it that you have to kill, aren't you frightened?''

With a contemptuous snort at the naivety of my question, she declared: ''Frightened? Of course I am! If they strike me I will get sick.''

Her dream battles were not, she revealed, undertaken alone, but with the aid of her deceased husband and mother-in-law. In a case of serious illness, she would summon the presence of these spirits to assist her:

''When people pay me to bespell them, I tell my mother-in-law and my husband, 'I have bespelled the sick person and you also must bespell them. You must bespell him and then at night when I go to search for his dream-self I will call you together and we will go together and search out the dream-self and take it and bring it back.' I tell them that. When I say that and then that night I lie down and their dream-selves [of her dead husband and mother-in-law] come. We go and search for the person. When we go down into the water—oh! there is a lot of fighting [with the water spirits]! They all fight. Then my mother-in-law and my husband go and take hold of the dream-self of that person and they give it to me saying, 'You go to the village, we will stay here and fight.' Then while they are fighting, I take the dream-self and bring it back. I *run* back to the village.''

Although Josephina does not mention it, summoning the spirits of the dead, even one's own relatives, is considered a matter not to be undertaken lightly. Anyone can do so who has some physical relic of the deceased (e.g., hair, fingernails, or simply some cloth worn next to the skin), but most people, including many with ritual knowledge, do not dare to undertake such a conjuration. Keeping relics of the dead about one's house is often interpreted as the cause of illness, since the spirits' presence are attracted by them (examples are given in chapter 7). Josephina's ritual practice puts her at risk from these different sources of danger. Why does she, particularly at her age, expose herself? In the first place, as her manner makes clear, she feels in control of the situation—she is not intimidated or overwhelmed by the forces she encounters. She knows each of the water spirits by name; they are familiar figures to her and she is confident in this familiarity. She is aware of the dangers, but she indicates no anxiety about them. Josephina did not mention dreams associated with illnesses of her own. Despite her advanced age, she rarely suffered from even minor complaints such as a bad cold (which, in any case, were never serious enough to prevent her from talking with me). She conveyed an air of totally calm confidence and grandmotherly authority.

When I asked Josephina about dreaming in general, she replied she only dreamed after she performed healing or divination rituals. Later she conceded that she did occasionally dream without ritual inducement, then shortly after she would that learn that the person she had seen in her dream was sick. Thus the action of her dream-self leaving her body is something she controls through ritual. The infrequency of her spontaneous dreaming is, of course, in accordance with her belief that frequent dreaming that is not ritually controlled is potentially harmful. The rituals of *feuapi* enable her consciously to direct the action of her dream-self, but these rituals do not give her unqualified control over the dream-self. That is to say, she cannot employ them in any way she chooses. For example, when I asked her if she could converse with the dead in dreams and obtain knowledge from them, she replied that this was not possible for her. She can direct her dreaming to one end only, that of locating and bringing back the dream-selves of sick people.

Her ritually conferred ability to direct the actions of her dream-self has a double edge to it, as do all the traditions of secret knowledge. It gives her an advantage over other people in that they lack this valuable skill to heal the sick. At the same time, it places a special responsibility, and burden, on her. If, as she herself pointed out, she did not undertake these perilous dream journeys, people would die. Likewise, if she did not instruct the relatives which men of sorrow to approach the sick would die. Therefore she must be paid for her services; she expects compensation for undertaking dangerous tasks on behalf of others. Furthermore, possession of this special knowledge places her in a situation where she cannot really refuse to employ it. This double aspect of ritual knowledge as both burdensome and prestigious underlies all situations. It becomes particularly evident in the transmission of knowledge; parents often hesitate to load offspring with an inheritance that might bear unwelcome consequences. On the one hand, *feuapi* is a precious gift, as Josephina explained, which was given to her by her mother-in-law in reward for tending her in her last illness. Yet, if improperly handled, it can lead to injury, sickness, and or possibly death—even for the practitioner.

A Timorous Dream Diviner: Janet

The hazards involved in *feuapi* were made more evident in the responses of another, less confident practitioner. Janet, a middle-aged married woman, was much less renowned as a dream healer than Josephina, although her father, from whom she acquired the rituals, was a well-known expert. I had only one interview with Janet; she seemed anxious about her rituals and about discussing them with me. The discussion began on a pessimistic note. She described a recent case: after treating a sick child she dreamed she was successful in bringing back the dream-self of her patient and returning it to the mother, but just as she did so, it managed to run off again. The child died the next evening. This brief account of an unsuccessful cure exemplifies the tone of her response. She also recounted dreams occurring when she herself was seriously ill; they were of water-spirit lovers luring her away to live with them. Janet openly confessed her anxieties: ''I don't go to the river because I am frightened of the water spirits. At night I see them in dreams—I am very frightened they will strike me and make me sick.'' She added: ''My father taught me the spells and now I bespell people and I get money. They give us money because the water-spirits hit us and make us sick. We have to suffer a lot!''

Janet is caught between her own fears of the water-spirits, with whom she must struggle to win back the captured dream-self of her clients, and her desire to meet the responsibility the knowledge entails. She seems overwhelmed by these forces. She confided she put out money and food offerings for the spirits of her dead father and mother so that they would assist her in her dream tasks. At night one could hear the clatter of the forks and spoons on the plates as they ate the food, she said, and she laughed a little, commenting that these noises during the night frightened her husband, who did not know what they were. Janet herself appeared less than comfortable about the visitation, unlike Josephina, who found reassuring the spirit aid of her dead mother-in-law and husband. Indeed Celestina, with no ritual means at her disposal, and whom nobody identified as a dream healer, had more confidence in her dealings with the spirit world than did Janet.

All three women, Josephena, Janet, and Celestina, reported dreams in which they dive into the water to seek out the lost dream-selves of sick people. One noticeable difference in the reporting of the ritual experts, Janet and Josephina, was that they found it difficult to recall many actual examples. As they both separately explained, it was difficult to remember specific dreams because they had so many of a similar kind. I found ritual experts in general could remember no more than a few specific examples. It was necessary to record their dreams soon after they occurred, before they faded from memory and merged with the continuous stream of interaction with the hidden world that a ritual expert undertakes. Many ordinary people such as Celestina and Maria recalled dreams from several years and presented carefully constructed dream histories.

Janet consented to describe the medicines (*fu'a*) she used to induce dreaming; they had been revealed to her in a dream by the *faifai* water spirits themselves. But she firmly refused to divulge the spells used in her rituals, stating that her own father had not given them to her until she paid him for the knowledge. Perhaps she was hinting at what she wanted in return, but I never paid people for what they told me. If they were reluctant to part with their secrets I did not insist. All she would say about the spell she used was that it was directed to the *faifai* water spirits. Janet's *feuapi* ritual, like Josephina's, consisted of bespelling the patient and then rubbing the patient's body with the medicines, which she later put under her pillow when she wanted to dream. In identifying the medicines, Janet gave me part of her knowledge. The medicines alone are expected to induce the appropriate dreams although the spells add greater effectiveness to the procedure. By keeping the spells to herself she ensured that she retained the more powerful form of the ritual, granting me only a weaker means of guiding my dream-self to explore the underwater realm of the *faifai* spirits.

A final point to be noted is that although Josephina and Janet emphasized the dangers of their dealings with the spirits in the dream realm, Josephina (who was the only one of the two I questioned on this point) denied that her rituals necessitated any rigorous dietary or sexual restrictions (*gope*), such as are required for many major rituals. Even when her husband was alive, she was able to practice dream healing. Since dream healers are often married women it is evident that prolonged celibacy and isolation are not prerequisites. Some women practitioners of other minor rituals, however, stated they abstained from eating meat as a preparation, since the spirits of the dead were offended by its odor on the breath. If one wished to attract their presence, one avoided meat for the duration of the ritual.

A confident, expert practitioner like Josephina is able to maintain a dual existence in separate but vividly experienced worlds—the everyday round of safe, female household activities and chores, and the strange journeys and fearsome encounters in the spirit realm. She deals with both with equal aplomb and does not allow one to intrude upon the other. Janet, on the other hand, is apprehensive lest her nighttime world of water-spirit lovers and spirit snakes invade the daytime reality of going to the river to bathe or fetch water. She fears that her attempts to rescue others from the dream realm will result in being captured, or "hit," herself, and that her bodily self will become ill as a result. For Janet, only a very uneasy accommodation of the roles is available to her two different selves. She is not really able to cope with the ritual means she has been given to empower her hidden self. Yet given time, experience, and greater maturity, she may acquire more confidence and greater command. If she survives to attain Josephina's venerable age, she too will probably achieve similar renown.

Feuapi is not confined to women, yet Josephina was generally regarded as the most prominent practitioner in her own community and in surrounding ones. As noted in the previous chapter, several other women in the community are known to be dream healers, whereas men rarely have a reputation for this alone. People never expressed any opinion as to the comparative abilities of male versus female practitioners. Reputations such as Josephina's seem to depend on the healer's performance over time. Like a male adept, Josephina's advanced age certainly enhanced her position, yet in one respect she was regarded very differently. Men possessing ritual knowledge, especially as they enter old age, are feared by others. Although this fear does not extend to the open avoidance displayed toward the man of sorrow, younger people, both male and female, behave very circumspectly toward male elders known to have secret knowledge, and they evidently feel uncomfortable in their presence. During my early fieldwork I found it difficult to obtain good interpreters for this very reason. There were any number of young men who could speak and write excellent English, but none were prepared to act as intermediaries with the elders. "You have to know how to talk to the old people," I was told. Only married men in their thirties or forties would agree to undertake the task, and they did so with some trepidation. Female elders, even those, like Josephina, who possessed important rituals, were never spoken of or treated in the same way. Certainly Josephina was highly respected and was paid some deference, especially by her family, but no one seemed to fear her or avoid her. This is in keeping with the general attitude described previously that women perform rituals with positive intent. Although the dream healer's interaction with the forces of the spirit realm puts herself at risk, she is not seen as endangering others thereby. Like all the rituals of secret knowledge, *feuapi* is very specific in intent: it enables the adept to bring back lost dream-selves but it does not confer the ability to control destructive forces or actions in the dream realm. Women may indeed become more successful dream healers and diviners than men. Female adepts do not, however, undertake *gope,* the ritual regime necessary to perform destructive rites. The significance of this in relation to self-identity will emerge later.

11

Two Men of Knowledge:
Alex and Francis

Alex and Francis exemplify the man of knowledge (*ikifa auga*), described earlier, who has at his disposal major traditions of secret knowledge, yet is not openly identified by the community as a ritual expert even though other adepts are well aware of the nature and extent of his abilities. Both are the sons of men publicly identified as ritual experts, yet neither is the eldest son (who would be expected to assume the father's position) and no one so much as mentioned them as being versed in esoteric matters. It was not until each volunteered to tell me something of their secrets that I became aware of this other aspect of their identity. It then became evident that other men and women of knowledge, such as Aisaga, had always known what came as a surprise to me. I have chosen to discuss interviews with these two men because the descriptions they give of their practice illustrate in some detail the various components of specific procedures, the nature of the performance, and the subsequent effects upon the practitioner. Their rituals are more complicated and more perilous for the practitioner to undertake than those of the two dream diviners, and thus afford a point of comparison. Alex and Francis differ from each other in that one commands ostensibly productive, the other destructive, rites; each reveals a markedly different attitude toward his status. Alex finds himself, almost against his better judgement, placed in a position where he cannot escape the unwelcome burden that secret knowledge imposes, whereas Francis relishes his role.

Alex: A Reluctant Rain Magician

Alex has already been introduced (chapter 4). Son of the redoubtable George, he was heir to an important body of secret knowledge pertaining to rain, fish, and the *faifai* water spirits. Yet no one referred to him as a man of knowledge. Indeed, he was so nervous about the situation that he preferred to conceal how much he knew; his reasons will become clear shortly.

Alex assisted me in innumerable practical ways throughout my entire second fieldwork. He was not afraid to visit me, as so many of my old friends now were, nor did he hesitate to come and talk with Aisaga (which should have alerted me to the possibility he possessed ritual expertise). He was one of the very few people who cooperated in reporting his ongoing dreams. He took the initiative in introducing me to a famous man of knowledge, a distant agnatic relative from another community, and persuaded him to tell me the esoteric versions of some important myths. Alex also imparted in precise detail spells, medicines, and other information necessary to implement secret traditions referred to under the general heading of *kinapui* and *faifai,* which includes rites to bring rain, to stop rain and bring out the sun, to bring floods, to call fish up the river from the sea, to control the course of the river, to cure ailments caused by the water spirits (*faifai*), and to inflict such illnesses. This is not to say that Alex commanded all these rites, but that he was versed in this general area. He volunteered the information. He showed me the ritual implements required and identified the special plants and medicines used, often by bringing actual examples so I could see what they looked like freshly cut. On a later field trip in December and January 1981–82, he spent many hours taking my husband through the bush and identifying the ritual medicines and substances (*fu'a*).

Work experience in various parts of Papua New Guinea has given Alex an understanding of other cultures. He speaks Pidgin fluently and has a good basic grasp of English. My interviews with him were usually in English, except when I specifically asked him to recount dreams, myths, and similar material in Mekeo. It was undoubtedly easier for him than for most people to comprehend what kinds of information I was seeking and why. Nevertheless, his schooling was rudimentary and he is very much a man of his own culture. In his late forties when I interviewed him, he is not part of the new educated elite, and one should not overestimate his understanding of the wider world, intelligent as he is.

The material to be presented is drawn primarily from one interview lasting about five hours. Coming as it did in the midst of many discussions with Alex concerning dreams and other topics over several months, it was revealing in many ways and was typical of the guarded manner in which ritual knowledge was usually imparted. This was no casual, spur-of-the-moment revelation, it required careful planning. In order to tell me the spells, show me the powerful objects employed, and explain their use, Alex had to arrange several things. First he had to ensure that he was in a state of preparedness to handle the potent objects, and he had to ensure that his wife and children would not be endangered by them. This meant not sleeping with his wife for several days and making sure that the children were not present when the objects were exposed. He also had to have on hand certain leaves and medicines that might be required in case, despite his precautions, one of the family was accidently affected and would have to be cured. In addition, he needed to modify his own diet for a few days, including in it quantities of ginger and chili to fortify himself—to make his body "hot"—so that he would not succumb to the influence of the powerful forces with which he would be dealing. Having achieved all this, he needed to arrange a location and a time when we would not be disturbed by others.

The interview finally took place at his invitation at his house. He explained we could not talk at my place for fear Aisaga might overhear something. He was not concerned Aisaga might acquire the knowledge, because he believed he already had it. What he did not want Aisaga to discover was how much he, Alex, knew! Furthermore, Aisaga would not himself tell me these things, even though he knew them, Alex explained, because then he, Alex, might take revenge against one of Aisaga's sons or their families for revealing things rightfully his. These levels of subterfuge are typical. I was told to come in the morning; when I arrived, Alex was alone on his veranda. The children had gone to school and the older members of the family had left for the gardens. He explained his wife was visiting Port Moresby for a few days to sell betel nut and that he had been waiting for this opportunity to prepare himself. A few neighbors and their children were still dawdling around as we spoke. Alex waited patiently until all had departed for the day's work.

A Fish-Calling Ritual

Our discussions that day provided a clear and comprehensive outline of the elements comprising a particular ritual, one that is indicative of the general structure of all types of secret knowledge. The basic structure has been described briefly (see chapter 9). Here I wish to pursue in more detail the components of a specific ritual as described by the practitioner. This can be done without revealing the actual wording of the spells or precisely identifying the ritual medicines and objects.

The healing techniques implemented by Josephina and Janet involved the recitation of spells and the ritual use of certain plants, which are not consumed or ingested, to induce dreams wherein the dream-self of the patient is restored. Alex described a more complex procedure, involving several additional elements, to call fish from the sea so there would be many large fish for the village to eat. He explained that usually only small or inferior fish could be found in the river and swamps of the Mekeo plain, but with the correct rites one could call the big fish from the sea. Heavy rain was required to flood the area, then the fish could ascend the river and be washed into the creeks and swamps. Calling the fish involves separate procedures to bring rain and to influence the *faifai* water spirits; both rituals are counted as major types of secret knowledge. Alex learned the ritual by helping his father perform it shortly before the old man died: "My father was bringing the rain and calling the fish. And the fish

were *everywhere!* Everywhere there was fish. So I knew—you say the words
and you think it will not happen, but it *does* happen!''

My discussion with Alex was too lengthy to reproduce verbatim. I shall
briefly outline the steps Alex described and then discuss each component
separately. After explaining why he did not want to tell me these things at my
house, and again stressing the need for secrecy, Alex began by recounting a
myth (*isonioni*), the story of the first fish trap (*ogopu*). Briefly summarized, it
relates how a man made a fish trap and placed it in the water, but failed to
include various essential parts. Each night the trap climbs out of the water onto
the bank and dances and sings a song. The man spies on it, hears the song, and
thus learns some essential part is missing. He adds the missing part and waits
to see what happens. This is repeated several times until at last the trap is
complete. The man goes to the river in the morning and finds it full of fish.

Having finished his recital, and without giving any explanation of it, Alex
announced, ''Now I'll bring the things for you to see.'' These things were
contained in a metal box which he brought out from the interior of the house.
Among them were various small packets of unrecognizable dried substances
including the ritual ''medicines'' (*fu'a*) and the bones and scales of various
sea fish, which are used in the preparation of a charm used in the first stage
of the ritual. There was also a small oval container (*polo*) about four inches
long made out of a coconut shell, the mouth of which was stuffed with bark
cloth. The first step was to make the charm, which would be floated down the
river. Alex, demonstrating, took a few scraps of the bark cloth with the other
dried substances and put them on a coconut husk. This would then be taken
to the river, the charm set alight, and the whole floated downstream. It was,
according to Alex, a message to the fish; it floated down to the sea, inviting
them to come.

The next thing, Alex explained, is to summon the rain and floods. After
setting the coconut husk in the river, the practitioner returns to the house and
summons the presence of the myth people. To do this, he must know the special
names of these beings. He recites the list of names and then burns pieces of
bark cloth, circling the smoke in front of him to summon the spirits. When I
asked about the meaning of the names he recited, Alex replied:

''Those are the names of the old people—the old people who were with
A'aisa—so when you call their names, it's just like sacrifice, like when Father
[the Catholic priest] makes a sacrifice, he thinks of God, or people think about
A'aisa. So when you do something [perform a ritual] you remember those
people. You mention their names and remember them. And then you burn bark
cloth so they will come—like straight in the night to tell you in a dream, or
something like that.''

Having summoned these presences, you must, he said, bring out another
larger and much more powerful charm (*polo*). This consists of a mixture of
many medicines and powerful substances held in a large coconut shell container, or bamboo tube, or—as Alex had—a metal billy can which had the

advantage, he noted, that it did not rot like traditional receptacles. This combination of powerful medicines and substances, including the container itself, is usually referred to as a *polo* (which also is the word for "ball"). A long list of ingredients is required for this particular *polo,* and these ingredients may take many months to acquire. Only when the charm is complete and to hand can the ritual begin. Alex explained that, having burned bark cloth to summon the spirits, he makes a fire and places the *polo* near it. Then he must sit by the fire and sing the spells to call the fish. He begins with the song sung by the fish trap as it stood on the bank—the song incorporated in the myth. Then he must call all the names of the fish of the sea, and follow this with another spell entreating the fish to come to him. As he sits in front of the fire, singing the spells, the rain should begin to fall. This will be heavy rain, falling for several days and bringing floods. He must stay in front of the fire, singing the spells, for two or three days and nights and must not leave the house until the fish come up the river with the floods. The spells invite the fish to come to a great feast. Another small *polo,* similar to the large one, must be placed in the water at the location designated in the spell in order to draw the fish to the precise spot where the fish traps are set in readiness.

Once the large *polo* has been prepared, the whole ritual takes no more than two to three days, from the sending of the burning coconut husk down the river to the arrival of the fish with the floods. All the actions described are performed in private and in secret. It was not necessary, Alex said, to hide the singing of the spells from his wife and children, as they could not understand what he was singing (the spells are in a special language which appears to combine elements of different languages, including archaic elements),[1] but he never performed them in the open or in public view. He had to explain to his spouse that he would sleep by himself for several nights.

Set out in this manner as a summary of Alex's description of the actions he was taught by his father and performed under his direction, one has little sense of the experiential aspects of the performance or of any meaningful connection between its parts. Inevitably, a step-by-step account of how to implement the ritual, either reconstructed on the basis of an informant's verbal account, as here, or even a first-hand observation of the performance, is likely to convey little more. How are the practitioner's actions understood to influence the rain and the fish? Spells and substances are the means of attracting both, and spirit beings are also invoked. Here, it seems, is the magical power of the word and the attraction of like to like, or part to whole, that is so familiar from countless anthropological studies of magic beginning with Frazer's *The Golden Bough.* But the processes of thought involved are more subtle and complex than is usually recognized.

I now must go back over the components of the rite to draw out some of the implicit information contained there. Alex tells us he invokes certain spirits (he gives their names) at the beginning of the ritual. These spirits, he says, come bringing the rain, and rain should start to fall shortly after the invocation. Do Mekeo believe that certain spirits control the rain and thus can be influenced by a human agent? This is far too simple a reading. Mekeo do not rely on spirit beings to regulate or maintain the natural world. What then is the purpose of the invocation? This can be answered by looking more closely at what is involved. The summoning of spirit presences—referred to in general as *ipi iuma* ("to burn bark cloth")—is a crucial part of every major ritual of secret knowledge. The presences summoned vary according to the nature of the rite. Any person is said to be able to summon spirits of their own dead relatives if they have some physical relic such as hair, fingernail clippings, or clothing worn by the deceased. The dream healers Josephina and Janet claimed the assistance of dead relatives in their battles in the dream realm, but neither specified how she summoned them. The usual method is to burn a tiny fragment of some relic of the dead with a little bark cloth while calling their names. In the case of major rituals, other spirits as well as one's own dead relatives are invoked, according to the specific tradition of knowledge. Thus Alex's rain ritual involves spirits associated with rain and the sun, whereas a hunting rite would call on different spirits. Only those who possess a particular tradition of secret knowledge know the names of the spirits associated with it and are able to call them. It should not be thought, however, that these entities are in any sense gods or even nature spirits controlling the natural world. They are, as Alex explained above, "the old people who were with A'aisa"—the "myth people" (*isonioni papiau*).

In addition to A'aisa there are numerous other myth people, and they are all associated with the origins of specific traditions of secret knowledge. These beings are referred to as "people" (*papiau*) and are believed to have once inhabited the same natural world as that occupied by human beings; they are not the creators of this world, but rather beings who brought about changes or transformations in it. They did not create, nor do they maintain, the natural order of things; what they achieved was a means to impose their will or realize their desires in specific circumstances. In other words, the myth person was able to find a way to achieve what is now desired by the human practitioner.

This makes more comprehensible the often seemingly trivial nature of the myths, such as the story of the myth person who made the first fish trap and succeeded in catching many fish, which is the starting point for Alex's ritual. This myth person is not thought of as having some kind of controlling function with regard to fish, he is simply the originator of a successful means of catching them. Yet this is not to say that he is merely the historical founder of a technological discovery—not at all. Take another myth Alex referred to but did not disclose in full. It tells of an old woman who wanted to stop the rain falling but could find no way to achieve her end. Finally she tried to climb a tree, and her dog began to follow her. To discourage him she twisted his ear, and the dog howled loudly, whereupon the rain suddenly stopped. This recounts the origin of a ritual to stop the rain. The old woman and her dog and the man with the fish trap are not nature spirits, but people (*papiau*), although certainly people with abilities and powers beyond those of ordinary human beings. These people were responsible for mysterious transformations and extraordinary achievements. Thus I think it is appropriate to refer to them as heroes, not gods—human beings with special powers and knowledge now made available to present-day adepts via the rituals of secret knowledge.

When Alex says that the myth people "bring" the rain after he invokes their presence, he does not mean that they are supernatural agencies or powers responsible for the weather. They are the heroes who were first able to bring rain by using the techniques Alex is now implementing. They are representations of success and effectiveness in a particular task. The myths recount the exploits of the *isonioni papiau,* give their names, and incorporate their words in formulas and songs. It is perhaps true to say that these myth heroes provide a model for the adept, who shapes his words and actions according to the mythic pattern they established. But I am not referring to some mythic participatory mode of thought (e.g., Leenhardt 1979). In some sense the adept does identify himself with these mythic heroes, but it is not his *bodily* self and conscious awareness that is able to interact with them but, rather, his hidden self. When the adept summons these entities, as Alex points out, they come to him in a dream. He summons their *dream-images* to assist his *dream-self* in the task.

In addition to the myth people, Alex would also invoke the dream-self of his dead father, burning a little of his father's hair with the bark cloth. Having summoned these spirit beings, the adept should wait for a sign that they have arrived before proceeding. They may appear in a dream, as Alex noted; alternatively, the appearance of fireflies at night or a fly during the day may be taken as a sign of the presence of the summoned spirits. Then the adept continues with the ritual, confident that the spirits will be there to assist him. These spirits are experienced by the adept as powerful presences actually assisting not his bodily self, but his *hidden* self.

If the spirits do not bring the rain in any instrumental sense, but, rather, are associated with success in performing rain rituals and are experienced by the adept as powerful helpers, then the question still remains: how is the rain brought and the fish called? There are also, as noted earlier, spells to bring the fish which are sung following the spirit invocation and the placing of the *polo* (the container of medicines and powerful substances) near the fire. Alex stressed that the most important element of the ritual was the *polo*—it was this that brought the rain and the fish. Without it, nothing would happen. Just as the invocation of spirits (*ipi iuma*) is a crucial part of every major ritual, so is this repository of powerful substances. The substances contained in the *polo* vary according to the intent of the ritual, but the combination follows the same general principles. Alex listed twenty-two ingredients obtained from plants, animals, reptiles, and fish. They fell into three groups: those associated with rain, those associated with the *faifai* water spirits, and those associated with the fish to be called up river. The link of association between the substances and the intention of the ritual suggests the mistaken connections "like attracts like" and "part attracts whole" that are considered typical of "magical thought." The symbolic associations certainly are based on metaphor and metonym, but the nature of the connections involved are worth pursuing further.

The substances associated with the rain include the blood from several black animals and a vine stalk which, when crushed, releases much watery sap. Alex explained that the blood of black animals is used because the sky must become black with clouds before heavy rain can fall. The vine stalk, mentioned in the myth recounting how to bring rain, produces sap like rain and was used by the myth hero. None of these things, it should be added, are thought to be powerful or in any way effective alone; it is the combination of ingredients in the appropriate context that creates efficacy. The substances to attract the water spirits include the blood of reptiles and large fish, which are the bodily forms *faifai* are believed to take, and the dried flesh of a special swamp creature, believed to be a particularly powerful *faifai* spirit, that features in the myth of a widow who found water and fish to feed her children. Among the plant ingredients is a special vine that the widow in the myth employed as a rope to pull the fish out of a spring. The remaining substances are the blood, scales, or flesh of all the different fish and sea creatures summoned to come up the river.

The association of black animals with black clouds and of the watery sap of the vine with rain are simple instances of a perceived similarity, a metaphorical link. Underlying these links is the presumed efficacy of the bodily substance of an entity—human or animal or spirit being—as a vehicle for gaining influence over it. *Faga ofuga* (literally "body dirt") is the term used to describe these substances. They play a key role in all the traditions of secret knowledge. A clear instance is the summoning of the assistance of dead relatives. The dead once existed in the human world, where they left some physical remains to which they are believed to be attracted. For this reason, people who keep relics of the dead near them can expect to be bothered by spirit presences. The burning of small pieces of some physical relic of the dead, along with the bark cloth, is used to summon the spirit. I need to specify here an important distinction made in Mekeo but not in English: it is the hidden/dream-self (*lalauga*) of the spirit (*isage*) that is summoned.

The myth people and the water spirits also are believed to have left various kinds of physical remains in this world. They have been transformed or changed in various ways so that, unlike the relics of the dead, they are not immediately recognizable as such; special knowledge is required to identify and use them. The adept may employ them to summon the hidden/dream-selves (*lalauga*) of the myth people who, like the human dead, are attracted to their former physical remains. They take many forms and have varying degrees of effectiveness.

Certain objects are taken to be the actual bodily remains of a myth person or a *faifai* spirit, turned to stone; such are referred to as *kepo* ("stones"). Some substances are believed to be the blood or other bodily fluids in dried or only slightly changed form. In many instances, the heroes, or parts of their bodies, are revealed in the myths to be transformed into some natural species of bird, insect, reptile, animal, or even plant. In fact, when investigated, nearly all the ritual medicines (*fu'a*) turn out to be the transformed body substance of myth heroes. For example, the hero who established the ritual to bring rain dies at the end of the story, and his body is transformed into a tree or plant used as "medicines" to bring rain. The products of these transformations are considered much less powerful and dangerous than the physical remains of the hero's dead body.

In the case of a living human being, the same attraction between the hidden/dream-self and the physical body—or some substance abstracted from the body—operates. The hidden/dream-self may leave the body during sleep, but usually returns to it in the morning, only failing to do so if something is preventing its return. Thus by obtaining some substance that was formerly part of a person's body—blood, excreta, sweat, fingernail clippings, and the like—one is able to attract the hidden/dream-self of that person. Possession of the body dirt of a living person gives the adept the means to summon the hidden self of that person in the dream realm.

Alex's container of powerful substances primarily held the body dirt of *faifai* spirits and of the fish to be called up the river. It also contains the body dirt of black animals that represent the black rain clouds and of plants established by the myths as associated with rain, being either the transformed body substance of the myth heroes or the means they used to implement their rituals. That is to say, these powerful substances represent varying degrees of transformations of the bodily substance of, or the bodily substance of things associated with, the entities the adept is attempting to draw to him. The *polo* brings together the body dirt of the *faifai,* the myth people, the fish, and the rain (or of entities associated with each of these). This collection of various kinds of body dirt is intended to draw the hidden/dream-selves of all these entities to the hidden/dream-self of the adept. The "work," the "action" of the ritual, takes place in the dream world.

This is indicated in Alex's response to my question as to whether the adept dreams during the performance of the ritual:

"You are going to dream like, ah, you went to the gardens and you got many bananas or taros. Or you went and got [were given] lots of betel nut from somebody else. Or sometimes you'll dream about the canoes—oh, you will see many canoes coming up the river or many canoes were racing—if you see that you know the fish are coming."

He recalled that when he assisted his father, he did not dream himself, only his father did:

"The old man had a dream. But I was new [this was the first time he had assisted in the ritual] so I didn't know what it was. He told me that dream. He said, 'Oh, I saw many canoes were racing in the sea.' So I thought to myself, what's that? And he said, 'Maybe the fish are still coming. Maybe tomorrow or tonight they will reach the shore. Tomorrow the young girls will go in the morning to fetch water and see the fish coming.' And it was true!"

This dream of the racing canoes is directly linked to the spells that are sung to call the fish. They address the fish as people, telling them to bring all their relatives to the feast that is being held up river; they are told to paddle their canoes up the river, to paddle by day and paddle by night. Here the images conjured in the spell are visualized by the adept in his dream. The other dream-image Alex mentions, of taking food from the garden or taking betel nut, is a standardized dream symbol indicating success or good fortune in any enterprise. About two weeks prior to this, Alex came to tell me about two recent dreams and we asked Aisaga for his interpretation. One dream was about going to market to sell betel nut. Aisaga commented:

"The betel nut is the fish. They want to come but who will call them to come? The name of the fish is *maikua,* they come up the river from the sea. They are not coming now. Old George [Alex's father] used to call them. On rainy days like this he used to call them. Now rain is coming but this fish is not coming. The fish would come, but nobody is calling them. . . . When old George used to set a fish trap he would dream of betel nut and then in the morning he would go and find the trap was full of fish."

George and Aisaga were colleagues and friends; they shared many ritual secrets, including dreams. When induced in such a ritual context, the dream is not so much an omen of what might shortly happen as the adept's perception of actions achieved or completed in the dream realm.

To sum up, the link between part and whole, which operates in the notion of the effectiveness of a subject's body dirt as a means of influencing that subject, is not understood as a connection operating in the human world. The bodily substance of the fish does not attract the fish. It is the dream-selves/images of the fish that are drawn to the dream-self of the adept. In other words, the symbolic link of metonymy between fish blood and living fish is used to invoke dream imagery of fish. There is no mistaken connection between part and whole in the bodily world of waking reality, it operates only in the dream realm (here psychoanalysis would surely agree!). Once the dream-images of the fish are summoned, their bodily selves are believed bound to follow. The connection between the ritual substances and the fish coming up the river thus depends upon a much more complicated train of thought, underpinned by the idea that what takes place in the dream realm is later realized in bodily reality. One might say the adept does not reason falsely in relation to metaphorical connections operating in bodily reality; although perhaps he overvalues the influence of dream imagery on his waking existence.

Alex's *kinapui* procedures provide us with an example of three important elements absent or little stressed in the rituals described by the two dream healers: the myth associated with the ritual, the repository of powerful substances (*polo*), and the ritual preparation (*gope*). Not one of the many people I questioned could recall a myth associated with the origin of dream healing. The spells for it refer to the *faifai* water spirits, but no myth concerning *faifai* is told in relation to this rite. Nor is any repository of powerful substances used in dream healing; only a few (usually two) medicines are required. These medicines are believed to be the transformed body substance of a *faifai* spirit, hence their purpose is to summon dream images of the *faifai,* but these plant transformations are not considered to be very dangerous. Furthermore, no ritual preparation in the form of food restriction and sexual abstinence is necessary. The need for ritual preparation is related to the dangerousness of the medicines and other substances used. Just to take out and show me the *polo,* Alex had to prepare himself by avoiding sexual contact for a few days and making his body "hot."[2] If he were performing the ritual he would have to undergo more lengthy preparation. He does not have to segregate himself entirely from his family, as a yet more dangerous ritual might necessitate.

Unlike the repository of powerful substances, and the preparatory regimen, the myth is not essential to the performance. Yet it plays an important role in providing a context of meaning that links in narrative form the powerful beings associated with the rite, the words of the spells, and the nature of the powerful substances used. It provides a "master image," organizing and integrating all the imagery the practitioner seeks to induce.

The Dangers of Secret Knowledge

At this point, I wish to turn to other issues raised in the interview. I have characterized Alex as a reluctant rainmaker. Why should an apparently beneficent ritual, such as one ensuring a bountiful supply of fish for the community, create misgivings? Why is Alex reluctant to assume the role of ritual specialist?

In the first place, implementing rituals involves risk to his family, particularly his wife and children, and also to his neighbors. The *polo,* the container of powerful substances, is so potent that if it is not handled with great care it can affect all those who come into proximity. Since the bodily substances of the *faifai* spirits are contained in it, they are attracted there. Alex was taught the spells and medicines to cure *faifai*-caused illness in case of trouble, and the *polo* is stored in a special strong metal box hidden well out of the children's reach. Precautions were necessary, as he explained:

"You have to keep it the right way . . . in a special place, like that. I'm keeping it in a special box. Not to hurt us. So it won't hurt us. . . . The old man [his father] told me a spell to keep it away from us. . . . I hold the ginger and

I say the spell before I blow on the ginger and then I rub the [sick person's] skin. Say somebody's skin [flesh] is swollen up, then I blow on the ginger and rub it on his boil . . . and he will get better. When I do that I go and take the leaf [the medicine] and bring it and I dream. If I dream I have killed a snake [the form harmful *faifai* are believed to take], that means that thing [the *polo*] is hitting us.[3] If I dream I kill a pig or a wallaby or anything, I know that thing [the *faifai* spirit] has left us. But if I don't kill it, if I see any white man or an old woman, or an old man with a beard [all forms taken by *faifai* spirits], when I see those, I know the thing [*polo*] is getting us."

In this speech Alex reveals that he can perform healing rituals virtually identical to those of the two dream healers. The difference is Alex's own actions, which draw the *faifai* spirits close and thus make his family and neighbors sick. There is no such implication in the recounted experiences of Josephina or Janet. The physical person of a man of knowledge becomes infused with the *faifai* spirits' presence and is thus harmful to others. One ingredient in the *polo*—the key ingredient—is so powerful the practitioner has to fast for months before even attempting to obtain it. Alex stressed there was grave danger to his wife if he did not avoid sexual contact with her when he was handling the *polo*. She might fall sick with swelling and boils. If pregnant, the situation was even more grave; she would suffer severe, possibly fatal, complications in childbirth. Provided he observed the necessary *gope* restrictions, Alex said he was not concerned for his own safety. The risk was rather to his wife and children and others in close contact with him who were not protected.

What Alex was most anxious about on his own account was the likelihood of arousing the jealousy of other people. The two dream diviners mentioned their fears of being attacked by the men of sorrow should they disclose the identity of an assailant. But Alex's fears were much more acute. He was quite open about them:

"We want to call the fish. That's how we start. The old man [his father]—he told me how to do it while he was alive, and I have done it and it was right [i.e., the rituals worked]. But right now I'm a bit scared to do it [perform the ritual]. Because . . . ah . . . I'm still young yet and if I do it people will say, 'Oh, *he* is the man that is making magic to have rain or to call the fish.' So somebody might be jealous of me and *kill* me."

Alex was convinced others would have no hesitation in having him killed, either by *ugauga* sorcery or some physical means such as poison, should his activities arouse anger or jealousy. His fish-calling rituals bring floods which are likely to destroy gardens, ruining food and cash crops alike. On the occasion when Alex was taught the rituals, the flooding was so severe that everyone's gardens were destroyed, including his own, and there were no vegetables to eat for months. Shortly afterward old George died—a result, Alex believed, of community anger over the floods. Some people claimed that Aisaga, ostensibly the old man's friend, was responsible because the floods had destroyed a large crop of sweet potatoes his family had planted for a commercial contract. It was also rumored George had taught Aisaga all he knew, so now Aisaga was ready to get rid of him. This was the usual custom, Alex explained: if you teach someone outside your own close family, once they have acquired what they want they try to do away with you so as to be sole possessors of the knowledge. Alex was not, however, persuaded that Aisaga was responsible for his father's death; he suspected those who were spreading the rumors against Aisaga were themselves the real assailants. He claimed he had good reason to think this because his father told him, just before he died, that he had been poisoned. Someone crept in while the old man was asleep and rubbed poison on his mouth; he woke up, but not quickly enough to identify the culprit as he slunk off into the dark.

Alex exposes here a number of related fears: that the destructive effects of the floods will anger people and thus cause them to take action against him, that people will simply be jealous of him because he has powers they do not, that other men of knowledge, like Aisaga, desire to acquire his rituals and, if they succeed, will dispose of him. Alex's generalized fears are given a concrete focus in the death of his father. He was convinced his father died *because* of teaching him the rituals; people wanted the knowledge to die with George and not be passed on. Now, he believed, many people wanted to see *him* dead.

In the midst of all this unease concerning his ritual inheritance, Alex confessed that he still wondered whether his father had entrusted him with either the correct information or the full version of it. He did not pay his father before he died, as he should have, for the transfer of knowledge. Thus the old man may have withheld the final secrets. On the other hand, since he had implemented many of the rituals himself and they worked, he felt more or less reassured that he had effective command of them. Yet he was not absolutely sure; his narrative petered out into silence accompanied by a worried frown. As I listened to his vacillations and doubts, I was inclined to think him a rather weak, indecisive individual, unsuited to the responsible role of a major ritual expert. His suspicions of everyone—including his own father—seemed to border on paranoia. I felt a little impatient with him and thought that he was turning out to be a weak replacement for the formidable George. I now realize I was mistaken. What I took to be his personal fears and anxieties were recurring cultural themes associated with the transmission and acceptance of secret knowledge. Looking back, with hindsight, I must admire Alex for his honesty and even be grateful to him for trying to explain to me something that I understood only later: the sorrows of acquiring knowledge.

Although he was then in his late 40s, Alex insisted he was still too young to take on his father's ritual mantle:

"You see, we younger people [i.e., not of the most senior generation] are too frightened to do these things for fear of the jealousy of other people. So lots of younger people know these things but they won't do them when the old people are still alive. When they become old themselves, then they will do it."

If Alex survives into old age, he, too, will probably become a formidable adept (recall the earlier discussion of the significance of age to ritual power in respect to Josephina). Indeed, this is what he was trying to communicate to me.

Francis: Ulcer Infliction and Some Other Things about Dreams

Some time after the interview just described, Alex mentioned that his brother-in-law, Francis, had some things he wanted to tell about dreams but, like many other people, was reluctant to come to my house because of its proximity to Aisaga. I knew Francis from my first fieldwork; he was now in his late forties or fifties with a grown-up family. Several of his sons had received higher education and now occupied well-paying positions with the government and private industry in Port Moresby. I thought I knew him well, but I had no inkling he possessed any kind of esoteric knowledge. He had never even hinted at this, nor had I heard anyone refer to him as a man of knowledge. He seemed an ordinary, somewhat stolid person, not likely to have much to say about dreams or other esoteric matters. On Alex's suggestion, I called on him. He appeared delighted by the visit; we chatted for a while, then suddenly he announced: "Ah, yes! I wanted to tell you some history!" "History?" I enquired, a little doubtfully. "Yes, some history about how ulcer sorcery [*kua*] came down from our grandfathers and great-grandfathers, and I'll tell you the spells and the medicines, too."

Ulcer infliction! I was stunned. This is considered one of the most horrendous forms of disease infliction, causing terrible pain, disfigurement, the loss of a limb, and finally a grotesque, lingering death during which the victim's rotting flesh stinks so vilely that he or she is abandoned even by close relatives. I knew the ritual for ulcer infliction was the hereditary possession of Francis's family, that two generations ago his patrilineage broke away from the major founding clan of the village because of an internal quarrel over its use. I had no idea Francis possessed, let alone practiced, it. His father was a feared ulcer sorcerer, publicly acknowledged as a man of sorrow, and the leader of a brief outbreak in 1929 of the so-called Vailala Madness (Stephen 1974): He set up tall poles next to his descent group's meeting house, claiming to communicate with God via strings attached to them. I interviewed Francis about these happenings, and other people, during my early fieldwork. These events took place before Francis was born, and his father died only a few years later. In the absence of anything to the contrary, I assumed the father had died before passing on his ritual knowledge to his sons, neither of whom were identified as men of sorrow. Consequently, I did not know whether to be more astonished by Francis's open admission of such dangerous knowledge—or by the fact that he was volunteering to teach it to me!

He would not be ready for a few days, he said, instructing me to return on Saturday morning, when most people had gone to their gardens or to market. We met as arranged, but this time we did not sit talking at his house. He led the way to the meeting house. It was deserted, and no one approached us for the several hours we spent there. Normally, to meet there is to invite others to come and join you; Francis had instructed family and neighbors to leave us alone. He needed no prompting or persuading to describe in full the requirements of ulcer infliction. When he had done so, he moved on to the use of dreams in love ritual and for obtaining favors from others, and a range of other techniques.

One might assume that a technique as feared, even despised, as ulcer infliction would be a radical departure from the essentially positive activities discussed so far. Francis's account of ulcer infliction plainly indicates the underlying similarity with other major rituals—a similarity of structure already asserted, although not fully demonstrated, in chapter 9. His discussion further reveals the role of the adept's hidden self in the ritual action. I will take each point in turn. Although the *kua* rituals described by Francis are directed to entirely different ends from those of Alex's *kinapui* rituals, their basic components and structure are identical. They involve a) invoking the spirits by taking out their physical relics, burning bark cloth, and calling their names, b) the preparation and heating near the fire of a container of ritually powerful substances, c) the reciting of spells while the practitioner remains secluded by his fire, and d) a ritual regimen, which begins before the ritual is implemented and continues for some time afterward. The only essential differences lie in the precise nature of the medicines put in the container, the identity of the spirits summoned, the wording of the spells, and the severity of the restrictions the practitioner must observe.

The container of powerful substances (*polo*) for ulcer infliction contains four categories of ingredients: plants that scratch, pierce, or irritate the skin; animal species with sharp spines, sharp beaks, or sharp teeth that pierce and gnaw; filings of an axe, a knife, or pieces of broken glass; and some body substance of the intended victim. The container is made of a bulb of very hot ginger into which a hole is made and the other substances placed. It is prepared first, but before it is completed and put near the fire, the spirits must be summoned. Without their presence, Francis emphasized, nothing can be achieved. He must have relics of his dead relatives, such as their hair or nail clippings. He catches a firefly and a fly, putting them together with the relics, then sets alight a piece of bark cloth, which is circled around the relics while he calls upon the dead (*ipi iuma,* literally, ''burning bark cloth''). He explained the purpose of these actions (Francis speaks adequate, if rather clumsy, English and most of this discussion was in English):

''That is to get those [dead] people to come. You put them [the relics and the flies] there to one side. You keep them aside. Then you burn bark cloth and you call them—the [dead] people's names—to come and join you and to help you at that time. Tell them that that *polo* is ready. You have to call those [dead] people—to say the names—to come to help you make that person sick.''

Having summoned them, the adept must wait for a sign of the spirits' presence. Just as Alex described, this will take the form of a firefly or a fly circling close by or, alternatively, a dream omen. Francis continued:

''If you burn the bark cloth at night, you will see a firefly coming first, you will see the action coming, you will know that the [dead] person came now. But if you sleep you'll have a dream. You'll see the face of the [dead] person you called. Or in the daytime the blue fly will come to you. . . . You can't go out. You have to stay here. You have to wait for those [dead] people to come. . . . They will come to see what you need, to help you. . . .

''At that time you don't stay with your family. And you don't have any other person watching, you just stay by yourself. Like this—no people around. And when you start to turn the bark cloth around, the (dead) person will come to join you. . . .

''You make the fire and you sit there for three days, and after that I can go out. What time will it happen? But it *will* happen [i.e., the victim will get sick].''

These *kua* techniques are not linked to a particular myth, and unlike those of *kinapui,* neither the spirits summoned nor the powerful substances require a myth to identify them. Francis calls upon only the spirits of his own ancestors, not mythological heroes or beings, and the substances used in the *polo* have an obvious metaphorical connection to piercing and eating away the victim's flesh. In this respect, they are simpler than Alex's *kinapui* rituals, which require many different and difficult-to-obtain ingredients, as well as knowledge of the esoteric names of several myth people. On the other hand, *kua* ritual requires more stringent preparation and seclusion. It cannot be performed safely in one's domestic residence with the rest of the family present. Furthermore, to protect himself, the practitioner must undergo a rigorous *gope:* he may partake sparingly only of hot foods and liquids, he cannot wash in cold water, and he must observe the restrictions for at least several weeks before and after implementing the rite. Alex, in contrast, could operate in his own house with his family around him and he did not have to observe lengthy *gope,* although he did avoid any sexual contact for a few days and ate and drank ''hot'' things.

The knowledge of *kua* ritual includes techniques to cure ulcers. Francis recounted these as soon as he finished describing the means of inflicting them. The curing ritual involves summoning the spirits to his aid and reciting spells that reverse the destructive imagery of infliction. Powerful ''medicines'' are also employed; these are actually applied to the ulcer and are said to make it close over. The healing techniques also require the practitioner to observe dietary restrictions; should he eat meat, for instance, the ulcer will not heal.

During our interview, Francis evidenced his understanding of the ritual as something operating not externally on the physical world but upon the hidden realm of dream imagery. He told of how his bodily self remained in front of the fire, singing the spells, while his dream-self, in the company of the spirits, went to attack the victim. This he expressed rather clumsily, but unambiguously, in a mixture of English and Mekeo: "*Imaumu* [your body] is here but those [dead] people are getting your *lalauga* [dream-self] and your soul is going there with them." He is not necessarily consciously aware of the actions of his dream-self, yet he knows the attack on the victim is taking place. That is to say, he does not attempt to visualize it literally, but he will probably dream in symbolic form of the action of his dream-self. Once he receives a sign of the spirits' presence—be this a dream or a waking omen—he will begin to dream of the victim (whose body substance is included in the *polo* precisely for this purpose):

"A pig—when I dream of that, when I take the knife and cut the pig or spear it. I know it will be happening [the ritual has taken effect on the victim]. . . . That person you are making sick—you dream of a pig or a dog. That's *palapole* [disguised dream imagery]. Not killing them, but shooting or spearing them."

If he himself does not dream, which is often the case according to Francis, one of his relatives would. He would recognize this as a favorable sign, while letting on nothing to others:

"In your family, your people will let you know what they dreamed. They will say, 'Are you doing something? I dreamed this way.' 'Ah, no, I don't know'—you tell them lies!—'Nothing, I'm not doing anything.' When it happens, then they might know you were doing something. When the person gets sick and then worse."

When I asked what kind of dreams these might be, Francis replied that his dream-self might be seen carrying a bow and arrows or a spear near the house of the intended victim. Although the victim was unlikely to dream at this stage, his or her relatives might because the ancestral spirits would be trying to warn them of the impending danger. Such dreams would be reported to the victim, with advice to take special care (there are several examples in previous chapters). But provided the rituals were performed correctly, Francis assured me, the warning was of little use since action in the dream realm was already well underway.

Francis is informed in conscious awareness by omens or by his own symbolic dreams and those of others. He thus learns that the desired action has been implemented in the dream realm. When he dreams of piercing with a spear (a bullet, a knife, or an arrow) a domestic animal (a pig or a dog), he knows the ulcer (a hole in the flesh) has been inflicted on his victim—that is to say, the wound has been suffered by the victim's hidden self.

Each element of the *kua* ritual is directed to inducing and guiding the practitioner's inner imagery. The invoking of the spirits summons their dream-images, which then "take with them" the dream-self of the adept to attack the hidden aspect of the victim. The container of powerful substances, in addition to parts of plants and animals associated with scratching, piercing, and gnawing, also includes the filings from an axe or knife. At first I could not understand what Francis was saying when he spoke of the knife filings because, with his limited English, he said, ''you put in the *faga* of the knife,'' using the Mekeo word *faga,* which means ''skin, bodily substance.'' This underlines, as pointed out previously, that the powerful ''medicines'' constitute the bodily substance of things or entities whose dream-images are sought by the adept. The metal filings are intended to invoke the image of the victim cutting him- or herself to provide a site for the ulcer to develop; the body substance of the victim is included to conjure his or her hidden self. The *polo* the adept prepares can thus be understood as the means of creating or drawing together specific imagery in the dream realm. The words of the spells the adept sings by his fire reiterate in verbal form the same imagery of flesh, body, and organs being slowly consumed in various painful and ingenious ways.

There is no intrinsic difference between a presumably constructive, beneficent ritual such as dream healing and a destructive rite such as ulcer infliction. Both take place via the adept's dream-self in the dream realm. Both are potentially threatening to the practitioner, whose own dream-self may be injured or lost. When spirits and the myth heroes are encountered, the adept risks being attacked or injured by them. The intent (constructive or destructive) of the ritual is not what determines its risk.

The purpose of this rather tediously mechanical examination of each element of the rituals has been to establish as clearly as possible, on the basis of detailed ethnographic evidence, that they are intended, and explicitly understood by practitioners, as the means of shaping events in the dream realm. I have labored the point because it is easily obscured, or simply overlooked, when practitioners are asked to describe in abstract the operation of their rituals. The experiential context is crucial, yet because of the extreme privacy involved, there is little to observe. I had to rely primarily on people's statements about the effects of their rituals. One could not ask that rituals be implemented unless the outcome was actually desired. I could not insist Francis perform his *kua* rituals, not without designating a victim and being prepared to face the consequences of this action—including compensating Francis for the weeks or even months of privation he would have to undergo. Nor could I expect Alex to undertake his rituals, with all their serious consequences, just to satisfy my curiosity; nor could they be performed except at the appropriate time of the year. Merely to recite the incantations or to expose to view the powerful objects is considered dangerous, hence the precautions both Alex and Francis took when providing me with this information.

The Adept's Sense of Self

Surprisingly perhaps to an outsider, of the four ritual experts discussed so far, Francis has the most positive and least anxious attitude to his ritual role.

Ulcer infliction, however, is not his only forte. He told me of numerous other spells and charms, including a favorite technique for winning favors from influential people, to which he attributed his success in obtaining several government grants and subsidies for his various business ventures. As he talked on and on, enumerating with a kind of complaisant satisfaction his abilities to bend others to his will and to obtain what he wanted from them, I could not help but gain a sense of not exactly of revulsion, but of decided unease. Did this man really believe himself possessed of so many means to manipulate, control, and even destroy others? Clearly he did. Yet there was no ranting boastfulness, just a pleased, rather sly conspiratorial air. He was not merely trying to impress, which would have been understandable and thus not really offensive. What bothered me was the absolute confidence he exuded in his power—and right—to exercise his individual will at the expense of others. And he was including me in his secret, conspiratorial world, for he was not merely telling me about, but actually giving me, effective command of some of his most important secrets.

Listening to Francis gloat—the word is not too strong—about his powers, one might be inclined to suspect he suffered from some form of megalomania. In this respect he reminded me of Richard (chapter 9), whose endless boasting about his abilities did seem excessive. Indeed both men appeared to engage in prolonged fantasies of power to control others. Yet neither Francis nor Richard are deluded concerning their powers in the eyes of their own community—only when taken out of cultural context do their statements appear immoderate.

The four adepts I have described illustrate something of the varying perceptions of self that are developed by the man or woman of knowledge. Each emphasized in his or her own way the risks, the responsibilities, and the rewards of practicing their rituals. The risks are many and stem from the intrinsic danger of contacts with the powerful entities of the hidden world and from provoking the anger and jealousy of other people. Yet ritual knowledge also brings social respect and concrete rewards: payments for one's services, and the power to impose one's will on others.

Some are overcome by their encounters in the hidden world, like Janet, who was terrified of being seized and destroyed by the *faifai* spirits. Since the rituals aim to conjure powerful interior imagery one might suspect that already troubled persons would be unable to face the imagery generated by their ritual practice. Strength and courage are necessary to deal with the hidden world. Some, like Alex, are more bothered by the social consequences of the role. Ordinary people resent those who have major ritual knowledge. Experts regard each other as rivals, and to share the knowledge empowers others and thus diminishes oneself. Adepts guard their secrets jealously, and many will not hesitate to kill off a competitor. Alex also pointed to a significant difference between his position and that of the dream healers: whereas the latter are paid by their clients, and usually receive comparatively small payments, the *kinapui* expert operates at the behest of the men of kindness, who must reward him handsomely for his services. The exercise of all major rituals affecting the community as a whole is, in principle, under the control of the men of kindness, who should ensure they are employed only in the interests of the public good.

Whereas a weak or timorous person may be unable to face these perils, a strong, assertive person knows that secret knowledge is the means of fostering an even greater sense of inner power. The calmly confident Josephina and the almost smugly boastful Francis exude this inner forcefulness. How powerful the hidden self becomes through ritual practice depends upon the extent of the adept's knowledge and the nature of it. No one described so far observes continual isolation from the rest of the community. Josephina and Janet, the two dream diviners, move in and out of the hidden realm at will. They do not observe *gope* restrictions, as do the male adepts; they are not required to isolate themselves from their children, spouses, or family, nor are they held responsible for causing damage to others as a result of their rituals. They are not dealing with the most potent substances or spirits, yet their dealings with the other realm are by no means weak or passive. Alex and Francis are individuals who might in their old age become real men of knowledge. Now they live in a normal domestic situation, only occasionally segregating themselves as required to deal with the hidden world. Different adepts have varying capacities. Only a few become so threatening to others that they must largely withdraw from normal social interaction.

The accounts of these four adepts reveal the nature of secret knowledge, its experiential aspects, the burdens attached to it, the special sense of inner forcefulness it confers, and its variations and degrees. Yet none of these men and women of knowledge exemplifies, or dramatizes, its many aspects as does Aisaga, the man of sorrow. To present my encounters with Aisaga in isolation, without placing him within a broader cultural matrix and the spectrum of personal and private experience examined here, would distort equally the representativeness of his role and his personal uniqueness (Wikan 1990:243–244; Keesing 1987). The role of the man of sorrow, as I shall argue in the following chapters, represents the consequences of secret knowledge pushed to the extreme. In my dealings with Aisaga, I was continuously thrown off balance by what I discovered, yet had I paid closer attention to what I was told by Josephina, Alex, Francis, and others, I might have anticipated the direction they would take.

12

Observing a Man of Knowledge: Aisaga

A sequence of disturbing dreams followed my interview with Francis on ulcer sorcery. I woke in the morning unable to shake off nightmare images of rotting flesh and the nauseating odor of decay. I decided to ask Aisaga about them. His invariable response to questions about dreams was to ask about mine, but often I could not recall any. This time I was a little apprehensive because one seemed to depict *his* death. Nevertheless, I plucked up my courage and went over to Aisaga's house, where as usual he sat alone on his veranda. I told him I had been bothered all night by frightening dreams. One, I admitted, seemed to depict his death. In the dream (replicating the waking events of that and every other morning) I found him sitting on his veranda. I greeted him but he made no response, so I tapped him on the shoulder. To my horror, his flesh began to fall off his body and he became a rotting corpse. Aisaga responded to this grisly imagery with a dismissive smile. The dream was not about him dying, Aisaga reassured me. If one dreams of the death of an important man such as himself it means someone will kill a large pig; the dream was in fact a favorable omen. I persisted, however, in describing the recurring visions of decaying flesh and the overpowering stench that permeated several dreams throughout the night. Suddenly his dismissive expression changed; he asked sharply, "Did Francis teach you about ulcer sorcery when you went to see him yesterday?"

Aisaga always kept an eye on my whereabouts and he knew I had visited Francis the previous day; I never told him what other people disclosed, nor, of course, did I repeat my discussions with him to anyone else. Had I betrayed these confidences, soon everyone would have avoided me. I had inadvertently alerted Aisaga to what had transpired the day before. Although I previously had no inkling of Francis's esoteric prowess, it was now obvious Aisaga was fully informed on this score. Subsequently I discovered he possessed the very same rituals; he knew from his own experience the gruesome images conjured by the powerful substances and the spells used for ulcer infliction—and the horrible smell of the victim's rotting flesh. In his view, my nightmares had been caused by the spells I wrote down, and the *polo* (the container of powerful substances) he assumed I was shown. As a result, my hidden self was driven out of my body, encountering frightening images in the dream world. Aisaga observed that since I had awoken feeling nauseated from the smell of decay, perhaps my hidden self had suffered damage, in which case I would get seriously ill. We would simply have to wait and see what transpired. His disapproving manner implied that I had acted foolishly in undertaking such risks; it would be up to him to cure me if I had done real damage. Fortunately for me, there were no subsequent incidents he could point to as resulting from my exposure to the *kua* rituals.

Aisaga was the only person who asked, or even suggested, that I share my dream experiences. Other people might refuse to discuss their dreams, deny recalling any, or agree to discuss the topic only in very general terms, but none, not even those people who reported their recent dreaming, asked me to recount my own dreams (although some asked whether I, and other Europeans, did in fact dream). This is indicative of the position Aisaga assumed in relation to everyone. He was always in control of the situation. He assumed prior knowledge of whatever was taking place, and responsibility for the outcome. Of the several men and women in the village who possessed important ritual knowledge, he was by far the best known, the most feared, and the most respected. He has already figured extensively in this account, and is by now a familiar figure. In this and the next two chapters, I will examine at closer range his role as exemplifying the most powerful ritual expert found in Mekeo culture.[1]

The circumstances leading to Aisaga's assumption of the role of a man of sorrow (*ugauga auga*) were outlined earlier (chapter 9). Strictly speaking, he does not represent the man of sorrow in his most dangerous ritual state (which is sustained for only a limited period) but rather an intermediate state, wherein he has continuous contact with the realm of spirit forces but is not entirely removed from human society. Aisaga referred to himself more often as a man of knowledge (*ikifa auga*)—a title which gives a better idea of his various capacities.

During my first period of fieldwork, he lived away from the village and I had little opportunity to observe his activities. There were then two other acknowledged men of sorrow in the community, Augustine and Opu (chapter 3), both elderly widowers living alone in small *gove* on the outskirts of the village. Augustine was in his seventies and arthritic. Opu was believed to be dying as a result of not obeying the *gope* restrictions while performing *ugauga* sorcery. I assumed, therefore, that their inactivity and isolation was due primarily to physical incapacity and old age, yet whenever I talked with them they were alert and sharp-minded. Sitting in solitude day after day with apparently nothing to do, they conveyed not an impression of aimless inactivity but rather of controlled, watchful aloofness. I often wondered what passed through their minds, I found it difficult to understand why the whole community regarded these two apparently harmless, indeed physically feeble old men as figures of menace. Aisaga was neither sick nor physically incapacitated, yet he conducted himself in much the same manner. He was virtually isolated from the rest of society, even his own immediate family (chapter 4). His small widower's house (*gove*) was hidden away at the back of the village, its garden merging into the surrounding bush. Rather incongruously, it seemed to me, the front of it was painted a brilliant shade of electric blue, and showy red poinsettia bushes grew along the front fence. I was intrigued by these apparently frivolous embellishments, just as I was by the many flowers and decorative plants in his garden, and put them down to personal idiosyncrasy. In this, as in so many things having to do with esoteric matters, I was way off the track.

It would be easy to assume, as I had of Opu and Augustine, that Aisaga eked out a dismal, uneventful existence, partly because of increasing age and partly because of the social constraints imposed on those identified as men of sorrow. Gradually, I began to perceive something of what passed behind the aloof mask Aisaga presented to the world and of the many vital concerns filling his apparently empty hours and days.

The Daily Concerns of a Man of Sorrow

The circumstances of our dialogue and the context of ordinary daily activities within which it took place can be conveyed more directly in the following entries from my field diary which recount events over a few days approximately five weeks after my arrival. I do not, of course, include all the day's happenings, but only those which relate in some way to Aisaga and his dealings with hidden things.

November 30, 1980

Aisaga had two visitors this evening apart from myself. First, one of his teenage grandsons came to have a sore eye treated. The usual procedure followed: Aisaga muttered a spell under his breath, blew into a cup of water, and gave it to the boy, who drank it and then left. This started Aisaga on an explanation of another powerful *ikupu* (a ritual technique usually used to protect property) of the same kind as the rituals for bleeding he revealed a few days ago—one employed to cause and to cure blindness. It was, he stressed, a highly valued secret known only to his family line in this village and that if anyone outside his family wanted to learn it they would have to make a huge payment in riches and money in order to obtain it. It was also highly dangerous to those who possessed it. He recalled that his paternal grandfather's wife went blind, and so did the wife of the now deceased man of sorrow, Opu, who was Aisaga's junior agnate; this was because both his grandfather and Opu had not taken sufficient care to protect their wives and families while using the rites. Like the bleeding *ikupu,* this rite was used primarily to protect crops and property. The adept prepared a potion which was painted on his betel nut trees or other property, then when the thief came in contact with it, he or she would become blind. The blindness could be cured by the appropriate healing spell, but the sufferer had to pay handsomely for the cure.

The technique can be used to cause blindness to any person he wished to punish for some reason, Aisaga said. His second son, who lived in town, asked Aisaga to use it on the vegetables planted in his garden to protect them from being stolen by neighbors, but one of his own children became affected. Aisaga then had to be called upon to heal the child's eyes and remove the *ikupu* before it caused more harm to the family. The user had to take great care, Aisaga explained, not to touch the potion with his hands or to let it fall on his skin; he himself used a long feather to paint it on the place where the victim would be sure to touch it. Yet despite his care over the years, he added, his own eyes had been affected and he was now having difficulty seeing in the evening and at night. (Incipient cataracts are in fact visible in Aisaga's eyes.)

Following this discussion, and warning, he did tell me the ingredients of the potion used to cause blindness, but firmly declined to tell either the spell to inflict blindness or the spell to cure it.

As we sat talking, a truck from Port Moresby drew up and a boy got off. The young man, a bachelor (*o'oae*) in his late teens or early twenties who was a member of Aisaga's lineage and his classificatory grandson, came over to us. He talked to Aisaga briefly, handing him a small bottle, which proved to be a bottle of trade-store scent. Aisaga nodded with approval and the boy left. It turned out he had asked Aisaga for a love charm to get a girl friend; Aisaga promised to help if during his next trip to town he bought a bottle of scent and gave it to him. Since the boy had done as he asked, Aisaga explained he would use some of the scent to prepare a love charm and keep the rest to use in other potions. This young man had a slight disfigurement in that one side of his face was partly paralyzed; he thus perhaps had special need for ritual assistance in finding a partner. (When I asked Aisaga about this disfigurement, he attributed it to the effect of another kind of *ikupu,* similar to those used to inflict bleeding and blindness; the boy had stolen someone's crops and thus had been affected.)

In the past, young men were very keen to obtain love charms as that was the only way they could get brides, but now with money so freely available, Aisaga observed with some disgust, boys could easily buy girls' favors with money! This, however, was not the only young man who sought love magic from Aisaga. He provided his own sons with charms, he admitted, but since they were married and he did not want them involved in troublesome adulterous liaisons within the community, he only allowed them to use such charms when they visited the town or other places. Tomorrow he would gather various magical medicines (*fu'a*) and crush them up with the scent to make the required potion. This the young man would surreptitiously wipe on the hands or clothes of his partner at a dance, causing the girl to dream of him and thus to fall in love with him. When I asked about the ingredients, Aisaga replied that it was dark and he could not show them to me now, but that he would in the morning when he made the charm.

December 1

Today Aisaga actually volunteered to tell two important love spells, and described the medicines he would use to make the love charm for the boy who visited yesterday. He also told a curing spell for *faifai*-caused illnesses and described the medicinal potion to be drunk by the patient. But there was no mention of the spells for blindness.

December 2

I was determined to ask about the blindness spells this morning but I picked a bad time. Aisaga was clearly not in a good mood; he was reluctant to talk and seemed preoccupied, almost morose. When I reminded him he had told me the medicines but not the spells for the blindness rituals, he warned me very sharply that I must never make this information public, as it was the special property of his family line, and known only to them. He then said it was impossible to tell the blindness infliction spell now because he had already eaten this morning and if he said the spell its influence would enter his body and harm him. He could only say the spell when he had not eaten and his stomach was closed (*kaisapua*). Finally, after all these warnings and objections, he did tell the curing spell.

Thinking that my request for the spell had angered him, I asked him outright whether he was annoyed with me for some reason. He then began to complain that because he was the only old person who knew *ugauga* sorcery left alive in the village, every death was blamed on him. He explained he had a visitor yesterday, whom I did not see, a man from the clan of the recently dead woman, Ruth (her death is described in chapter 4). The visitor informed him that a rumor was going around the village that Aisaga had caused her death. Aisaga was clearly annoyed and upset by this information.

December 3

I found Aisaga still in a bad mood this morning so I did not stay long talking. About 11 A.M. visitors arrived from across the river to discuss with him the installation of the man of kindness being held this Sunday.

Late in the afternoon I was typing up my fieldnotes inside my house when Aisaga came to the door. He was apologetic for disturbing me, but there had been a serious accident. Henry, his daughter's husband, had fallen from a coconut palm in the gardens and had lain there several hours before anyone found him. People were now trying to find a truck to get Henry to hospital, but none were available; could I go in my utility? We set off together at once. The injured man had by now been carried to his garden house, and this was where we found him. He was fully conscious, and although evidently in some pain, was able to converse with the relatives and neighbors who had gone to his aid. Aisaga swiftly took charge, instructing the women to prepare food for the patient and prepare hot water with which to wash him. Then he examined all the limbs of the injured man and pulled all of his joints, including the fingers of each hand and the toes of each foot; meanwhile, he muttered spells and blew on all the joints and on places where the patient indicated pain. From what I could tell, there were no broken bones, but Henry had fallen on his hip, and it was very painful and probably dislocated. After examining him and bespelling him, Aisaga spoke with his son-in-law for a while. I suggested Henry should be taken to hospital without further delay, but everyone said that he must be fed and washed first, then they would take him. Henry himself seemed to be less anxious than when we arrived, and somewhat soothed by the attentions given him. As it began to get dark, people finally decided it was time to take him to the mission hospital. We returned to the village, where later that night the word was brought that Henry was being sent to Port Moresby for X-rays and treatment.

I wondered what interpretation Aisaga would put on Henry's accident. As we drove back to the village, he remarked Henry had told him he had a warning of the accident in a dream last night but had ignored it. Thus, when he went to climb the tree the next day, he had felt heavy and clumsy, and fell. Aisaga, I noticed, never seemed to jump to conclusions about sorcery or other destructive rituals as the cause of illness or misadventure. In fact, his first consideration, since he was always in the position of having to handle the situation, was to determine the nature of the symptom—what hurt, and where, what part or organ of the body was malfunctioning or damaged—then he selected a treatment to deal with the pain or damage. If the patient had sore eyes, he said spells and gave potions intended to remove the redness and inflammation and take away the pain. If the patient was hemorrhaging he said spells and gave medicines to stop the flow of blood. Yet the patient never heard the spells, nor knew the contents of the medicines he or she was given to drink.

December 4

A chance remark today gave me a new slant on the man of sorrow's dilemma. A few days ago I gave Aisaga a spare air mattress because he had been complaining about his uncomfortable bed. When I asked him about it this morning he said it was no improvement because it would not sit firmly on his bed. I suggested he should put it directly on the floor and then it would be perfectly stable. That was no use, he replied, no man of sorrow could sleep directly on the floor for fear of being speared through the floor boards at night. Men of sorrow such as himself placed sheets of corrugated iron under where they slept and made beds of solid planks to guard against being speared or knifed while they slept. I was most struck by this, since ordinary people often talk about the danger of men of sorrow spearing them or stabbing them through the floor boards at night, yet as far as I have observed, they place their sleeping mats directly on the floor, without any of the precautions Aisaga described. Certainly I had always done so myself, and no one had ever commented on this or warned me to act otherwise.

December 5

The presence of the spirits of the dead can sometimes be indicated by distinctive smells and perfumes, Aisaga noted this evening. (I was asking him about the strong odor possessed by many of the plants he used as ritual medicines.) The smell of hospital disinfectant always alerted him to the presence of the spirits of his deceased daughter and her husband, both of whom had died in hospital. When he smelled this, he knew that Thomas, their young son, would get sick, so he would formally invoke the spirits and ask them to leave the child alone. And he would also tell the little boy not to think about his parents because this made them come to him.

My daily contact with Aisaga, as reflected in these brief extracts from my diary during the early weeks of fieldwork, afforded the opportunity to observe closely his activities. The most frequent ritual activity he undertook was healing. Scarcely a day passed when he was not called upon to deal with some illness or injury. The very day I arrived in the village, an adolescent boy from a neighboring community was being treated for a *faifai*-caused illness. Aisaga told me to go and talk to the boy about his illness; he let the boy himself explain in English so I would understand better what was going on. The patient seemed relaxed and calm, in fact not at all ill. He told me he had been there a few days and that Aisaga had given him medicines to drink and said spells over him, and now he was feeling better. He had bad pains in his abdomen, he said, which were caused by a *faifai* python. Aisaga had seen the python in his dreams, the boy explained, so it was certain a *faifai* spirit was causing the trouble. Over the next several weeks, I saw Aisaga treat both serious and minor cases, including hemorrhaging following childbirth, a dislocated hip, severe diarrhea, fevers, headaches, and sore eyes. Yet in all of these instances there was no public performance or dramatization of his role as healer; in many cases Aisaga did not even have direct contact with his patients, but simply sent them bespelled potions via an intermediary.

Healing was not the only beneficent ritual action he undertook. He performed gardening rituals for his family and descent group and hunting rituals to ensure a good supply of game; on request, he prepared love charms for the young men of his lineage and charms to win at cards for his sons. He could, others assured me, secure the village rugby team's success—if they paid for his services—by employing rituals formerly used in warfare! He commanded such a wide range of ritual knowledge that there was scarcely any activity in which he could not offer success, or provide help and protection.

In addition to the many rituals he performed for the benefit of his family, his lineage, and other members of the community, he acted as an adviser in several capacities. He carefully watched over the activities of his immediate family, counseling them in everything, and although they did not always relish his advice, they always turned to him when trouble arose. As senior member of his lineage, he also advised on the affairs of his descent group, despite the fact his eldest son was now the official lineage head and responsibility for public action fell to him. Aisaga refrained from appearing at the ceremonies of other descent groups held in his village. He was, however, invited to officiate at the installation of a new man of kindness in another village. In short, he was called upon to function as an expert in all fields of traditional knowledge, etiquette, and ritual. Whether it was a matter of a bad dream, a child's stomachache, the need for a charm to ward off spirit presences, the installation of a new man of kindness, important deliberations over marriage payments, or an imminent death, Aisaga had to be ready to deal with the situation. His counsel, and ritual intervention if necessary, would certainly be sought.

It was in this context of ordinary happenings that Aisaga began to impart some of his ritual knowledge. What he told me usually emerged out of a practical situation. It was characteristic of his methods that he rarely revealed all elements of a ritual at once. He would usually begin by identifying the medicines (*fu'a*), or by telling the myth if there was one associated with the rite. Only later would he give the spells (*mega*), and he was always more reluctant to divulge the negative spells than the positive ones (as shown in regard to the blindness *ikupu*). When I asked other people, such as Alex, about this reluctance and seeming hesitation to disclose the full information, they replied this was how the old people always passed on their knowledge. It was done gradually, bit by bit, and one could never be sure whether one had or had not been told everything. Aisaga drew my attention to the fact that when he requested his sons or grandsons to collect medicines for him, he always saw to it that they did not learn the correct combinations; he asked one to bring this medicine, another to bring that one, and made sure he himself collected the key components. Younger people, like Alex, impressed on me that I had to keep asking for information if I wanted to learn about esoteric things. If I gave up, or was satisfied just with what I was told, I would not get far. I must keep badgering them (*fo pagaga*), so I was told. It was difficult to know where to draw the line between offensive insistence and an appropriate determination.

Often Aisaga would remark with exasperation, "You keep pestering me [*lo pagaga alogaina*], so now I have told you!" His tone of voice would seemed to imply, "Let the blame be on you then."

Aisaga often deliberately deceived me. This was something I found particularly disconcerting; my own cultural assumptions intervened to distort my perceptions of what was entailed in the transmission of secret knowledge. I expected guidance and trust, whereas Aisaga would tell me one thing one day, and then with total unconcern tell me a few days later that what he had previously said was false. He would assure me at length that the particular spell, myth, or whatever it was I wanted to know was not part of his repertoire and that he would tell me if he knew it. Subsequently he would reveal the very item he professed not to know. When I challenged him on this, he would simply reply, "Yes, I didn't want to tell you that, but now I have told you." There was no regret or embarrassment at being caught, as I might have expected; his tone of voice and manner emphasized his benevolence in now deciding to give me something he would have preferred to keep for himself.

There was nothing exceptional in Aisaga's actions, it was simply the old people's method of transferring secret knowledge, so Alex and others reassured me. The directness with which both Alex and Francis had explained their rituals was exceptional in this respect. They were both familiar with European ways, spoke English, and had some understanding of my reasons for collecting this information. But Aisaga was one of "the old people," and as far as he was concerned, the only reason to acquire secret knowledge was to put it to use. At every turn he impressed upon me the danger of what he was imparting, both to myself and to others. Although Aisaga allowed me as close an access to him as anyone in his family, he always kept the upper hand—with me as with everyone else—by never revealing more than he chose to, often diverting and confusing me by deliberate dissimulation and disguise when he deemed it necessary. I was forced to be ever alert and suspicious, which was perhaps part of his intent.

Emerging here is a theme already emphasized by other ritual experts: the dangers of being a man of knowledge. Alex, for example, attributed the death of his father to other people's jealousy of his ritual knowledge, and now he feared for his own life. Aisaga, on the other hand, conveyed an air of absolute calm and control—but he was evidently careful to take appropriate precautions to protect himself against the many hazards he encountered in his role.

Almost every day throughout this fieldwork, I was able to observe some ritual action Aisaga was called upon to perform for others. Yet there was no public enactment or dramatization of his role (except for the installation feast, which is described in the next chapter). The veranda of his small bachelor's house was center stage; there were never many actors, nor much action to observe, nor usually any audience apart from myself. Even in the case of a healing rite the patient was rarely present. The actions Aisaga performed, the spells he recited, and the substances he manipulated were not revealed to others, indeed were deliberately kept concealed. There were many aspects of Aisaga to observe and many facets to be revealed. The more devious, shadowy side, which at first was not apparent to me—although clearly prefigured in his constant deception with respect to imparting ritual knowledge—began to emerge only later.

His Interaction with the Spirit World

All Aisaga's ritual activities, regardless of whether he is healing someone or preparing a dangerous *ikupu* to inflict blindness or hemorrhaging, connect him in some way with the disembodied world of spirit beings. Indeed, his seemingly empty hours are pervaded by an intense interaction with it. Dreaming or awake, he is continuously alert to subtle signs and influences which give him awareness of happenings in that other realm.

The rituals of secret knowledge are intended to bring about changes in the disembodied world which subsequently influence happenings in the embodied world. The task to be achieved, whatever its nature, is implemented in the disembodied realm through the action of the adept's hidden self, aided by the spirits. (In some cases the nature of the contact with spirit entities may be somewhat different, as in divination.)[2] Thus the majority of rituals are believed to bring the adept into direct contact with the spirits, via the medium of his or her hidden self—a situation fraught with potential danger. This much has been shown in the accounts of even minor adepts. Aisaga clarified another important point: the practitioner's hidden self does not easily or safely leave the body at will to accompany the spirits, as one might perhaps assume on the basis of statements given by minor adepts in previous chapters. On the contrary, it is driven or forced out (*papealaisa*). The spells used to summon the spirits, the objects, and the medicines, which are the spirits' physical substance transformed in various ways, bring about a violent separation of the adept's bodily and hidden selves. The more potent the spirit entities invoked, and the more intensely charged with their physical substance are the objects and medicines used, the greater the impact on the adept's hidden self—and the greater the risk to the bodily self, since the hidden self may not be strong enough to withstand direct contact with the spirit presences. It was for this reason Aisaga was concerned about the nightmares I reported after interviewing Francis on ulcer infliction. My hidden self had been jolted out by my exposure to the *kua* rituals, as evidenced by the gruesome dream imagery, and it was likely these destructive images would now affect my bodily self, instead of that of the victim toward whom the rite was directed.

The nature of the spirit entities invoked, and the potency of the substances and relics used to attract their presence, determine the intensity and duration of the adept's engagement with the hidden world. For example, a gardening ritual which involves summoning the presence of Lagama Papie, one of the myth people, is attributed with great efficacy and is as dangerous to perform as many forms of destructive ritual. Aisaga possessed some of the most powerful (and therefore potentially most dangerous to the practitioner) forms for virtually every area of ritual competence. Every time he performed a ritual, he knew he was sending his hidden self out into the disembodied world.

That this was not simply a matter of belief, but an experiential reality, is indicated in many ways. As one would expect, dreams provide a key source of insight into the activities of the adept's other self. Of the dreams Aisaga discussed with me, he attributed most to the influence of recent rituals. A dream of killing visitors from the coast, for example, he interpreted as an indication of the success of his hunting charms; the dream-images of killing people represented the successful actions of his dream-self in killing game animals. Other instances he interpreted as the consequence of revealing spells to me. Likewise, he interpreted many of my dreams as the result not of actually using a particular ritual, but merely writing down or recording a spell (as I found with the nightmares that followed my instruction in the ulcer rituals). There was nothing remarkable in such dreams, from Aisaga's point of view, since it was precisely the function of the spell and powerful substances to drive out the dream-self of whomever was exposed to them, adept and victim alike. A few of his own dreams he interpreted as unsolicited omens—messages from the spirit realm not deliberately induced by ritual performance—very much as did laypersons such as Celestina or Maria. Aisaga's dreams incorporated similar themes and motifs, and were interpreted along the same lines, as those of laypersons.

Dreaming is a commonplace activity for Aisaga, and for other adepts. In contrast, laypersons such as Celestina or Maria experience their dreams with a quality of wonderment—a quality they indicate in their manner of reporting and in the fact they can recall significant examples occurring years before. In Aisaga's case, there is such a constant moving back and forth between the two realms—that of waking and dreaming—that "significant" dreams, revealing matters of life and death, have no novelty for him; they occur all the time. Yet this is not to suggest he exists in a state of mental confusion somewhere between these two "realities." His is a very pragmatic view; he is concerned with the ways in which the hidden world influences the concerns of the living, and not in the hidden world per se. He has no interest in spinning elaborate dream narratives; his dream reports usually consisted of a single, simple motif from which he extracted a specific meaning. He focuses his awareness upon the hidden world because he wants conscious knowledge of what will eventuate in bodily reality. As a man of knowledge it is his responsibility to know what is likely to happen, and thus what should be done to manage events in waking reality. He maintains a lucid awareness of himself as a thinking, knowing embodied self—an embodied self trained to be aware of and to guide the actions of that other self.

Aisaga's contacts with the spirit realm are not limited to dreams, but take place through several modalities. His waking hours are permeated with an awareness of the other realm. In fact, for a man of knowledge such as Aisaga, almost everything that surrounds him in the physical world is imbued with special significance that links him with the myth hero A'aisa, the many other myth people, and the spirits of his ancestors and the dead.

The little garden of colorful plants surrounding his widower's house (*gove*), which he originally told me was just "for decoration," was, as I might have guessed, a rich herbarium furnishing most of the ingredients of his medicines and potions. Each plant and tree is the transformed body substance of some myth hero, each with its own myth and associated rite. An enormous black butterfly with trailing, frilled wings floats past as we talk; this, he notes, is the beautiful widow clad in black, and the swarm of brightly colored smaller butterflies pursuing her are the unmarried youths who desire her. Those who know can use her to make a love charm. For the man of knowledge, almost everything he encounters has some special use. On a short walk through the bush we might see the vine the old woman in the myths used to pull out fish from the first river and the tree that furnished the firewood in which little A'aisa, the myth hero, was found by the old woman Epuke—the same tree that became A'aisa's canoe when he stole the women. A handsome stag fern was once a woman from whom Amue, the dog, stole fire; another plant is a "medicine" to make dogs fierce for hunting. Further on we come across a plant with dark red leaves, which grew from the blood of a myth hero, and a tree with fruits shaped like breasts, which was once a beautiful maiden; both plants can be used to ensure success in love. Birds, animals, insects, reptiles—any natural species, any significant feature of the landscape—all are woven into a richly figured mythological tapestry for the man or woman of knowledge. Aisaga has a seemingly endless fund of myths and ritual uses for what he finds at hand in the natural world. Everything takes on a secret significance, a potential to realize his will. Of course, many people know some of these things; what distinguishes a man like Aisaga is the depth and extent of his knowledge.

Signs and omens of various sorts, such as the cries of certain birds, the appearance of bats, cicadas, and various other creatures referred to as the "messengers of A'aisa," bring warnings to the man of knowledge. Aisaga observed that the presence of spirits of the dead might be sensed in the appearance of flies or fireflies (as was discussed in the previous chapter). Even the internal sensations of Aisaga's own body—a ringing in the ears, the throbbing of blood in particular veins, sneezes!—he attends to as signs that can be read to reveal future events. A poisonous taipan snake emerging out of the bush he acknowledged as the presence of the myth hero A'aisa. When a large python came one evening to my back fence to take a fowl, Aisaga recognized it to be a *faifai* spirit drawn to my house by a powerful charm he had given me. It was Aisaga who had to deal with these intrusions from the other world.

After the squawking of the terrified fowls aroused the whole household and his sons went out with lamps and shotguns, Aisaga calmly motioned them aside and told them to stand back. He walked up to the python that hung from the branch of a tree, a blood-soaked fowl in its coils, its pewter eyes glittering coldly at us, and addressed the fearsome creature courteously. He asked it to take its prey and leave peacefully or else he would be obliged to kill it. To destroy such a creature thoughtlessly would bring sickness on the family or neighbors. Snakes are not necessarily spirits, but spirits may take the form of snakes. The hidden forms of the spirit realm may become visible in apparently natural entities; it is up to the man of knowledge to discern which is which—and deal with them accordingly.

In waking hours, particular scents or smells might reveal the presence of the spirits of the dead. Aisaga explained that just as one can tell the presence of a living person by their smell, so spirits can be detected in the same way, even when they cannot be seen. He often heard the muttered voices of spirits near his house and the rapping sounds they made inside the house at night. He did not, however, mention seeing visions of spirits during his waking hours; when I asked about this he replied he had occasionally in the past seen processions of spirits coming up from the river toward the village—the spirits of those killed by crocodiles—but that he no longer saw them. The crocodiles, prized by European hunters, had disappeared from the river many years ago. Often, though, he glimpses shadowy forms around his house at night. He has an intimate sense of the continuous presence of the spirits around him. Frequently at night I would hear Aisaga's voice from inside his house formally addressing the spirits of his forefathers (*isage e pamagogo*).

It is not only that he sends out his hidden self to participate in the disembodied realm and is ever attentive to a host of omens, signs, and other more subtle indications of events there, the spirits are close to him whether or not he is actually engaged in some ritual performance. The relics of the dead and of other powerful nonhuman spirits that he keeps near him ensure this. Aisaga possesses bones, teeth, and other physical remains of dead agnatic relatives, and many stones and ritually powerful substances believed to be the transformed bodily substance of the myth people. These relics are necessary for the performance of his various rituals, but even without any intentional activation they are considered highly potent, and their presence will attract spirits. For this reason the spirits come to him in the form of snakes or fireflies, or reveal themselves in muttering voices, unidentifiable smells, and rapping on the floors and walls.

In order to withstand the dangers of this continuous intimate contact with the influences of the hidden world, Aisaga is never able to totally relax his *gope* restrictions, unlike lesser practitioners, who abandon the *gope* restrictions once their ritual task is accomplished. I found almost every adept gave a somewhat different account of *gope*. In Aisaga's case I was able to observe his actual practice. He explained the regimen varied according to the rituals he was performing. Now only a modified version was necessary of the rigorous restrictions he observed when, in the years following his wife's death, he lived outside the village as a practicing man of sorrow. The rituals of *ugauga,* he said, required the practitioner to eat each day no more than one or two plantains heated over a fire with grated ginger or chili to make them "hot." One could drink only hot liquids, and as little as possible, and one could not bathe or wash at all during the most rigorous form of *gope.* Chewing betel nut was avoided because it produced liquid in the mouth, and all sexual contact was avoided because of the fluids produced by one's own body and by one's partner. One also had to avoid consuming or coming into contact with all cold, wet things. The intention was to reduce the moisture of one's body, rendering it light, dry, and "hot," and also the flesh, leaving little more than bone (*unia mai'ini*). Since he had observed a rigorous *gope* for many years, he was used to it, he said; he now ate some meat and chewed betel nut, and he did wash, but only in hot water, and he continued to live alone as a celibate widower. The most important aspect of the *gope,* he stressed, was to avoid all cold, watery foods and substances, to eat and drink sparingly, and to eat only hot things. He did not starve himself but he carefully observed this modified regimen, and his tall frame remained spare and fleshless.

Ordinary people, who did not observe the *gope* restrictions, had, Aisaga said, heavy, cold, watery bodies that were vulnerable to the potent heat (*isapu*) possessed by spirit entities. When a living person came into contact with a spirit entity, or with the body substances employed by the adept to summon its presence, he or she was exposed to its "heat."[3] If the *gope* restrictions were observed, a person's body was hot and dry and thus able to withstand this heat without suffering serious injury (although, as I have noted, the contact is sufficient to bring about a separation of the two selves). But in the case of someone unprepared, the heavy, moist, vulnerable flesh would be violently struck (*e auga*) by the powerful heat, and the hidden self would be jolted out of the body in fear and confusion, subsequently resulting in sickness or even death for the physical body.

When I asked Aisaga, as I had asked Josephina, Alex, and other lesser practitioners, about the dangerous forces he encountered in the disembodied world, he replied: "Why should I be afraid? I always take care to observe the *gope* restrictions." Those too careless or too weak to observe the appropriate regimen could expect to meet with disaster, but for one as long practiced and accustomed to self-control as Aisaga, the denizens of the spirit world were almost familiar companions, in whose company he spent as much time as he did with the living. The closeness of his relationship with the spirits is indicated in the following reply to my questions about what he did when he addressed the spirits at night alone in his house:

"I say the names of my fathers and grandfathers, and A'aisa's name, and the names of his people—Oipau, Kalokau, Ofaofa, Aisamo, Kopamo—those people. Our custom is you put some meat or food in a plate so at night they can eat it. Now the spirits take the dream-image (*lalauga*) of that food and when people dream, they give them that food and they eat it. Then they get sick. When I want to do sorcery (*ugauga*) I put food in a plate and I tell the spirits, 'Eat some and take the rest and give it to that person to eat.' Then that person dreams that I or the spirits of my grandfathers came and gave him food to eat, and that he ate it. Then he knows he will get sick. . . . If I was making sorcery no one would eat with me, because I would be sharing my food with the spirits.''

Of course no one did eat with him, except me. Yet recall that even the timid dream diviner Janet put out food for the spirits who aided her. Aisaga's intimacy with the spirits is not so much different from minor adepts in kind, as it is in degree. His interaction is continuous, his isolation from society more complete, and the potency of the spirits and their physical substance, to which Aisaga is constantly exposed, are much greater than those dealt with by lesser adepts. Although Aisaga did not express fear on his own account, he had to take cognizance of the effects on his family. It was for this reason he never encouraged his married sons or their wives and small children to spend time with him, and he never visited their family residence. At first I assumed his reluctance to tell me destructive spells and show me dangerous relics, which he said was on account of the danger to his family, was merely a trumped-up excuse. But I learned from experience he had to take responsibility for every sickness, minor or major, suffered by his sons, their wives, and children.

Aisaga is not only a man of sorrow—the one who undertakes the most intense and the most dangerous encounters with the spirit realm—he is also the *oldest* man so identified in his community. Age confers a special aura on the ritual expert, as in the case of the venerable Josephina. Middle-aged and young people speak with respect, deference, and above all, fear when they refer to the ''old people.'' The expression *au apaoi* includes the ancestors. When Aisaga, who is a member of the oldest living generation, refers to the *au apaoi,* he means the people of the generation senior to him, who are now dead. He is the closest to them. Most of his own generation, as well, are now dead. He often reported seeing and speaking with his deceased friends in his dreams; they, along with the spirits he so frequently summons, are those with whom he now spends most of his time, so little social contact does he usually have with the living. He knows more than any younger person, he has the most complete version of the secret traditions, and he uses that superior knowledge to hold the advantage over others. Only the dead know more than he—and, in any case, they are his constant companions.

It was, Aisaga confessed, the aim of the man of sorrow to become as much like the dead as possible. For this reason one reduced one's flesh until it was as dry, as light, and as hard as the spirits' remains of bone and stone. One did not wash so that one's body would come to smell as bad as the dead, thus attracting them to one. Fasting also had the effect of making one's physical body weak and feeble, like the dying. The physical frailty of old Augustine and Opu, which had seemed to me so incongruous with the community's fears of them, now emerge in a rather different light. Their appearance was a clear demonstration of their affinity with the denizens of the spirit realm—and of their capacity to interact with these powers. In fact, according to Aisaga, the man of sorrow deliberately feigns physical feebleness and age in public, limping around hunched over with a stick, yet under cover of darkness he moves about swiftly and vigorously. Like the myth hero A'aisa, whom he emulates, the man of sorrow always deceives people; he can disguise himself, and he has spells and potions to make himself invisible while attacking his victims (many techniques involve some direct contact with the victim).

Aisaga was adept at changing his appearance. I have seen him with almost white straggling hair, dressed carelessly in old faded clothes, sitting hunched up, his face crumpled, his eyes unfocused—to all appearance a withered little old man. At other times, he would dress carefully in black, his hair tied back in a widower's snood, emphasizing the stony planes of his face, his back held ramrod straight, his eyes commanding—his whole presence forceful, intimidating. When he visited town with me, another persona emerged: his now black hair was carefully combed into an apparently luxuriant mass, handsomely framing a smoothly composed face, a jaunty scarf encircled the neck, and he sported new clothes. Tall, straight, walking vigorously, he appeared twenty years younger than he had in the village. When I commented on these transformations, his reply was that this was how the man of sorrow, like A'aisa, deceived people. People who did not know him well often failed to recognize him in these different guises, or so he claimed. He gave an example of an occasion when he still lived away from the village. People from a different village came to ask him to treat a woman who was seriously ill from snakebite; when they arrived they found Aisaga working in the garden and took him for someone else. He told them to wait there, returned to his house, changed his clothes, and then sat awaiting the visitors while one of his sons went to fetch them. When they were ushered into the presence of the forbidding man of sorrow, they had no idea this was the nondescript worker they had encountered earlier. Perhaps I looked unimpressed by this anecdote, so he reminded me of the time many years previously when my husband and I had visited him at the same place (chapter 3); both of us failed to recognize him when we came across him mending a fence, until he spoke to us and announced himself. As always, Aisaga was right.

13

Learning "Sorcery" Unawares

In Mekeo society, everyday events are interwoven with imaginal products such as dreams, visions, omens and divination. The general description of Aisaga's engagement with the hidden world offered in the previous chapter fails to give an appreciation of this state of affairs. The two areas intertwine in a fashion that is disconcerting to Western rationalistic modes of under-standing. A Western observer might object that, given the idea that dreams are indications of the actions of one's hidden self in the disembodied world, any dream is an experiential confirmation of the belief system as a whole, and that, furthermore, the methods of dream interpretation allow the interpreter to find whatever meaning suits the situation. Indeed, Aisaga might have been enter-taining himself by making up stories to fool me. Placed in the context of actual events, however, seemingly ephemeral fragments of fantasy weave into an experientially powerful and convincing fabric.

Instead of providing further isolated instances, I will take up the narra-tive thread of happenings (begun in chapter 4) that included Aisaga's offici-ating at the installation of a new man of kindness in early December. The circumstances of this important social occasion and of subsequent events revealed many things, including more sinister facets of Aisaga's role and the complexity of his awareness of different levels of self. This narrative will also reveal my own increasing entanglement in the interweaving of fantasy and event.

My intention is not to dwell upon my own experience, but from this point onward my involvement is crucial to what I learned about Aisaga's personal role and about the role of the man of sorrow as a cultural construct. In this and the next chapter I deal with the uncomfortable task of facing my part in events that I did not fully understand at the time. The consequences of this I perceive only now, as I retrace the pattern of events, and it is not pleasant to have to face my lack of foresight. Even in the "new ethnography," I think, the ethnographer is expected to take the stance of an almost omniscient observer—a narrator of boundless sensitivity, foresight, and wisdom. For me, "reflexivity" requires recognition of my own ignorance and confusion at so many points (cf. Favret-Saada 1980). I was merely an actor in these events, not the director or some *deus ex machina* looking down from Olympian heights. How little I knew about the concealed aspects of events will become painfully evident in the following pages.

The community in which the installation of the new man of kindness was to take place was only a short distance across the river, but several miles by road. The senior members of the descent group holding the feast were linked by several ties of friendship and marriage to Aisaga's family; it was with them Aisaga had sought refuge when forced to leave his own community two or three years before. They had invited Aisaga to play a key role as "supervisor" of the men of sorrow who would attend and witness the installation. The grand public feasts held on these occasions have been described elsewhere (Hau'ofa 1981; Seligman 1910; Stephen 1974), and the details of the public performance are not of concern here. The climactic point of the ceremony is the official presentation to the new man of kindness of his insignia of office: a special lime pot and stick, a special string bag and, most important of all, the knife with which he must ritually cut up the skin of a pig which is distributed to the guests. The role of the men of sorrow is to observe that everything is performed according to the appropriate procedure. Any mistake, especially in the distribution of pork and food to the guests (a most complicated matter that is determined by the relative status and seniority of the guests and their respective relationships to the hosts) can result in the death of the man of kindness or his close relative via rituals implemented by the men of sorrow.

It was Aisaga's role to watch all with a hawklike eye, and to direct the other men of sorrow to do likewise. Important male guests were received at the clan meeting house of the hosts; other platforms had been specially constructed for female visitors and children. Aisaga spent the day at the meeting house, presiding over events, while a deputation of half-a-dozen men of sorrow, dressed in their forbidding black widowers' weeds, their faces painted with black, stood silently at the sidelines on the periphery of the village—watching. Only late in the evening were they invited to enter the back of the meeting house and receive their shares of food and meat. As usual on any public appearance, Aisaga was very carefully dressed all in black, his hair wrapped in a widower's snood, in the manner of the myth hero A'aisa. He had also painted his face, which I had never seen him do before, blacking out his broad receding forehead in a manner that accentuated in a fearsome manner the skull-like appearance of his face.

The public, visible role Aisaga played as adviser at the feast had another, concealed side to it. I was alerted to this before the ceremony. Aisaga explained that at such ceremonies the men of knowledge engage in a covert contest of ritual power (see also Hau'ofa 1981). For this purpose they carry on their persons potent charms intended to harm whoever comes in close proximity. Ordinary people stand well away, and are careful not to sit near the men of sorrow and other important elders. The men (no women of knowledge engage in these activities) carrying these potentially lethal "weapons" undertake a period of rigorous *gope* to protect themselves from the influence of their own charms and those being carried by others. The test is to see who will be overcome by whose powers. The charms are carried in the small bags in which people usually put their betel nut, lime pot, and other personal paraphernalia. When the men of knowledge are seated at the clan meeting house, each carefully places his bag next to the bag of his neighbor to counter the forces emanating from it.[1] They wait to see who, over the long day, will succumb. Should a man be forced to leave the meeting house because he feels ill or faint, or should he collapse on the spot, he will have obviously been bested; alternatively, he might be taken ill shortly after the feast. In any case he would know who had struck him down. Ordinary people, even though they do their best to maintain their distance, might suffer illness or injury from some inadvertent contact with the dangerous charms; moreover, since they are not ritually prepared through the *gope* regimen, they are much more easily overcome.

The competing men of sorrow, Aisaga explained, aim to injure both rivals and ordinary people. The reason for injuring the latter was simple: people affected by a man of sorrow's powers would have to pay him to be cured. This was in fact a way to make money. By attending feasts in other villages, a man of sorrow can make people sick, then they come to him to be cured. These people would be unrelated, so the adept was not concerned about hurting them and was glad to take their valuables or money in payment. I was taken aback by this admission and his smiling, almost sly manner. Although I had been told years before about the contest of ritual powers between important men, never before had I heard of illness and injury being inflicted on innocent bystanders merely to make money! That was what all men of sorrow did, Aisaga assured me with apparent satisfaction.[2]

Aisaga confided that he would be taking "something" powerful to the feast, since it was essential for his own protection—without it he would have no defense against the other men of sorrow who would be trying to best him. Then he asked what I would do. I replied, mendaciously, that I would take my own charm. If I admitted I had nothing, or asked for a charm from him, he might simply refuse my request and insist that I keep well away from him during the ceremony. Since I had never witnessed the installation of a man of kindness before—such expensive ceremonies were rare events—I did not want to give up the chance to observe at close range Aisaga's part in it. Perhaps he thought it would teach me a lesson if I got sick as a result of coming in contact with his and others' powers. In any case, he accepted my assurances and raised no further objections. (It is evident that while I accuse Aisaga of tricking and deceiving me, I have little compunction in lying to him!)

The ceremony went well, as far as I could judge. Aisaga played his public role with great aplomb. He seemed in exceptionally fine spirits the next day. His manner was always so controlled and dignified that subtle variations in his usual inscrutability gave evidence of his moods. He revealed so little, it kept me constantly on guard. This time, however, his satisfaction in the events of the previous day was apparent in his enumeration of the joints of meat (which were being divided up at the clan meeting house as he spoke) presented to his descent group in his name, and in his comments on the organization of the feast and the part he played in it.

After discussing various aspects of the ceremony, Aisaga remarked that Philo, the wife of his third son, who had recently given birth to a baby girl, was frightened by a spirit (*isage*) while we were at the feast. She had gone into the bush behind the houses to relieve herself when she was startled by an old man dressed as a widower. She did not get a good look at him as he quickly covered his face with his hand and disappeared. Hearing Philo's screams, a young unmarried man, a member of Aisaga's lineage, ran to her aid, whereupon a taipan snake came out of the bush after him. He threw a bottle at it to scare it away. Neither the young man nor Philo had been physically harmed in the incident, but the spirit sighting had affected Philo, who was still in the vulnerable *megomego* state following childbirth,[3] and she was now ill.

No one was quite sure what Philo had encountered; there were, Aisaga pointed out, several possibilities. It might have been a human being, perhaps a man of sorrow from some other village, or a spirit of some kind. On the other hand, he said, it could even be his own hidden self. It was possible his hidden self stayed to look after the place while his bodily self attended the feast; men of sorrow, he remarked, could do this. On the other hand, it was also possible that she had seen the spirit of her own dead father (himself a redoubtable man of knowledge), come to tell her of the death of a relative that took place that day. The most likely possibility, he considered, was that she had encountered A'aisa, the mythic hero. Her description of the apparition—a widower with a big mop of hair, light skin, and of medium to short stature—suggested it was indeed A'aisa. Moreover, when he brought out the potent charm to take to the feast in the morning, Aisaga said he had invoked the presence of his forefathers and of A'aisa and the other myth people. Being summoned, A'aisa had come looking for us, but we had left quickly in the truck so he could not find us. The snake that came out of the bush when the young man went to Philo's assistance (the *augama*, a deadly poisonous snake) was A'aisa himself. Snakes always appeared when one took out these dangerous charms, Aisaga said, and reminded me that on the way to the feast a large *augama* had in fact come out of the bush and crossed the road just in front of our truck. (While these highly venomous snakes are said to be plentiful in the region, I rarely saw them, and their appearance in the village or on the highway was not common.)

It was not until later that I discovered the precise nature of the potent charm referred to here, but in order to appreciate the fit between Aisaga's interpretations and subsequent events, more information concerning it is needed. I was now observing in action, although I did not realize it, *ugauga* sorcery. The powerful "thing" Aisaga took to the feast was a container of dangerous substances, medicines, and relics called a *polo,* and was essentially similar in nature to those used for rain magic and for ulcer infliction (chapter 11). This was the *polo* used for *ugauga* sorcery; it was intended to summon A'aisa's presence and the presence of other angry spirits, invoking images of harm and sickness. It was highly charged with "heat" (*isapu*), which is said to strike or pierce the body of victims, driving out the hidden self, whereupon the angered spirits can attack it. This particular container is simply a smaller and weaker version of the *polo* used to kill a specific victim. Its intention is to make people sick indiscriminately, rather than inflict fatal illness on a designated victim.

The presence of the myth hero A'aisa, the most powerful of all the myth heroes and the originator of *ugauga,* is ensured when either *polo* is used, since both contain his transformed bodily substance and that of his son, Isapini. A'aisa appears as a widower, or as a person in mourning (according to the myth, A'aisa is in mourning for the death of his son), the usual state also of the human man of sorrow. A'aisa not only originated *ugauga* sorcery, he sent his henchmen to teach human beings how to use it. According to the myths, *ugauga* was first taught by Muki (cicada), one of A'aisa's messengers, to the people of Bebeo village and was used to cause death by snakebite. A young man was bitten by *afi* (death adder) and a young girl by *augama* (taipan); then Muki taught the people how to cure snakebite by bespelling the victims and giving them medicines. *Ugauga* sorcery always brings death by snakebite or by internal illness. The spirits invoked, including A'aisa himself, may take the visible form of a snake and attack the victim, or may invisibly inflict the victim with some fatal illness. Whereas pythons are always associated with the *faifai* water spirits, venomous snakes, in particular the deadly *augama* and *afi,* are associated with A'aisa and the spirits of the dead. As Aisaga pointed out, the *augama* snakes that appeared the morning of the feast were the visible presence of A'aisa, as was Philo's vision of the widower. From Aisaga's perspective, these were not random events.

In the evening I heard Aisaga singing softly to himself on his veranda. When I went to eat with him, as I usually did, I asked what he had been singing. He confided these songs were the spells used to call the spirits to make people sick. He said he could sing them softly because no one else knew what they were or what they meant. I could not understand a word, but I was to hear them often enough to learn to recognize them. I did not, however, understand their significance at that time. These spells "to make people sick" were in fact the spells used for *ugauga* sorcery. What he was doing was calling on the spirits, urging them to continue to attack any persons who had fallen victim to his powers the previous day.

Aisaga's intent, to score a number of victims, had been indicated in a seemingly unimportant detail of his appearance on the day of the feast: his painted face. Although I had observed other men of sorrow with distinctive facial painting at public events in the past, I had never seen Aisaga paint his face before. When I first asked why, he said it was to make him look impressive, to frighten people. With the whole of his broad forehead blackened, he did indeed look fearsome. Later he confided the real reason was so he would be identified in the diviner's dreams when people were trying to identify the man of sorrow responsible for causing their sickness. Since many attended the feast, the one responsible would have to be determined by divination (*feuapi*—the form of ritual undertaken by Josephina and Janet). He wanted to make sure the diviners would know who it was when his face appeared in their dreams, so he marked it to make it stand out from the rest.

This admission left me flabbergasted. Dream diviners, like Josephina and Janet, express the greatest fear of incurring the wrath of the men of sorrow should they identify them. When I put this to Aisaga, he dismissed it as merely "talk"; the man of sorrow *wanted* to be identified because he wanted to be paid for the cure. Men of sorrow not only painted their faces when they went to public gatherings, they made sure their dwellings were distinctive in some way so that the diviner, in her dream search for the place where the dream-self of the victim was imprisoned, would recognize immediately to whom it belonged. Had I not noticed his own house was painted a brilliant blue and that he had planted bright red poinsettia along the front fence? This was to make certain the dream diviners would recognize his house in their dreams. I had naively assumed these decorations to be mere whimsy on his part, although I had asked if the red bushes were used in medicines or for other purposes. He had replied nonchalantly that they were introduced plants, brought by Europeans, and had no mythic significance—making no mention of any other use they might serve. A minor point, one might think, yet typical of the way in which I was always left wondering what lay behind Aisaga's latest disclosure.

My impression remains that the dream diviners are genuinely afraid to identify men of sorrow. If this were not so, one would have to suspect complicity between the men of sorrow and the diviners, and there was never any evidence or suggestion of this. What is particularly remarkable is Aisaga's explicit understanding of the possibility of deliberately creating associations in order to influence the diviner's dream imagery. His subtle awareness of different levels of being—the embodied and the disembodied dream realm—become apparent here. He is concerned with the power inherent in the realm of imagery, recognizing that it shapes, and can be shaped by, actions in the embodied world. He is highly sensitive to the existence of his own hidden self, the significance of its actions, and the possibility of guiding them. When his bodily self goes to the feast, his hidden self may remain behind to guard the place. While his bodily self officiates at the feast, his hidden self is in the company of angered spirits that attack any person who comes in proximity to the lethal charm. The next night, as he sits alone on his veranda, he sings spells to send out his hidden self and to urge the spirits to continue their attacks on those who fell victim at the feast. Meanwhile he waits to be identified in the dreams of the diviners.

Were there any victims on the day of the feast (December 7)? And what of the covert play of powers between the assembled men of knowledge? I was keen to hear what Aisaga had to say. (In what follows, the reader must keep in mind that these events took place during the first six weeks of my fieldwork in 1980, when I did not have the information and understanding I now possess in hindsight.) Philo, Aisaga's daughter-in-law, was evidently one victim. Her unfortunate encounter was unintended, but none the less confirmation in Aisaga's view of the potency of his rituals, regardless of whether what she saw was his own hidden self or that of A'aisa, the myth hero. I suspected there was at least one other incident that might be attributed to the lethal *polo* Aisaga carried to the feast.

When we arrived at the meeting house of the descent group installing the new man of kindness, Aisaga arranged that I, from whom he did not fear harm, was seated to one side of him, while I was seated next to a man of sorrow from another village whom I had met previously. He was the senior living member of the most famed lineage of *ugauga* sorcery in the entire Mekeo region. While acknowledging his illustrious forebears, Aisaga was rather contemptuous of this man, who, he pointed out, claimed to be a man of sorrow, yet his heavy frame and pot belly indicated he observed no more than a token *gope* regimen. Aisaga instructed me to place the bag I carried next to that of my neighbor and watch what transpired. I noticed Aisaga positioned his bag away from me. I followed his example, keeping watch on the man next to me. After a while, perspiration started to bead my neighbor's upper lip, and as the day wore on, sweat began to drip down his face. He looked increasingly uncomfortable, rubbing his forehead frequently and shifting his position. In this hot, humid climate there is nothing remarkable in a man sweating, but when I glanced at Aisaga and the others, no one else gave indication of being distressed by the heat. Nor was I experiencing any unusual discomfort. I wondered if my neighbor's fidgeting had been noticed, but the faces around me were the composed masks Mekeo assume in public.

None of this, of course, had escaped Aisaga. When I raised the topic the next day, he pointed out my unfortunate neighbor had risen abruptly and left as quickly as he could the moment the climatic part of the ceremony, the handing of the knife to the new man of kindness, was over. This man had been promising to visit me to talk about the rituals of secret knowledge, but Aisaga assured me he would not come now, as he would be too frightened—unless he came to be cured! Who had bested whom, I wanted to know; was it Aisaga's *polo* or what I took with me? He gave no direct answer to this, but merely said, "You won and he lost." Inadvertently, by my very presence, I had become part of the contest. Of course, what my presence among the men of knowledge asserted, as I did not fully appreciate at the time, was that I possessed powers at least equal to theirs. How Aisaga interpreted the situation I am not certain, but I am inclined to think, on the basis of later developments, he judged his own rituals to have bested his rival, while my "powers" served mainly to protect me from harm.

Several months later I encountered another man at a feast in a different village whom I had met first at the installation ceremony. He said he had wanted to visit me for a long time, but did not dare. Surprised, I asked why. He replied that when I shook his hand after being introduced to him, I made him sick; he had taken my "power" (*isapu*) and now he wanted me to heal him. By this time, I was becoming accustomed to such occurrences, although they always discomforted me. How ironic to think back to the man of sorrow who, several years before, held out his hand to me saying, "I can kill you if I wanted just by taking your hand" (chapter 3). Now the situation was reversed. Like Lévi-Strauss's (1972a) reluctant sorcerer, I was acquiring "powers" that were effective *despite* my own lack of faith. I might also have reflected on Lévi-Strauss's (1972b) notion of the "effectiveness" of symbols. By associating myself with a well-known and feared man of sorrow such as Aisaga, on an occasion when roles of power were being acted out in public, I had linked my image with his much in the same way as he created distinctive dream-images of himself by painting his face and decorating his house. I was not fully aware of what I was doing, but undoubtedly, as I realize now, these actions were giving shape to my hidden/dream-self in the imaginations of others.

Aisaga, of course, always knew what he was doing. I cannot be sure of all his reasons, but in retrospect it is clear that this was a turning point in the transference of secret knowledge. Up until then, although he had given me much important information, including the spells, myths, and medicines used for a wide range of purposes, he had not revealed any of the secrets of *ugauga* sorcery. He claimed he had destroyed all his *ugauga* materials some time ago because of sickness suffered by several members of his family. Consequently, I did not realize the "powerful thing" he took to the feast was the *polo* used for *ugauga* sorcery. Once again, he had deliberately misled me. In fact, he had not destroyed the paraphernalia for *ugauga,* and shortly I was to be shown more.

The installation ceremony provided an opportunity to test whether it was safe to teach me more. Because of the risks involved to his family, and potentially to me, I doubt he would have otherwise revealed so much about *ugauga* sorcery so early or, perhaps, at all. His part in the ceremony necessitated the *ugauga* rituals, for to have attended without them would have risked not only supernatural harm, but his reputation as a man of sorrow. Since he had no choice, and he could not avoid some risk to those in proximity to him, the opportunity was there to find out how I would react. He warned me of the dangers, but if I paid no heed to them, he could not prevent me from accompanying him to the feast. Either I would get very sick, like poor Philo, which would finally make it clear to me, as well as him, that I simply was not strong enough, or I would publicly demonstrate to all that I could withstand confrontation with the destructive forces of the hidden world. My reaction would settle the matter. I imagine he must have been reasonably confident of the result, otherwise he would have made stronger objections. His own eldest son, as I relate in the following chapter, fell seriously ill when Aisaga tried to teach him hunting ritual, let alone *ugauga*. He would not have wanted to repeat that situation. Another test was to come in a few days' time. Once again I did not realize its significance until after the event.

Throughout the morning as we talked, Aisaga was increasingly bothered by a running nose and frequent sneezing. This was unusual, but when I asked him about it, he appeared annoyed, dismissing my questions with the comment that he had breathed in the smell of meat and blood at the feast and this had made his nose "watery." Later that day he gathered plant medicines, demonstrating how he crushed up the leaves, and then strongly inhaled them to stop the running nose; shortly his sniffling and sneezing stopped. The relevance of this minor detail will emerge shortly.

For the next several days Philo's illness became of increasing concern, a circumstance not unrelated to Aisaga's next revelation of *ugauga*. The day following the feast, when I first learned of Philo's illness, Aisaga promised he would tell me the spells he was singing to himself that evening. The next day, however, he refused on the grounds that Philo was feeling worse; if he recited the spells, he warned, the spirits would come and harm her. Cynically I thought he had not worried about that yesterday, but this merely reflected my lack of understanding. He, of course, was called upon to cure Philo. He had that very morning bespelled her and given her medicines; having just performed rituals to heal, calling upon the help of the spirits to do so, he could not counteract them with the reverse ritual action, the spells to bring sickness.

I questioned Philo and the youth who had gone to her assistance. The boy had seen nothing but the *augama* snake which darted toward him out of the bush (these creatures can move very fast). Philo was emphatic that what she had seen was a spirit (*isage*) because, as she returned to the house, she could still hear footsteps behind her, but when she turned around there was no one to be seen. She made no attempt to identify the spirit; as far as she was concerned, she had encountered something from the hidden realm and was now sick. She did not speculate further on the matter. Her illness was causing everyone concern. Her mother and sister, from the village across the river, visited her that afternoon. They spoke briefly with Aisaga, who told them what Philo had encountered was not a man of sorrow from some other village, as the rumor was, but a spirit—probably the spirit of her own dead father come to tell her of the death of a relative which had occurred the day of the installation. He had mentioned this to me previously as a possibility, but not a possibility he seemed to find very convincing. This interpretation suited his purposes as it directed the in-laws' attention away from himself. At the same time, it relieved the general anxiety that Philo, in her weakened *megomego* state, might be the object of an attack by a foreign man of sorrow.

Philo's husband, Michael, spent some time that evening discussing matters with his father in my presence. Aisaga repeated the explanation he had favored the day before: because he had taken out "powerful things" to go to the feast, and had called upon A'aisa to go with him, Philo accidently encountered A'aisa himself. I suggested Philo might be sick as a result of eating meat from the feast that had started to go bad in the heat. Michael emphatically rejected this, insisting, "No! She is sick because she saw spirits. She didn't eat any meat; she is sick because the spirits have given her bad food and it won't stay in her stomach, it just goes straight out." He complained he had not slept the night before because Philo had to wake him so many times for help to go outside to the toilet. He eagerly accepted my offer of some tablets that might help her diarrhea. As I left to get them, Aisaga went inside his house to burn bark cloth to summon the spirits of his ancestors and ask them not to harm Philo; he could be overheard speaking softly, as if to someone in the house. Meanwhile, Michael was sent to collect certain plant medicines which would be burnt to frighten away the spirits.

People often asked me for European medicines, and if I had something suitable, I gave it to them. Like many other Papua New Guineans, Mekeo see no contradiction in employing both European and traditional remedies. Even ritual experts such as Aisaga seemed to fear no competition; he did not hesitate to send people to hospital after he had treated them (for example when his son-in-law fell from a tree and dislocated his hip). I asked Aisaga if my tablets would help Philo or whether only his spells and medicines do the job. He replied: "It's like this, if you use both European medicines (*mulamula*) and our medicines (*fu'a*), the sickness will stop quickly; if you use only one by itself, it will take longer."

Such pragmatism was typical of him. I was confident the tablets would relieve Philo's symptoms, and that Aisaga would not see my offer of them as an intrusion. I was also uncomfortably aware that my gesture might be interpreted by Michael, Philo, and the rest of the family as some kind of admission of responsibility on my part. In admitting it was the *polo* he had taken to the feast that summoned the spirit encountered by Philo, Aisaga informed Michael that I, too, carried something "powerful" with me, which implicated me as well. In any case, Michael must already have assumed something along those lines since he commented on how surprised people attending the feast were to see me sitting among the men of knowledge. He said they asked him: "Since she is a woman, won't she get sick, and if she doesn't get sick, why is this?" Later, when we were talking alone, Aisaga added to Michael's comments. People at the feast believed I was a *faifai* water spirit because they heard me speaking their language and eating their food. Surely a real white woman would be afraid to stay alone by herself, they argued, suggesting that Aisaga should look in my house at night to see whether I turned into a snake, or whether the place where I slept was empty because my hidden self had gone elsewhere (implied here is that I was not an embodied entity but a spirit; similar expectations concerning me were harbored even by close friends such as Maria and Josephina).

The following day, December 10, Philo's diarrhea was reportedly better, but now her head was aching. I noticed Aisaga early in the morning coming back from the bush with a packet of leaves. He showed me the medicines, which were for Philo's fever. Then he pulled out of a small tin a live beetle he had captured. This large, light-green insect was similar to a cicada but had a pungent, offensive smell. It was used, he explained, in another charm men of sorrow often took to feasts; the beetle was placed with other medicines (*fu'a*) and powerful objects in a container. When the container was unstopped, people standing near would be overcome by the smell and collapse. There were, as I was eventually to learn, many different variations on this theme.

Philo's illness attracted less attention during the next few days. Rumors that she was the victim of an *ugauga* attack prompted a visit on December 11 from female relatives of Aisaga's eldest daughter-in-law. He reassured them that no foreign men of sorrow were involved, but that his own ancestral spirits were the cause as a result of his summoning them the day of the feast. By now this interpretation must have spread widely. The next three days were occupied by two events involving virtually the whole community: an all-day card game, attracting participants from neighboring villages and, two days later, a large marriage payment (*kopakopa*). In the midst of all this activity, I heard little more of Philo, except that she had not yet recovered, and that one of Aisaga's adolescent grandsons had taken sick. Aisaga took no part in the card game, nor the marriage payment, but the rest of his family was active in both. As usual, he remained alone on the veranda of his *gove,* aloof and distant from the hubbub.

The evening of December 14, having spent most of the day observing the marriage payment, I went to see Aisaga. There had been a new development in Philo's case and her condition had suddenly worsened. That afternoon she went to hospital for treatment and then to her own village to see her brother. Since their father's death, Philo's brother, James, had begun to practise *ugauga* rituals. Although a young married man, James lived apart from his wife and observed a strict *gope* regimen while mourning his father's death. He had the rituals to kill infants and make women sick during and after childbirth. According to Aisaga, he had cut off a finger from the dead body of his father and dried it, which he now used to summon his spirit to bring sickness. Philo, on Aisaga's instruction, had gone to ask James to call off the spirits troubling her. Aisaga also revealed that two days before Philo gave birth, he had dreamed her dead father visited him, saying that he wanted to see Philo. He did not tell me about the dream, but informed his son Michael, because it indicated they could expect difficulties with or following the birth.

This put in a different light an earlier interpretation, that Philo had encountered the spirit of her own father. In giving this first explanation to Philo's mother and sister, Aisaga was informing them he was aware of the brother's intent to harm Philo. She had previously lost two infants. This reflects a common cultural theme: dissatisfaction with marriage payments or other grievances between in-laws is often believed to be the reason for infant deaths and difficult births. If people do not possess the rituals themselves, they hire the services of someone who does. Aisaga had been expecting trouble from the in-laws all along. Thus at first he entertained several possible causes of Philo's indisposition. By the evening of the second day (if not before), he insisted his own actions in summoning the spirits were the cause; this was the interpretation given to Philo's husband, and to the in-laws of his eldest son. Now he appeared to have changed his mind. When I questioned him, he replied that his own actions had originally made Philo sick, but this new development was something different, caused by her own relatives. By instructing Philo to see her brother, Aisaga made this new phase of events a matter of public knowledge, since, of course, everyone in both communities would be able to read the reasoning behind Philo's visit.

There is little doubt Aisaga employed divination in this case, even though I did not witness it, nor hear any reference to it. In all serious or prolonged cases of illness, he would perform divination with the bone and shell (*logu*) before attempting a cure (as described in chapter 4). Indeed he commonly performed divination to decide anything he was uncertain about. He would not have continued to bespell Philo, give her medicines, and entreat the spirits on her behalf, as he had done every day since the feast, unless divination confirmed this was the appropriate course of action. Had divination revealed the cause of this new development? Why was he so certain something different was involved?

There was one other small piece to this puzzle. The morning of these new developments, Aisaga's cold had come back. Just as the morning after the feast, his nose was running and he could not stop sneezing. I refrained from commenting because he had been annoyed when I questioned him the previous time.

The next day, December 15, I learned that despite Philo's visit to her brother, she had been ill during the night and had collapsed with bad stomach pains, whereupon the family roused Aisaga to bespell her and give her medicines. I wondered if she would be sent back to her own village again, but there was no suggestion of this. I spent the day elsewhere, observing various activities stemming from the marriage payments the day before. When I returned in the evening, Aisaga was evidently keen to speak with me and seemed to have something on his mind. After discussing various matters, he finally announced, with an evident sense of importance, that yesterday he had gone to fetch from the bush, where he had hidden it, a very powerful thing used for *ugauga* sorcery rituals. It was *this* that had made Philo sick again, he explained, and that also had caused his running nose and sneezing. He had me really confused now! I protested he had said Philo's brother was making her sick, which was why she visited him yesterday. Quite so, said he with a smile—he was putting the blame on the in-laws. But what really caused the worsening of her condition was the powerful thing he had brought out of the bush yesterday. He had fetched it to show it to me; I would see it soon, but exactly when was left up in the air.

This powerful thing was another *polo,* like the one he took to the feast, but much larger and much more potent—it was the *polo* used to strike down and kill a specific victim. It had been hidden in the bush along with the smaller, less powerful *polo* taken to the feast—and Aisaga had been exposed to it when he removed the smaller polo. Although its potency was now much diminished from when it was assembled, it was nevertheless this that had affected him the day after the feast, causing his streaming nose and eyes, and it had affected him in the same way yesterday. Being ritually prepared through his *gope* regimen, he was only slightly affected. In contrast, poor Philo, already in a physically and ritually weakened state after giving birth, was now seriously ill, even though she had no direct contact with the *polo* and neither she nor anyone else was aware Aisaga had brought it into the village. At this point I realized why Aisaga deliberately deflected attention to the in-laws. He knew his family would be angry if they discovered he was putting Philo and themselves at even greater risk by bringing such a highly dangerous object to the village. His reason for doing so, or so he said—thus implicating me in whatever was to follow—was to show it to me. No one, especially his own family, must find out, he impressed upon me.

The next morning Aisaga had a remarkable dream to report. I will save discussion of it until the next chapter, noting only that it followed, and was evidently related to, his announcement he had decided to show me the large *ugauga polo.* He again warned me most seriously of the dangers to myself, saying he was frightened I might become seriously ill like Philo. Finally he announced he would bring the mysterious object to my house first thing in the morning, before daybreak so that no one would know. I was to take it inside the house and examine it there by myself.

As promised, a metal box was deposited outside my door the next morning before it was light. I did not see Aisaga until later, after I had gone through

the contents by myself. Following all this build-up, the mysterious box proved
to hold nothing very horrifying in appearance. There were three small *polos*
made from small oval-shaped coconuts and incised with geometric designs, to
all intents identical in appearance to the small *polo* Alex used for fish calling.
There were also three large worn human teeth; three roughly tooth-shaped
stones, each approximately one-and-a-half to two inches long; a large piece of
bark; a lump of bright red material resembling plasticine and about the size of
a joint of my thumb; and a considerable residue of dirt, dried plants, and other
unidentifiable substances. Everything inside the box was dry, and there was no
bad smell as I had expected, but rather a vaguely perfumed scent like dried
herbs, similar to the plant medicines used to induce dreaming that I had been
shown. (Recall the reports of the Resident Magistrates of the former colonial
government, which listed countless similar inventories of articles found upon
the persons of arrested ''sorcerers''; the reports were presented with the laconic
comment that there was, in these supposedly deadly collections, little but
childish hocus-pocus and harmless rubbish.)

If the contents of the box were an anticlimax, other circumstances gave the
day an appropriately sinister cast. On leaving the house I came across what I
assumed to be a huge scorpion in my backyard. At first I thought it was a frog,
as its body was about the size of the palm of my hand, but when I got closer
I saw it had nippers like a crab and an upturned tail like a scorpion; it was the
color of a mottled, decomposing leaf. As I had in the past witnessed the pain
of sufferers from scorpion bites who came to me for medicine, I kept well clear
of this nasty-looking creature. Then I recalled Aisaga had mentioned a scorpion
charm used to protect property. This *ikupu*, he said, was placed under the steps
of your house; if anyone entered while you were away they would experience
the terrible pain of scorpion bites. So I went to ask him about the creature I
had just seen. ''Go and catch it and we will make the *ikupu*,'' was his reply.
His son, Michael, who was talking with him when I arrived, said one never saw
scorpions in the village and asked me what it looked like. Both of them shook
their heads over my description, saying it was not a scorpion (*aipa*). I went back
to find it but was rather relieved when it was nowhere to be seen; I was not
looking forward to catching it. I returned, empty-handed, to be informed by
Aisaga that what I had seen was not a scorpion at all but a spirit (*isage*) attracted
to my house by the powerful things in the box. It could have taken the form
of snake, he observed. He then added, pragmatic as ever, that since the rainy
season was beginning, many insects were abroad at this time of the year!

Less than an hour later, the young girl who helped me with household chores
slipped and fell down the steep ladder-steps of my house while carrying a heavy
container of water. She scraped her arm and hurt her leg, and seemed somewhat
shocked; after bandaging her abrasions, I sent her home to rest. Aisaga witnessed the accident from his veranda—but it was no accident in his view. He
warned me again that I must say nothing to anyone about the box, which was

still in my house. The spirits attracted by it had pushed the girl off the steps as she tried to enter the house. She might now get really ill, he chided me, in which case he would have to be on hand to bespell her. I guiltily realised I could be held to blame for allowing her near the house when I knew the offending box was there. He then observed, as he had of the "scorpion," that the girl had fallen because it was raining and the steps were slippery, but he immediately added that she had carried many buckets of water before, under the same conditions, and this was the first time she ever lost her footing. About 11:00 A.M., several hours since I had opened that Pandora's box, I was working on my field notes when suddenly my nose started to stream as if I had a chronic cold! It was an exact repetition of what I observed with Aisaga, which he had attributed to the effects of handling the *ugauga polo*.

That evening I asked Aisaga to explain what the box contained. There were the bones of A'aisa, the myth hero himself, the bones of A'aisa's people, A'aisa's fingernails, and his blood—*egeva* (literally, "ochre" or "paint"), the red "plasticine" I had seen. *Egeva* was one of the most potent and dangerous ritual substances and one of the most difficult to obtain, the essential ingredient for the major forms of *ugauga* rituals. Also in the box was a snake-stone used to summon spirit snakes, dried human brains, the teeth of Aisaga's forefathers, dried human skin, cinnamon bark, and many other medicines (*fu'a*) required for the rituals. Aisaga pointed out there was much less heat (*isapu*) contained by the *polo* because the ingredients were no longer fresh, otherwise I would have been immediately overcome when I opened it. For Aisaga, who knew what was in the box, its contents were very potent indeed—a veritable repository of ancestral, mythic, and spirit power. Likewise, the events of that day were in no sense random; for Aisaga they were the expected consequences of coming into close contact with this distillation of destruction.[4]

After the disquietening events of that day, it was not surprising I had a vivid dream that night. The dream had no manifest link with the day's events yet was so striking I decided to solicit Aisaga's interpretation. The dream was of finding myself at the top of a massive tree, thousands of feet tall—something like a great pine tree—and in the dream I knew I had to get down somehow or else die. I sat there at the top, watching jet airliners fly past below; I shuddered to think how high I was. With horror, I realized if I stayed where I was, I would fall to my death as I got gradually weaker and weaker from lack of food and water. How was I to get down? It seemed impossible, but finally I resolved to try because there was no chance of survival otherwise. I managed to move down a few branches, then stopped and looked down, too terrified to move any farther. After a while I summoned the courage to climb down a few more branches, then stopped again, paralyzed with fear. This went on for a long time until, at last, I reached the ground safely despite my terror.

As I finished describing my dream, Aisaga began to nod approvingly, muttering almost to himself, "You are a strong person." Finally he announced this was a highly significant dream. If I had stayed at the top of the tree, or fallen in trying to climb down, I would get seriously ill and probably die. The cause of the dream, he explained, was the *ugauga polo*. I had touched all the objects in it and inhaled their smell. If it had been fresh, instead of buried in the bush for several months, I would have been seriously affected. If my dream-self stayed at the top of the tree, my bodily self would be unable to eat, he said. I would get sick and my bodily self would refuse all food because my hidden self was starving at the top of the tree. (Recall my first realization in the dream, that I would starve and then become weak and simply fall.) Had that happened, Aisaga would have to bespell me and try to bring back my hidden self. His dream-self would climb the tree in a ritually induced dream, and at the top he might find a bird or a bat. He would capture this creature, my hidden self, and bring it down from the tree. But since my hidden/dream-self was strong enough to descend on its own, it had suffered no harm.

That huge tree where I had found myself was, Aisaga declared, A'aisa's tree. According to the myth, A'aisa became a tree and carried away the women of his village. This happened at night, so when the women woke up they did not know where they were. (The tree is mentioned only in esoteric versions; in public versions, which I already knew, a mountain grows up and carries A'aisa and the women away.) Aisaga asked me if I remembered how I got to the top of the tree. I said I did not, and he replied this was because it was at night that A'aisa became a tree, while the women were asleep. When he himself was young, he continued, his uncles and grandfather tested him in a similar manner. The time he was first shown the *ugauga polo* he dreamed he found himself at the top of a coconut palm. He managed to get part of the way down, then fell. Because he fell only a little way, he was sick for a while and eventually recovered. Many people, he assured me, had similar kinds of dreams when being taught the *ugauga* rituals. Yesterday when I opened the box I touched the bones of A'aisa himself—that was the cause of the dream.

The following day, I left the village for a planned few days' break in Port Moresby over the Christmas period. Events had reached closure for the time. The girl who had fallen down the steps to my house recovered without further complications; Philo's condition had not worsened, and by the time I returned had recovered. What I did not fully understand was how significant the events of these few weeks had been. Unbeknown to me, I had been put through two *Tests* tests: the covert contest of powers at the feast, involving indirect contact with the smaller *ugauga polo*, and the exposure to the major *ugauga polo*. I emerged from both without mishap. Although Aisaga had explained the "powerful things" to which I had been exposed, I did not understand, for several reasons, that in essence this constituted the revelation of one of the most important aspects of the rituals of *ugauga*. I will return to this point shortly.

In this and the previous chapter I have tried to depict the complexity of Aisaga's role: His apparently empty days are filled with many unseen dramas.

He must observe a constant ritual preparedness to deal with any intrusion from the hidden world. He maintains a state of alertness, almost of vigilance; he is sensitive to every subtle sign or communication—dreams, omens, vague perfumes, muttered voices—which allows him to monitor that other world. His *gope* regimen not only serves to protect him from dangerous contacts with the forces of the hidden world, it also attracts spirit presences to him. A man like Aisaga believes himself to hold powers of life and death.

Chapter 12 provided an account of the more positive aspects of Aisaga's role as healer, helper, and adviser; a very different aspect of his role—and of his personality—emerged when circumstances necessitated his using *ugauga* rituals. The extent of his duplicity and his ruthlessness in endangering others, even members of his own close family, and his readiness to implicate me in these activities has, in this chapter, become evident.

As this darker aspect of Aisaga is revealed, so too is his awareness of the divisibility of self. His interaction with the spirit realm is through the medium of his hidden self. His rituals enable him to send out his hidden self in the company of the spirits of the dead and A'aisa himself, while his bodily self attends a feast. While his bodily self is sitting harmlessly on his veranda, his hidden self may be in the dream realm attacking his victim. People may catch sight of Aisaga and not know whether what they saw was his bodily self or his hidden self. He does not claim full conscious awareness of the doings of his hidden self, but he possesses complete confidence in his ritual ability to guide its actions in accordance with his conscious will. Waking or sleeping, he is able to direct his hidden self to accomplish his ends in the hidden world. What for the layperson or minor adept is a problematic and vulnerable part of the self, becomes for a man like Aisaga a most potent instrument of his conscious will. In the next chapter I will unveil yet more of this hidden self and its intense powers.

I now wish to return to the point just raised concerning my ignorance of the significance of the *ugauga polo*. In being shown it and having its contents explained, I was receiving knowledge of how to implement *ugauga* rituals. The irony was that I had heard so much rumor and gossip about the nature of the *ugauga* rituals (chapter 3) that when they were shown to me, I did not recognize them for what they were! I assumed that viewing the *polos* had been merely some kind of preliminary. What I did not know was that in being told in detail the contents of the *polo,* and in surviving contact with it without suffering ill effect, I had received all the information necessary to construct such a deadly charm for myself (provided I could get access to the appropriate ingredients). Furthermore, I had demonstrated my ritual strength (or the strength of my hidden self) to employ this dangerous instrument without destroying my bodily self. The spells appropriate to the ritual had not been given, although I had heard Aisaga singing them. I assumed, as many people had told me in the past, these were the key. Laypersons also placed much emphasis on the importance of special powerful "stones" (*kepo*) wherein *ugauga* power resided, but no one had said very much about the ritual substances of various kinds that were used. The public rumor about *ugauga* sorcery served to disguise its real nature from laypeople and make its implementation simpler for practitioners, since ordinary people had rather different expectations about what the rituals entail.

There is yet a further irony. The wily old man of sorrow, Augustine, who was such a favorite of mine during my early fieldwork, in fact gave me a full list of ingredients and instructions to make an *ugauga polo,* but I only now, with the benefit of Aisaga's instruction, recognized it for what it was. Augustine would be so amused if he knew it had taken me more than ten years to discover the real value of his information. What a fine joke, even better than that perpetrated by jovial George! Aisaga asked me shortly after I arrived what Augustine had told me about *ugauga,* and I replied he had divulged very little specific information on the topic. Aisaga responded by asking me why, then, did the young man who had acted as my interpreter during my sessions with Augustine (he was the only person brave enough to agree to interpret when I was interviewing Augustine!) subsequently claim that Augustine had taught me *ugauga,* and thus him as well, and as a consequence, had to kill a large pig and present valuables in payment? I was quite dumbfounded by this and protested I really could not explain why, as nothing very important had been revealed. At this point the reader might be inclined to think that I was rather dumb! But I was deceived by experts: the man of sorrow is nothing if not a trickster like A'aisa himself, the mythic trickster.

There is one final point to be dealt with, another that does not reflect well on me: my increasing involvement—a kind of unconscious complicity—in Aisaga's interpretations. Credulity and gullibility are not too strong to describe my own reactions during the events just described. I am reminded of Jung's (1978) statement to the effect that if a white man (or woman) subjected himself to a shaman's or a magician's rituals, he might expect to experience the same visions sought by the shaman or the magician. Had I been overtaken by floods of conscious imagery, I might have been content with Jung's conclusions and interpreted the situation as an activation of archetypal forces from the unconscious. But I was overtaken by no florid visionary experiences. My sense of ordinary reality was challenged in much more subtle ways. It was the mundane nature of events confirming Aisaga's worldview that startled me. The "scorpion" was no ten-foot-high impossible monster; it was simply a large, ugly, nasty-looking insect I had not seen before. There was nothing unnatural about it. Snakes are sometimes, although rarely, seen in the village. There was nothing exceptional in a young woman who had recently suffered the rigors of childbirth feeling unwell; nothing very remarkable about someone sneezing and having a runny nose. That a girl carrying a heavy load should lose her footing on steep steps is hardly surprising, nor is it remarkable for an important man to appear hot and worried at a feast (although it is unusual given the cultural emphasis on presenting a smooth, impassive exterior). There was nothing really disturbing about my dream of being at the top of huge tree. Out of context, not one of these events is in any way exceptional. Yet they fitted together in a sequence that persuasively supported Aisaga's interpretations.

Perhaps other circumstances might have served just as well. Not just any event would suit his purposes, but a range of events might. Any mishap occurring that day would be attributed to the dangerous box. Any sickness in the family might be attributed to it. On the other hand, although none of these events were unnatural, they were unusual. What is clear is that Aisaga read actual events as indicating hidden significance, then acted on that "informa-tion." If, for example, no mishaps or illnesses had occurred, he would have concluded that the *polo* had lost its potency. In that case, my dream would be interpreted differently, indicating I was sensitive to even the slightest exposure to a weakly charged charm and therefore unfit to learn anything more of *ugauga.* Put another way, I could say Aisaga read a psychological significance in people's actions and responses. Certainly he demonstrated a remarkable capacity to invest actual events with a significance that confirmed his own view of them.

Everything that took place up until my dream of the tree could be interpreted without difficulty as Aisaga's clever manipulation of meanings. But the dream brought me face-to-face with a new and inescapable realization: my own fantasy constructions were cooperating with—indeed contributing to—the interweaving of event and interpretation. Was this *folie à deux,* countertrans-ference?[5] I could no longer avoid the fact that some part of myself outside conscious awareness was colluding in the process. Truly a "hidden self" had come to the fore, but activated by what? The answer to this question will, of course, depend on one's specific theoretical stance, or lack of it. It could be pointed out from a Freudian perspective that the dream revealed that my own unconscious wishes to confirm Aisaga's occult powers were grounded in a specific context of infantile dependency needs (Freud 1933). The sexual con-notations are so obvious: the tree, the mountain "that carries away" the women. From a Jungian perspective this may be the "cosmic tree" (Jung 1967, 1976), and thus a classic shamanistic initiation dream, indeed closely fitting the Mekeo interpretation. But what such explanations tend to do is close the matter—prematurely, in my view. Also involved is a dialogue, a process of communication, one which cannot fail to intrigue the culture theorist as well as the psychoanalyst. My dream displayed such a neat fit with the context of actual circumstances of events, the A'aisa myth (which was well-known to me, although the esoteric version Aisaga referred to was not), and Aisaga's inter-pretation and expectations as determined by the cultural context. It brings to mind the dialogue analysts often observe between the theoretical stance of the analyst and the dreams produced by the analysand, wherein the dream imagery fits the expected models of the therapist. My unconscious fantasies were somehow responding to and reproducing the symbols required by the Mekeo cultural context.

Recall that, according to Aisaga's belief, his rituals were specifically intended to activate and direct the self that dreams. For him, as for the other ritual experts discussed, the powerful spells, relics, and substances activated inner imagery in such a way that he had a vivid experiential sense of another realm of powers beyond waking reality. The adept focuses upon subtle indications or perceptions of a reality that is not that of the physical world, nor of his or her conscious thoughts, but that somehow exists outside either. This is a realm without bodily form, yet perceptible in images, smells, and sounds, a realm existing independently of conscious, deliberate thought processes. One which he or she experiences and believes to be invested with extraordinary powers, destructive and creative, not found in the ordinary world of waking existence. It is, of course, such subtle influences, such fleeting glimpses of an inner fantasy world, that Westerners are taught to ignore and dismiss as meaningless.

I have endeavored to show how the rituals of secret knowledge guide inner imaginative processes of the adept, whether this be a minor practitioner, like the dream diviner, or the most knowledgeable, like Aisaga. One can also identify here, I think, some form of feedback effect from inner "realities" to outer experience, so that the adept's view of a waking, mundane reality is shaped according to these inner certainties. One can discern a dialogue between conscious and unconscious levels within the individual, and a parallel dialogue of fantasy productions operating between individuals, as dramatized in my own case when my dreams took up themes and motifs appropriate to a cultural context of belief of which I had only incomplete conscious understanding at the time. Such an imaginative process, which operates outside consciousness yet is responsive to external cues and direction, and which communicates to and from deeper levels of self, was described in chapter 5. In my view, the rituals of Mekeo secret knowledge are a culturally elaborated means to put to conscious use what I identify as autonomous imagination.

The Sorrows of
Acquiring Knowledge

Placed betwixt the world of the living and the world of the spirits, Aisaga mediated between the two, and was a full participant in neither. So far I have focused on his interactions with the spirit realm and the nature of his ritual practice. It is time to describe his relationships with the living: with his family, with his lineage and descent group, with friends and colleagues. I will also examine the transmission of knowledge to his heirs, in particular his eldest son, and the perceptions of self and the complex self-identity that emerge in these various contexts. On the one hand haughty, aloof, and maintaining a strict physical separation from others, even his own children and grandchildren, Aisaga was immersed in his engagement with the dangerous forces of the hidden world, seemingly beyond the reach of ordinary human desire and emotion. Yet, on the other hand, he was deeply concerned with the affairs of both family and descent group, even though he rarely directly participated in them. Despite the destructive powers he wielded, he was forbearing with others and sensitive to their feelings. These seeming contradictions were different aspects of one formidable personality.

A Man of Sorrow and His Family

Aisaga's relationship with his own family—his four sons, a daughter, their spouses, and his many grandchildren who ranged in age from young adults to babies—was one of deep, indeed passionate concern, yet he maintained a strict, almost total, isolation from them. He ate by himself and never joined family members when they gathered together to relax and talk. The women and children left food for him; the grandchildren were brought to him only if they were sick; his sons called to consult on daily tasks or crises but never stayed chatting just to pass the time of day. Unlike many elders, whom I often interviewed while they held a small grandchild on their lap, Aisaga never fondled his grandchildren or even allowed them to play near him. This physical isolation was not a reflection of his own preferences, but was imposed on him by the need to protect others. Philo's illness, described in the previous chapter, illustrates the serious consequences of failure to maintain sufficient distance between the two worlds.

Although he had to stand apart from his family's daily activities, he supervised, where he could, every detail. The eldest of his four sons was in his forties, the youngest about twenty-five. The second son worked as a tradesman in the town, where he lived with his wife and five children. The other three sons, with their wives and children, lived in a large family house (*e'a*) built a few yards away from Aisaga's widower's house (*gove*). Of his three daughters, one died in infancy, and a second died in her late twenties after marrying and giving birth to two children. The eldest daughter, a married woman in her late forties, lived with her husband and children in a house built away from the village, near their gardens. On the whole, relationships among the members of this large family were good; there was little quarreling, even among the numerous children. Without exception, they were physically strong, lively, and intelligent—a handsome, numerous, easy-going family in which any patriarch might take pride. There was only one blemish on this attractive surface: a recent lingering illness suffered by Matthew, Aisaga's official heir, now the functioning head of the family and lineage.

For Aisaga's taste, his sons spent too much time drinking, gambling, and just idling around, but in this respect they were certainly no different from the other men. Occasionally, the youngest son tried to beat his wife or got into a scuffle after drinking too much, but his two elder brothers, who never behaved violently even when drinking, restrained him from going too far. Aisaga would be visibly annoyed when, after a night's card playing and drinking, the men of the household spent the morning sleeping and lazing around instead of rising early to work. The day often began with the stillness of the early morning broken by a loud harangue from Aisaga. It was usual for people, especially respected older men, to air their views in public in this way, criticizing others for improper behavior and advising them to mend their ways. Aisaga would scold his eldest son for making himself sick by drinking beer and warn the youngest son that, since he was now married and had produced a child, he and his wife must work each day to make their own gardens instead of relying on the rest of the family for food. The third son he would chide for not going hunting to provide his children with meat. Whatever the daily or seasonal tasks to be performed, in these early morning lectures Aisaga exhorted his family to get on with their jobs, sternly castigating their laziness and tardiness.

Unfortunately, Aisaga had objectives that his sons had neither the incentive nor energy to implement. He was keen to take advantage of the many government-sponsored programs for local agricultural development offered in the 1960s and 1970s (Stephen 1974), and he planned to raise pigs and grow vegetables for commercial sale. The family possessed plenty of good land, and with three strong adult sons living in the village to provide the labor, there appeared to be every prospect of success. The family started a pig farm, only eventually to abandon it because the sons and their wives wanted to return to live in the village. Then, on Aisaga's prompting, they decided to plant sweet potatoes on a commercial scale, and they secured a government loan to buy a tractor. But by the early 1980s, when I arrived, they had lost interest and the tractor had broken down.

Aisaga now urged the tractor be repaired so that the family could take up rice planting, which was again being encouraged by the Department of Agriculture after endless vicissitudes promoting it in the 1940s and 1950s (Stephen 1974). He had seen many other families in the community succeed in business ventures and was deeply disappointed in his sons' lack of achievement. Finally he did persuade them to get the tractor repaired, and rice planting was begun. He was delighted the day the family went out to work on the rice plot, demonstrating his pleasure by purchasing several tins of meat for the workers to eat that night. Just how deeply his hopes were invested in these plans was indicated when I asked what had been the most important dream he could remember within the last few months. It was hardly what I expected: instead of some life-and-death matter, or a portentous message from the ancestors, he recalled a dream in which the tractor had broken down and he was weeping bitterly. Shortly afterward his fears were realized. He had pinned so many hopes on the tractor, he said, and they had struggled so hard to raise sufficient money to get the loan, that when it did in fact break down, he was as inconsolable as he had been in his dream. What a strange image—the inscrutable Aisaga weeping over a broken tractor!

No doubt Aisaga found it galling to see the sons of men of lesser standing get ahead. Furthermore, none of his offspring had made a place for themselves in the new educated elite, which many of the young men and a few women of the community were entering. His youngest son did not even bother to finish his plumber's apprenticeship, whereas other men's sons were becoming lawyers, degreed diplomats, and high-ranking government officials. Except for the youngest, Aisaga's sons were too old to take full benefit of the education and job opportunities that opened up in the mid-1960s; he was looking to his grandsons to succeed here. His concern with his family, however, extended far beyond this desire for educational and economic success. Aisaga did not simply seek to extend his own prestige through his offspring, rather, I think he was concerned what their future might be without him to urge them to improve their lives.

His surveillance of family life included even the intimate relationships between spouses. As head of the family, it was Aisaga's responsibility to ensure that postpartum sexual taboos were observed, neglect of which is believed to threaten the life of the newborn child. He also supervised the *megomego* restrictions applying to new mothers. In the past, following the birth of a child, the husband slept for several months in the clan meeting house, but this practice had not been observed for at least two decades. Nevertheless, in households like Aisaga's, the senior members insist that spouses sleep apart for the required period, and Aisaga strongly disapproved of the younger generation's preference for the husband to remain in the family house following a birth. He believed everyone was better served by the system prevailing in his youth: wives were spared the burden of too-frequent births, while husbands could enjoy the pastimes of bachelors, whether indulging in secret love affairs or devoting themselves to ritual activities. To resume sexual relations too soon after a birth is also believed to endanger the health and proper development of the new infant. Aisaga could no longer insist that all the old ways be followed, but he did his best to impose his views. Although intimate sexual relations, marital or otherwise, belong to the domain of the private and hidden, a couple's sexual activities affect not only themselves but also the welfare of their child and thus the whole family. Sexual congress, even between spouses, is believed to be damaging to the crops if performed in new gardens (menstrual blood is also considered to be damaging to crops); newly married couples are to refrain from sexual relations until their first gardens are cleared, planted, and brought to fruition. Young people are taught to control and regulate their sexual appetites for the sake of others, as well as themselves. Being the most senior of the family, this was Aisaga's responsibility.

Aisaga complained if he thought his grandchildren were not fed properly, or if their safety was neglected. He was enraged when the children were allowed to play with an adolescent, mentally deficient boy who was known to have molested other children—Aisaga believed him capable of killing a small child. Despite constant warnings, the family fed the boy and let him hang around. One morning Aisaga finally delivered a scathing public lecture, threatening that if the parents' lack of foresight resulted in the death of one of his grandchildren he would, with his own hands, beat the parents with a heavy stick until he broke bones. The retarded boy was not encouraged after this. If Aisaga was continually urging, criticizing, and lecturing his family, it should be noted that he never complained on his own behalf. He might be left all day without food or betel nut, but he would voice no objection. His public exhortations always related to the welfare of others.

He took particular note of the care given his two orphan grandchildren, the children of his dead daughter, a girl of about eight and a boy of six. They had been born and reared in Port Moresby, Aisaga explained, and were not used to village ways or village food. He often bought biscuits and other delicacies craved by the two town-reared children, observing that they were thin and not eating properly because they disliked village food. He would call one of them over and ask the child what he or she wanted, then supply some money for a purchase at the store. And he kept a sharp eye on the adults to see that they treated them fairly. The care of these children was not in fact the responsibility of Aisaga's family, but of the family of their (deceased) father in this patrilineal society. But as Aisaga explained, he was pleased to keep these offspring of his dead daughter with him for as long as possible so he could be sure they were looked after properly. There was genuine kindness in his concern.

Aisaga was not tyrannical or unfeeling in his dealings with others, and it would be false to give that impression. I was often surprised by his delicacy of feeling. He was careful, for instance, never to berate his daughters-in-law, but always directed his anger at his sons. He explained this was because wives came from other families and places; if their feelings were hurt, they would have no one to turn to for comfort. He often emphasized that one must take care not to offend or embarrass anyone heedlessly. Should I object that a particular person's behavior hardly merited such consideration, he would reply, "Nevertheless, he or she is a human being" (*isa papiau, e*). And this, recall, is from a man who confesses to inflicting sickness and death on others just to make money! There were many facets indeed to Aisaga.

Alongside the dream-image of him weeping over the broken-down tractor, let me place another image drawn from his waking life: Aisaga is telling me of his desire to see his eldest grandson, Matthew's heir, properly installed as a war leader. As he describes his plans, I am startled to see his eyes filling with tears; finally they brim over as he continues to speak, tears running down his face unheeded. This is no sobbing, heaving, histrionic performance. He sits straight-backed, dignified, and as impassive as ever. His motionless face and calm voice give no indication of weeping. Yet there can be no mistaking the depth of emotion evoked in this steely individual by the very thought of presiding over his grandson's formal investiture as head of his lineage—an event that would mark the final achievement of Aisaga's own life and the ensuring of the line into the next generation.

Aisaga's Relationship with the Wider Community

I have shown that Aisaga was not only a man of sorrow but also the war leader and head of his clan section (chapter 9). According to custom, he was installed as war leader shortly after his marriage. His father died during the Second World War, and for the next twenty years or so Aisaga acted as head of his lineage. When his wife died in the early 1960s, he was obliged to withdraw from society for the period of mourning. Matthew, now officially installed as the war leader, took over in his stead. Because it was well known that Aisaga possessed the knowledge of *ugauga* sorcery, the community expected him to practice it during his mourning, and he did so. He explained to me that not only was it expected of him, but if he failed to observe the appropriate ritual preparation, other men of sorrow would have tried to kill him. After two or three years, when he ended his seclusion from society, he might have chosen to remarry and enter normal society again. Instead, he remained a widower and a man of sorrow—a life he had now followed for more than twenty years. Why did he choose such a hard and lonely path? There can be no single answer, but to a certain extent, I think he felt he had no choice.

Aisaga continues to act as the lineage head, advising in all important matters affecting the lineage as a whole, despite the fact that his eldest son is officially installed as the war leader. Aisaga's attitudes to his role as head of his clan section clearly reflected the values and ideals people commonly attach to the men of kindness.

As the senior member of the most senior line of his lineage, the junior clan, Aisaga held familial responsibility for, and authority over, his "younger brothers." The members of the senior and middle sections of the clan were his "elder brothers." In theory at least, he was bound to respect the authority of the man of kindness of the senior section in matters concerning the clan as a whole, and he had no direct responsibility for the affairs of the other two sections (although in years past he would have in times of war). His own lineage was in effect his extended family, and he watched over the activities of its members in much the same way he monitored the activities of his sons and their wives. Since one's kinsmen are also one's neighbors, Aisaga could keep an eye on most of the goings-on in his clan section from his vantage point at the back of the village, where his raised voice could be heard in most of the nearby houses. He did not lecture his "younger brothers" as frequently and as severely as his own sons, but he did not hesitate to lay down the law when necessary.

One morning, for example, he delivered a sharp reprimand to Henry, his classificatory son (*gauga*), a married man in his thirties. The previous day Henry had held a small feast to celebrate putting an iron roof on his house, events he had been saving for, and Aisaga was dissatisfied with the amount of meat distributed. This was a serious matter. The men of kindness traditionally hold the right to use certain building materials for their own houses, and several deaths in the community were attributed to people building houses with corrugated iron roofs without first obtaining permission (Stephen 1974). The practice developed that anyone who intended to use iron on their roof should first kill pigs and send the meat to all the men of kindness of the village to seek their approval. Aisaga's rebuke to his "son" was not aimed at getting more meat for himself or his family but at ensuring that the other leading men, and the community as a whole, would have no cause to complain that Henry had been stingy and had not "paid" for his roof. Whatever Henry's views on the matter—I shall shortly describe how his relationship with Aisaga was strained—that very morning he killed another large pig and quickly distributed the meat.

On another occasion Aisaga delivered a stinging lecture to his lineage when he learned the husband of a recently deceased woman of the lineage (Aisaga's classificatory daughter, *gauga*) was not observing the appropriate mourning procedures. The husband, as a brother-in-law (*ipa gava*) of Aisaga's lineage, came under his authority at this time of mourning. It was up to the dead woman's agnatic relatives to ensure the husband behaved appropriately. Aisaga had heard reports that the recently bereaved husband, who should have been secluded from society and fasting rigorously, was participating in drunken carousals about the village. Outraged, Aisaga demanded these scandalous events be stopped and the widower brought to him for supervision and punishment. The widower was not handed over, as demanded, but there was no further news of improper behavior on his part.

When he was younger, and still married, Aisaga contributed heavily to the marriage payments of several of his lineage members. He also made frequent gifts of meat to various households of his lineage (he was then an energetic hunter and an expert in hunting rituals). This help was acknowledged by younger kinsmen, who now reciprocated by sharing with Aisaga the marriage payments made for their sisters. As the senior member of the lineage, he would be involved to some degree in all these marriage negotiations, but people I spoke with referred to specific obligations to him personally that arose out of the help he had given their parents. One of the benefits of belonging to a family possessed of major ritual knowledge, Aisaga often pointed out, was that one could acquire wealth. His father and grandfather had amassed much wealth in the form of traditional valuables (*efu*) in this manner; he had done the same, using it to finance the marriages of his classificatory younger brothers and sons and, later, his own sons.

Aisaga had also financed two marriages outside his own lineage. For some reason, the elders of the two more-senior sections of Beach clan were unable or unwilling to provide for these marriages, so Aisaga stepped in. He hoped thereby to attract both men to his own clan section. Yet although it was publicly recognized that these two families owed their origin to Aisaga's generosity, they maintained their separate identity as members of the second section of Beach clan. Over the years, bad feeling had developed between Aisaga and one of these two men. Joe (chapter 8), the man in question, was several years younger than Aisaga. His children, born in the 1950s, were able to take advantage of the expansion of educational facilities in the 1960s and early 1970s. All his sons received tertiary education and in the late 1970s were occupying important, well-paying positions in the town. Aisaga's own sons, in contrast, had been born more than a decade earlier and were content to be subsistence farmers. By 1980, Joe's increasing affluence enabled him to buy a truck and to set up a well-stocked village store, complete with refrigeration and electric light provided by a generator. The contrast with Aisaga's family was evident to all, and could not fail to be an irritant to Aisaga. Having financed

Joe's marriage, and thus contributing to the very existence of his sons, Aisaga felt Joe owed him some obligation. On the other hand, Joe's educated and independent sons were little inclined to take much notice of the debt.

Undoubtedly the community as a whole had done much to stir up ill feeling between the two men. Many people warned Joe that he was incurring the envy of a powerful and dangerous man, and, at the same time, stressed Joe's failure to meet his obligations to Aisaga and pointed out Joe's deliberate flaunting of his new wealth. I heard many rumors from various sources concerning threats of sorcery from Aisaga against Joe, and attempts by Joe to hire men of sorrow from other villages to deal with Aisaga. Both men denied these rumors, but that did not stop them from spreading. Joe was well aware he was a target of others' envy because of his new affluence. The quarrel with Aisaga was just one aspect of the situation. To make matters worse, Joe began to drink to alleviate his anxieties and, when drunk, he was prone to behave in an abusive and scandalous way, creating further troubles. The situation had long since reached the point where Joe and Aisaga were not on speaking terms.

Under the circumstances, Aisaga was very forbearing. He observed that many people had complained to him about Joe's behavior and had suggested he should be punished. A colleague from a neighboring village informed him that Joe had tried to hire his services to kill him (Aisaga). The colleague wanted to know if he should do away with Joe instead. Aisaga refused to give permission. His identity as lineage head comes to the fore here: "I refuse to use *ugauga* sorcery against my younger brother, even if he quarrels with me," he declared. Then he added, "A *lopia's* anger is short; only ordinary people hang on to their anger."

The Anger of a Man of Sorrow

The tensions underlying Aisaga's relationship with his kinsmen, and how he managed things to contain these tensions, were dramatized in events taking place in January 1981 in which Joe, Henry, and I all played a part. On January 11 Aisaga announced he was worried because the previous two mornings he had heard the bird, *ifi,* singing in the bush at the back of the village. This was an omen of imminent death in his lineage. The following day, about midday, news reached the village that a married woman in her late thirties had collapsed on her way to the gardens and had died of hemorrhaging. This woman, Helen, was the daughter of one of Aisaga's classificatory younger brothers (*akina*) and a member of his lineage. The death was unexpected and a source of great sorrow to the lineage, and to the whole community, as she was well liked and respected. Such a death, of an adult in his or her prime, could be expected to be attributed to *ugauga* sorcery, but I heard little mention of it at first, as the relatives were preoccupied with the funeral and mourning procedures. Feeling ran high at the funeral, which I attended, and a scuffle broke out between the agnatic kinsmen of the dead woman and the relatives of her husband, who were accused of working her too hard and not taking proper care of her (a usual occurrence in these circumstances). Aisaga's sons were prominent in this outburst. As usual, Aisaga himself was not present at the funeral, but the father of the dead woman spent much time consulting with him, and he generally kept an eye on activities. Since responsibility for the funeral and other rituals associated with death and mourning falls to the senior man of kindness of the descent group's senior section, Aisaga was not directly involved even though Helen was of his lineage.

The morning of January 19, before it was light, I woke to hear Aisaga angrily shouting from his veranda. I could not follow what he was saying and later in the morning went to enquire. I found him energetically clearing the bush behind his house and evidently not in the mood to talk to me, and I did not call back until evening. Had I understood, he asked me then, what he was saying to his lineage members that morning? He was rebuking his classificatory son, Henry, for accusing him of causing the recent death in the lineage. According to Aisaga, Henry had spoken first, announcing to the lineage that Joe attributed the death of their clan sister to the fact Aisaga was teaching me *ugauga* sorcery. Incensed by these accusations of sorcerizing his classificatory daughter, Aisaga responded by berating both Henry and Joe. He was clearly very angry and upset, which was why he had avoided me earlier in the day.

I was shocked. First, it was disturbing to find I had become so closely identified with Aisaga that people whom I knew well were ready to believe me responsible for sorcerizing them. Second, although private gossip and rumor concerning sorcery were ever-present, open accusations were, in my experience, extremely rare. Had things changed, or had I previously not been this close to events? It should be noted that in this instance no public meeting had been convened specifically for the purpose of accusing or identifying a sorcerer (such as found in the witchcraft moots described by Riebe 1987). Nevertheless, the statement was made in a public context, and this was sufficiently offensive and unusual to provoke Aisaga's justifiable anger.

Why had Henry been so rash as to speak out against his "father" in this manner? His relationship with Aisaga was complicated by the circumstance that he himself had hereditary claims to *ugauga* sorcery. His father, Pukari, was a renowned sorcerer, but he had died while Henry was an infant. Pukari and his issue represented the junior line of Aisaga's lineage, to whom the practice of *ugauga* sorcery was usually passed by the senior line (i.e., Aisaga's father and grandfathers). Henry thus believed himself entitled to ritual knowledge, including *ugauga* sorcery. Aisaga accepted this and had already taught Henry a little, and intended to teach him more. Understandably, Henry was resentful of my presence and the fact that I, a white outsider, was apparently being given knowledge still withheld from him.

Henry was a moody, difficult character. I knew him quite well during my first fieldwork, and as he spoke good English, he was put forward as a likely interpreter. Despite his apparent willingness and obvious intelligence, he proved unreliable and sullen, so I soon turned to others more cooperative. He might then have been described as a young man with a chip on his shoulder; now older, he seemed to have become even more truculent. He was not a noisy troublemaker, but his manner was always subtly resentful and sullen.

Henry felt he had a grudge against Aisaga, and given Joe's long-standing quarrel with Aisaga, it was not surprising that the two should support each other in siding against him. Furthermore, Joe not only drank to excess himself, but plied his kinsmen and friends with liberal amounts of drink at public gatherings. No doubt the men had been drinking when Joe made, or reportedly made, his rash statement about the recent death. In repeating this accusation, Henry not only risked bringing Aisaga's revenge on himself and his immediate family, he could not fail to be aware he was also cutting himself off from any possibility of learning from Aisaga what he desired. It may be that Henry was counting on another source. There were rumors that Henry's father's sister, Ann, now an elderly, childless widow, had been instructed in *ugauga* sorcery by her brother, so the knowledge could eventually be passed on to his son (a common practice in such circumstances). Ann now lived with Henry and his wife and children, which perhaps added fuel to the rumors. Why else, people would ask, should the family support and feed the useless old woman? Whatever the reasoning behind his action in speaking out against Aisaga, Henry was soon to regret it.

The next day I sought out Joe. Since I was implicated in the accusation, I did not consider myself to be meddling in things that did not concern me. Joe talked with me calmly and reasonably—when sober he was a perceptive, kindly man. He denied he had made or supported any accusation against Aisaga and myself. Perhaps he had forgotten what was said while he was drunk, but I was convinced of his sincerity in not wanting to perpetuate the quarrel. He said that other people were always trying to stir up ill feeling between Aisaga and himself. I told him it was unlikely Aisaga would be performing *ugauga* sorcery now, since he lived close to his family and the danger to them would be too great. I also pointed out it was unlikely I, as a woman, would employ *ugauga* sorcery to kill someone. He agreed, insisting it was Henry, not himself, who was making trouble with unwarranted accusations. I reported our discussion to Aisaga, who likewise agreed other people were always trying to worsen the situation.

The stage had been set, one might assume, for some kind of showdown between Aisaga, Joe, and Henry. As was usually the case in this community, however, emotions that seemed about to burst through the surface calm of social relationships were kept in check. Aisaga was angry but, having publicly rebuked Henry and Joe, was not prepared to take further public action. Despite the serious provocation, he insisted in our private conversations, it would be wrong to use sorcery against his younger brothers even though the rest of the community would see it as justified. Like a chess player, Aisaga was satisfied to wait for the next move.

Three weeks passed before the matter surfaced again. In the interim, other disturbing events took place. The night of January 21, Aisaga dreamed his eldest son, Matthew, decorated himself and danced in front of the house of Joe's neighbor and lineage member, Arthur. The same night I dreamed of talking with people at the clan meeting house, which was on the opposite side of the village but almost directly in line with Arthur's house. Both dreams are considered classic omens of death (chapters 4 and 8). Aisaga had no doubt they indicated a death in that part of the village, that is, in the lineage to which Joe and Arthur belonged (the second section of Beach clan). Four days later, on January 25, the body of a grandchild of Arthur's younger brother, who shared his house, was brought to the village for burial; the child had died in the village of its mother's descent group.

The hammering of workmen making the child's coffin and the wailing of the mourners echoed through our section of the village. Aisaga observed to me that this was the death indicated in the two recent dreams. I wondered whether we would be blamed for it, and whether people might interpret it as a warning to Joe since the child was a member of his lineage and his classificatory grandchild, but I did not voice my fears. The paternal grandparents blamed the mother for taking the child to visit her relatives and they had tried to beat her, Aisaga told me. In fact, he added, they themselves were responsible because they had failed to make payments of bride wealth to the mother's family; thus, in anger, the mother's relatives brought about the child's death. Both Arthur and his younger brother were notoriously lax in making their sons' marriage payments: only a few weeks previously Arthur had lost a grandchild (chapter 4), and the death was attributed to the same cause. This—attributing the deaths of infants and small children to disgruntled maternal relatives—is a common cultural theme, but I wondered whether in this instance other people, especially those of Joe and Arthur's lineage, would accept Aisaga's interpretation.

The whole village section was depressed the day of the child's funeral. A death affects everyone; even those who are not the immediate mourners and closest relatives are always visibly distressed. This was not simply a matter of social convention, but an almost palpable atmosphere of shared grief and loss. Aisaga reflected this mood when the death was in his descent group: his normally straight back would be hunched, and he would seem drained, distracted. That evening, two of his own grandchildren were sick and were brought to him for treatment. Matthew, his eldest son, was also ill, and Aisaga had been asked to call on the spirits to leave him alone. The previous evening Matthew also had been troubled by a dream in which the spirits of Joan, his dead sister, and Helen, the woman who had recently died, came and embraced him, then wept. This dream badly frightened him, and he had been ill all day.

A death in the community has the effect of bringing the living into contact with the normally hidden realm of unseen powers. It is a time when anyone might experience dream omens, sightings of spirits and ghosts, and feelings of lassitude and depression, or even illness. For Aisaga, ever in contact with the other realm in one way or another, a death in his descent group affected him even before it occurred. He invariably had prior knowledge of it. Although he never said so, he conveyed to me the impression that he somehow felt responsible. Following an omen (for example, the bird *ifi* calling in the bush before Helen's death), he would become tense, his attention focused elsewhere, waiting for further indications. When the death occurred, he would seem defeated, as if he felt a deep involvement or complicity in the death. At the time, I took the sickness of Aisaga's grandchildren and Matthew as part of the usual reaction to a death in the descent group, although I dimly sensed that Aisaga felt some responsibility here, too. Nothing more was said about the incident with Henry and Joe. What I did not realize was that Aisaga's covert anger was the link running through all these and subsequent happenings.

A few days later, Aisaga did something very surprising: he not only told me certain dangerous spells for *ugauga* sorcery, he actually sang them for me to record. Previously he refused to recite these spells because of the extreme danger to his family and other people. If he recited them in the village, he objected, people would get ill or those already ill might die. Yet on this day he made no objection, despite the fact that Matthew was still ill, and that he and the rest of the family were sitting only a few yards away. Aisaga did insist, however, on the recording being done at my house, which was a little further removed. I interpreted his actions as proof that he had not wanted to give me the knowledge before and that the rest had been mere excuses. Thus I missed the significance of his actions. Aisaga was still angry. The spells imparted were those to drive the angry spirits to attack people. It was because of Aisaga's continued, but now concealed, anger that he sang the spells.

Two days later, on February 14, another death occurred, this time in Aisaga's own lineage. Once again our section of the village was filled with the sound of funeral dirges. An old woman was found dead in her house early in the morning. She turned out to be none other than Ann, Henry's paternal aunt, who was rumored to be teaching him *ugauga* sorcery. The old lady had been left alone to mind the small children while Henry and his wife were visiting elsewhere. It was wrong of Henry and his wife to leave the old woman on her own, Aisaga observed, noting that Opu, the ailing man of sorrow, Henry's uncle, had died alone like that and had been found hours later in the same condition as Ann—naked and huddled in a fetal position.

The old lady was buried early in the day, without waiting for mourners to arrive, for no one knew how long she had been dead. As an elderly, childless widow, the loss of Ann was felt less than that of Helen. Nevertheless, she was a daughter of the clan and was mourned as such. As always following a death, the whole village section was depressed and dejected. On such days the heat always seemed especially oppressive, mosquitoes and other biting insects coming in swarms. Aisaga referred to such days as *kina apala*, an "ugly" or "bad" day. Although he discussed the death in a matter-of-fact manner in the morning, when I returned to see him in the evening he looked tired. He had not slept well the night before, he said; he knew something was amiss because there were voices under his window all night, but when he lit the lamp and got up, there was no one there. These were the voices of the spirits coming to take away the old woman, he said. He had also dreamed of being visited by a friend of his, a man of sorrow long dead. Aisaga looked so tired, like a shrunken old man, and I wondered if there were more rumors about this death, and whether we were to be accused once again, but said nothing for fear of upsetting him further.

We talked a little. I told him of certain strange scents that had bothered me the previous night because I could not determine from where they were coming. I suspected Aisaga himself may have placed some strongly perfumed plant medicines under or near the house, as the smell reminded me of some of the plant medicines he had demonstrated. But he denied this and suggested the scents were associated with the presence of the spirits come to take away the dead. Finally he observed, somewhat peevishly and in an accusatory tone, that he had not wanted to sing the *ugauga* sorcery spells two days ago, but since I insisted on recording them, he had sung them for me; it was because of this the old woman, Ann, had died suddenly. Once again, I was stunned. Here was Aisaga himself telling me we were both responsible for the old lady's death: I for urging him to sing the lethal spells, he for performing them!

I also felt confused. Did not one have to direct the rituals at a particular victim to cause a death? Had Aisaga deliberately intended to do away with his clan sister to punish Henry, and thus prevent the younger man from any chance of obtaining his inheritance? Was Aisaga really as double-faced as that? Had his earlier denials of using sorcery against his "younger brothers" been mere subterfuge? Perhaps Henry's original accusation about Helen's death was not so implausible. What was really going on? I was still not yet aware of how much dangerous knowledge I had already been taught: Philo's illness, after all, proved to be minor, and she was now fully recovered. I did not imagine that Aisaga would perform on my account any ritual threatening the lives of his family. At one level, I found it difficult to take seriously his refusal to show me certain things, or recite certain spells, because of the danger involved for other people. On a deeper level, I was becoming entangled in the Mekeo belief system.

What I failed to understand was that Aisaga did not have to implement rituals deliberately to inflict punishment on his kinsmen. His anger alone was sufficient. This was made finally clear to me in Henry's response to this death, and to the illness of his youngest child, which shortly followed.

The day after the old lady's funeral, relatives from other villages arrived to pay their respects and were received in the lineage meeting house. Aisaga was present on this occasion to talk with the visitors (as usual, he had not attended the funeral, which was held at the meeting house of the senior man of kindness). By now, Henry had word of the death, had returned home, and was present. He sat silent and sullen; his eyes flashed occasionally with anger but he held his tongue. Much to my amazement there were open jokes among those assembled, led largely by Aisaga's third son, about Aisaga and me performing *ugauga* sorcery—obviously these were directed to Henry. I am not certain of the intent of these jokes; Henry made no response to them, but they probably served to bring things out in the open and relieve tension. Certainly the tone of the group conversation was quite relaxed. But the scene had for me an almost surrealistic air: the public jests about us making *ugauga* sorcery indicated how ludicrous the imputation was, yet in secret Aisaga had admitted to me his responsibility, and revealed my complicity, in the latest death!

Who knows what was going through Henry's mind as he listened to the taunting of his kinsmen? Certainly he knew all hopes of ever obtaining his father's inheritance of secret knowledge were now dashed. There was no one apart from Aisaga from whom he could obtain it. Had he interpreted his aunt's death as a warning? Whatever he thought, this time he kept it to himself; there were no further public accusations. But Henry made no attempt to apologize or make redress.

There the matter rested for a few days, until Henry's youngest child, an infant of about six months, became ill. Twelve days after the death of Ann, Henry's wife came to Aisaga with a substantial payment of money and traditional valuables, asking him to bespell her sick baby. This was done in strictest privacy, as such things always are. In ordinary circumstances, Aisaga might be called upon to treat someone of his lineage without any expectation of payment. How was Henry's action in sending the valuables to Aisaga to be interpreted? Was this in fact a payment to the man of sorrow one suspects is responsible for an illness? Was Henry thus covertly accusing Aisaga of sorcerizing his child? Was Henry simply cowed by Aisaga's superior powers and ready to capitulate before the child died too? Was Aisaga in fact trying to kill the child? Both Henry and Aisaga, I discovered, viewed the situation rather more subtly: involved was a question of legitimacy and moral right that Henry had to concede.

Henry had made no accusations about being sorcerized, Aisaga assured me. Instead, he admitted that because Aisaga was justifiably angry with him and had publicly rebuked him (*lo'u e penia*), the spirits of their lineage forefathers had made the child ill. Realizing I was finding this difficult to grasp, Aisaga elaborated:

"The spirits of our fathers and grandfathers are with me. Their spirits come to my house. I have their hair and bones there, so they come. I do not see them when they come—though we can see them in dreams—but they are there. I was angry with Henry, so they struck his child.''

The following evening, when it was dark and Aisaga and I were talking alone on his veranda, Henry appeared. It must have taken a good deal of courage and considerable swallowing of pride to come and face us. He was nervous and anxious but spoke with sincerity and much contriteness. He reiterated that he knew Aisaga had done nothing to his child, but that because his ''father'' was angry with him, the spirits of the lineage dead had hit his child. Only Aisaga could tell the spirits to leave the child alone. Since Aisaga's treatment, the child had improved a little, he said; the mother had taken the child back to hospital and his temperature had fallen a little. Aisaga discussed the child's condition with Henry for some time and then asked about the umbilical cord and whether it was possible that this could have fallen into the wrong hands (the dried cord can be used for various charms, and if it is obtained by a man of sorrow it can be used to kill). Henry assured him it had been properly disposed of. The conversation was of a conciliatory nature, Aisaga indicating his concern, Henry his regret for bringing about the crisis by opposing Aisaga.

Henry's stance was by no means groveling or terrified, but it was an admission that he was in the wrong. The payment of valuables to Aisaga was acknowledgment of this, and an indication of Henry's sincere desire to heal the rift he had caused. Aisaga's moral authority as lineage head was at last acknowledged; this was what he had been waiting for. Once the first move toward reconciliation had been taken, he was ready enough to forgive Henry. The child was brought for treatment a few more times, and he finally recovered. For the remaining months of my stay, there was no further trouble with Henry.

In Aisaga's view, the rift with Joe needed to be settled in the same way. He was prepared to forgive his ''younger brother'' for past insults, but it was up to Joe to acknowledge he was in the wrong. Aisaga was not alone in this view. Other people confirmed that Aisaga had paid for Joe's marriage with his own pigs and valuables. Even the widow, Maria, who was a close friend of Joe's wife, and might be expected to take his part, considered him at fault. Following the incident with Henry, I began to ask people why Joe had not suffered similar punishment from the lineage spirits as a consequence of Aisaga's justifiable anger. Had he not, they replied? Why did I think Joe, formerly a highly respected, hardworking, sensible man, had become such a useless drunk?

The events just described revealed a new aspect of Aisaga's role as mediator of the powers of the spirit realm. His relationship to the spirits of his dead forefathers was such that whoever incurred his anger was in danger of supernatural injury. Simply to oppose his will was sufficient to endanger any member of his family, lineage, or descent group. The full implication of this entailment was soon to become apparent in another crisis which, like an abscess, had been slowly festering until it reached a painful head. This was the illness of Aisaga's eldest son, Matthew.

The Man of Sorrow and His Heirs

Matthew was a tall, powerfully built, handsome man in his early thirties when I first met him. He was evidently something of a ladies' man; he was considered to have a fine singing voice and to be an accomplished performer of traditional dance, talents important in wooing and winning female admiration in Mekeo culture. His somewhat broad face was given distinction by high cheek bones and well-shaped features, and he moved with the fluid, sinuous grace cultivated by Mekeo men. Although there was a certain hauteur about his appearance, he was easygoing and a rather quiet man, with a light pleasant voice and an engaging smile. He had married early and already had several children. Aisaga held the ceremonies necessary to install him as the war leader when Matthew was in his early twenties. He was liked and respected by the whole community, and he carried out his official duties with appropriate dignity.

In 1980 Matthew was in his forties. He now had ten children, the eldest a girl of marriageable age. His eldest son, and heir, was a young man just completing secondary school. Matthew was now heavy and lethargic, his once handsome face puffy, almost bloated—he had changed a good deal. Although still good humored, he rarely laughed. He spent a great deal of his time sitting and lying around the house, occasionally stirring himself to attend a card game or a beer-drinking party. He explained he had been seriously ill on and off for the past two years or so, but no one, it seemed, knew what was wrong or could cure him. He asked me to examine the medicines prescribed for him by private European doctors in Port Moresby (many people who could afford it now preferred to see private doctors than attend the public hospital clinics). None of these fancy treatments had done him any good, he said. I wondered why Aisaga was not called upon but hesitated to ask directly. It was evident Aisaga was concerned, but his interest seemed to involve no more than periodically lecturing Matthew for staying out all night drinking. When I first broached the topic, Aisaga replied in some disgust it was entirely Matthew's fault. If he got up early and went to his gardens and did a little work, he would feel better. This was only common sense, and there did not seem much wrong with Matthew apart from lethargy and the occasional hangover.

As the weeks progressed, however, Matthew's health deteriorated. I heard various rumors as to the reason. Some people avowed injudicious love affairs had aroused the ire of powerful men whose wives and daughters he had seduced (the same explanation as given for the death of the handsome Mark, also a well-known ladies' man and expert in love ritual; see chapter 10). If this were the case, why could not Aisaga counteract their attacks? Aisaga himself maintained he was scrupulous about allowing his sons access to love ritual for the very reason they might use it inappropriately. He confided to me that Matthew became ill when trying to learn hunting rituals. Many powerful, highly dangerous relics and substances are used in the major rites and are no less injurious than those used in *ugauga* sorcery. Poor Matthew, it seemed, was unable to withstand contact with them and had become ill as a result. (Recall here my experiences in being shown the sorcery *polo* and the *kua polo;* a similar container of powerful substances is used for hunting.) When I asked Aisaga whether he could cure Matthew, he replied indeed he could, but Matthew first had to come to him to be bespelled, and this he had not done.

Several weeks later, when chatting with a Mekeo friend in Port Moresby, himself a formidable man of knowledge, the truth finally dawned. "Don't you understand?" my friend asked me. "Matthew's illness is due to his father." Everyone knew very well the source of the problem: there was a long-standing quarrel between Aisaga and his son, but Matthew refused to make it up. As a result he was seriously ill, and—my friend added this matter-of-factly—he would die if he did not mend his ways. "Aisaga is killing his own first-born son?" I asked incredulously. "Yes," was the emphatic reply.

Unbeknown to me, the quarrel, which extended back over several years, had recently worsened. Several frightening dreams were linked to Matthew's deteriorating health, and it was difficult to tell whether the dreams reflected or in fact contributed to it. For example, in late January, a week after the death of Helen, Matthew's classificatory sister, he dreamed that the dead woman and his dead sister came and kissed him, then wept. He awoke feeling ill and frightened; for the next several days he complained of pains and general debility and did not leave the house. Aisaga meanwhile seemed to do little about the situation, although in late March he delivered a scathing morning lecture to Matthew as he had been bothered that night, and for several days before, by numerous omens of death (mainly the calls of particular birds from different directions of the village); he interpreted them as warnings about Matthew. Shortly after this rebuke, while Aisaga was absent from the village, Matthew was troubled by more nightmares. All I could gather later from him was that he saw his father in the dreams, whereupon his illness got much worse.

At the heart of the matter was not simply a quarrel but a battle of wills between father and son. Although I discussed the situation with Aisaga many times, and with Matthew and his family as well, no one made explicit what perhaps they assumed I knew. Evidently it was a painful matter; perhaps neither side liked to discuss it with me, quite understandably. But matters were soon to be brought out into the open. The morning of May 2, Matthew told me of a dream he had had that night. He did not hesitate to tell me his dreams when I enquired about them; I suspect he did so to communicate indirectly to Aisaga (I always asked if I could relate the dream to Aisaga to find out what it signified). In this case, to ensure Aisaga learned of it, Matthew also sent one of his sons to report it to him.

The dream, recounted in chapter 6, was of the small, fierce mountain men chasing and spearing the dreamer. Aisaga seemed alarmed by it, and he hurriedly bespelled some water, called Matthew's wife to take it to him, then sent someone to the bush to collect plants to make a protective charm (*fogea*). Finally, he withdrew into his house to ritually invoke the spirits of his forefathers (*isage e pamagogo*) and entreat them to stop bothering Matthew. He told me only that the dream showed Matthew was being attacked by the spirits and that he must drive them away as quickly as possible. This flurry of activity and concern rather surprised me, since Aisaga had seemed little prepared to do anything for Matthew until now. Was he alerted to a new or more serious development?

Four days later, the silence of the early morning was rent by angry shouts hurled between Aisaga's house and the main house occupied by his sons. I listened anxiously for a while, but could not make out what was going on, except that Aisaga was extremely angry over something. I was used to his early morning haranguing of family and lineage, but this was different. Later I called on Aisaga and learned that there had been open quarreling over the family tractor. Instead of accepting Aisaga's rebukes for not getting on with preparing a plot for the season's rice planting, as he normally would do, Matthew responded this morning with abuse, telling his father he did no work but just ordered others around, so he should keep quiet and leave his family alone. Finally, according to Aisaga, Matthew threatened violence if he did not shut up and leave them alone.

Aisaga related all this with a dignified but tragic air. He was deeply shamed (*ofuege*) he insisted; his son's public abuse, defiance, and open threat to kill him—what Matthew really meant was that he would shoot Aisaga—was unforgivable. He did not know what to do; he would leave the village and go elsewhere; he would take his esoteric knowledge with him, and his sons, his family, his lineage would have none! In recounting his anger and his shame, he wept, as he had when he told me of his plans to install his grandson as war leader of the clan. I wondered where would he go and who would have him. Aisaga often remarked to me it was too dangerous to travel around the region now; being such a feared man of sorrow, many people would try to shoot or spear him if they could catch him on the road or in the bush alone. I recalled the incident only a few years ago when his own clansmen forced him to flee the village for a time. The friend and colleague with whom he had taken refuge was now dead, and his family was not likely to welcome such a dangerous visitor. Aisaga's fears were supported by stories related by other men of knowledge. Recently I had been talking with the sons of a man of knowledge from Waima on the coast; they told of how they surrounded their place with barbed wire and kept fierce dogs because there were so many attempts on the old man's life. Alex's uncle was a man of knowledge in another village; I had gone to visit him a few weeks before, only to find that his house had burned down and that the old man had taken refuge with relatives in another village. If Aisaga was determined to leave his family, he was surely bent on self-destruction. Such was his shame, he declared, that his fate did not matter (cf. Young 1983 and the concept of *unuwewe*). He would leave Mekeo altogether and go to his grandmother's people on the coast, he finally announced. These comments were evidently intended to provoke guilt, but there was no one but me there to listen.

Perhaps I should not have, but at this stage I decided to intervene. I would drive him to the coast to visit his relatives, I suggested, as in this way he would at least arrive there safely. He agreed, then barred the gate to his little house and locked his door, as if he were departing for good, and we set off. I cannot say what his Waima relatives made of the unannounced arrival in their midst, but they treated him with great courtesy and prepared an elaborate meal for us. He told them of his shameful treatment at the hands of his eldest son while I went off with some younger guides to explore the village, which I had not seen before. When I decided it was time to return home before it got dark, Aisaga, to my surprise, announced he was returning too. His mood had changed. I know not what had transpired but he seemed mollified by his Waima relatives' reception. Perhaps he judged his departure from the village had given his family and lineage sufficient fright. In any case, we both returned that evening.

My intervention defused the immediate situation, but this was by no means the end of the matter. Although Aisaga returned, he refused to have anything to do with his sons and their families from then on. Each morning he pointedly threw out the food brought by his sons' wives as if he were accusing them of poisoning him. Soon various senior men of the village came to speak with him privately, urging him not to leave the village, attempting to soothe his wounded pride. After a few days, he regained his usual equanimity—but as far as his son Matthew was concerned he remained implacable.

Once the quarrel was made public, Aisaga spoke with me more freely about it. In his view, the trouble had its origins in his, Aisaga's, ambitions for the family to establish some business or enterprise to make money. But Matthew and his two younger brothers never really had their hearts in it; they were not keen on hard work and saw little need for greater effort since they could, like everyone else, easily raise cash by selling betel nut in town. Aisaga's disappointment led to ill feeling between him and his eldest son in particular. The recent crisis arose because Aisaga had been urging his sons for some time to prepare a plot for commercial rice planting but, instead, Matthew lent out the tractor—the family's one achievement—for other families to use, and had not even asked for payment. Aisaga's dream of the broken tractor now emerged in a clearer light. It represented not only his broken ambitions for his family, but, more deeply, the fractured relationship with his eldest son.

Aisaga explained that just as in the case of his classificatory son, Henry, defying him, so his anger alone was sufficient to bring about Matthew's illness. It was not a matter of performing any ritual with the intention of harming his son; the very act of arousing his anger caused the spirits to attack the object of his anger. Despite his shame over the recent incident, Aisaga did not wish his son to die. But, he insisted, it was up to Matthew to make the first move. If he would only apologize, kill a pig, and present it to his father, the healing could begin. Once Aisaga was appeased, the spirits would no longer attack Matthew. Things could not be solved by a conscious decision on his part to forgive Matthew. As long as Aisaga's hidden self continued to be angry, the illness would continue. It was for this very reason, he stressed, that one had to pay a man of sorrow to cure. Only when the hidden self of the adept was pleased by a substantial gift would its dangerous actions cease. The trouble was that Matthew balked at taking the first step. It did not matter how often Aisaga tried to cure Matthew, his actions would have no effect as long as his hidden self remained angry.

Now that the quarrel was a topic of general speculation I heard many different versions of it. Not only was everyone aware that Aisaga's anger was the root of Matthew's illness, I learned this conflict between father and son was a common occurrence. Aisaga himself told of how his best friend, also a man of sorrow, was threatened with violence by his eldest son, of the illness the son suffered as a result, and of the irreconcilable conflict that ensued. Now, Aisaga pointed out, he was to endure the same fate. Another senior man of knowledge described the hatred between himself and his father and how they quarreled over who had greater powers; he went so far as to claim to have caused his father's death by ritual means. It was a well-known phenomenon, people assured me, this anger between a man of knowledge and his heir. The conflict taking place between Aisaga and Matthew was not, I began to realize, a purely personal crisis—it was a recurring cultural theme of personal tragedy.

The pattern of Aisaga's anger runs through events from late January onward, beginning with the death of Helen and the accusations of Henry and Joe against Aisaga and myself, and the subsequent deaths of Henry's aunt and the small child (all three deaths from Aisaga's clan). The matter with Henry was resolved by the end of February. Joe still remained something of a thorn in Aisaga's side, but there was no further overt trouble. Meanwhile, the quarrel with Matthew was building up, reaching a crisis by the beginning of May. There is another thread to this pattern that I have not revealed: Aisaga's growing anger against me. I began to sense he resented me going to other people for information, as I did increasingly from March onward. He also became noticeably annoyed when I asked him to go over spells and other esoteric material he had already told me. By now my competence in the language was much greater, and I wanted to check out earlier understandings. At first I assumed his irritation was impatience with my slowness to grasp things obvious to any member of the culture. But he admitted he felt angry when I asked to revise material, because he then realised how much valuable knowledge he had given me. Late in March he reported a dream in which his grandfather sternly rebuked him for divulging so much of the traditions of secret knowledge to me, an outsider who would soon leave.

A few days later I was planning to go to Port Moresby to buy supplies. Aisaga asked to come, explaining he could no longer go to town because people were too frightened to take him in their truck; when they did no one else would dare travel in the same vehicle. The morning we were due to leave, Aisaga announced, in an almost accusatory tone, he was not going. Realizing something was wrong, I decided to wait and discuss things with him, even though I was packed and ready to go. After some time he finally admitted what was on his mind. He asked me quietly and seriously: did I intend to kill him now that he had given me the knowledge I wanted? That he said, was the custom; if you teach an outsider the major rituals of secret knowledge, they will then try to kill you (recall Alex's comments on this score in chapter 11). Aisaga suspected this was why I had agreed to take him to Port Moresby.

By this time I was used to dramatic and sometimes horrifying pronouncements from him, but this latest revelation stunned me as nothing else had.[1] Aisaga believed I was planning to kill him, yet we talked and ate together almost every day, and he continued to teach me the knowledge he thought motivated my desire to murder him! (I knew, of course, this was how people said even ordinary social relationships operated. I think back to my early fieldwork and the friend who startled me with his admission we had just been chatting with the man responsible for his child's death; see chapter 2.) Up until this point, I had continued to maintain certain romantic Western notions of what learning esoteric knowledge involved, despite the comments of people like Alex. Now, at last, my eyes were being opened to the sorrows of acquiring knowledge. As was the case with other events that seemed to point to some dramatic showdown, such as the accusations of Henry and Joe, Aisaga's growing anger toward me was kept contained. I, of course, never knew what might happen next, but when his conflict with Matthew flared up at the beginning of May, his attention was deflected from me to his son.

The anger of a man of sorrow is a complex personal and cultural construct. Aisaga had good reasons, in his view, for anger and annoyance—with his kinsmen, his son, with me. At the same time, he gave expression to this anger by deliberately singing and reciting (and allowing me to record) the dangerous spells intended to make the spirits strike down people with illness and death. He rather relished this undifferentiated expression, his anger acting randomly through his ritual action. Thus conscious anger seems to feed unconscious levels: self and hidden self set up a reinforcing circle of mounting anger. My presence and involvement in the situation was both cause and effect in the process. It contributed to the situation, exacerbated it, provided an excuse for Aisaga to perform his lethal rituals; at the same time, the very nature of Aisaga's position and his relationships with his family, kin, and community was such that the events I describe are but part of the ongoing pattern of his life, a pattern that would find expression in similar events, with or without my presence.

The Sorrows of Knowledge

It is little wonder people wish to avoid contact with the powerful will of the man of sorrow and strive to insulate themselves from it. Aisaga is totally cut off from others; he can have no casual social interaction with anyone. I have shown how he avoids physical contact even with his own grandchildren—for their sake. He is not only cut off physically, but also psychologically; he can trust no one, not his family, his lineage, his eldest son, nor me, to whom he is giving his knowledge. He cannot trust other men of sorrow. When one man of sorrow visits another for any purpose, he explained, both must sit up all night, neither daring to fall asleep, for if one does the other will kill him—that is their way, he said. When I asked why he had not married again and returned to normal life, he replied he could not, even if he wanted to, because all the other men of sorrow would then know he was no longer observing the *gope* regimen, and thus would kill him in his newly vulnerable state.

The man of sorrow is also in danger of physical attack or poisoning at the hands of many ordinary people. For this reason, Aisaga, whose eyesight was deteriorating from cataracts, avoided traveling about the region or even the village. To prevent anyone from killing him by thrusting a spear or a knife through the floorboards of his house while he was asleep, he placed his bedding on sheets of corrugated iron. Not only the men of sorrow, but all important men of knowledge risked physical assault. Alex, for instance, believed his father, George, was poisoned by someone creeping into the house at night and smearing poison on the old man's mouth while he was asleep. He also claimed that shortly after his father's death, someone tried to knife him through the floorboards, but he woke up in time and frightened off the assailant.

A man such as Aisaga is threatened from all sides; he must never let his guard down. In his relation to the spirit world, too, he must be cautious all the time, as he interacts with destructive forces that might destroy him. When preparing his powerful charms, be they for hunting, weather, or any task, he must take the utmost care not to damage his own hidden self. Many are the men of sorrow who come to grief because of their inability to withstand the effects of the forces they unleash—as in the case of Matthew when he tried to learn hunting rituals. Even as steely a character as Aisaga is not immune to the dangerous forces he attempts to control. His failing eyesight, for example, he attributes to his use of techniques for inflicting and curing blindness. He also suffers from pains and rheumatic swelling in the knee joints that he blames on a particularly effective hunting ritual originated by a lame boy (a form taken by A'aisa); continued use of it can render one a total cripple, he declared. A twisted, deformed fingernail on his right hand he blamed on contact with the python blood he used for various potions. Every time the man of sorrow prepares his lethal charms, he risks harming his own hidden self, despite all the precautions he takes. Should he merely allow his shadow to fall across the container of powerful substances he is preparing it will be trapped there—and destroyed. It is only the strongest who can bear the isolation, privation, and constant dangers faced by the man of sorrow.

In the transference of esoteric knowledge I saw something of how such a sense of self is developed. I have described at some length the continuous deception I faced from Aisaga; it served to make me suspicious and distrustful and angry, as no doubt was intended. The man of sorrow can depend on no one. Many other people, including my friend Alex, repeatedly assured me this was the way all the elders acted; they never give secret knowledge easily, one must keep asking for more. Even when elders become angry and refuse, one must keep badgering them. One must demonstrate the desire for the knowledge and the ability to handle it. I was forever warned that one never knew whether the final secrets had been received, and to lack them could be disastrous. A friend said to me, "It is only when you hold your father in your arms to hear his last dying words that you know he has told it all." But, of course, an adept still may withhold something, there is no way of finally knowing (cf. Barth 1975). The tensions and difficulties inherent in the transference of knowledge pervade the material presented so far, but there was a deeper level for which I was not prepared.

With the mounting pressure of Aisaga's anger from March onward, I at last came to understand that a full transference of secret knowledge involved nothing less than the recipient destroying the giver. This was the underlying significance of Aisaga's conflict with his son, and of his growing anger toward me. Anyone who feels tempted to undertake a similar study should keep this firmly in mind. I was involved with no idyllic path of enlightenment or self-discovery: Mekeo secret knowledge is dangerous knowledge. The reason many parents prefer not to pass on their knowledge may well be to avoid this final ruthless encounter. I had been caught in the trap unaware.

Although I had been given a vivid warning as to the underlying psychological significance of the transference of knowledge, I recognized it for what it was too late. The day after Aisaga's announcement that he would show me the sorcery *polo* (chapter 12), he also told a significant dream that had occurred the night before. In other words, the dream immediately preceded his revelation of *ugauga* sorcery. The dream was of me asking to take his photograph so I could show it to people in Australia. I—my dream-self—told him I wanted to photograph him in traditional dress, the *ipi* (which is no more than a brief perineal band). He objected, saying that he felt awkward about being photographed like that because most people, including himself, nowadays wore clothes (shorts, ramis, and shirts). But I continued to press him, until finally he agreed, providing the photograph was taken inside the house. I said he would have to go outside because the photograph would only come out properly if taken in the sunlight. Once again he protested that he felt embarrassed to be photographed in such scanty dress, but I still insisted. Then he woke up.

This dream might be given many different interpretations, but the context points to a self-evident significance. In asking for esoteric knowledge (the photograph I want to show to people in Australia), I am stripping—denuding—him of his secrets. It also indicates his fear, which he often expressed to me, that I would make this secret knowledge public. It also depicts my persistence in getting what I wanted (something others had advised me was imperative). The contrasts in the dream between inside and outside, darkness and sunlight, private and public, secret and hidden—the key cultural themes outlined earlier—are all present in the dream imagery (indeed this brief dream of Aisaga's encapsulates the main themes of part I). And what of this image of an old man being stripped of his precious cultural knowledge in the rapacious and exploitative manner assumed of all whites? Surely this image is so poignant, and so pointed, that it should have given me reason to pause, to reflect upon the callousness of my actions. Yet, at the time, what struck me was that this seemed an oddly vulnerable image Aisaga presented of himself—one very out of character.

Aisaga offered no explanation—did he assume it was self-evident? Was it in fact a dream or a message couched as a dream? When I asked what the dream signified, he replied he was not sure, perhaps it meant he would get sick since I wanted to take his *lalauga* away with me. The play on words here is, of course, highly significant: a photograph is also *lalauga,* so in taking his photograph I was taking his hidden/dream-self (*lalauga*), stealing the very locus of his power. The dream warned that if I proceeded with my intention of acquiring his secrets, I would inevitably arouse his shame and anger. What I failed to take into account at this stage, because I did not know of it, was the nature of that anger. The image of Aisaga shamed by me, which struck me initially as curiously inappropriate, takes on a different meaning when the implacable and autonomous nature of the anger of a man of sorrow is understood. To shame a man such as Aisaga, as his son Matthew did with his threats to shoot him, can lead to only one end: a battle of wills wherein the weaker will be destroyed.

In the final weeks of my fieldwork I came to empathize with Matthew, whom I had prematurely judged to be lazy and weak-willed. Matthew was always very patient with me, allowing me to record his dreams, discussing his sickness and the quarrel with his father, all without losing his temper or even seeming irritated by my meddling. Perhaps this stemmed from his greater awareness of the painful dilemma which, in a sense, we shared. He had a much fuller understanding of the situation than I, and no illusions about his ability to withstand his father's anger. He spoke plainly and honestly on this score when I tried to persuade him to make up the quarrel. He knew he would eventually die, but his death, he said, was of no consequence since his eldest son was old enough to replace him and to look after the family. He did not have the knowledge or the strength to best his father; thus there could be no competition of powers (similar to those described in other cases). He could do nothing—except refuse to give in. I realized Matthew was indeed helpless against his father; the only means of salvaging some shred of his manhood and dignity was to refuse reconciliation, and accept death as the inevitable consequence. In this way, he would succeed not only in defying his father, he would punish him, for his death would be a loss to Aisaga and a diminishing of his lineage.

Aisaga's anger with me stemmed from the inherent nature of the transmission of knowledge. This was indicated not only in his suspicions of me, but in accounts I had of many battles between fathers and their eldest sons. Obtaining the major rituals of secret knowledge requires nothing less than the ruthlessness to kill the giver—and usually that person is the father. In the nature of things, the son usually does replace the father, but this is not always the case. Aisaga, for example, acquired the major lethal rituals not from his father, but his uncle (his father's classificatory brother), because his father did not wish to burden Aisaga with this dangerous knowledge. Often important rituals are given by grandfathers rather than fathers. The man of knowledge who claimed to have killed his own father obtained his powers in this manner. Since he was instructed by his grandfather, he believed he had received fuller, more-complete traditions, and thus was able to destroy his father. We have seen that all people are reluctant to part with their ritual knowledge, even the minor rituals, and tend to pass on the final secrets to their heirs only when close to death. In the case of the holders of major powers, self seems so invested in them that to transfer even part is to strip the self—as was imaged in Aisaga's dream. This is so because secret knowledge is, above all, the instrument of individual will, allowing the adept to shape his or her hidden self into a powerful means of controlling others.

Should we point to a classic Oedipal conflict underlying all this? Clearly, such is not strictly applicable in the sense of sexual jealousy over the mother as the pivot of an Oedipal triangle. The conflict taking place is of will against will, self against self. Only when the father feels close to death does he willing transfer all his secrets to his heir.[2] The individual determined to obtain major secret knowledge must gradually strip the giver of that which constitutes the core of his powerful self. According to cultural ideals, and usually in fact, this inherently destructive transaction takes place between father and son. But once the father is dead and a spirit inhabiting the hidden world, he becomes a powerful helper. In order to call upon the spirit of his father, the son must take some physical relic from his dead body. Aisaga instructed me on his death to cut off a finger from his body before it was buried and use it to summon his spirit. He told of how, as a young man, he and his classificatory brother were told to exhume their grandfather's skull after his death. Aisaga still keeps this relic. He also described the ceremonies following his father's death. After the body was buried in the cemetery, they (Aisaga's two uncles, both men of sorrow, himself, and his cousin) exhumed the body during the night, taking it to a place in the bush where it was dismembered, and the flesh, organs, and bones used to prepare various ritual weapons and charms. In these final grisly mutilations of the father by his heirs, I find reflected Freud's (1961b) fundamental insight that patricide—symbolic or otherwise—lies close to the heart of the attainment of ritual and religious power in the human imagination. In the Mekeo context, the man of sorrow turns this psychically powerful motif into an instrument of ritual power to destroy others. It is the spirit of his father, and of his forefathers, whom the man of sorrow calls upon to aid him in his deadly rituals.

As the end of my fieldwork drew near, I became increasingly oppressed by the awareness of just how implacable, indomitable, and dangerous a will was possessed by a man like Aisaga. I had seen more than enough of it, and the consequences of crossing it. I confess, though it does me little credit, that I felt relieved when his attention was deflected to poor Matthew. From then until I left in June, dealing with Aisaga became increasingly difficult for me and for everyone around him. He remained angry with us all. Matthew's condition did not change much; he continued to be ill but not, it seemed to me, significantly worse. In the days following the outburst in May, Matthew's children began to fall sick one after another. Aisaga had cause to reprimand the wife of his youngest son; two days later she, too, took ill. Although he did not refuse to bespell the sick and administer medicines to them, everyone was well aware of his attitude. Lest the significance of all this escape me, Aisaga pointedly asked why I thought the family was suffering such a sudden spate of illness. Every evening now I could hear him singing softly by himself on his veranda, the songs I now recognized as spells to provoke the spirits of the dead to attack. It was during this time, mid-May, that a man from another descent group was bitten by a taipan snake (*augama*). A dream linked to this event, in which Aisaga was identified as the attacker, was mentioned earlier. Taking care not to reveal the identity of the dreamer, I was bold enough to ask whether the omen was correct. Although I was nervous about provoking Aisaga further, I really wanted to know how he would respond. He listened quietly to what I had to say. I feared an outburst, but he mildly replied, after due consideration, that he performed no ritual with the express purpose of harming the man in question, but since he had been angry for several weeks, and had been singing the spells to invoke the spirits to bring sickness and death, it was entirely possible the responsibility lay with him. When the man of sorrow calls upon the spirits, he reminded me, they usually assume the form of snakes and may bite people (recall the snakes that appeared after the sorcery *polo* was brought from the bush). Indeed, the spells he was singing, as I now knew, included many symbolic references to the dreaded *augama* snake.

Aisaga was not one to boast of his powers. He had no need to, except perhaps to me, an arrogant outsider who failed to take proper heed of him and the situation I found myself in. In his view, no doubt, he was exceptionally patient and forbearing. He quietly cautioned me against thinking I could best him at his own game. He knew it was difficult for me to grasp all that was going on. His long ritual practice, he observed, resulted in him becoming more like a *faifai* (water spirit) or a powerful spirit (*isage*) like A'aisa himself, than a living human being. Indeed, he had partaken of the body of A'aisa himself by ritually eating the flesh of the *augama* snake, the bodily form taken by A'aisa. His anger had become like the *augama* snake, striking at others and destroying them. He kept with him the bodily relics of his father, his grandfather, and all the powerful men of sorrow of his lineage. He was not only imbued with their power, but was in constant communion with them; his own hidden self acting in concert with them, even without conscious direction. His bodily self, long hardened and reduced by a strict *gope* regimen, had become like the imperishable stone relics employed in his rituals—totally unlike the vulnerable fleshy bodies of ordinary men and women. Many people had tried to kill him over many years, he said, and none had succeeded. "I will stay until my spine becomes bent right over—like my grandfather—and then I will die," he said. "No one will kill me."[3]

I had reached the point where all I wanted to do was get away—to return to my own world and reality, to leave behind this grotesque battle of wills. Aisaga sensed this and complained anew that since I had gotten the secret knowledge I wanted, I was looking forward to leaving with no regard for him. What I have referred to as the burden of the gift had become far greater, far more intolerable than I ever imagined. My appreciation of Matthew's courage grew; I could leave, he could not. There was no resisting Aisaga's singular will. He was not maliciously evil, he acted within the moral boundaries of his culture, but no one could oppose him. I felt chilled contemplating the culture that created such an implacable will.[4]

The traditions of secret knowledge bring sorrow to those who possess them, to those who wish to acquire them, and to those who lack them. Aisaga is indeed a man of sorrow, laden with greater ritual powers than any other living person in his community. He bears the burden of the sorrow he must bring others, and himself, with great fortitude. His is both a heroic and a tragic role, a role of mythic stature he plays with consummate skill.

15

A'aisa's Gifts

Having explored the compelling inner worlds of actual men and women, I now return to a more analytic examination of the representation of self in cultural symbolism. Although not primarily intended as an examination of the contingent nature of ethnographic understanding, this text describes a richness and variety of social practice and individual understandings that give lie to normative statements concerning the nature of the Mekeo spirit realm and cosmic ordering. Investigations into subjective experience and esoteric knowledge did indeed disclose things not available to me during my first fieldwork. This raises a host of important theoretical and methodological issues currently being energetically debated within anthropology. I do not hope to resolve these issues, nor even face them head on, although I shall offer some passing comments, the first of which being that I believe Western anthropologists must learn to work within an awareness of the indeterminacy of our knowledge without being overwhelmed or obsessed by it.

This chapter draws together and brings to a close my ethnographic material by arguing that Mekeo cosmological orderings can be understood more richly when considered in relation to the self, and that Mekeo culture structures some of its key symbols around the existential problems of self-differentiation. This necessitates going over ground already covered in order to draw out new insights. In the process, I hope to clarify, at least in part, the nature of the contradictions discovered between public, manifest representations of the cosmic order, and its concealed aspects. I shall focus on three interlinked topics: the potentials of self imaged in the symbolism of the adept's ritual regime; the roles of the man of kindness and the man of sorrow; and the nature of death, its place within the cosmic order, and its link to the emergence of self-consciousness.

Creating the Invulnerable Self: *Gope*

Vivid images of the different potentials of self are to be found in the symbolism of *gope, the preparatory regimen necessary for implementing major rituals.* Yet without the knowledge of the experiences of actual persons such as Celestina, Joe, Josephina, Alex, Francis, and especially Aisaga, the symbolism of *gope* cannot be read with the same conviction. What follows is not simply my decoding of the "cryptology" (Sperber 1975) of Mekeo symbolism; the stonelike invulnerability of the adept, and the fluid, vulnerable self of the ordinary person have already been powerfully enacted in individual lives.

In practice, as I have observed, the requirements of *gope* vary, from Alex's brief seclusion, to the much more stringent requirements for Francis's rituals for ulcer infliction, to Aisaga's continuous but modified observance. Women do not undergo *gope,* and the reasons for this will become apparent later in the discussion. The most rigorous form of *gope* is that imposed on the man of sorrow when he prepares himself for the first time, or after a long break, to undertake *ugauga* rituals. Although the process has already been outlined, I will now examine it more closely, as it is only now that it can be appreciated within the context of actual lived experience.

According to the adept's account, the body of the ordinary person, male or female, is heavy (*meau*) with watery (*veivei*), cool (*kekea*), soft (*mamea*), and abundant flesh (*faga e alogai*). The purpose of *gope* is to render the body light (*ilikae*), with a minimum of flesh (*unia maini*), so that the whole body becomes dry (*ogogo*), hard (*inoka*) and hot (*isapu*). Stringent *gope* requires a radical reduction of flesh and muscle, so that a strong, muscular man becomes skin and bone. Aisaga explained that as a young married man he was similar in size and appearance to his eldest son, Matthew; thick-necked, heavy-shouldered, and powerfully built. He spoke of his relatives weeping when they saw him emerge from seclusion after first practising *ugauga* rituals following the death of his wife, because his formerly powerful frame was reduced to a mere skeleton. To achieve this, the trainee not only limits his food and drink, but consumes various emetic and purgative potions to rid the body of its wastes and to reduce the watery content of the flesh. Food intake is reduced to the absolute minimum, allowing each day no more than one or two plantains charred in their skins. Liquid intake is kept to a minimum and only hot liquids may be consumed. As well as ridding the body of its fluids, it must be made hot by the ingestion of hot "medicines" such as ginger and chili. To preserve heat and dryness, the body must not be washed or come into contact at all with cold water. The practitioner cannot chew betel nut because this produces saliva in the mouth. Sexual intercourse, since it produces semen from the body and exposes one to the sexual fluids of the partner, must be avoided. Even seminal emission at night during dreams is dangerous under these extreme conditions. Finally, the adept's body reaches a condition in which it becomes so dry, hard, and hot it produces no liquids (neither sweat, saliva, nor sexual fluids) nor scarcely any wastes. After this stage is achieved, usually after several months, it is safe to handle the remains of the dead and the relics of spirit beings. The adept's hidden self is still sent out (*papealaisa*) of the body by contact with these powerful substances, but now it is able to act in concert with the spirit beings.

The adept understands *gope* as the means of transforming his body into a state wherein it can withstand contact with the dead and the spirit beings. There is an implicit opposition between living bodies and the bodily remains of spirit beings (human and nonhuman). Paradoxically it seems, living bodies are seen to be passively vulnerable to the active, piercing power inherent in the bodily substance of the dead. Death is a transformation which empowers the hidden self while dissolving the body. Similarly, *gope* reduces all the soft, fluid, permeable, vulnerable parts of the body to the point that it becomes a fleshless skeleton, stopping just short of death. The adept's identification with the spirits and the dead is explicit; recall Aisaga's observation that his many years of ritual practice had made him like a spirit himself. By not washing his body, the man of sorrow even comes to smell like the dead, thus attracting them to him. *Gope* is further acknowledged to make the practitioner *physically* weak, lacking the bodily strength to move around or work, just like a dying man.

The meaning of the term *gope,* as Mosko (1985:86ff.) observes for the Bush Mekeo, is "to tie up" or "bind." The action involved in binding something up with rope, or fastening it with vine, is described as *gope*. Mosko suggests "tightening" the body as a translation. I would suggest that "closing" or "binding" the self comes closer to the meaning intended. Undoubtedly, the aim of *gope,* as Mosko puts it for the Bush Mekeo, is that nothing should go into the body and that nothing should pass out of it. In other words, the fluid boundaries of the physical self are closed and hardened—nothing can be introduced into it, nothing alienated from it. The adept becomes, ideally, as hard and invulnerable as the stone relics he employs in his rituals. He neither takes from, nor gives to, others: he becomes totally self-contained.

If at one level, this ritual closing of the self is an imitation of death in life, an identification with the dead and the spirits and their transformative power, at another level it represents a severing of self from the living. While the adept, like Aisaga, tends to emphasize a positive identification with the spirits, the cutting off of self from others is apparent. Ideally, like the dead, the *ugauga* adept does not eat, nor does he engage in work to produce food. What little he consumes should be stolen by himself or his assistants. He is removed from the domestic ties and social obligations wherein food is produced, shared, and exchanged. Not only is his body reduced to the minimum of flesh, but he ceases to owe his bodily sustenance, and thus substance, to others. He must physically segregate himself from society, his only occasional contacts being with other celibate males living outside society like himself. His body is closed to sexual exchanges, he can allow no part of his bodily substance to be given to another. In fact his body becomes so dry (*ogogo*) that it produces nothing that can be appropriated.

By this means, the unstable, divisible flux of bodily substance that makes up an ordinary, living human being becomes hard, impermeable, and closed—invulnerable. It is defended against all intrusions and alienations. Laing (1965: 46ff.) has written of the petrification of the self in Western psychology. Mekeo *gope* seems to put such a process into effect ritually; it is not solely a physical mortification of the flesh to gain spiritual power, although it is that as well. It is equally a psychological process involving the hardening of the boundaries of self against other. *Gope* is a process leading to that immovable, inexorable, indomitable will so strikingly exemplified by Aisaga. If Aisaga's story helps us to appreciate the human reality behind the symbol, then the symbol itself also underlines the representativeness of his life and situation.

Mosko (1985:84–90) presents *gope* as an integral part of the opposed reproductive ritual cycles of male and female in Bush Mekeo culture. He shows that men and women throughout their reproductive life ritually "tighten" and then open their bodies to sexual partners. Much of Mosko's description and analysis applies also to the Central Mekeo, yet I sense a significant difference in emphasis which may, or may not, stem from Mosko's avowed intent to analyze the belief system abstracted from social practice. Central Mekeo women today still observe the *megomego* restrictions following childbirth (or a modified form of them), but their husbands do not, as a matter of course, undertake *gope,* nor do they remove themselves to the clan meeting house (*ufu*) during this time. Nevertheless, the spacing of births in most households support claims that husband and wife normally cease sexual relations until a child is weaned. Elders observed that in the past husbands removed themselves to the *ufu,* but they did not refer to men as necessarily undertaking *gope* at this time, as Mosko describes for Bush Mekeo. If a man wanted to use or acquire ritual knowledge, *gope* would provide the opportunity, but major rituals are not available to all. Only specialists manipulate the dangerous substances necessitating rigorous *gope;* less strict regimens, however, might be undertaken by ordinary men implementing minor rituals such as various forms of love ritual.

Mosko acknowledges that for Bush Mekeo the purpose of *gope* was to prepare a man to handle the substances used in esoteric ritual, but he implies all men engaged in such activities while segregated from their wives, and thus it was part of the ritual cycle observed by every man. In contrast, for Central Mekeo, *gope* is the distinguishing characteristic of the male adept, and in particular the man of sorrow. In the past, ordinary men who removed themselves to the *ufu* following the birth of a child might engage in minor rituals, or act as assistants to experts, requiring them to undertake modified forms of *gope*, but this was a matter of choice, not necessity. Prior to European contact and pacification in the late nineteenth century, it was necessary to maintain ritual preparedness for warfare, which did require *gope*. Some men are said to have devoted their lives to war and rarely cohabited with their wives, but the majority only reluctantly undertook *gope* when they knew attack was imminent. The attitude is that *gope* is something ordinary men prefer to avoid and undertake only when circumstances demand it.

Nor is this attitude surprising in view of the levels of meaning just explored. *Gope* is not simply a kind of ritual, prophylactic hygiene, as Mosko seems to come close to arguing, but the means of creating death in life. It is not something for the ordinary man, except under extraordinary circumstances. Yet Mosko's point that *gope* is essentially masculine is applicable. Women, even those who practice various forms of esoteric ritual, do not undertake it. No one ever asserted women could not, or should not; women practitioners simply said they did not observe *gope*. Since women do not implement destructive rituals, they do not have to manipulate the most dangerous substances and relics, although this is not to say that rituals such as dream healing and divination involve no risk for the practitioner. Furthermore, it would clearly be impractical for women to close their bodies to others. Following the birth of a child, a woman does refrain from sexual intercourse until the child is weaned, but during this time she is giving her bodily substance to her child in the form of milk. Her body is still open to others. Women who produce food and milk for children cannot close themselves. Even postmenopausal women, such as Josephina, did not undertake *gope*.

The female self, as discussed earlier, is thought to be inherently altruistic— always caring, giving. Thus the quality of femaleness, when applied meta-phorically to land or inanimate objects, indicates productiveness, fertility, multiplicity. Females are associated with life, birth, the production of the material, the living body. They are "mother," "matrix," "materia."[1] Mekeo understand both the living body and woman to be passive and acted upon by the active, destructive power wielded by male ritual experts. We are evidently dealing here not only with male and female reproductive cycles, but with much broader cosmological oppositions to which female and male, life and death, passive and active, and corporeal and noncorporeal are all linked. The physical, embodied world is seen as primarily female. *Gope* is essentially masculine in that it involves the transformation of the passive, corporeal self, dependent for its existence on others, to a state wherein the hidden self realizes its maximum potential for independence and for destructive power. Thus *gope* aims at destroying nothing less than the feminine aspect of self.

It becomes difficult to distinguish between what is generally known and what is known only to ritual experts. Ordinary people are well aware of the ritual use of body substance, and of the dangers posed by the body substance of the dead. They are also aware of *gope* and its function to render the body of the adept "hot" and thus capable of withstanding the destructive "heat" possessed by the spirits. But only the adept has a precise and detailed knowledge of all just described. I found laymen's description of *gope* stressed heat, and the necessity to build up heat in the body (see also Hau'ofa 1981), whereas I found the adept stressed the importance of dryness and hardness. Watery things were to be avoided not simply because they cooled one's heat, as the layman would emphasize, but because they were wet—that is, matter in flux, fluid, and liable to decay. It is perhaps appropriate that the layman should stress the expert's destructive powers while the expert himself lays stress on his own indestructibility. The ordinary person, I think, is not so consciously aware of the very flesh of his or her body as inherently unstable and liable to dissolution. Yet their general sense of vulnerability to the power of esoteric ritual, and to the destructive influence of the spirit world, is profound. The adept's more intimate knowledge of the significance of bodily substance serves to give a heightened conscious awareness of the layperson's permeable, vulnerable body boundaries, and of the imperviousness of his own, an awareness evident in Aisaga's comments that as long as he observed *gope* he had nothing to fear from the spirit world or from the living.

The management of body substance as represented in *gope* could be illustrated also in the deployment of body substance in other contexts. The vulnerability and permeability of the living body to the influence of others, both living and dead, is vividly represented in the ritual use of body dirt (*faga ofuga*) as described in chapter 11. To pursue this further would underline the arguments just made, but it would not develop them in any new way.

Potentials of the Self: The Man of Kindness and the Man of Sorrow

The symbolism of *gope* draws attention to the way in which the ordinary person is perceived, at least by the adept, to be inevitably caught up in transfers of matter taking place between human bodies. The bodily substance of a person is unstable in two directions: it may be appropriated by others, yet it is equally the result of contributions by others. Social relationships are based upon transfers between living bodies in sexuality, marriage, and reproduction to create new bodies, and upon transfers of vegetable foods and meat to maintain bodily existence. A child is produced from the "body dirt" of its parents, and once born it is fed by them. Thus, raising a child, whether by natural or adoptive parents, is referred to as *pafa'a*—to make large by feeding. The growing body of the child is sustained and derived from the food given to it by others, to whom it owes its existence. When a person reaches adulthood, he or she continues to consume food, especially meat, derived from others through gifts and exchange. Gifts of food are much more than temporary contributions to a person's well-being or pleasure, in the Mekeo view they are additions to a person's physical substance, to the continuing flow of matter that is a living person. Those who provided wealth for one's parents' marriage helped to create one's physical existence: the flow of wealth led to the exchange of body substance which produced one's own body. It is not just that the bodily self can be intruded upon or appropriated by others, as in esoteric ritual, the entity I call "my body" (*imauu*) is in essence a flow of the gifts of others.

The significance of food as a gift, in Mauss's (1966) sense, in Melanesian societies has been a dominating theme of the anthropological literature for decades. What has come to impress me in the Mekeo situation is the intimate sense of food as an incorporation of others into self (cf. Meigs 1984). In accepting a gift of food, one does not simply recognize a social tie or obligation, but makes that "other" part of self. Mekeo do not engage in the competitive exchanges of wealth characteristic of many Melanesian societies (part I); their exchanges aim at reciprocity and are not primarily a means of establishing dominance in political relationships. The generosity publicly displayed by the man of kindness can be seen to express the value and necessity of transfers of matter perpetuating social relationships and creating new life. The giving and receiving of food manifests the openness of self to others. (The apparent paradox that the most important feasts and food exchanges are linked to death will be dealt with shortly.)

The man of kindness is most obviously associated with the smooth, harmonious surface of the social body and the physical body. But the material world has a double aspect: a visible surface of controlled forms, and a concealed interior of matter in flux. Viewed from the "inside," the embodied world can be understood as a series of transformations and transfers of matter between different states and bodies.[2] It might seem that this is most obviously associated with the man of sorrow. Hau'ofa (1981:chapter 8), for example, explicitly identifies him with the inside of the body. In contrast, I have asserted he is representative of the disembodied realm. It is the man of kindness, who functions as the center of the descent group's hospitality, conviviality, and food exchanges, who must be understood as the mediator of the flow of matter between bodies in social interaction.

Ordinary people are often referred to as the "eaters" (*aniani aui*) since they eat the food at feasts. The men of kindness are not supposed to consume anything on public occasions, although today they usually do. In the past, so it is said, they wore distinctive nose ornaments extending over the mouth, intended to make eating and drinking impossible. While the man of sorrow abstains because he has cut himself off from life, the man of kindness demonstrates his role as giver rather than consumer. In contrast to ordinary men and women—the eaters—the man of kindness does not consume the flow of substance, he generates and channels it. Paradoxically, it might seem, ordinary people are also commonly referred to as *ulalu aui*, those who are deprived or who lack something. They are thus at the same time both the "eaters" and the "deprived." What they lack is the means to impose their will on others, that is, they lack the rituals of secret knowledge, while their role as "eaters" emphasizes their immersion in the flux of life processes.

The ordinary person must somehow define his or her existence between two extremes. One's body is owed to others, and threatened by others. It remains open, vulnerable, permeable. Yet one also has self-consciousness and is aware of existence as a complex of private, hidden thoughts and emotions, and of a yet more hidden self. Through the rituals of secret knowledge a person can develop this inner/hidden self to exercise will power and exert it over others. But the more developed the hidden self, the more one must be isolated from ordinary society and human companionship. The ordinary person, of course, really has no choice. Although drawn to the pleasures of sociability, the "eaters" are unable to achieve the ultimate expression of altruism and generosity. They are envious, mean, and would hold back what they could. They desire secret knowledge, but lack the opportunity, and the necessary self-control, to exercise it.

Here, perhaps, is the pull of eros and thanatos (Marcuse 1969): everyone has potential in both directions. One may develop the hidden self, but this leads to a kind of death in life. Or, one can open oneself fully and give one's self to others in the flow of matter, but life, paradoxically, is vulnerable to death. In the forbidding, stony self of the man of sorrow and the benevolent figure of the man of kindness, Mekeo culture leaves little doubt as to which of these two potentials is more desirable. Hau'ofa (1981:302) also observes moral potentials for the self in the symbolism of "chief" and "sorcerer," but couches them in terms of ethical oppositions of "good" and "bad," which, in my view, imposes inappropriate Western categories. The man of sorrow is not simply "bad" in moral terms (recall the discussion in chapter 2 of the different connotations of bad). What is "bad" is if all people were to follow the same path. The ordeals the man of sorrow must undergo are symbolic expressions of the suffering endured by all who seek personal power via secret knowledge. He represents not how ritual power is in fact exercised, but how it *should* be used within the constraints of human society, so that the proper ordering of human relationships and cosmic processes is maintained.

Death, the Nature of the Cosmic Order, and the Emergence of Self-Consciousness

The nature of death, and its significance within the total cosmic order, is clarified by what dreaming reveals of the existence of a disembodied realm. The public symbolism asserts a total separation of the realms of the living and the dead, with the man of sorrow the sole mediator of the two. This would suggest a simple opposition between life and death which masks the more complex and multilayered cosmic ordering, wherein living and dead both possess material and nonmaterial aspects, and both are engaged in two different yet interpenetrating processes, one consisting of a flow of material substances, the other of immaterial forms.

From this perspective, Westerners can better appreciate that death, in the Mekeo view, is not so much a question of destroying the body (as we look at it), but rather of achieving a permanent separation of the bodily self and the noncorporeal self. Mekeo take more seriously than we the proposition that matter can be neither destroyed nor created. Death brings about a transformation of the body, but its constituents remain part of the flow of matter. Furthermore, the separation of the corporeal self and the noncorporeal self must be achieved first.

Death, as it is revealed in the esoteric versions of the A'aisa myths, is something extrinsic and introduced by an external agent to the embodied realm. It was A'aisa himself who brought death, along with his gifts of secret knowledge. Prior to his appearance among human beings, people did not die. A'aisa is not attributed with the creation of the bodily world, which existed before him, and there is no account of its origin. Two myths, however, deal with the origins of death. The first is the story of the *imala,* a word used to describe the sloughed skin of a snake, a tortoise's carapace, or the shell of crab or shrimp. Desnoes (1941:381) also gives a secondary meaning: "to last forever, to be immortal" (durer toujours, être immortel). According to this myth, death came into being because people failed to heed A'aisa's words. When A'aisa threw down from the mountain the various stones and implements to be used in the rituals of secret knowledge, he also threw down the *imala* of a dead human being, instructing the people at the bottom not to drop it or let it touch the ground. Foolishly, they ignored A'aisa's warnings and let it fall. Whereupon A'aisa declared that if they had caught the *imala,* human beings would not have to die, but merely change their skins like snakes and thus renew themselves. Because of their failure human beings would have to die. (The *imala,* which was said to be like a great stone, broke into pieces and became one of the many different kinds of "stones" used in destructive rituals.) The second myth recounts the adventures of a man whose pitiful lamenting of the loss of his dead wife so moved A'aisa himself that he agreed to take him to the land of the dead and give him back his wife. A'aisa instructs him that he must not touch or try to have sexual congress with his wife until they have planted a new garden together and seen it come to fruition. The husband, however, soon forgets A'aisa's warnings and, as a consequence, the wife returns to the land of the dead. From that time on, all possibility of the dead returning to the living was lost.

The first myth suggests that death, as introduced by A'aisa, need not be a permanent change in state, since people could simply renew their physical bodies, as reptiles do their skins. The second myth proposes that even with the creation of death, and the separation of the living and the dead, there might still be a movement from death back to the living, embodied state. But because of people's disregard of A'aisa's word, this becomes impossible. Both myths emphasize that death, as a state, is introduced from outside the material, physical order and that it is a transformation taking place in one direction only, from the embodied to the disembodied. Matter—the physical world—is thus prior.

The transformations brought about by death bear upon both aspects of the self. In life, the hidden self can leave the body and act independently for a while, but must return if the person is to operate as a healthy, purposeful physical entity; the physical self and the hidden self are closely linked. Death can take place only when the hidden self is unable to return to the embodied self. But death is not immediate, it may take some time, during which the body sickens. Death comes about first as a result of the abstraction of the hidden self, and only second as a result of the physical body undergoing changes which eventually lead to the disintegration of its boundaries and the transformation of the substances composing it. Once separated from its body substance, the hidden self still retains a certain attraction to it. But following death the body is no longer a single, integral entity enclosed by a skin, or surface form: it becomes part of the generalized flow of substance.

I have now identified the following cosmological divisions. There exists a visible outside of bodily forms and a concealed inside of unstable matter in flux. External forms may undergo change, but the flux of matter which they contain continues to exist and may take on new forms. The disembodied realm also consists of a partially visible outside and a concealed interior; though, of course, in contrast to the physical world, the whole of the disembodied is a hidden world. The imagery accessible in dreams and similar states of consciousness represents that aspect of the other world which is knowable, at least to some degree, to the living. There is as well, Aisaga often impressed upon me, another aspect that is entirely obscured from the living. That is to say, there is a yet more hidden, indeed an entirely unknown inside to the disembodied realm.

The embodied and disembodied realms are linked by the force of attraction that draws the dream-self back to its body substance, which, alive or dead, remains in the physical world. (To my knowledge, Mekeo do not conceptualize this force in abstract terms, nor do I know of any single term to describe it; but its existence is implicit in everything that has been described here. People would simply refer to the dream-image self leaving the body and then being drawn to its body dirt.) The dream-self, it should be recalled, is conceptualized as normally existing *inside* the body (people speak of it not leaving, but coming out from inside [*pealaisa*] the body). Or it may be attracted to body dirt produced from the *inside* of its body, or even to transformed matter which was once part of its body substance. Thus it is clear, I think, that the noncorporeal self is linked to the concealed flux of matter comprising the physical world. This is to say the "inside" of the embodied world is linked to the "outside" of the disembodied,[3] as shown in figure 1.

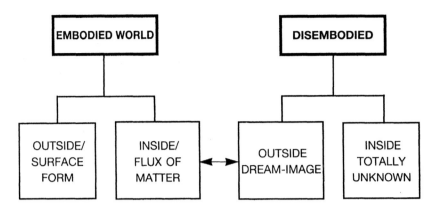

Figure 1

How then do the various layers of self identified earlier relate to these cosmological divisions? We have seen that the person consists of a) an inside self (*alo*) concealed from others, this is the experienced self of conscious thoughts, desires, and emotions; b) a public "face" (*maaga*) visible to others, that is, one's actions which are observed by others; c) a physical body form and surface (*faaga*); d) a body interior of unstable matter (*faaga ofuga*) which is concealed; and finally e) a noncorporeal self (*lalauga*) which participates in the hidden, noncorporeal realm, as shown in figure 2.

The inside self is linked to the concealed interior of the body, as is the hidden self, but the latter is not bound by physical existence. It is in the concealed thoughts and desires of the inside self and in the concealed flux of the interior of the body that the rituals of secret knowledge find their subject—but it is *via the hidden self* that they must operate.

Mediators of Life and Death

I can say, then, that the rituals of secret knowledge are based upon the concept of an embodied and a disembodied realm linked by the attraction of the noncorporeal self to the interior of its corporeal substance. Is it going too far to translate this as the attraction of incorporeal form (dream-image) to corporeal formlessness (matter in flux)? If not, then perhaps I can propose that the rituals are a means of bringing about transformations of form in the material world, via the relationship of incorporeal form to formless matter.

The rituals employed by the adept cannot create matter but they can change the forms it takes. The myths describe the many transformations of shape and surface form that have come about in the material world. One tale of A'aisa explains that originally there were no animals, birds, reptiles, or insects, only

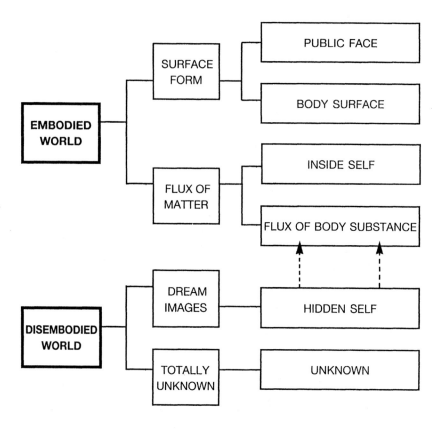

Figure 2

people. Because there were too many people, A'aisa transformed some of them into other species, including plants, and thus it was that these other living entities came into being. Many of the myths relate how a particular myth hero changed on death into some plant, animal, or bird. These transformations are of the greatest significance to the adept who understands them, since these transmuted bodies become the "leavings" (*fu'a*) which are the basis of the powerful "medicines" he employs in his rituals.[4] They become the means of attracting the dream-images of the myth heroes to help the adept bring about new transformations. A'aisa himself was a great shape-changer—he might appear in the form of a snake, a wild pig, a cassowary—and it was his appearing before his brother, Isapini, in the form of a little boy, that led to the misunderstanding and anger between them, and thus to the origin of *pikupa* ("jealousy") in human society—and of *ugauga* sorcery. The man of sorrow, like A'aisa himself, is a trickster who can change his appearance and even become invisible, so it is believed.

The cultural emphasis on controlling surface appearances and on disguise and trickery are evidently connected in that both are the means of changing forms or the appearance of form. But whereas the ordinary person desires only to maintain existing entities, the adept aims at shaping them to his own ends. The most drastic, far-reaching transformation is to bring about the death of a living person. By permanently separating the hidden/dream-self of the victim from his or her body, the man of sorrow brings about the dissolution of the bodily self. All then that is left of the form (image) that person once had is his or her dream-image/self.

It is death, as an existential fact and as an event, that is the pivot, the focus, of the roles of the man of kindness and the man of sorrow. The culture hero A'aisa created death, along with the rituals of secret knowledge; because of this, all human beings must die. Through A'aisa's intervention, death becomes an aspect of the cosmic order. It is the function of the man of sorrow to bring about the transformation of death. He is in this sense A'aisa's agent and is explicitly identified with A'aisa. The man of sorrow manipulates body substance of the dead to bring about a transformation of the live body of a living person. His existence necessitates the existence of the man of kindness, since the flow of physical matter must be maintained despite the disruption of death.

In the mortuary feasts, the man of kindness can be seen to operate in reverse to the man of sorrow. The death of a member of the descent group is the occasion on which important food gifts are made by the man of kindness to other clans, in particular the *ufu apie* (chapters 1 and 2). That is to say, he takes body substance of the dead—the corpse of a member of the lineage—and turns it into gifts of meat, which contain potential for life in the nurture of living bodies, and these gifts are given to other groups, in particular those from whom wives are received. Thus the man of kindness perpetuates the flow of matter in the physical world in the face of death. Since the mortuary feasts, in particular the termination of mourning (*umu pua*), are the most important occasions for food exchanges, and given the significance of food exchanges as an expression of the flow of matter in social relationships, this interpretation does not really require further justification. But there is in the A'aisa myth's explanation of the origins of the death feasts an explicit association of the corpse of the deceased with the gifts of meat made to other groups. This association is made only in the esoteric versions, never the public versions, of the myth (cf. Mosko 1985 on the same myth). It describes how, stricken with grief over the death of his son, A'aisa travels to the coast carrying the dead body with him. As it decays, the putrefying juices fall in various places, thus creating various powerful things used in the rituals of secret knowledge. Finally A'aisa decides to dispose of what is left of the body and end his mourning. He buries the remains, and at night they turn into wallabies that eat the plentiful grass growing over the grave. A'aisa then instructs the people who allowed him to bury his son's body on their land that they might kill and eat this meat sprung up from the corpse of his child. He then bids the human world farewell and travels west to Kariko, the village of the dead.

This is typical of the transformation of bodily substance described in many myths that explain the origin of different kinds of esoteric ritual. On the death of the mythological hero, his or her body substance is transformed into some other living species, death bringing about a change in surface form but not destroying physical matter. The adept employs these transformed substances to create further change in the material world. In the death feasts, the man of kindness ensures that despite the changes wrought by death to the forms of the embodied world, the flow of matter continues in life to sustain the group. The meat, which the body symbolically becomes, cannot be consumed by the relatives of the deceased, since it is their very own body substance (A'aisa declined to eat the game animals sprung from the corpse of his son although he declared them appropriate meat for his hosts). The meat is used to sustain the flow of material substance between this group and those groups which provide wives, and thus the bodily substance of the next generation.

Death is inevitable. Nevertheless, human agents—the man of sorrow in consultation with the man of kindness—are those that decide when it shall occur. They can control the transformation of death in the interests of the group by determining that lawbreakers and miscreants (or their close kin) die early or in their prime, while protecting the righteous as long as possible. The man of sorrow brings about death by attacking the victim's noncorporeal self and separating it from the body. Once death has taken place, it is the role of the man of kindness to deal with the ensuing disruption to the material flow. Both, therefore, are the necessary agents of transformations in and between the embodied and disembodied worlds. Ritually, they function to maintain the cosmic order instituted by the myth hero A'aisa. They do not just represent a cosmic order, they function to maintain the flow of cosmic processes in the interests of the living.[5]

Mosko (1985:160) observes that the senior "chief" is termed by Bush Mekeo the "owner" (*gome auga*) of a death in his descent group, and suggests that this is because his permission must be given before such a death can be brought about. Central Mekeo use the same expression. The term *gome* also means "root," for example the root of a tree, and thus metaphorically the origin of something. As we now know, the role of the man of kindness originated with death, as did the roles of the man of the spear (*iso auga*), the man of cinnamon bark (*faia auga*), and the man of sorrow. If the man of kindness is seen as the root, origin, or foundation of death, it is surely because his role is to regulate the movement between the embodied and disembodied realms. Of the four dignitaries only the man of kindness is concerned with perpetuating the flow of physical matter that is life, which is why he takes precedence over the others.

At this point I can perhaps also clarify the significance of the war leaders. Hau'ofa (1981:218) represents the *iso* and the *faia* as related to each other as the man of kindness is to the man of sorrow. According to my information, the cinnamon bark man did not answer to the spear man, but to the man of kindness (Mosko 1985:160 confirms this for Bush Mekeo). His main function, it was insisted, was to determine who on his own side would die. Since death does not originate in the material world, it must come about by ritual action. Even violent deaths and death in warfare require ritual mediation by a human agent, who must act in consultation with the man of kindness, since it is he who deals with this disruption to the flow of matter.

Prior to the imposition of colonial rule, I suggest that peace and war constituted different phases or states wherein the normal relationship between the inside and the outside of the embodied world was reversed. The traditional symbolism of the *iso auga*, the war leader, is clearly the reverse of that of the man of kindness. The war leader decorated himself with the black feathers of the wild cassowary, the ornaments of the man of sorrow. His face and body were said to be hairy, a characteristic considered bestial and repulsive by Mekeo standards. His *ufu*, in contrast to that of the man of kindness, was the place where weapons and the dangerous relics and substances used for war ritual were stored. Should a stranger enter by mistake, instead of being received with generous hospitality, he would be killed on the spot. In war blood is shed—that is, the inside, concealed flux of matter is revealed, and surface forms are destroyed. Private hatreds and desires are brought into the open. Destructive urges are given free reign. Evidently the man of kindness could not be part of this. Yet his interdependence with the man of the spear is represented in the exchanges of meat that took place between them. When the *iso auga* was rewarded by his allies with gifts of meat at feasts held following peacemaking, he would present the major part to the man of kindness (of his village-based clan). In turn, the man of kindness always presented meat to the *iso auga* when the recipient of gifts at feasts held by other men of kindness. These reciprocal gifts indicate an explicit recognition of the necessity of both phases of existence, of a continual movement between peace and war, order and chaos, harmony and conflict. All, it should be noted, are states existing in the material world. It is the function of the man of kindness to make peace and to restore order—surface form and harmony. The man of the spear disrupts this harmony, turning it inside out. Yet even chaos and conflict are not enough to cause death. This must be achieved through the rituals of the *faia*, and in the absence of physical violence, through the action of the man of sorrow. Death is what links these four: *lopia, iso, faia,* and *ugauga*. And it is the cosmological divisions of embodied and disembodied states that create and necessitate the fourfold structure.

A'aisa's Gifts

Since death involves the separation of the embodied self and the noncorporeal hidden self, A'aisa's introduction of death to the world can be understood as an action whereby he separated, or differentiated, two parts that had formerly been united, thus creating two separate realms of existence—the embodied and the disembodied. Once the two had been parted, one could act upon and influence the other. The force of attraction that remains—presumably stemming from their original unity—serves to link the two. In the rituals of secret knowledge, which A'aisa gave to human beings along with the legacy of death, he bequeathed the means to bring about transformations between the two realms.

What then is meant by the idea that A'aisa "introduced" death, which brings into being two separate, but linked, states of existence? I would suggest that A'aisa's introduction of death signifies the origin of self-consciousness. The realization of death—of the end to the self in a particular bodily form—emerges only as human beings achieve self-consciousness. Prior to this, as the A'aisa myths tell us, human beings were aware neither of beginnings and ends, nor even of themselves as differentiated from the other forms of life. It is A'aisa who breaks up this original unity of identity, telling some creatures to be plants, some insects, some animals, and some people. Furthermore, he bestows upon human beings one of his greatest legacies—the rituals of secret knowledge—as the ultimate means of differentiating self, of hardening the boundaries of self in the indeterminate flux of matter in life, as the ultimate instrument of the individual will. The origins of esoteric knowledge, of death, of the man of kindness and the man of sorrow are woven together in the origins of self-consciousness. Death, secret knowledge, and self-consciousness were A'aisa's gifts to humankind.

Manifest and Concealed Aspects of the Cosmic Ordering

Key symbolic elements—body substance and the adept's ritual regimen, the rituals of secret knowledge, the roles of the men of kindness and the men of sorrow, the death feasts, the principal A'aisa myths—can all be read from the perspective of their significance to self-concepts.[6] Furthermore, each in a different way focuses upon the existential problem of differentiating self as this task arises out of the dawning of self-consciousness in the mythic beginnings of human society. It is not simply that any cultural concept might be read for its significance to self. The inevitable conflicts between personal power and social relatedness that arise out of A'aisa's threefold gifts constitute for Mekeo the central dilemma of the human condition. The nature of the self, its potentials within the cosmic ordering established by A'aisa, are a core around which the entire cultural system of belief pivots.

It should be evident by now that I do not regard the public, manifest representations of the cosmic ordering as sham, disguise, or merely the artifact of my own misunderstandings. They are part of a system of cultural meanings more intricately layered than I realized until I started to explore the inner experience of actual persons. The disjunctions between the public and the concealed aspects of the cosmic ordering are, from the Mekeo viewpoint, the expected, natural, order of things. Westerners tend to assume that a "spirit realm" is purely a cultural construct, that it has no empirical reality and hence must be brought into being through public symbols. This assumption overlooks the ways in which spirit forces and powers impinge upon the everyday lives of ordinary people. My focus on individual experience in earlier chapters has emphasized the experiential basis of Mekeo constructs concerning the hidden self and the hidden world. Yet, of course, it is true that a system of shared cultural representations exists to describe and put to use these inner psychological processes and needs; I have explored these at length. Two different levels of shared cultural representations are at issue here.

The question remains: why is one kept concealed? Why do Mekeo hide what they know on another level to be true? Having posed this question, it seems impossible to ignore the arguments of Bourdieu (1977) whose studies of the Kabylia of Algeria subtly explore the ways things that all in the community know to exist may be deliberately hidden. He demonstrates the mystifying nature of ideology and symbols, such as the Kabylia honor system, that must assert what is in fact not so. Kabylia ritual serves not to mediate opposites but to legitimate the bringing together of things that should remain opposite according to the category system. In his emphasis on practice as opposed to informants' rationalizations and symbolic expressions, Bourdieu exposes a reality of practice that informants do not themselves see, or if they do, must hide. Marriages, for example, are made to appear to fit stated ideals once a particular partner has been chosen for quite other, practical, considerations. One of the important correctives his study has to offer lies in his insistence that other cultures are not exclusively cognitive symbolic discourses. We must, he urges, deal with actual people involved in practical situations, people who are trying to get things done as best they can within a given context of material conditions and cultural guidelines (habitus), operating over time. My use of data based on practice—individual action in precise social contexts and individuals' opinions and subjective experience—makes Bourdieu's theories of particular relevance.

The similarities between Mekeo and Kabylia cultures are evident, yet I am struck by the fact that with Mekeo culture I encountered a quite explicit awareness of two, or more, levels of discourse relating to the spirit realm. The degree of conscious concealment, deliberate secrecy as a cultural strategy, and the clear separation of what D'Andrade (1984) identifies as the representational and directive functions of cultural symbolism, are particularly striking. If we consider the nature of the differences between the public and hidden aspects of the Mekeo cosmic ordering, we see that one represents the perceived nature of things, and the other the proper ordering of them. The concealed discourse concerning dreaming and other matters relating to the spirit realm, the many ordinary people who ritually interact with it, and the beneficent aspect of the man of sorrow—all are aspects of culturally constituted "reality." They are cultural representations of experience—of what is, what does happen. On the other hand, the manifest, public symbols do not represent what *is*, but what, given the nature of "reality," *should* be. I am not suggesting this is an empty ideal, rather it is a symbolic means of creating order. I have traced this desire to impose order in the pervasive emphasis on controlled exteriors and uncontrolled, dangerous interiors as they pertain to human social relationships, to the individual person, and to the physical body. Mekeo seek to impose order on the manifest aspects of their world; yet, at the same time they clearly recognize that much of experience lies beyond their control. Secrecy screens disorder, and in doing so, helps to create manifest order.

This ordering is not a preordained state of affairs in the Mekeo view as much as an achievement accomplished through ritual. There is a keen awareness that the nature of reality is always more complex, more inexplicable, more changing and various than suits human desire and understanding. The chaos of actual events does not, however, vitiate the proper ordering of things as represented in the roles of the man of kindness and the man of sorrow. This helps us to understand the capacity of the system to survive and adapt with change, why over a century of colonial rule and externally imposed change has not destroyed the necessity for such roles. My ethnography highlights just how easy it is for the external analyst to be dazzled by the public symbols. Wikan (1989, 1990), in her studies of the Balinese, has examined a similar situation. Focusing on the actual experience of particular individuals necessarily gives a view different from that engendered by normative statements. The problem during my early fieldwork, compared with Wikan (1990) for example, was that I could not get access to anything other than normative and symbolic statements. People's interactions with the spirit realm were private, deliberately concealed, and took place largely in the form of inner experiences; this was true of both ordinary people and ritual specialists. We see here precisely the effectiveness of secrecy in creating a symbolic order.

If, as many would have it, cultures are texts, there is nothing exceptional in encountering different readings of the same text by different persons (or even, as in my case, by the same person). Yet I have argued that attention to subjective experience reveals important things otherwise obscured. This is not to claim an exclusive stake on "correctness" of interpretation: I am satisfied simply to demonstrate that my investigations into subjectivity reveal other levels. Nor do I deny the possibility of yet further strata, since this is something Mekeo cultural logic always posits.

Poet Octavio Paz (1976) describes all knowledge as a form of domination. The postmodernist view, in ethnography as in other disciplines, seeks a more pluralistic approach. I find this less conquistadorial stance not simply more congenial, but more in touch with the evidence of experience. It is hardly surprising that Hau'ofa, Mosko, and I all interpret aspects of Mekeo culture differently. How could it be otherwise? Their independent evidence (and the differences between them) forced me to come to terms with the reality of the different layers of cultural understandings I encountered. I might have succumbed to the temptation to look for some single underlying "truth," and thus do away with the complexities of presentation with which this book has wrestled. Mosko finds in Bush Mekeo culture a formalistic quadripartite structure. Hau'ofa describes a dual epistemology for Central Mekeo. I present a dualistic view further divided by the crucial cosmological division of embodied and disembodied—a division which, of course, necessarily creates many fourfold structures (or sometimes threefold with the fourth element left unknown). My primary concern has not been with the underlying logic of symbolic elements, but with the meaning and significance they hold for members of the culture.[7]

I refer to "data," but this is not to suggest ethnographic observations constitute scientific "facts." The task of coming to terms with my own shifting interpretations of Mekeo culture, and of reconciling them with the accounts of other ethnographers (which include not only Hau'ofa and Mosko, but also Seligman 1910; Williamson 1913; Egidi 1912; and Belshaw 1951), firmly convinces me of the accuracy of Clifford's (1982:125) observations:

> It is at least necessary to stop thinking of social science as a process of collecting and analyzing data. Anthropological "specimens"—texts and artifacts—brought back from the field should not be seen primarily as evidence of a distinct other reality or even as signs, traces to be interpreted, of the "native point of view." Rather, anthropological data must be seen as referring to the research process itself, reflecting its specific dialectics of power, of translation, of interpersonal exchange.

This being so, I take comfort from the fact that, despite our differences in approach, in personality, in interpretative frameworks, the disjunctions between our accounts are not greater than they are, and that they largely reflect the richness of the culture we attempt to describe.

The new "self-reflexive" ethnography urges the locating of the author within the text. In these explorations of Mekeo inner experience I have found it impossible not to put my own experience to the fore, yet I have endeavored not to dwell upon it but to use it as a means of deepening my insight into Mekeo worlds. What is for me primarily a methodological necessity might, from another perspective, be seen as little more than an extension of the classic "participant/observer" techniques originally advocated by Malinowski (1961) and, ever since, a touchstone of ethnographic practice. Yet just how far should one go in placing oneself in the reporting, as distinct from the collecting, of ethnographic data? In the end this must be a personal decision, and I attempt to make no prescriptive formulations. My criterion for deciding what of my own experience to include was simple: whether it contributed to a closer under-standing of the ethnographic data. I do not assume that my reactions, thoughts, or feelings were identical with those of the Mekeo men and women described here, but only that what I encountered might point to new formulations from which to question more deeply their unique subjectivities. If my methods are grounded in empathy as a mode of reaching out to the ''other,''[8] I employ it as a mode of communication, not as a mystical transcending of boundaries. For anyone who might feel tempted to undertake a similar study, a final warning note should be struck, one which underlies this whole narrative and is most painfully illustrated in my dealings with Aisaga: intruding upon secret and hidden things leads to dangerous knowledge. I realized too late how burden-some this can become.

Part IV

Conclusion

*The poetic process is not different from conjuration,
enchantment, and other magical procedures. And the
poet's attitude is very similar to the magician's. . . .
Every magical operation requires an inner force,
achieved by a painful effort at purification. The
sources of magic power are twofold: formulas and
other methods of enchantment, and the enchanter's
psychic power, his spiritual refinement that permits
him to bring his rhythm in tune with the rhythm of the
cosmos. The same occurs with the poet. The language
of the poem is in him and only to him is it revealed.
The poetic revelation involves an inner search. A
search that in no way resembles introspection or analysis: more than a search, a psychic activity capable
of bringing on the passivity that favors the outcrop-
ping of images.*

Octavio Paz, *The Bow and the Lyre*

16

Magic, Self, and Autonomous Imagination

This study has presented an extended analysis of Mekeo cosmological symbols as they relate to the self, and to the problems of self-differentiation in the flow of social relationships. It has examined the kinds of personal experiences, feelings, and desires informing these symbolic representations, and the interplay between subjective experience and the system of cultural beliefs, pointing to the role of private fantasy in the generation of symbolic forms. Although we have traveled by very different routes, the conclusions I reach lend support to Barth's (1987) arguments concerning the role of cosmological symbols in relation to the self in Melanesian cultures. Two final tasks remain for this chapter: to consider what the experience of ritual experts adds to the understanding of Mekeo self-concepts in a comparative, cross-cultural perspective, and to draw out more explicitly the connections between magic, the self, and what I refer to as "autonomous imagination."

Permeable and Impermeable Selves

If the selves of ordinary Mekeo men and women appear to be exemplary divisible entities, with highly fluid, permeable boundaries (similar to those described in many other studies such as Marriot 1976; Leenhardt 1979; White and Kirkpatrick 1985; M. Strathern 1988), we must also take cognizance of the opposite potential achieved by the man of sorrow.

A connection between "sorcery" (as distinct from "magic" in general) and personal power is well recognized (Douglas 1970), and has been especially noted for Melanesian cultures (Patterson 1975; Zelenietz 1981; Lindstrom 1984; Knauft 1985; Stephen 1987b). Part of my argument here emphasizes points made elsewhere (Young 1983; Stephen 1987b; Lawrence 1987), that sorcery beliefs should be understood within the total cosmological order of a culture, and that they cannot be separated as a topic relating only, for example, to social conflict; it may well be illuminating, however, to consider the operation of sorcery beliefs within the context of conflict management (Patterson 1975). Sorcery—that is, death-dealing rituals—may be the ultimate expression of one person's power over another, but magic of all kinds is an exercise of will over other, be that "other" the external environment or a human subject. (No Western practitioner of the occult would be in any doubt as to the link between magic and personal power; see, for example, Luhrmann 1989.) The importance of the management of knowledge, both ritual and practical, as a basis of power in many Melanesian cultures, especially those such as Mekeo where status is not achieved on the basis of economic exchanges, has been examined by Lindstrom (1984). Much of the data presented here supports his arguments, but my concern is not primarily with these undoubtedly important political ramifications, which have been dealt with extensively by Hau'ofa (1981).

The point I wish to emphasize is that Mekeo esoteric knowledge is not simply a basis for political stratagems, although it is that, but is equally a psychological investment in self. For a man like Aisaga, ritual knowledge is not simply a means of obtaining power in any social sense, for he is largely isolated from the rest of society. His knowledge is so intimate a part of self that to transfer it to others involves nothing less than the ultimate destruction of self. Knowledge is undoubtedly power, as Foucault (1980), Bourdieu (1977), and others remind us, but it is not simply a commodity in Mekeo culture.

The knowledge of a man like Aisaga becomes self-substance, like body substance. It is perhaps, therefore, emotionally appropriate that it is usually only transferred to one's offspring, who are the product of one's body substance. It also may be given to those who have intimate contact with one's body substance—a spouse, or a person who nurses one in sickness or old age. The proper transmission of a major tradition requires a special relationship: the giver must be prepared to bestow all that is required, and the recipient must be sure that what is received is a full and accurate version. A suspicion always remains that something has been withheld. And payment, even to one's parents, is needed to placate the hidden self of the giver so that it does not resent, and thus obstruct, the transfer. Only at the point of death, and the dissolution of the bodily self, is the man or woman of knowledge prepared to relinquish the self-substance of knowledge, allowing it finally to flow on to another.

Secrecy undoubtedly protects the value of knowledge, but it also protects the self. It seals in the self-substance of knowledge, preventing its alienation. For Mekeo, knowledge is anything but a freely imparted commodity; it is part of self, hence the emotional investment in it that is so distressingly revealed in my dealings with Aisaga.

Younger people fear to use secret knowledge until the death of the giver and until they themselves have become senior members of the community. Increasing age lends greater authority and prestige. The term *apaoga,* meaning "old" but also "big, important, fully developed," is particularly applicable here in that old people are those richest and most adept in secret knowledge. Younger people contrast themselves with their elders; they are little, unimportant—*kekele.* Men like Francis and Alex do not at present have reputations as men of knowledge. As they grow older, particularly if they become widowers, they will, of necessity, become the next generation. Just as Aisaga was forced by circumstances into becoming a man of sorrow, so Francis and Alex will be unlikely to avoid a similar fate. Even the diffident Alex, as well as the more confident Francis, will, I believe, develop the stony self and implacable will exemplified by the true man of knowledge. It is impossible, of course, to read the future, but there is no doubt that another generation of men and women of knowledge requires only time to come to full maturity (*apaoga*); since the traditions of secret knowledge, and the cosmological order of which they are part have survived a century of external changes, there is no reason to expect they will disappear for a long time to come.

The ordinary person's sense of vulnerability to external influence and control is, of course, the other side of the coin. Merely through the commonplace experience of dreaming, every Mekeo person is aware of the existence of the hidden world and the dangers it holds. The fluid boundaries of the self of an ordinary Mekeo person depicted in cultural symbolism reflect the realities of actual persons' experience amidst the flow of social relationships. It is precisely the aim of secret knowledge to stabilize this flux and gain control over the hidden self. I might perhaps say Mekeo do not easily experience themselves as clearly bounded entities, but that they *desire* to do so.

Mary Douglas (1966; 1970) and many Melanesianists following her insights (e.g., Lindenbaum 1979; Lederman 1981) argue that a concern with body boundaries, such as is found in Mekeo notions of body substance, primarily expresses a concern with social boundaries. Defining the self may also, by extension, involve the defining of social boundaries.[1] But the point I wish to emphasize, which has been little considered so far, is that self-boundaries are likely to be a much greater focus of attention—and source of anxiety—in small-scale societies. Here people are immersed in an endless and inescapable flow of face-to-face social relationships. This is in sharp contrast to our own Western culture, where so much is given over to individual rights, privacy, personal space, and individual choice and taste (Moore 1984; Heller, Sosna, and Wellbery 1986). I suggest that it is this very embeddedness of person and self in social relationships in Melanesia, and in similar societies, that results in the differentiating of self becoming a vital concern.

Self-boundaries are not usually regarded as difficult to define in Western cultures. If they are, some kind of pathology is assumed. I think here particularly of Laing's (1965) descriptions of the two polarities of the self in schizophrenia, polarities that seem to come remarkably close to Mekeo notions of the permeable and the stony self. Yet, Mekeo too aim at a self-ideal situated between these two poles. Only the man of sorrow achieves the petrified self, and only the troubled and ineffectual person feels constantly at threat. Most Mekeo are able to draw insight and wisdom from the glimpses they have of other layers of self. Mekeo understandings encourage a sensitivity to aspects of self that our culture persuades us to ignore (except, of course, in psychotherapy). Yet do *we* really experience ourselves as firmly bounded unitary entities (Ewing 1990b), or might it not be truer to say, in common with Mekeo, we only *desire* to be? Perhaps the difference is that Mekeo culture focuses much more explicitly on the tensions inherent in the desire.

In these images of permeable and impermeable self boundaries, we encounter themes to be found in places far removed from Mekeo, as in the Western psychiatric theories of Laing. Within Melanesia, Michael Young's study *Magicians of Manumanua* (1983) provides portraits of several powerful individuals, especially Iyahalina with his vengeful self-destruction, that closely parallel the formidable Aisaga. Both Iyahalina and Aisaga become figures of mythic proportions in their lived performance of the role, and in their ultimate confrontation and destruction by their sons. If the concept of *unuwewe* is not as explicitly developed in Mekeo culture as in Kalauna, the psychological force is clearly much the same. In contrast, Bercovitch's (1989) study of the Nalumin witch reveals an exemplary permeable, vulnerable self—not a figure comparable to Iyahalina or Aisaga.

Far removed from Melanesia, Favret-Saada's (1980) study of witchcraft in modern French provincial communities provides models of selves (the individual and his domain) that are invaded by the excessive force of another (a witch) and thus depleted of strength. Favret-Saada shows how the system of belief works in action to become a highly persuasive discourse, but does not attempt to explain how or why such a view of the vulnerable self holds conviction. Her fieldwork experience reflects my own. Like her, I was drawn into the system unaware; I encountered the same secrecy, suffered the same confusion, and had to come to terms with the fact that being given knowledge meant people assumed you were using it. Her involvement in fantasy processes reflects my own, and she too came to recognize, if in different ways, the sorrows of what she calls "poisoned gifts."

The similarities between witchcraft in modern rural France, as encountered by Favret-Saada, and Mekeo concepts and the notions of self attached to them only underline a basic difference. In the Bocage, it is denied that the person who has power to protect (the unwitcher) also has power to invade self. People focus on their vulnerability to the destructive desires of others, on the fragility of self to unseen influence, and pin their hopes on the ability of some external figure to restore the integrity of self. While the Mekeo vulnerable, fluid self is much the same, what stands out is the figure of the man of sorrow, whose secret rituals are intended precisely to create a self capable of penetrating, controlling, and if necessary, annihilating others.

This difference further emphasizes a polarity that, as I have previously argued (Stephen 1987b), should be recognized in the jumble of beliefs anthropologists label "witchcraft and sorcery."[2] Both sorcery and witchcraft can be understood as beliefs concerning the unseen powers of human others to penetrate and influence the self. In certain configurations, which I would term "witchcraft" (such as in the Bocage), this ability is rejected and despised. Whereas in "sorcery" configurations (such as in Mekeo) this presumed power to penetrate other selves is not only accepted, it becomes a focus of ritual elaboration and ultimately the basis of a socially powerful and influential role. Divisible, fluid, open selves are common to both cultures, but the stony, impermeable self capable of intruding, controlling, and destroying others is not.

Although he refers to "sorcery" in a situation where I would identify "witchcraft," Knauft's (1985) analysis of Gebusi action and beliefs provides a striking illustration of this very contrast. In Gebusi culture, individuality is muted (Knauft 1985:72). Anger is considered to be reprehensible self-assertion, and the angry person is feared. Cultural values stress equality and "good company," and there is in fact no hierarchy of status or inequalities of any kind. Yet present in this very egalitarian culture is a high level of homicide against accused sorcerer-witches. Knauft stresses that good company is not simply a value or an ideal, it is an experienced reality. It is therefore, one might say, a shared psychological style of experiencing self. Sorcery/witchcraft violence is the "flip-side of good company": it is the denial of conflict, not conflict per se, which results in accusations (Knauft 1985:3). Gebusi are friendly, dependent on one another, and trusting on a conscious level. Fears or envy of one another are inadmissible, and when they surface they are projected onto a scapegoat in the community. The more one is constrained to love, give, and be open to others, the more, it seems, the task of self-differentiation becomes difficult. The Gebusi do not, like the Mekeo, *consciously* desire a more differentiated self. The Gebusi self should not be cut off from others, since a closed, hard, angry self is feared and despised. But this cultural valuing of the openness of self creates feelings of extreme vulnerability to the destructive powers of others. Beliefs such as those of the Gebusi, wherein the "witch" who threatens to invade others is killed, might be understood as a means of defending the boundaries of society and self against others. In contrast, with Mekeo and similar systems, varying degrees of legitimacy are given to the invasion of self by more powerful others. Clearly we are talking about the exercise of power, but on a psychological rather than an institutional level. For Knauft (1985:344), Melanesian sorcery/witchcraft is associated primarily with male status differentiation. I take a somewhat different view, although I do not deny the salience of issues of status and hierarchy.

Why in these multifarious beliefs, and in their seemingly endless variations, does a person see him or herself "depleted" as the result of the "force" (Favret-Saada 1980) of another human being? The answer, I believe, lies in the psychological difficulty of constructing a firm sense of self. Its continuity is constantly being interrupted, argues Ewing (1990b). There are many parts, scripts for self, or complexes, as Jung (1978) would say, waiting in the wings to take over. The task of consciousness, to decide who and what is self and what is not, is no easy one (Noy 1969, 1979; Roheim 1955). There is the fear of consciousness being overtaken and devoured by the unconscious, the devouring mother (Jung 1967). As Laing (1965) has shown, the self is always threatened by disintegration from the many external pressures acting upon it. We might also consider Bateson's (1973) insights into schizophrenia. These various arguments do not necessarily assume a unitary bounded self, as experienced in Western culture, to be a human universal.[3] They posit only a pervasive *desire* for a well-defended self—a desire vividly and insistently expressed and realized in Mekeo culture; a desire we find repressed and then erupting in violent homicide within the community among Gebusi.

Similar points concerning the anxieties created by establishing self-boundaries have been made by Roseman (1990) in a different context. In describing the "sociocentric," fluid, and divisible self-concepts of the Temiar of Malaya, Roseman shows that awareness of the self's permeability generates concern over the observance of appropriate boundaries between selves. Temiar seek to protect themselves, and one another, from the damage caused when one self intrudes upon another, which, given their permeability, is easily done. Roseman observes that this multiplicity and separability of the components of the self found in other Southeast Asian peoples—and many other cultures—has its cost: anxiety concerning the integrity of self. In Western cultures, she suggests, the normative emphasis on a unitary self overlays a sense of multiplicity (1990:236):

> Temiar interactions with one another and the cosmos are driven by a dynamic tension that celebrates the potential detachability of self while guarding the integrity of self. The cultural subscript of sociocentric interdependence, then, is the continual reinstatement of an independent, bounded self. Similarly, in societies commonly characterized as egocentric, such as contemporary mainstream United States, the emphasized cultural value on the independent, individuated self exists in tension with a cultural subscript that values interdependence in the family, in the community, in nationalism, in employer-employee relations, or within unions. And the seeming indivisible is variously divided into a multiplicity of selves.

This adds further support to the arguments of Ewing (1990b) and McHugh (1989) discussed in chapter 7, which point to the exaggerated dichotomies that are set up when normative values concerning the self are isolated from actual practice and individuals' subjectivity (see also Wikan 1989, 1990). Roseman suggests, as I have argued for Mekeo, that *desire* for self-integrity is common to both "sociocentric" and "egocentric" cultures, but how that desire is modulated, expressed or repressed, justified or devalued, varies enormously across cultures.

For Mekeo this desire finds its ultimate cultural expression in the indomitable will (a personal and a cultural achievement) of the man of sorrow. In achieving an impermeable self, the man of sorrow becomes just that: not merely he who causes sorrow but he who *suffers* from his invulnerability. This leads back to the pathology of the self in Western culture where selves are so rigorously bounded, or should be, that all must suffer from painful isolation (DeVos, Marsella, and Hsu 1985:13–14; Johnson 1985). Both realizations are the consequences of self-differentiation pushed to its extreme.

Yet, of course, the Mekeo man of sorrow can in no sense be assimilated into the modern Western notion of self. The stony invulnerability achieved through his ritual regimen is balanced by his ritual empowerment of the hidden self, expanding it and extending its reach, so that it becomes an instrument of his conscious will acting upon others regardless of time, space, and the limitations of embodied existence. No one may cross his self-boundaries, but via the hidden self they are infinitely extendible. Of course, everyone possesses a hidden self, but only ritual knowledge enables a person to gain control over it. The man of sorrow carefully develops this projection of self into a force capable of destroying others. The formidable Aisaga, in all his uniqueness, exemplifies a cultural ideal. The man of sorrow is not simply a callous manipulator of a system designed in his own interests, employing secrecy and concealment to achieve symbolic mystification of the status quo, nor is he simply the victim of some delusion of grandeur. The self-indulgent fantasies of power in which some adepts, such as Richard, engage have been noted. Why did I exclude Aisaga from similar condemnation? An important difference is that these adepts do not isolate themselves from society, as Aisaga must, nor live out their days in intimate contact with the dangerous forces of the hidden realm. Aisaga commands respect because his mastery over life and death is achieved only at great cost to himself. If he has emerged in these pages as heroic, it is because his shaping of self is an heroic task, one which few men achieve.

Ultimately, however, Aisaga is a chilling figure. This is hardly surprising in view of the intent of his ritual practice—to create a self ruthless enough to destroy others. Westerners tend to assume, I think, that desire for power is some kind of human universal, a given that needs no explanation. We have failed to understand that in cultures where selves are open and permeable to others, extraordinary measures are needed to create a will as individuated as that of Aisaga.

Magic and Autonomous Imagination

Anthropology has long debated the nature of "magical" thought and its
relationship to a "primitive mentality" (see Tambiah 1990 for a survey), but
there has been little consideration of magic as the means of creating a particular
self-concept. Durkheim (1915), of course, did stress the individuality of the
"magical" versus the collective nature of the "religious," but this is not a
distinction many later scholars have found useful, especially for Melanesia (see
Lawrence 1973:201–203). Roheim, however, in a posthumously published
work, *Magic and Schizophrenia* (1955), outlined a view of magic as a universal
mode of human thought that in certain respects appears similar to the view I
have put forward concerning the rituals of secret knowledge and the shaping
of the self in Mekeo culture.

Roheim revises the orthodox psychoanalytic theory that magic reflects the
unconscious conviction in the power of thought based upon infantile experience
of the mother's responsiveness to her child's demands and needs. Roheim
doubts that the infant feels all-powerful, suggesting rather that the experience
of the mother-child relationship, the "dual-unity," creates a confidence one's
desires and wishes will be realized in the external world. This, he suggests, is
essential for the individual to operate at all upon reality. In the ego's battle to
deal with reality, the demands of the id, and the negative and punitive influence
of the superego, the ego needs confidence that it can win its battles; it is here
that magical thinking prevails. Roheim proposes that along with the pleasure
principle and the reality principle we should posit a third—the magic principle.
And he contends it is a necessary basis for all healthy ego activity. We have
moved a long way from magic as infantile wish fulfillment, although not as far
as I think we need to move.

Evidently, Roheim's position has various affinities with Noy's (1969, 1979)
revision of the primary process as discussed in chapter 5. Whereas both Roheim
and Noy argue that fantasy and unrealistic thinking contribute positively to ego
development, and to the construction of a secure self-identity, I see the rituals
of Mekeo secret knowledge as creating a particular view of self. Mekeo
cosmological symbols create specific images: the vulnerable self and the
all-powerful self. The symbolism of Mekeo secret knowledge draws extensively upon oral, anal, and phallic themes; witness the importance of body
substance in the rituals—an importance which is of course well established for
magic in general. With regard to points raised earlier concerning body substance and defining the boundaries of the self, I might add that oral, anal, and
phallic themes are not just stages of libidinous development but equally stages
of self-definition as the child learns to distinguish between self and other, and
parts of self, and self-products. In the case of magic, we are, of course, dealing
with culturally elaborated complexes of belief and ritual. Yet these do seem to
follow basic patterns identified long ago by Frazer (1913). Are we dealing with

a universal human affective structure arising out of prolonged infancy and the mother-child (dual-unity) relationship? Or with a distinctive mode of thought, whether a primary process or autonomous imagination? Or with both combined?

Like Roheim and Noy, I see the establishment of self as a well-integrated entity to be a very difficult psychic task. Our culture demands a highly differentiated and unified self. Many of our cultural institutions and rituals contribute to this, art being one of them, as Noy argues. This takes us back to arguments just raised concerning variations in self-concepts. If the concept of self varies cross-culturally, so must the nature and difficulty of the task of achieving self-identity. Ewing's (1990b) work emphasizes, along with Roheim and Noy, the inherent difficulties of self-construction as a psychological process. We might assume that in non-Western cultures where "divisible" (Marriot 1976) selves are constituted primarily in social relationships, the task of self construction is less demanding. Instead, I have found that the very embeddedness of self in relationships creates acute concern in Mekeo culture with defining and defending self-boundaries. Roseman's (1990) study of the Temiar comes to similar conclusions. It may be that in cultures sharing much the same kind of face-to-face social relationships and cultural notions concerning self, cosmological symbols and esoteric knowledge reflect similar needs.

It is clear, I hope, that I am not suggesting that the traditions of Mekeo secret knowledge are only a means to differentiate self within a particular kind of social structure. I have equally attempted to demonstrate that they provide access to an especially compelling and powerful mode of thought imagery. The ritual practice of Mekeo men and women of knowledge is anything but a mechanical performance, wherein mere recitations of certain words or the manipulation of various substances is believed to have an automatic effect on external reality. For Josephina, for Francis, for Alex, for Aisaga, ritual provides access to that other realm of disembodied powers, where they, as men and women of knowledge, can shape the possibilities of dream-images soon to be realized in the embodied world. Their engagement with the spirit world, although private and not dramatized in any form of public performance, is no less immediate or powerful than the shaman's. Indeed once we consider the nature of their inner experience, the distinction between shaman and magician begins to fade (a point I have argued elsewhere; see Stephen 1987a).

The adept in no way confuses the disembodied images of the dream realm with the physical substance of material entities; the very language of dream reporting consistently distinguishes between the two in ways which avoid the ambiguity often arising in English when describing such experiences. We do not here find people overwhelmed by their inner imagery, disoriented as to materiality of the apparitions they encounter. These are not persons confused by "magical thinking" where the normal distinctions between subject and object, cause and effect, space and time, disappear—they are experts deliberately engaging in the events of the dream world where, as Freud (1900) showed so clearly, these distinctions are nightly dissolved for all of us. Let me reiterate: the traditions of Mekeo secret knowledge are a means to deliberately invoke and direct this symbolic mode of thought, not an unconscious immersion in it.

At this point I am reminded of Clifford's (1982:137) contrasting of Malinowski's view of magical/instrumental thought in Trobriand culture and Leenhardt's (1979) concept of mythic participation pervading the Canaque Melanesian world. As Clifford observes, these views reveal the totally contrasting approaches of the two ethnographers. The purely instrumental approach of Malinowski is inadequate to capture the powerful sense Mekeo adepts have of participation in the mysterious forces of the dream world and, especially, to understand the intimate communion between Aisaga and the spirit presences of his ancestors and the myth heroes. Yet, on the other hand, Leenhardt's diffuse mythic participation seems to go too far in the opposite direction, allowing for no discrimination of different states of awareness or for the degree of control that is involved in using them. The rituals of Mekeo secret knowledge are instrumental in that they are directed toward quite specific goals, yet they equally involve a special kind of participation in realms removed from material reality. These Western dichotomies of rational/irrational, instrumental/magical are given lie to by the ease with which Mekeo explore, and play upon, the dynamic relationship between different components of self.

Leenhardt's term "mythic participation" might perhaps be preferable to the term "magical," which still seems tied to its evolutionist origins within anthropology, denoting an inferior or rudimentary stage of thought gradually eschewed as cultures emerge from the early stages of primitive barbarism. Drawing on Leenhardt, Tambiah (1990:105–110) has proposed that in place of the conventional contrast between magical and scientific thinking, we recognize two orientations of "causality" and "participation" operating in all cultures.[4] "Mythic" thought or "participation" is at least a mode we might be able to perceive within ourselves as it touches upon an aesthetic and transcendental participation in nature, and even spiritual concerns. Whereas the label "magic" inevitably distances and exoticizes other cultures (Said 1978; Abu-Lughod 1989). For this reason I have thus far avoided it in describing Mekeo beliefs and rituals; I now need, however, to invoke the concept.

The prevailing climate of opinion, of course, tends to run magic and religion together under the general heading of "symbolic" thought and action (e.g., Beattie 1972:202ff.; Middleton 1967:ix–x; Douglas 1966:1–6, or "participation," Tambiah 1990:109). It is often pointed out, especially for Melanesia, that there is no indigenous separation of magic and religion (Lawrence and Meggitt 1965; Lawrence 1973). But then I know of no Mekeo terms for "economy," "exchange," or even "kinship," yet this does not prevent anthropologists from employing them. The absence of emic categories does not usually prevent the external observer from applying different analytical ones. The problem is in insensitively applying our own commonsense (cultural) labels without concern for, or awareness of, how these distort indigenous understandings. "Magic," in view of its negative connotation, might be better supplanted by more neutral terms such as "ritual." Yet here one faces the difficulty that Mekeo traditions of secret knowledge are not just any ritual, or just any set of cosmological beliefs or magico-religious beliefs—they are of a specific and recognizable kind, one that has been described over and over again in the anthropological literature as "magic." The Mekeo traditions of secret knowledge are virtually identical to the Trobriand magic Malinowski describes (which is not surprising in view of the many cultural similarities between the two groups), and they fit entirely comfortably within Evans-Pritchard's (1967) comparison of Azande and Trobriand magic. All three systems of belief employ identical elements: spells, magical substances, and the ritual condition of the practitioner.

What is magic, one might well ask? So often the meaning of the term is simply assumed (e.g., Winkleman 1979 provides virtually no discussion of definitions). There is, however, a general understanding of the concept that pervades the literature, one clearly and simply stated. Middleton, for example (1967:ix), cites this understanding in separating magic and religion:

> We may say that the realm of magic is that in which human beings believe that they may directly affect nature and each other, for good or for ill, by their own efforts (even though the precise mechanism may not be understood by them), as distinct from appealing to divine powers by sacrifice or prayer. Witchcraft and sorcery are, therefore, close to magic, as are processes of oracular consultation, divination and many forms of curing.

I offer the following as a summary of magic as it applies to the Mekeo situation and is recognizable in innumerable other ethnographic studies. This is not intended as a formal definition of a term but as a description of a widespread variation on a broader theme. In this formulation, magic involves the belief that the material world can be altered by nonmaterial means via rituals that usually employ words (spells), substances (magical medicines and objects), and ritual actions and special preparedness on the part of the practitioner. The ritual words, substances, and actions and preparation required are related to the intention of the rite by symbolic links of similarity (sympathetic magic, metaphor) and/or of contagion (part for whole/metonym). Magic is often the personal possession of a particular individual, and usually a closely guarded secret. When it is performed on the behalf of others, the practitioner is usually rewarded in some way for her or his services.

Mekeo cosmology is based upon very specific beliefs in such magical ritual and knowledge. It is the belief that the rituals of secret knowledge give specific individuals the capacity to impose their will upon others, which sets up the potentials for self-development I have described. It is conviction in the power of particular persons to influence others that confers the capacity for self-differentiation. It is "magic" in the sense of Malinowski (1961), Evans-Pritchard (1937), and even Frazer (1913), that is linked so powerfully to self-definition and the assertion of self at the expense of other. It is magic which is bound up with the anxiety over self-boundaries and the desire to experience self as a differentiated whole, which is the concomitant of the emergence of self-consciousness as described in the A'aisa myths. It is magic in this sense that is the ultimate expression of the individual's will, as exemplified by Aisaga. It is this classic, if old-fashioned, formulation of magic which describes the pivot of Mekeo cosmology.

Magic has always been understood as a desire to control the external world, hence the "mistaken science" approach of the early evolutionists. What I am suggesting is that magic in general might be understood as a means to develop inner desire to exert control over others. I do not see this as a simple will to power: it is part of the involved and lengthy psychic process of achieving full self-awareness, and resisting the desire to be merged back into the unconscious matrix from which it emerged. I think here of Jung's (1967; 1976) descriptions of the process of individuation and the difficulties the psyche faces in achieving self-differentiation. "Magic" in the classic sense, as used by Roheim and others, provides, in my view, a means of achieving a sense of self-boundedness and a capacity to assert self over others, a refusal to be engulfed by the flux that is material existence and social relationship.

The Effectiveness of Symbols

In view of the special characteristics of autonomous imagination identified earlier—its vivid, seemingly autonomous imagery, its greater freedom and richness of inventiveness, its more extensive access to memory, its high degree of responsiveness to external suggestion, and especially its capacity to influence levels of mind and body beyond conscious control—I cannot brusquely dismiss Mekeo claims that the rituals of secret knowledge "have the power to change your mind," nor assertions that they both harm and heal. From such a perspective, magical thinking does not originate from a distorted or inferior mode of thought as Western analysts have so frequently assumed. Nor does it arise primarily out of "preoperative thought" (Hallpike 1979), or "obviation" (Wagner 1972), or merely infantile wishful thinking (Freud 1916b). Rather, I would suggest, magic consists of rituals that are culturally devised to put to use a special mode of symbolic thought present in all individuals in all cultures.[5]

Does magic work? Or do I think that it does? It is perhaps not surprising that these are questions people often ask me. Much that has been described in this book underlines the powerful effects of the rituals of secret knowledge on both the practitioner's and the subject's experience.[6] Or is it merely that I want magic to work, as Freud (1933) might point out? And not just I, but others as well. If the "sorcerer's apprentice" narrative has become almost an accepted genre in current ethnography, it reveals perhaps not only a new and more open approach to what was formerly denigrated as the irrational but also that unconscious desire in all of us for miracles.

Some anthropologists are prepared to argue in favor of the existence of psi and other paranormal phenomena (Winkleman 1979). Even the highly rationalistic Freud (1933) was prepared to take seriously the possibility of telepathy occurring in the psychoanalytic situation. Should we appeal to Jung's (1973) notion of synchronicity? It would, for example, account for the apparently synchronistic sequence of events described in chapter 4. But such a theory takes us outside our existing explanatory framework. Yet, in a sense, I think all anthropological explanations and theories of magic have assumed that it *does work*. The question is: How? The concern with rationality and the nature of the "primitive mind" that dominated earlier approaches seems rather outmoded in the context of contemporary cultural anthropology's awareness of the culturally created nature of all "realities." Yet whether it is the fallacy of misapplied logic that is invoked, or the power of collective representations, the functional bolstering of self-confidence to survive in a hard world, infantile dependency wishes, the force of deadly words, or the inescapable web of culturally constructed meanings, no anthropological theory has really doubted the power of magic; they have disagreed only as to the source of its efficacy. Roheim (1955), following Frazer, reminds us that magic is something found everywhere, at all times, among all people (although it does not, of course, provide the central focus of all cosmological systems). It is as universal a phenomenon in human cultures as we are likely to find.

My aim has not been to explain paranormal phenomena nor to focus on the marvellous. I am concerned with something long observed in the anthropological literature but rarely tackled explicitly; Lévi-Strauss (1972b) refers to it as the "effectiveness of symbols." Despite anthropology's fascination with the evident capacity of symbolic modes to shape, mediate—even create—moods, emotions, and inner states within individuals (Geertz 1975b), most studies nevertheless emphasize the generation of cognitive and intellectual meaning in symbolic forms. Comparatively few (for example Lévi-Strauss 1972b; Turner 1967; Schenchner 1986; D'Aquili, Laughlin, and McManus 1979; Herdt and Stephen 1989) have been prepared to take more seriously the effectiveness of symbols as a means of shaping inner experience, of communicating to affective and somatic levels. Yet I would be dismayed to see such approaches based on the assumption, for example, that emotion is divorced from cognition and located not in the cortex, but in the reptilian brain (Schenchner 1986). I endorse D'Andrade's (1984) arguments that emotion needs to be understood as not in opposition to, but allied to cognition. Or, as Jung (1976) has said in quite a different way, but pointing to the same understanding, feeling (by which he does not mean raw emotion, but something closer to *sensibilité*) is a significant aspect of the mind's capacity for dealing with sensory information from the external world. As the culture theorists properly insist (Shweder and LeVine 1984; Stigler, Shweder, and Herdt 1990), emotions are complex things shaped and mediated by culture, not mechanical responses determined purely by physiology (which is not, of course, to deny that emotions have physiological concomitants).

Since, in my view, magic and magical thinking represent particular kinds of uses of autonomous imagination, it is useful to distinguish them from other ritual and symbolic modes. Yet this is not to say that they constitute something essentially different in kind. Myth, ritual, and cosmological beliefs, I suggest, are cultural means to represent and deal with those invisible forces that impinge on the self. They are ways of dealing with the creative and destructive powers of the irrational. Through its rituals, a culture provides the self with an orientation toward these hidden powers. In doing so, cosmology naturally tends to help shape a particular view of self and of the forces that beset it. These may be conceptualized as forces of nature, as in Mountain Ok cosmology (Barth 1987), but they are also forces within the psyche itself. Since, as I have argued, symbols possess the unique capacity to point to the unknown and represent that which is just beyond the reach of consciousness, they provide the means by which culture deals with these forces. Religious beliefs are not in themselves irrational (projected id desires), they are symbolic means to relate to the irrational. Symbols communicate to that part of mind and self outside consciousness; they also emerge from hidden and deeper parts of self, mediated by autonomous imagination. Their "effectiveness" becomes more comprehensible in view of the special characteristics of autonomous imagination I have identified.

Autonomous imagination, Herdt and I have argued (Herdt and Stephen 1989), is a vehicle of cultural production, reproduction, variation, and innovation. Operating in all persons, all cultures, and underlying religious phenomena in general, it is a process whereby self and culture shape each other, a means of creating harmony between inner desires and the external demands of society and physical environment. It is no less than a means of creating culture, and of creating self. From this perspective, the seemingly curious juxtaposition of magic and the self with which this study began no longer appears totally incongruous, or even strange. The rituals of Mekeo magic can thereby be understood as a way of drawing upon basic symbolic processes from which self and culture are woven.

There is one final point to raise, one that indicates the direction for future explorations. In the struggle to define the self that Mekeo cosmological symbols depict, can we not discern something of much broader patterns of the human psyche? Do we not find the Mekeo self pulled between forces that more than echo Freud's eros and thanatos, in his view the two ultimate directions for psyche? Shall we fail to discern in the figure of the man of sorrow, who "always deceives people" like his prototype A'aisa, the ultimate trickster—Jung's archetypal trickster who, surely not coincidentally, is identified with the process of differentiating self from the matrix of the unconscious?[7] In the battle of wills between the man of sorrow and his heirs can we ignore the recurring mythic motif of Oedipus's struggles? Is it so surprising that, despite infinite varieties of cultural expressions, the human psyche continues to face similar basic challenges in the task of self-realization? From a more open-ended perspective, perhaps we might view these different psychic images not so much as shreds torn from rival theories and incompatible views of mind but as enduring insights into the recurring patterns of a uniquely distinctive imaginative mode. The "mytho-poetic," "hypnomantic consciousness," "autonomous imagination"—whatever we choose to name it—its contours have only begun to be clearly delineated in our Western theories of mind and culture.

Notes

Introduction

1. The current popularity of the self as a topic of anthropological investigation (see Whittaker 1992 for a review) possibly owes something to its rather comfortable looseness of fit and definition: it can mean different things to different writers. For some, it seems to be a new label for the old categories of character and personality, and thus it becomes a kind of catchall for studies that would previously have fitted the "culture and personality" school of psychological anthropology. My usage falls to the phenomenological end of the spectrum, emphasizing the individual person's experience of "self," that is, self as self-awareness. My emphasis is more on understanding states of consciousness and individual experience than normative definitions of what a "person" or a "self" might be in a particular culture, although the two cannot, of course, be entirely separated.

2. Mosko's (1985) study of Bush Mekeo symbolic structures has called into question various aspects of Hau'ofa's analysis but not points of central concern to my study. Furthermore, I consider Mosko's criticisms to rely too heavily on a yet-to-be-established correlation between the two groups. Evidently the cultural similarities are great, yet one cannot simply overlook the considerable differences in contact history, habitat, and scale and settlement patterns. In 1970 Bush Mekeo had a total population of 1,841 divided into eight communities (Mosko 1985:15); Central Mekeo had 6,500 divided among fourteen communities, with nearly half the total concentrated in three large villages: Beipa, Aipeana, and Inawi.

3. Neither Hau'ofa nor Mosko, of course, were unaware of the multilayered nature of Mekeo culture. As Hau'ofa (1981) stresses, there are always two sides to everything in the Mekeo view, and Mosko (1985) presents an even more complex underlying quadripartite structure. Indeed, from their perspectives (despite their differences), the layers of concealed things I was to stumble across might have been expected or predicted. Yet many of these concealed things are passed over by both ethnographers, and they remained invisible to me throughout my early fieldwork.

Chapter 1: The Visible Ordering of Things

1. See Hau'ofa (1981) and Mosko (1985) for similar versions of the same myth. Like any oral tradition, the myth has many versions and variants, especially esoteric versions. When told in public, parts not essential to the basic narrative are omitted, certain episodes are excluded, and the sequence may be changed in various ways. Sometimes a person may privately recount a version that combines some esoteric aspects, yet without disclosing any important secrets. In other words, any standardized version of the myth is a construction of the ethnographer. The episodes which explain how A'aisa brought death into the world are omitted here since they are usually not included in public recitations; I briefly outline them in chapter 15, where they become essential to my arguments.

2. Hau'ofa (1981:31) refers to the oral tradition that tells that the Pioufa and Ve'e first arrived from the sea in big canoes and settled on the mountains which were then part of the coastline. Later, when the water receded from the plains, they left the mountains to occupy them. This may reflect a trace of the original migration of Austronesian peoples from the sea. Alternatively, it may represent a more recent incorporation of the biblical myth of the great flood and Noah's ark, of which I have collected various versions over the years.

3. The 1980 Papua New Guinea National Census, Preliminary Field Counts, National Statistics Office, Port Moresby, gives the total population of the Mekeo region as 7,114, including 155 non-Mekeo residents.

4. Hau'ofa (1981:53) refers to the *ango inaega,* literally, the belly or womb of the *land.*

5. My designation of the "backyard" differs from Hau'ofa (1981) in that I refer to the cleared space behind the domestic houses, he to the bush beyond this.

6. In Beipa, the village where Hau'ofa did fieldwork (1981:57ff.), youths continued to live in *gove* during the early 1970s.

7. The possible exception is the occasional outburst of anger and accusation between spouses or household members. In the heat of the moment, people may shout obscenities at each other, and intimate matters may be aired. Later they feel embarrassed, and those who habitually act in this way are regarded with amused disdain by others.

8. The literal meaning is of interest in relation to arguments about dual structures in Mekeo social organization (Mosko 1985), but I do not intend to pursue this here.

9. Perhaps Beipa village (where Hau'ofa conducted fieldwork) is particularly fond of such performances. I saw a very elaborate feast of this nature there in 1982, but have not witnessed such extremes elsewhere.

10. *Lopia,* although it includes the meaning "good," is not the term which would usually be used to translate "good"; this term is *velo.* The meaning of *velo,* however, refers more to attractive, smooth, and beautiful appearances or surfaces than to moral qualities. Thus I was cautioned not to say that a man was, in my opinion, *au velo* because this in fact suggested I thought him good-looking, and, coming from a woman, such a statement would imply erotic interest on my part rather than my appreciation of the person's moral attributes! See chapter 2.

11. On this point Hau'ofa (1981:218) asserts the opposite.

12. In Hau'ofa's (1981:46ff.) view, the cessation of tribal warfare may have led to radical shifts in the nature of Mekeo military and civilian chieftainships. While on the

face of things this seems plausible, and undoubtedly significant changes did occur, I argue that the man of kindness and the man of sorrow are less parts of a structure of political authority than roles with a primarily ritual and symbolic significance that has not altered in essence, despite European contact. This point is pursued in chapter 15.

13. Wikan (1990:xx), employing Appaduri's (1986) notion of "gatekeeping concepts," draws attention to the way in which understanding of Balinese culture has been distorted by the use of a theatrical model or metaphor. There is evidently the danger of distortion also in focusing on "key symbols" (Ortner 1973) so that they become a kind of stereotypical labeling. For Mekeo, "chiefs," "sorcerers," and "hierarchy" seem in danger of becoming just this.

Chapter 2: Manifest and Concealed

1. Evidently hospitality and competition are not necessarily mutually exclusive and may have different connotations within different contexts. My point is that compared with those Melanesian cultures where status and power are defined by exchange activities, Mekeo fall to the other end of a spectrum that Lindstrom (1984:304) identifies, where "material production and exchange, for whatever reasons, generate social equality rather than hierarchy." In the Mekeo situation, material abundance is so readily available to all that it is not surprising status must be established on other grounds.

2. I have not myself ever seen or visited such a place, but I was assured by my mentor Aisaga that such retreats existed in his youth. Aisaga had not for many years maintained a *fauapi,* although he did store the most dangerous objects required for his rituals away in the bush (see chapter 13).

3. These valuables remain essential components of traditional exchanges and payments, despite the incorporation of money into most transactions.

4. *Mefu* is a specific technique of death-dealing ritual which operates by binding the bowels of the victim, causing the abdomen to swell, and making defecation impossible. Its origin is associated with Isapini, the brother of the culture hero A'aisa, whereas *ugauga* is a different technique originated by A'aisa himself.

5. Hau'ofa (1981) interprets this concern with rights and dues as indicative of the inequality which he sees as characteristic of Mekeo culture. On this point I tend to agree with Mosko's (1985:241) criticisms that such inequalities in fact balance each other out for the system over all. That is to say, a person or group is only unequal to another on a particular occasion, which will later be reversed. The only permanent "inequalities" are between those with, and those without, hereditary office and, of course, esoteric knowledge.

6. I am struck here by the similarity of this brief anecdote and Wikan's (1990) extended story of Suriati. Admittedly in this case, the father had had some time to adjust to his grief over the death of his child, yet the basic management of emotion involved seems very similar. Mekeo, unlike Balinese, are expected to weep at funerals, but on other occasions they succeed very well in giving no hint of the dark suspicions and feelings they harbor toward others.

7. It seems ironic that Geertz himself has recently been criticised by Wikan (1989, 1990) on just this account. Wikan argues that Geertz's exclusive focus on the public aspects of Balinese culture distorts the reality of a much more complex Balinese experience of self.

8. Wikan's (1989, 1990) account of Balinese "face" and the importance in this culture of presenting a composed public persona has many resonances with the material described here. For Balinese, as well as Mekeo, the public face is by no means simply a mask or disguise but the very means of creating social harmony. Both the "turbulent heart" and the "bright face" are valid domains of experience in the Balinese view. A difference, however, lies in the emphasis the Balinese give to the effect of the "bright face" upon the emotional and even physical health of the individual. Mekeo are more concerned with the distance that is created by an inscrutable face; in contributing to social harmony, it also defends the "inside self" from the intrusions of others.

9. Notions concerning the body are, of course, also crucial in understanding how the self is defined in relation to other, how the bodily world of human beings is related to the realm of spirit beings, and the manner in which ritual is understood to mediate the two realms—but these issues must await later chapters for fuller investigation.

10. Mekeo make no special elaboration of the positive effects of semen, outside of normal heterosexual intercourse, compared with say the Sambia (Herdt 1981) and several other New Guinea cultures. Indeed, if ingested, semen, like any other type of body dirt (*faga ofuga*) is harmful. Similarly, if one's semen is obtained by another person it can be used to harm one. For this reason, sexual contacts are always fraught with some degree of danger since one's partner may take the opportunity to appropriate one's body substance; this applies regardless of gender.

11. The point is further emphasized by Hau'ofa's (1981) study, which makes little mention of body substance except in relation to sorcery. Blood, body dirt, and other substances discussed at length by Mosko do not even appear in Hau'ofa's index, a further indication of their absence as public social metaphors among the Central Mekeo. Whether this is a product of different cultural emphasis or of the different perspectives of the ethnographers is, of course, arguable.

12. In much the same vein, Hau'ofa (1981:96) refers to the "defensive privacy" which characterizes Mekeo culture.

13. This same sense of being shut out of things, of things deliberately screened, I can recall vividly from my early childhood. I also remember how I hated being tricked by adults. I was always determined to know more than them—an embarrassing admission for a scholar! Thus it may be, as Devereux (1967) suggests, that we each select a culture somehow influenced by unconscious personality factors: Mekeo with their emphasis on trickery and disguise resonating with my own long-forgotten childhood aggressions. Since investigating another culture places one initially in the position of a child just beginning to learn its own culture (chapter 3) it is perhaps not surprising that such buried emotions may be evoked by the fieldwork experience.

Chapter 3: From Visible Things

1. My undergraduate studies had been primarily in history and I was enrolled in the Department of Pacific History in the Research School of Pacific Studies, ANU. My experience in New Guinea and in Mekeo had convinced me that no purely documentary study could ever capture local events and attitudes as I hoped to do. My proposal to combine archival research with extensive ethnographic fieldwork intrigued the late Jim Davidson, then professor of Pacific history, a man who had never confined his own

distinguished Pacific career to archives and libraries. Fortunately for me, anthropologist Ben Finney (now professor and chair, Department of Anthropology, University of Hawaii), who was then working on recent economic changes in the New Guinea Highlands, had recently arrived in Davidson's department. He was to be my surpervisor and provide the necessary guidance to fill in the yawning gaps in my anthropological knowledge. I wanted to return to New Guinea immediately, but my new supervisor recognized that it would be many months, at the very least, before I had sufficient command of the ethnographic literature and grasp of theoretical concepts necessary to undertake the anthropological research I proposed. When at last, late in 1969, he deemed me ready to start, I returned to New Guinea to begin my first extended fieldwork. Gaps there no doubt still were, but I had now at least the foundations of an anthropological training and understanding on which to build. Certainly from this point my interests and methodology were to owe as much, or more, to anthropology. Two decades later, these disciplinary distinctions sound rather strained and old-fashioned given the current interest in historical perspectives in anthropology and of ethnographic perspectives in history (e.g., Marcus and Fischer 1986; Hunt 1989).

2. In all but trivial respects, these earlier accounts of sorcery and the beliefs associated with it tally closely with Hau'ofa's (1981) descriptions. Hau'ofa makes no claim to presenting the adept's perspective, and he explicitly states that he is dealing with oral testimony and the pattern of beliefs concerning sorcery (1981:220–221). The focus of his ethnography is the public ordering and public symbolism, as these relate to sorcery and the spirit world, and to social relations in general. My data and interpretations begin to diverge from his only following my 1980s fieldwork, when I started to investigate private and esoteric levels of understanding.

3. The versions that Mosko gives (1985:183–192) of the A'aisa (Akaisa) myth from Bush Mekeo includes several elements that for Central Mekeo constitute secret esoteric knowledge and are never included in public recitations.

4. Furthermore, despite the differences in Mosko's ethnography and his more complex view of the quadripartite structure of Bush Mekeo culture, his data differed little on the points raised here. The problem in comparing our findings centers on the fact that Mosko is dealing with another geographically and culturally separate group, the Bush Mekeo, and not the Mekeo of the central plains which Hau'ofa and I both studied. It is, therefore, difficult to be know whether our differences in our data are the result of actual cultural differences or of the fieldworkers' different perceptions and interpretations. But where they are essentially the same, the consensus is certainly persuasive. One fieldworker might have gone astray, but hardly could have three different people working in different communities, consulting different informants, coming up with essentially the same view with regard to the remote nature of the spirit realm, its mediation only by the forbidding men of sorrow, its separation from human society in general and from the benign influence of the men of kindness (Hau'ofa and Mosko both refer to "chiefs" and "sorcerers"). This does not seem probable. Differences in our accounts of Mekeo society there certainly were, but on these points, there was an agreement which emphatically argues for a consistency in cultural representation that goes way beyond my individual perceptions—or misapprehensions.

5. There is a black obsidian fragment of a sculpture of the head of King Senusret III (Washington, National Gallery of Art, C.S. Gulbenkian collection) illustrated in plate 105 (p. 313 for description) in K. Lange and M. Hirmer, *Egypt: Architecture, Sculpture,*

Painting in Three Thousand Years (London: Phaidon, 1956). This head quite remarkably resembles Aisaga's features and expression. Black volcanic glass, especially in view of the adept's aim to reduce flesh to stone, seems a perfect image for the man of sorrow.

6. Many fieldworkers in Melanesia and elsewhere dealing with similar systems of belief have come to the conclusion that fantasy alone is involved (Stephen 1987c). The difference in the Mekeo situation was that here, at least, there were actual persons who claimed to be the men of sorrow, but what they would tell me was always very guarded and tended merely to support the rumors and gossip of ordinary folk.

7. See Jung (1967:275ff.) on the horse as a symbol of unleashed power.

Chapter 4: To Hidden Things

1. Lawrence (1964:232ff.), among others, has eloquently pointed out the moral aspect of "cargo" in the so-called cargo cults of Melanesian. For the people of the Rai coast of Madang, he writes, cargo "became an index of their self-respect."

2. The now extensive cargo cult literature is replete with references to such beliefs (e.g., Lawrence 1964:2–4). For a recent discussion of the literature see *Oceania,* vol. 63, no. 1 (September 1992), "Alienating Mirrors: Christianity, Cargo Cults, and Colonialism in Melanesia."

3. These events were recorded in my field diary as they took place.

4. In psychological terms, it might be understood as an automatism along the lines of the automatic writing experienced by Western spirit mediums (Stephen 1987a).

5. Malinowski's classic Trobriand studies, for example, recognized that the "art of killing and curing is always in the same hand" (1961:75), although he did not further elaborate on this theme. Healing as an aspect of the Melanesian sorcerer's role has attracted little anthropological investigation, yet has been noted in many Melanesian societies (see Stephen 1987b).

Chapter 5: A Distinctive Mode of Imagination

1. I thank Bruce Knauft for underlining this point, one which he explores in his own analysis of Gebusi spirit mediumship (1985, 1989).

2. Bateson's (1973:101–129) discussion of primary process thinking and art makes an interesting comparison with Noy's. His is a much more positive view, both of the nature of primary process thinking and of the relationship of consciousness to the unconscious. Like Jung, Bateson (1973:118) sees consciousness as but the tip of the iceberg and as necessarily possessing only a partial and distorted view of the "systemic nature of mind" as a whole.

3. The concept of the "myth-dream" developed many years ago by Burridge (1960) in his study of Tangu cargo cults comes very close to Jungian and other similar views of the "mytho-poetic" function of the unconscious. Burridge bypasses the negative framework of primary process thinking, demonstrating by means of his ethnographic data the creative processes at work in the myth-dream. In my view, the myth-dream is a product of autonomous imagination.

4. Tedlock (1987a:14–17) comes to similar conclusions concerning the nature of dreams in reviewing recent neurophysiological studies of sleep and dreaming.

Chapter 6: Dreams

1. I recorded a large number of dreams occurring over the whole period of my 1980s fieldwork from Aisaga, and in an attempt to further elicit his methods of interpretation, I took to asking him to comment on my dreams. Thus I have a good volume of dream material obtained in the context of actual events as well as retrospective accounts. Both kinds of data reveal identical principles of interpretation.

2. The problems of collecting information raises issues discussed earlier (chapters 2 and 4) concerning the difficulty in Mekeo culture of gaining access to hidden things. Other dream researchers do not seem to have much to say on this score. Many, if not most, give the impression that information on the topic is readily divulged (e.g., Gregor 1981) and that there is no difficulty in obtaining any amount of material the ethnographer desires. Foster (1973) does refer to secrecy with respect to dream material, Kracke (1981) and LeVine (1981) discuss issues of trust and empathy, as does Herdt (1987), yet overall the Mekeo guardedness with respect to dreams seems unusual. Even Herr's (1981) study of Fijian nightmares, which emphasizes the highly negative cultural attitude to dreaming, makes little mention of difficulty of access to dreams once the ethnographer was well established in the community and had gained people's trust.

3. I refer, of course, to serious anthropological investigations, as distinct from various sensational and popular accounts of alleged shamanic initiation and the like.

4. Herdt (1987) and Kracke (1981, 1987) represent recent examples of investigators subtly negotiated into the therapeutic role; both are highly sensitive to cultural issues and complexities and to communicative aspects of dreaming. They recognize only in retrospect the extent of their involvement, and both examine their unease about accepting a role they considered they were not qualified to play at the time. Crapanzano (1980), in contrast, at first fiercely resists placing his own judgements on Tuhami's "narratives" but finally gives in fully to what he believes are Tuhami's expectations of a cure. LeVine (1981) simply assumes the researcher's position of authority, as does Kilbourne (1981b), bringing to mind the stance of earlier, less reflective workers such as Devereux and Roheim who saw themselves as analysts no less than ethnographers. Herdt and Stoller (1990) have sought to bring anthropology and psychoanalysis together in a new way, yet the assumption of authority with respect to the meaning of the dream remains.

5. On the other hand, the unwillingness of most people to report their ongoing dreams might be seen as a defensive measure to prevent me from intervening in their inner lives (meeting an equally defensive refusal on my part to become involved); but it had the positive effect of forcing me to focus my attention on emic understandings and uses of dream insights.

6. In this respect, Mekeo dream interpretation has close affinities with Jungian dream theory, as do many indigenous dream theories (Basso 1987).

7. Undoubtedly the manifest content of Mekeo dreams is as varied as that of any cultural group. My point here is that regardless of the actual dream content, Mekeo relate its meaning and significance to one of the topics listed. The underlying assumption is

that any dream is in some way connected to these matters and the task is to see how the dream imagery can be related to them. It is, in fact, not dissimilar from Freudian dream interpretation where the themes, although not the means of expressing them, are considered to be quite circumscribed. As Freud (1971:153) put it, "The range of things which are given symbolic representation in dreams is not wide: the human body as a whole, parents, children, brothers and sisters, birth, death, nakedness—and something else besides." Given the assumption that the dream is a disguised expression of an unconscious wish, Freudian interpretation assumes a very limited number of basic themes.

8. For example, Kilbourne (1981b) and Tuzin (1975). Kilbourne's apparently novel idea of submitting some of Freud's own dreams to Moroccan experts indicates his lack of sensitivity to these other levels of interpretation. He would have had to include a personal history for each dreamer, plus a sequence of other dreams or omens to provide the appropriate contextual and intertextual information. No wonder at least one of his dream interpreters refused to believe genuine dreams were being offered for examination!

9. These nightmares were dreamed by Matthew, Aisaga's son, and are associated with his ongoing illness which is linked to his difficult relationship with his father (see chapter 14). The first, in particular, provides a vivid image of this troubled situation. The cattle he fears are evidently the angry father; the barricade that prevents him from escaping and against which he repeatedly bashes his head is the inescapable dilemma of the relationship. In these examples the symbolism seems highly overdetermined since Aisaga is in fact both the father and the man of sorrow.

10. It seems surprising that Herr's (1981) discussion of Fijian nightmares, which in many respects parallel the Mekeo examples discussed here, makes no mention of the role of ritual influence, nor of sorcery or witchcraft.

Chapter 7: A Hidden Self

1. The term *kania e kieki* which means literally "head is painful" is used to describe a headache, the temporary madness or seizures just described, and the states experienced by participants in millenarian cults, several of which have occurred in the region (Stephen 1974, 1977). The old lady just described was involved in cultic activities during the 1940s, which spread following the preaching of a girl prophet, Philo, from Inawaia village.

2. This problem of finding an appropriate translation for the elusive entity that dreams is one that confronts all dream ethnographers. Careless and stereotyped equivalents such as "soul" or "spirit" bedevil the literature; see Tedlock (1987a:26–27).

3. A.J. Strathern (1977) cautions us against simplistic contrasts between "shame" and "guilt" cultures. He contrasts those emotions which Melpa feel on the outside of the body and those experienced on the inside. Mekeo have another expression, *meagai,* usually translated as "shyness" or "embarrassment," which seems close to the "shame" that Melpas feel "on the skin." See also Obeyesekere (1981:76–83) for an important discussion of the symbolisation of guilt in non-Western cultures, and Creighton (1990).

Chapter 8: Dreams and Self-Knowledge

1. The four case studies presented in this chapter are based upon interviews recorded in Mekeo, transcribed by me in Mekeo, and then translated by me into English. Because of the intimate and confidential nature of dreams in the Mekeo view, I could not employ others to transcribe or translate these materials. Only the interview with Michael, the church deacon (brief extracts of which are quoted here), was conducted in English.

2. Close relatives of the deceased (parents, children, and spouses) wear black clothes as a sign of mourning. They are usually only removed at the *umu pua,* the termination of mourning feast held about a year after the death. Whereas widowers and widows are always required to wear black and do so until they remarry, other relatives choose whether to adopt it, and may continue to wear it even after the *umu pua* as a mark of special attachment to the deceased. Since Celestina was not an immediate relative of Alice, but her classificatory sister of the same lineage, her mourning clothes indicate a particular fondness and personal affection for her. In view of this, forgetting to wear mourning in the dream, which provides the reason for not entering the city of the dead, seems significant in emphasizing her ambivalence toward Alice.

3. There is an esoteric version of the A'aisa myth which relates how A'aisa, annoyed by the apparent laziness of his wives, decides to make their life more difficult by causing masses of weeds to grow up in their food crops, forcing them to spend many arduous hours clearing their gardens of the undesirable growth. There is an associated ritual which can be used to ruin a neighbor's or rival's crops by infesting them with weeds. Does Joe know this myth or this rite? I have no idea, but it seems more than by chance that such a motif is incorporated in his dream vision of the punishments of the afterlife. This possibility further underlines the way in which his dream weaves together symbolic elements from indigenous and introduced sources.

4. Kilbourne (1981a: 167–169) relates "message" dreams to status, but in the Mekeo context, both message dreams and soul journey dreams are reported by everyone, without regard to status.

5. This returns us to issues raised in previous chapters concerning the ethnographer's unaware involvement in the fantasy lives of informants. On the surface, my interaction with Maria gave no hint of these underlying expectations, which might never have been expressed in another context. I had many other equally disconcerting experiences. For example, in interviews with two other women well known to me, it became apparent that they identified me with the *faifai* (water spirit) woman seen in the dreams of a husband and an adolescent son. In both cases, the dreams were linked to serious illness suffered by the two men concerned. Apparent here is the naivety of assuming that because the ethnographer has not in fact played an active role in events, or had much at all to do with a particular person, she or he is not involved in people's private fantasy constructions. In other words, the ethnographer may not have to play the part of analyst to provoke a transference (cf. LeVine 1981). This raises points made concerning the fantasies developed toward Europeans within millenarian movements—and the part played by Christian imagery and beliefs. My sense in penetrating Mekeo dream worlds was of coming upon a whole region of private fantasy somehow connected in a shared system that underlies people's thinking on many accounts yet is rarely, if ever, visible to European eyes.

6. Maria's dream of her daughter's death makes an interesting comparison with Kracke's (1981) account of the dreams of a bereaved father. Kracke admits his uncertainty as to whether the grieving father, Jovenil, would have worked through his mourning process on his own. In Maria's case, it is evident she uses her dreams to achieve this. The dream of Alice's death took place while I was away from the village, and I played no part except to provide the opportunity, years later, for Maria to relate the dream and its significance to me.

7. In my extensive interviews with Celestina, only a small part of which is related here, she revealed a similar propensity to create dream symbols and revelations with considerable revolutionary potential.

8. The association of dreams with knowledge, especially sacred or supernatural knowledge, is, of course, well established in the ethnographic literature. For reviews see Lincoln 1935; D'Andrade 1961; Von Grunebaum and Caillois 1967; O'Nell 1976; Stephen 1979a; Kilbourne 1981a. The therapeutic use of dreams is equally well acknowledged, but I think the significance of dreams as a form of self-knowledge has been largely submerged in this discussion. For example, the vision quest and berdache dreams of Amerindian cultures are obviously related to self-identity, yet are usually not explored from this perspective. They are treated as ritualized searches for social identity and as part of shared cultural beliefs, while the relationship between this "cultural template" (Ewing 1990a) and individual manipulations of it are rarely considered.

Chapter 9: The Traditions of Secret Knowledge

1. Mekeo "magic," as I describe it here, is quite similar in form and structure to that described by Malinowski (1935, 1961, 1974), Hogbin (1970), Lawrence (1973), Young (1983) and others. I am not asserting that Mekeo esoteric knowledge is unique in structure or nature. Yet what does seem unusual is the degree of secrecy that surrounds it—even its most minor forms. Many ethnographies routinely include the texts of spells, magical potions, descriptions of secret ritual actions, and native exegesis of esoteric symbols. Malinowski (1935), working in a similar culture, was able to fill volumes with the texts of incantations and ritual actions involved in garden magic alone. Why was information so difficult to obtain from Mekeo? Are we to assume ethnographers in other cultures had no problems gaining access to such material? Did they pay informants? It might have been possible to buy some esoteric secrets, but Mekeo have easy access to money and today place an extremely high cash value on everything. Had I tried to purchase what I wanted to know, I would quickly have run out of funds.

2. People's usual reticence on the matter of ritual knowledge in general and who possesses it is equally underlined in Hau'ofa's study. He (1981:215–216) notes the existence of other forms of "magic" in addition to sorcery but says very little about them.

3. For example, the special stones employed by the adept which are thought to constitute the actual, but petrified, bodily substance of a spirit being are said to contain *isapu* only if the spirit is that of a dead person or one of the myth people. A stone incorporating a *faifai* spirit, which is just as powerful and dangerous, is not said to have *isapu*. As with terms such as *lopia* and *ugauga* discussed in chapter 1, the word *isapu*

has been used extensively in attempting to communicate indigenous concepts to Europeans, especially, of course, to the Catholic missionaries, so much so that it is often used in ways that distort its primary meaning. Furthermore, laypersons are possibly not aware of the distinctions made here. Yet even ordinary people, when speaking their own language, do not refer to the *isapu* of *faifai* spirits striking them, as they would naturally of the spirits of the dead or their bodily relics. See also note 3, chapter 12.

4. The public ideal of male, patrilineal inheritance is stressed by Hau'ofa (1981: 216). He makes no mention of women possessing major rites, even of dream divination, which further underlines the public ideal.

5. Hau'ofa (1981) also refers to the importance of beauty ritual for males in courting, but makes no reference to equivalent female rituals. My sources assured me that some women did possess such knowledge, but that on the whole women did not need or bother with it.

6. I collected esoteric information from several women, especially Josephina, the community's most renowned woman of knowledge. Josephina in particular was very generous with what she imparted to me, yet although I spent a considerable amount of time with her, it is certainly true that I did not have the same opportunity to learn of her activities day by day as I did of Aisaga. It is possible that if I had spent all, or most of, my time close to a female ritual expert such as Josephina, I would have discovered more subtle aspects of female knowledge not available to males. Nevertheless, there is no doubt that life-threatening problems related to gynaecological matters are taken to male experts.

7. Over the duration of my fieldwork changes have occurred, with many of the older generation dying. My figures are based on my 1969–1970 data, when a thorough household census of the village was taken. Although the actual numbers have altered slightly, the overall picture remains much the same. The 1980 *Papua New Guinea National Census,* Preliminary Field Counts, gives the population of the community as 928, an increase of 57 persons on the total of my household census a decade earlier.

8. Hau'ofa observes the extent to which people suspected the men of kindness as being implicated in the deaths of members of their own community, but does not refer to them implementing destructive rituals themselves, but only via the men of sorrow. Hau'ofa (1981:250ff.) also describes in detail covert rivalry and battle for power between "chiefs" and "sorcerers," but sees the conflict in terms of the visible secular authority of the chiefs versus the invisible mystical powers of the sorcerers. My information suggests a different picture with yet more covert layers.

9. Perhaps at this point my differences with Hau'ofa's (1981) interpretations become clearer. In my view, he provides an excellent, detailed, in-depth description of the public/manifest (*ofakae*) layers of the roles of the men of sorrow and the men of kindness.

Chapter 10: Two Dream Diviners

1. "Riches" (*efu*) is the term Mekeo use to refer to traditional valuables made from shells, pigs tusks, dogs' teeth, and the feathers of various birds, especially birds of paradise. Small monetary payments may be made for minor services, but any major payment would include such traditional items of wealth, which are also a necessary

component of marriage wealth. These items continue to maintain their value, and in fact are more highly prized than money, which is easy for people to get nowadays. Ordinary people have access to *efu* only through marriage payments, thus ritual experts are in a privileged position in this respect.

2. The placing of a knife under the practitioner's pillow and its use in the dream to kill the *faifai* snake afflicting the sick person is typical of *feuapi* rituals. Many if not most people have of course heard *feuapi* diviners recounting their exploits in these terms to the patient or relatives. Even though such matters are always conducted in private, they are common enough for most adults to have had some direct experience of them.

3. It is interesting with respect to the special bush retreats reputedly maintained by the men of sorrow that diviners like Josephina refer to seeing the dream-self imprisoned in the *gove* (residence occupied by an unmarried male), and *not* the *fauapi* (bush retreat) of the man of sorrow. Of course the diviners would have no opportunity to see *fauapi*, whereas the *gove* are visible structures on the periphery of the settlement and known to everyone. It suggests, however, that the diviners believe that the men of sorrow are performing their deadly rituals there close to the rest of the populace, although the public statements discussed in chapter 2 deny this.

Chapter 11: Two Men of Knowledge

1. Although some spells (*mega*) employ ordinary Mekeo words, many spells are entirely foreign or archaic. Aisaga observed that most spells for *ugauga* sorcery are in Mekeo, but with substantial parts in the ancestors' language (*au apaoi ei mala*), whereas many spells relating to the *faifai* water spirits were in Waima language, and many hunting spells were in Bush Mekeo, as the knowledge had originated among these groups. I found most spells incomprehensible and had to ask the donors, after reciting them, to translate into current Mekeo. The use of arcane and foreign words no doubt helps to preserve secrecy, and makes the learning and acquiring of spells more difficult, keeping the apprentice dependent on the teacher for further instruction.

2. The aim of *gope* is not simply to make the body "hot" but rather to make it impenetrable and invulnerable, as I shall examine in more detail in chapter 15.

3. People commonly speak of the *faifai* spirits hitting or striking them. In the case of the spirits of the dead, or of the myth people, it is said their "heat" (*isapu*) hits or strikes one, but the same is not said of the *faifai*. However, I have heard people refer to a charm (*igove*) used to attract *faifai* spirits as having "married" (*akavania*) them, meaning it had caused them to become ill. This perhaps suggests that the penetration of self caused by *faifai* spirits is associated with sexual interpenetration, whereas the penetration of self by human spirits is seen more destructively, as piercing by "heat." As I have noted, the water spirits are thought to fall in love with human beings, luring away their dream-selves to their underwater abodes. Nevertheless, being struck down by them can prove fatal.

Chapter 12: Observing a Man of Knowledge

1. In focusing on such a remarkable figure as Aisaga, there is the danger of exoticizing him. Recent works have drawn attention to these issues (Wikan 1990:243–

244; Keesing 1987). To Western eyes, Aisaga will inevitably appear exotic with his mystical powers of life and death and his intimate engagement with the world of spirit beings. For this reason, I felt it essential to place him not only within his cultural context, but within the framework of ordinary people's understandings of the spirit world: the hidden self and dreaming. To have come upon him before encountering Celestina, Joe, Maria, and the others discussed in part III would be to render him much more extraordinary than he is. My intention is to take the apparently exotic and explore its grounding in everyday experience to reveal the sense it makes of that experience from the actor's point of view. I am reminded here of Wikan's (1982) description of the veil, or face covering, worn by the Omani woman, an object that appears intrinsically bizarre, ugly, and degrading to Western eyes, yet Wikan succeeds in exploring the significance of the *burqa* for the women who wear it in such a way that the reader's perception of it is, in the end, totally altered. Like Wikan (1982, 1990), I am drawn into a narrative presentation of material at various points as a means of uncovering meanings for actors in real circumstances.

2. In divination, for example, the spirits are said to "hold up the bone," implying a direct action upon the embodied world. But it must be kept in mind that the bone is their own body substance—an actual fragment of the arm bone of one of the adept's ancestors. It is also possible for spirit presences to be seen by the waking eyes of the practitioner. Yet the action of the spirits, I think it is true to say, is understood to operate via the immaterial or disembodied aspect of the object or victim. Of course not everyone understands this; a person with little knowledge might well implement minor procedures, such as employing a particular "medicine" (*fu'a*) to catch fish or to make a person sexually attractive, for example, without having any idea or even having thought about how the action they desire is achieved. Only the adept, who engages regularly with the hidden realm, is aware of the underlying principles at work. But this, as discussed in previous chapters, is not so much a matter of intellectual understanding as of experiential knowledge of interaction with the dream-imagery of the disembodied realm.

3. Spirits of the dead and of the myth people, such as A'aisa, are said to possess this "heat" (*isapu*). In contrast, the *faifai* water spirits are said to strike human beings, but not with *isapu*, as noted earlier.

Chapter 13: Learning "Sorcery" Unawares

1. In this case, the forces operating are properly referred to as *isapu*, "heat," since the objects and substances contained in the charm constitute the bodily relics or substance of spirits of the dead and the myth people, which are imbued with *isapu*.

2. In terms of the public ideals, this is denied. Nevertheless ordinary people do often express the view that the men of sorrow attack just to make money, but they also refer to the payments he receives from those who commission him to kill, implying that the offence caused to others is the underlying cause of his action. In this case, Aisaga reveals that the man of sorrow, of his own accord, simply strikes down any bystanders at feasts in the expectation of being paid to cure them. The charm he carries is not intended for a specific target, but affects anyone not ritually prepared who comes in close contact.

3. Most Mekeo women prefer to give birth in the mission hospital. This is seen to simplify the dangers of contamination for the rest of the family and to better protect the

mother and baby from the danger of the blood and other substances from the birth being obtained by the men of sorrow. The birth itself provides the greatest danger, both of harm to others through contamination and of harm to mother and child by appropriation of their body substance. For several weeks afterward (usually two to three months from my observance), the mother is considered to be in the special condition of *megomego*, wherein she continues to be contaminating to others (she must not prepare food during this time) and especially vulnerable to mystical attack via her own body substance. For a time she should sleep and sit near a hot fire and do no heavy work. Her diet is regulated to include "hot" foods and to avoid watery cold foods. This is similar to the *gope* regimen observed by male ritual experts, and the intention appears to be much the same: to close the body, to make it less vulnerable and less fluid. Sexual intercourse is harmful during this time, endangering both partners. For the sake of the child's health, marital relations between spouses should not resume until the child is walking.

4. Jung (1973) has written of "meaningful coincidences" wherein an underlying unconscious significance links apparently unrelated events in the external world.

5. It is no doubt comforting to have such labels to affix to our experiences, yet the problem of applying the concept of countertransference to my dealing with Aisaga is to decide where it belongs—with him or with me? It is usually assumed in the ethnographic context that the ethnographer, the elicitor of fantasy material, takes the role of the analyst, the informant that of the analysand. Such is evidently the relationship between Tuhami and Crapanzano (1980), Jovenil and Kracke (1981), Nilutwo and Herdt (1987). Aisaga, however, was neither a misfit ready to play whatever part the rich foreigner sought to cast him in nor a troubled and grieving father seeking to assuage his suffering, nor a deviant uncomfortable in the confines of his own culture. He was ever the man of knowledge, aloof in his superior control of every aspect of his world, visible or hidden. My dream of him as a rotting corpse (chapter 12) might be regarded as typical of a negative transference in which the analysand fulfills her unconscious wish for the death of the analyst. As I will show in chapter 14, Aisaga was convinced of my desire for his death, but this was grounded in his cultural expectations of what the transmission of secret knowledge involved, and was not primarily an intuiting of my unconscious fantasies. The next chapter reveals that the transmission of knowledge is itself a highly emotionally charged process. Any useful discussion of transference and countertransference would have to be grounded in the particular circumstances, cultural and practical, of these added complications.

Chapter 14: The Sorrows of Acquiring Knowledge

1. As in other such dumbfounding confrontations (for example, Maria's dream revelation that I was really the dead returned), there was no response I could make that could possibly resolve the situation. No matter how vehemently I denied any ill intent toward him, Aisaga was convinced of his superior insight into things. All I could do was deny any conscious plan to harm him, and this, for the time being, he accepted. It should be kept in mind that at the time of these events I did not appreciate fully their significance. Had I done so, had I then realized Aisaga's suspicions were inevitable and impossible to allay, I would have found my position intolerable.

2. When the possessor of secret knowledge is near death, he gives what he would never give up in life. A grandson often receives more knowledge than does a son, no doubt since when the father is close to death, the son is middle-aged and the grandson is still probably an unmarried youth who is ready to learn and to implement dangerous rituals.

3. A decade has passed since Aisaga, then in his late sixties, made this observation, so I suspect that this time has already passed.

4. Kracke (1981:273 and notes 8 and 9) refers to the informant mourning the departure of the ethnographer. His, I think, is a sensitive insight into the dynamics of the ethnographic encounter (see also Wikan 1990:200) which is little considered, no doubt because it is a painful one. I believe that Aisaga, in his anger with me, was also in a sense mourning my departure. He was not only angry, but he conveyed a sense of injury at my desire to be gone. A week or so before I was due to leave he announced he had a dream that I left: this meant my hidden self had already gone ahead of my bodily self. He had a special meal prepared for that evening—a "party to say goodbye"—and from then on made no further complaints and no longer seemed angry.

I left in June. In December that year I returned for a short stay of six weeks. The following year, 1983, Aisaga visited us in Australia for a month—but that is another story. His trip was at my expense; I did not want it to be said or thought that he received no substantial return for his gifts of knowledge. Nor did I wish to incur further debts, nor ultimately be placed in a position where Aisaga's death might be attributed to me. I had finally experienced enough of the sorrows of secret knowledge. I have not visited Papua New Guinea or seen Aisaga since, although I corresponded with his family for some years. In 1985, Aisaga's second son wrote to say that Matthew, the eldest son and heir, had died.

Chapter 15: A'aisa's Gifts

1. It interesting to see how the Latin roots of English words represent similar symbolic equivalents—mater, materia, matrix—so that it becomes easy to translate here from Mekeo to English. According to Jung (1976:75–110), such symbolism is universal, forming part of the "mother archetype."

2. It is thus Mosko (1985) has described and analyzed Bush Mekeo culture and social structure. His emphasis on body symbolism at first glance seems incompatible with Hau'ofa's (1981) descriptions, and my own (Stephen 1987a), both of which make little mention of body substance as *overt* social metaphors. Nevertheless, much of Mosko's description is recognizable as an account of the concealed "inside" of things, as described only by adepts like Aisaga.

3. Although I am dealing here with fourfold divisions, these do not seem to match the formal quadripartite logic Mosko describes for Bush Mekeo symbolism. If I applied Mosko's schema to this material, as I understand it, the following would result:

outside   :   inside   : :   inverted outside   :   everted inside
embodied   :   disembodied : :   flux of matter   :   dream-images

In this schema, flux of matter is directly opposed to dream-image. My proposition is that the embodied and disembodied realms are linked by inverted outside (flux of matter) meeting everted inside (dream-self/image). This more closely approximates the symbolism of body substance just described, wherein the dream-self is attracted to its former internal substance, suggesting that it is precisely at this point that the two realms are joined.

4. The word *fu'a*, according to Desnoes (1941:316), means "leavings; remains" (le reste; déchets). Almost every *fu'a*—or "medicine" as I have translated the term—turns out upon investigation to be the transformed body substance of a myth hero or a water spirit. These are clearly the body dirt (*faga ofuga*) of spirit beings, but only human body substance is usually referred to thus. In my opinion, the term *fu'a* represents a deliberate masking of the true nature of these substances. The adept, however, recognizes them to be the "leavings" or "remains," the body dirt, of spirit beings.

5. Hau'ofa attempts to distinguish between the functions and significance of "chiefs" and "sorcerers" on the basis of a "secular and sacred" dichotomy. He makes a similar contrast between "war chiefs" and "war sorcerers." My argument is that the role of the man of kindness is no less ritual or "sacred" in nature, and no more "secular" than that of the man of sorrow; both are mediators of the cosmic order and of the flow of life and death. The oppositions they represent are that of the embodied world and the disembodied world, as Mekeo conceptualize them, and not our categories of "secular and sacred." The roles of the leaders concerned with warfare can also be better understood from this perspective, as we are about to discover.

6. Although Mosko (1985:237) would argue for Bush Mekeo that "there is no single symbol or context that can necessarily be identified as dominant over the others," this, in the Mekeo case, ignores the public importance of the man of kindness and the man of sorrow, and the prominence given to esoteric knowledge in this culture.

7. That such symbols might be arranged according to a specific logic does not obviate their significance to affective and experiential needs. Indeed Jung (1969:41) has gone so far as to argue that numbers might be understood as an archetypal pattern of the psyche:

> It is generally believed that numbers were *invented* or thought out by man, and are therefore nothing but concepts of quantities, containing nothing that was not previously put into them by the human intellect. But it is equally possible that numbers were *found* or discovered. In that case they are not only concepts but something more—autonomous entities which somehow contain more that just quantities. Unlike concepts, they are based not on any psychic conditions but on the quality of being themselves, on a "so-ness" that cannot be expressed by an intellectual concept. Under these conditions they might easily be endowed with qualities that have still to be discovered. I must confess that I incline to the view that numbers were as much found as invented, and that in consequence they possess a relative autonomy analogous to that of the archetypes. They would then have, in common with the latter, the quality of being pre-existent to consciousness, and hence, on occasion, of conditioning it rather than being conditioned by it.

It is almost as if the whole impressive opus of Lévi-Straussian structuralism were a massive ethnographic exploration of this brief statement of Jung's! As for fourfold structures, Jung's works are replete with references to the symbolic significance of four (and multiples of four) as an archetypal symbolic expression of wholeness, especially, of course, psychic wholeness. One might perhaps ask: are quadripartite structures the product of logical arrangements of the mind? Or perhaps a repetitive pattern of the psyche, a motif, an aesthetic of wholeness, as Jung suggests? I confess, therefore, my partiality for quadripartite structures, but it has not been the task of this book to attempt to uncover them, nor to undertake the careful comparative work necessary to establish the correspondences between the Central Mekeo and the Bush Mekeo data.

8. I am thinking here of the concept of empathy as developed by Kohut (1971, 1977, 1985).

Chapter 16: Magic, Self, and Autonomous Imagination

1. As Mark Mosko has reminded me (personal communication).

2. I have argued (Stephen 1987b) that in the confusion of beliefs recorded in the anthropological literature one can identify two opposite poles, with a wide range of variations located in between. Following general anthropological usage of the terms, I refer to one extreme as "sorcery," the other as "witchcraft." Other terms might have done as well, my point is merely to identify the striking polarities in the ethnographic material. At one end of the spectrum, persons attributed with magical death-dealing powers are given high social status and are rewarded for their services, and they openly practice or claim to practice rituals with deadly intent. At the other end of the spectrum are individuals attributed with death-dealing powers who, although they deny any knowledge of such powers, are believed to be the agents of sickness and death within the community and are consequently ostracized or killed. Within these extremes are found many variations on the two themes which, I have suggested, need to be understood as cultural variations molded by external pressures as well as internal structures, and changing over time as a result of exogenous and endogenous factors.

My intent is not to ignore these complexities, nor, as Knauft (1985:345–346) suggests, to reduce them to an even more rigid dual classification that originally was asserted in Evans-Pritchard's (1937) classic distinction between sorcery and witchcraft. Knauft overlooks my explicit exclusion of the nature and symbolism of *belief* as a criterion for deciding whether a specific cultural complex more closely approximates the sorcery or the witchcraft end of the spectrum (Stephen 1987b:287–288). I point out that beliefs are not the basis of my distinction but the *social consequences* of the complex of belief and action, that is, whether being attributed with death-dealing powers results in social power and prestige, or the opposite. Knauft (1985:340–344) proposes a typology of Melanesian sorcery/witchcraft which, he acknowledges, is similar to mine and that independently identifies the move from one end of a spectrum of power to its opposite. In effect, we disagree only on terminology. Knauft wants to make no distinction between the two extremes, whereas I think it confusing to speak of the Gebusi "sorcerer" as if he or she were no different from the Mekeo man of sorrow. One might call one "sorcery/witchcraft/+ pole" and the other "sorcery/witchcraft/− pole," but our existing terms "sorcerer" and "witch" serve to highlight the differences.

3. In attempting to understand the decline of beliefs in magic, sorcery and witchcraft in the Western world (e.g., Thomas 1971), historians have yet to link the process to the changing nature of self-concepts and the growth of individualism in the sixteenth and seventeenth centuries. From this perspective, secularism and the decline of a magico-religious worldview may not alone account for events. In communities or cultures where

a divisible, sociocentric self-concept prevailed, beliefs in the powers of others to invade self for nefarious purposes would continue to retain their psychological salience and power, as indeed they do in some peasant and rural communities today in Europe. As Favret-Saada (1980) shows, education, or lack or it, is not the issue here, nor even is it one of epistemology, as Lawrence (1987:34–36) argues for present-day Papua New Guinea.

4. Tambiah (1990) proposes two basic orientations: causality and participation—seeing the external world as object and seeing it as related to self. He implies a conscious and deliberate movement between the two modes according to the intentions and purpose of the actor. Within participation Tambiah includes the self in relationship, whereas I have argued that the rituals of the Mekeo adept are directed precisely toward creating an impermeable self empowered by its separation from others. Yet it would be true to say that in this process, he or she engages in an intense participation with other-worldly beings and forces. Although I agree that all human beings employ modes of thought that are not strictly rational or causal but that are also governed by feelings and desires, I think it confusing to lump all such thinking under the heading "participation." We need greater differentiation between modes of cognition than are available at present.

5. Recent research by psychologists Nemeroff and Rozin (1989, 1990, 1992) suggests that magical thinking as evidenced in the "laws of similarity and contagion" operates in the reactions of educated Western adults, who would consciously deny any such beliefs. On the basis of various test procedures related to food preferences and disgust reactions, Nemeroff and Rozin propose that some underlying thought system, dominated by the laws of sympathetic magic, operates alongside rational, reality-directed thought processes in all human beings. Even where subjects intellectually understand, for example, the process of digestion from a scientific perspective, this does not obviate disgust reactions based on magical laws of contagion. While pointing to the negative aspects of such thinking, Nemeroff and Rozin (1989:66–67) also note its creative function. They point out that, unlike other researchers, such as Shweder (1977), who have argued for the existence of magical thinking in normal Western adults, their investigations do not indicate that its employment arises out of cognitive limitations—that is, substituting a more heuristic, intuitive approach in the absence of accurate scientific knowledge. Instead they argue that such thinking may prevail and influence emotions and behaviour even in situations where the subject has an accurate rational understanding of the situation. Thus they propose that "an actively competing thought system operates alongside the 'rational'—one that individuals may not be aware of, and that may even contrast with their explicit beliefs, but that nonetheless influences them." (1989:66). This has obvious parallels with my arguments concerning autonomous imagination. Since Nemeroff and Rozin deal specifically with eating and the incorporation of objects and essences into the self, their arguments also seem to support my contention that self-boundaries are an enduring and problematic theme of submerged imaginative processes in Western adults.

6. This, it should be emphasized, is not to argue that all magic is positive in nature. Clearly Mekeo rituals of secret knowledge are used to dangerous and destructive ends, as part III of this book constantly reiterates.

7. Mekeo cosmological symbols for the self cluster around what Jung (1967, 1976) would describe as the early stages of the process of individuation. The fluid self of the ordinary Mekeo person seems always in danger of being submerged back into the matter from which it emerged, that is, of returning to the engulfing mother, the unconscious. In the Jungian view, stone is always a symbol for the self, thus the Mekeo stony self represents the fully individuated self. Individuation seems especially tied to the shadow archetype in Mekeo culture, being closely linked to dangerous and destructive urges. The man of sorrow achieves the most differentiated self-consciousness, but he suffers in the process. Trickster, whom I would identify with the myth hero A'aisa, is, in the Jungian view, linked to the shadow, and one of the first steps on the path of individuation is to face the shadow. For Mekeo, it would seem, self symbols are strongly influenced by the potentials and dangers of the shadow aspect of their deeper selves.

Bibliography

Abu-Lughod, L.
    1989   "Zones of Theory in the Anthropology of the Arab World." *Annual Review of Anthropology* 18:267–306.

Appaduri, A.
    1986   "Theory in Anthropology: Center and Periphery." *Comparative Studies in Society and History* 28:356–374.

Arlow, J. A., and Brenner, C.
    1964   *Psychoanalytic Concepts and the Structural Theory.* New York: International Universities Press.

Barber, T. X.
    1979   "Suggested ('Hypnotic') Behaviour: The Trance Paradigm Versus an Alternate Paradigm." In Fromm and Shor 1979b:217–271.

Barber, T. X., Spanos, N. P., and Chaves, J. F.
    1974   *Hypnosis, Imagination and Human Potentialities.* New York: Pergamon Press.

Barth, F.
    1975   *Ritual and Knowledge Among the Baktaman of Papua New Guinea.* New Haven: Yale University Press.

    1987   *Cosmologies in the Making: A Generative Approach to Cultural Variation in Inner New Guinea.* Cambridge: Cambridge University Press.

Basso, E.
    1987   "The Implications of a Progressive Theory of Dreaming." In Tedlock 1987b:86–104.

Bateson, G.
    1973   "Style, Grace and Information in Primitive Art." In G. Bateson, *Steps to an Ecology of Mind: Collected Essays in Anthropology, Psychiatry, Evolution, and Epistemology,* 101–125. London: Paladin.

Beattie, J.
1972   *Other Cultures: Aims, Methods and Achievements in Social Anthropology.*
        London: Routledge and Kegan Paul.
Beattie, J., and Middleton, J. (eds.)
1969   *Spirit Mediumship and Society in Africa.* New York: Africana Publishing
        Corporation.
Belshaw, C. S.
1951   "Recent History of Mekeo Society." *Oceania* 22:1–23.
Bercovitch, E.
1989   "Mortal Insights: Victim and Witch in the Nalumin Imagination." In
        Herdt and Stephen 1989:122–159.
Bernstein, M.
1965   *The Search for Bridey Murphy.* New York: Doubleday and Company.
Boon, J. A.
1982   *Other Tribes, Other Scribes: Symbolic Anthropology in the Comparative
        Study of Cultures, Histories, Religions and Texts.* Cambridge: Cambridge
        University Press.
Bourdieu, P.
1977   *Outline of a Theory of Practice.* Cambridge: Cambridge University Press.
Bourguignon, E.
1968   "World Distribution and Patterns of Possession States." In R. Prince (ed.),
        Trance and Possession States, 3–34. Montreal: R. M. Bucke Memorial
        Society.
1972   "Dreams and Altered States of Consciousness in Anthropological Re-
        search." In Hsu 1972:403–434.
1976   "The Effectiveness of Religious Healing Movements: A Review of Recent
        Literature." *Transcultural Psychiatric Research Review* 13:5–21.
1979   *Psychological Anthropology: An Introduction to Human Nature and Cul-
        tural Differences.* New York: Holt, Rinehart and Winston.
Bourguignon, E. (ed.)
1973   *Religion, Altered States of Consciousness, and Social Change.* Columbus:
        Ohio State University Press.
Bowers, K. S.
1976   *Hypnosis for the Seriously Curious.* Monterey, Calif.: Brooks/Cole Pub-
        lishing Company.
1984   "On Being Unconsciously Influenced and Informed." In Bowers and
        Meichenbaum 1984:227–272.
Bowers, P. G., and Bowers, K. S.
1979   "Hypnosis and Creativity: A Theoretical and Empirical Rapprochement."
        In Fromm and Shor 1979b:351–379.
Bowers, K. S., and Meichenbaum, D. (eds.)
1984   *The Unconscious Reconsidered.* New York: John Wiley and Sons.
Breger, L.
1980   "The Manifest Dream and its Latent Content." In J. M. Natterson (ed.),
        The Dream in Clinical Practice, 3–27. New York: Jason Aronson.
Burridge, K. O. L.
1960   *Mambu: A Melanesian Millennium.* London: Methuen.
1969   *Tangu Traditions.* Oxford: Clarendon Press.

Cartwright, R. D.
    1969   "Dreams as Compared to Other Forms of Fantasy." In Kramer 1969: 361–372.
    1978   *A Primer on Sleep and Dreaming.* Massachusetts, Calif.: Addison-Wesley.
    1981   "The Contribution of Research on Memory and Dreaming to a 24-Hour Model of Cognitive Behaviour." In Fishbein 1981:239–247.
Chowing, A.
    1987   "Sorcery and the Social Order in Kove." In Stephen 1987c:149–182.
Clifford, J.
    1982   *Person and Myth: Maurice Leenhardt in the Melanesian World.* Berkeley and Los Angeles: University of California Press.
    1986   "Introduction: Partial Truths." In Clifford and Marcus 1986:1–26.
Clifford, J., and Marcus, G. E. (eds.)
    1986   *Writing Culture: The Poetics and Politics of Ethnography.* Berkeley and Los Angeles: University of California Press.
Codrington, R. H.
    1891   *The Melanesians.* Oxford: Clarendon Press.
Cohen, D. B.
    1979   *Sleep and Dreaming: Origins, Nature and Functions.* Oxford: Pergamon Press.
Cooper, L. M.
    1979   "Hypnotic Amnesia." In Fromm and Shor 1979:305–349.
Corballis, M. C.
    1983   *Human Laterality.* New York, London: Academic Press.
Crapanzano, V.
    1979   Preface to *Do Kamo* by M. Leenhardt. Chicago: Chicago University Press.
    1980   *Tuhami: Portrait of a Moroccan.* Chicago: University of Chicago Press.
Crick, F., and Mitchison, G.
    1983   "The Function of Dream Sleep." *Nature,* July 14.
Creighton, M.
    1990   "Revisiting Shame and Guilt Cultures: A Forty-Year Pilgrimage." *Ethos* 18:279–307.
D'Andrade, R. G.
    1961   "Anthropological Studies of Dreams." In F. L. K. Hsu 1972:308–332.
    1984   "Cultural Meaning Systems." In Shweder and LeVine 1984:88–119.
D'Aquili, E. G., Laughlin, C. D., and McManus, J. (eds.)
    1979   *The Spectrum of Ritual.* New York: Columbia University Press.
Davidson, J. M., and Davidson, R. J. (eds.)
    1980   *The Psychobiology of Consciousness.* New York and London: Plenum Press.
Davidson, R. J.
    1980   "Consciousness and Information Processing." In Davidson and Davidson 1980:11–46.
Davis, N. Z.
    1986   "Boundaries and the Sense of Self in Sixteenth-Century France." In Heller, Sosna, and Wellbery 1986:53–63.

Desnoes, G.
    1941   "Mekeo Dictionary." Three volumes, typescript manuscript. Veifa"a
            (Beipa) Catholic Mission.
Devereux, G.
    1967   *From Anxiety to Method in the Behavioural Sciences*. The Hague: Mouton.
DeVos, G., Marsella, A. J., and Hsu, F. L. K.
    1985   "Introduction: Approaches to Culture and Self." In A. J. Marsella, G.
            DeVos, and F. L. K. Hsu (eds.), *Culture and Self: Asian and Western
            Perspectives*. New York: Tavistock Publications.
Dimond, S.
    1972   *The Double Brain*. Edinburgh and London: Churchill and Livingstone.
Dixon, N. F.
    1971   *Subliminal Perception: The Nature of a Controversy*. London: McGraw-
            Hill.
    1981   *Preconscious Processing*. Chichester: John Wiley and Sons.
Doi, T.
    1986   *The Anatomy of the Self*. Trans. M. A. Harbison. Tokyo: Kodansha.
Domhoff, G. W.
    1985   *The Mystique of Dreams: A Search for Utopia through Senoi Dream
            Theory*. Berkeley and Los Angeles: University of California Press.
Douglas, M. T.
    1966   *Purity and Danger: An Analysis of Concepts of Pollution and Taboo*.
            London: Routledge and Kegan Paul.
    1970   *Natural Symbols: Explorations in Cosmology*. London: Cresset Press.
Dumont, J-P.
    1978   *The Headman and I: Ambiguity and Ambivalence in the Fieldworking
            Experience*. Austin and London: University of Texas Press.
Dumont, L.
    1965   "The Functional Equivalent of the Individual in Caste Society." *Con-
            tributions to Indian Sociology* 8:85–99.
Dupeyrat, A.
    1935   *Papouasie: Histoire de la mission (1885–1935)*. Paris: Dillen.
Durkheim, E.
    1915   *The Elementary Forms of the Religious Life*. Glencoe, Ill.: The Free
    (1947) Press.
Egidi, V. M.
    1912   "Le leggi e le ceremonie del matrimonio nella tribu di Mekeo." *Rivista
            di Anthropologie* 17:217–229.
Eliade, M.
    1972   *Shamanism: Archaic Techniques of Ecstasy*. Princeton: Princeton/
            Bollingen Paperback.
Ellenberger, H. F.
    1970   *The Discovery of the Unconscious*. New York: Basic Books.
Evans, C.
    1983   *Landscapes of the Night: How and Why We Dream*. New York: The Viking
            Press.

Evans, F. J.
1979   "Hypnosis and Sleep: Techniques For Exploring Cognitive Activity During Sleep." In Fromm and Shor 1979b:139–183.

Evans-Pritchard, E. E.
1937   *Witchcraft, Oracles, and Magic Among the Azande.* Oxford: Clarendon Press.
1967   "The Morphology and Function of Magic: A Comparative Study of Trobriand and Zande Ritual and Spells." In Middleton 1967:1–22.

Evans-Wentz, W. Y.
1967   *Tibetan Yoga and Its Secret Doctrines.* New York: Oxford University Press.

Ewing, K. P.
1990a   "The Dream of Spiritual Initiation and the Organization of Self Representations Among Pakistani Sufis." *American Ethnologist* 17:56–74.
1990b   "The Illusion of Wholeness: Culture, Self, and the Experience of Inconsistency." *Ethos* 18:251–278.

Favret-Saada, J.
1980   *Deadly Words: Witchcraft in the Bocage.* London and New York: Cambridge University Press.

Field, M. J.
1969   "Spirit Possession in Ghana." In Beattie and Middleton 1969:3–13.

Fishbein, W. (ed.)
1981   *Sleep, Dreams, and Memory.* Advances in Sleep Research, vol. 6. New York: Spectrum.

Fortes, M., and Evans-Pritchard, E. E. (eds.)
1940   *African Political Systems.* London: Oxford University Press.

Foster, G. M.
1973   "Dreams, Character, and Cognitive Orientation in Tzintzuntzan." *Ethos* 1:106–121.

Foucault, M.
1980   *Power/Knowledge: Selected Interviews and Other Writings.* New York: Pantheon Books.

Foulkes, D. W.
1966   *The Psychology of Sleep.* New York: Charles Scribner's Sons.
1982   *Children's Dreams.* New York: Wiley and Sons.

Frazer, J. G.
1913   *The Golden Bough: A Study in Magic and Religion.* London: Macmillan
(1980)   Press.

Freeman, D.
1967   "Shaman and Incubus." *Psychoanalytic Study of Society* 4:315–343.

Freilich, M. (ed.)
1970   *Marginal Natives: Anthropologists at Work.* New York, Evanston, and London: Harper and Row.

French, T., and Fromm, E.
1964   *Dream Interpretation.* New York: Basic Books.

Freud, S.

1900   *The Interpretation of Dreams.* Harmondsworth: Penguin
(1976)

1908   "Creative Writers and Day-Dreaming." *The Complete Works of Sigmund Freud,* The Standard Edition, vol. 9. London: The Hogarth Press.

1916a   "Wit and its Relation to the Unconscious." In *The Basic Writings of Sigmund Freud.* New York: The Modern Library.
(1966)

1916b   *Totem and Taboo.* In *The Basic Writings of Sigmund Freud.* New York: The Modern Library.
(1966)

1927   *The Future of an Illusion. The Complete Works of Sigmund Freud,* The Standard Edition, vol. 21. London: The Hogarth Press.

1933   "Dreams and Occultism." *New Introductory Lectures on Psychoanalysis.* In *The Basic Writings of Sigmund Freud.* New York: The Modern Library.
(1966)

1966a   "Three Contributions to the Theory of Sex." In *The Basic Writings of Sigmund Freud.* London: Allen and Unwin.

1966b   "The Psychopathology of Everyday Life." In *The Basic Writings of Sigmund Freud.* New York: The Modern Library.

1971   *The Complete Introductory Lectures on Psychoanalysis.* London: Allen and Unwin.

1979   *Case Histories II,* The Pelican Freud Library, vol. 9. Harmondsworth: Penguin.

Fromm, E.

1979a   "Quo Vadis Hypnosis? Predictions of Future Trends in Hypnosis Research." In Fromm and Shor 1979b:687–703.

1979b   "The Nature of Hypnosis and Other Altered States of Consciousness: An Ego-Psychological Theory." In Fromm and Shor 1979:81–103.

Fromm, E., and Shor, R. E.

1979a   "Underlying Theoretical Issues: An Introduction." In Fromm and Shor 1979b:3–13.

Fromm, E., and Shor, R. E. (eds.)

1979b   *Hypnosis: Developments in Research and New Perspectives.* New York: Aldine Publishing Company.

Galin, D.

1974   "Implications for Psychiatry of Left and Right Cerebral Specialization." *Archives of General Psychiatry* 31:572–583.

Geertz, C.

1975a   "Ritual and Social Change: A Javanese Example." In *The Interpretation of Cultures,* 142–169. London: Hutchinson.

1975b   "Religion as a Cultural System." In C. Geertz, *The Interpretation of Cultures,* 87–125. London: Hutchinson.

1975c   "Thick Description: Toward an Interpretive Theory of Culture." In C. Geertz, *The Interpretation of Cultures,* 3–30. London: Hutchinson.

1984   "From the Native's Point of View: On the Nature of Anthropological Understanding." In Shweder and Le Vine 1984:123–136.

1988   *Works and Lives: The Anthropologist as Author.* Oxford: Basil Blackwell Ltd.

Gell, A.
1979   "Reflections on a Cut Finger: Taboo in the Umeda Conception of the Self." In R. H. Hook (ed.), *Fantasy and Symbol: Studies in Anthropological Interpretation.* London: Academic Press.

Gerber, E. R.
1985   "Rage and Obligation: Samoan Emotion in Conflict." In White and Kirkpatrick 1985:121–167.

Goody, J.
1977   *The Domestication of the Savage Mind.* Cambridge: Cambridge University Press.

Greenberg, R.
1970   "Dreaming and Memory." In Hartmann 1970:258–267.

Greenblatt, S.
1986   "Fiction and Friction." In Heller, Sosna and Wellbery 1986:30–52.

Greenleaf, E.
1978   "Active Imagining." In Singer and Pope 1978a:167–196.

Gregor, T.
1981   "A Content Analysis of Mehinaku Dreams." *Ethos* 9:353–390.

Guis, J.
1936   *La Vie des Papous: Côte sud-est de La Nouvelle-Guinée (Roro et Mekeo).* Paris: Dillen.

Hadfield, J.
1974   *Dreams and Nightmares.* Harmondsworth: Pelican.

Hall, C. S., and Van de Castle, R. L.
1966   *The Content Analysis of Dreams.* New York: Appleton-Century-Crofts.

Hall, J. A.
1977   *Clinical Uses of Dreams.* New York: Grune and Stratton.

Hallowell, A. I.
1966   "The Role of Dreams in Ojibwa Culture." In Von Grunebaum and Caillois 1966:267–292.
1967   "The Self in its Behavioural Environment." In A. I. Hallowell, *Culture and Experience,* 75–110. New York: Schocken Books.

Hallpike, C. R.
1979   *The Foundations of Primitive Thought.* Oxford: Clarendon Press.

Hartmann, E.
1975   "Dreams and Other Hallucinations: An Approach to the Underlying Mechanism." In Siegel and West 1975, 71–79.

Hartmann, E. (ed.)
1970   *Sleep and Dreaming.* Boston: Little Brown.

Hau'ofa, E.
1971   "Mekeo Chieftainship." *Journal of the Polynesian Society* 80:152–169.
1975   "Mekeo." Ph.D. dissertation, Australian National University.
1981   *Mekeo: Inequality and Ambivalence in a Village Society.* Canberra: Australian National University Press.

Heelas, P., and Locke, A.
1971   *Indigenous Psychologies: The Anthropology of the Self.* London: Academic Press.
Heller, T. C., Sosna, M., and Wellbery, D. E. (eds.)
1986   *Reconstructing Individualism: Autonomy, Individuality, and the Self in Western Thought.* Stanford: Stanford University Press.
Herdt, G.
1977   "The Shaman's 'Calling' Among the Sambia of New Guinea." *Journal de la Société des Océanistes* 33:153–167.
1981   *Guardians of the Flutes: Idioms of Masculinity.* New York: McGraw Hill.
Herdt, G. (ed.)
1982   *Rituals of Manhood: Male Initiation in Papua New Guinea.* Berkeley and Los Angeles: University of California Press.
1984   *Ritualized Homosexuality in Melanesia.* Berkeley and Los Angeles: University of California Press.
1987   "Selfhood and Discourse in Sambia Dream Sharing." In Tedlock 1987b: 55–85.
1989a   "Self and Culture: Contexts of Religious Experience in Melanesia." In Herdt and Stephen 1989:15–40.
1989b   "Spirit Familiars in the Religious Imagination of Sambia Shamans." In Herdt and Stephen 1989:99–121.
Herdt, G., and Poole, F. J. P. (eds.)
1982   *Sexual Antagonism, Gender, and Social Change in Papua New Guinea.* Special Issue Series, *Social Analysis,* no. 12.
Herdt, G., and Stephen, M. (eds.)
1989   *The Religious Imagination in New Guinea.* New Brunswick, N.J.: Rutgers University Press.
Herdt, G., and Stoller, R. J.
1990   *Intimate Communications: Erotics and the Study of Culture.* New York: Columbia University Press.
Herr, B.
1981   "The Expressive Character of Fijian Dream and Nightmare Experiences." *Ethos* 9:331–352.
Hilgard, E. R.
1965   *Hypnotic Susceptibility.* New York: Harcourt Brace and World.
1977   *Divided Consciousness: Multiple Controls in Human Thought and Action.* New York: John Wiley and Sons.
Hilgard, J.
1979   "Imaginative and Sensory-Affective Involvements in Everyday Life and Hypnosis." In Fromm and Shor 1979b:483–517.
Hillman, J.
1975   *Re-Visioning Psychology.* New York: Harper and Row.
Hogbin, I.
1970   *The Island of Menstruating Men: Religion in Wogeo, New Guinea.* Scranton: Chandler Publishing Company.

Hogbin, I. (ed.)
1973   *Anthropology in Papua New Guinea.* Carlton: Melbourne University Press.

Howard, A.
1985   "Ethnopsychology and the Prospects for a Cultural Psychology." In White and Kirkpatrick 1985:401–420.

Hsu, F. L. K. (ed.)
1972   *Psychological Anthropology.* Cambridge, Mass.: Schenkman.

Hunt, H. T.
1989   *The Multiplicity of Dreams: Memory, Imagination and Consciousness.* New Haven and London: Yale University Press.

Hunt, L. (ed.)
1989   *The New Cultural History.* Berkeley and Los Angeles: University of California Press.

Johnson, F.
1985   "The Western Concept of Self." In A. J. Marsella, G. DeVos, and F. L. K. Hsu (eds.), *Culture and Self: Asian and Western Perspectives.* New York: Tavistock.

Jones, R. M.
1976   *The New Psychology of Dreaming.* Harmondsworth: Pelican.

Jung, C. G.
1967   *Symbols of Transformation.* Princeton: Princeton University Press.
1969   *The Structure and Dynamics of the Psyche.* Princeton: Princeton University Press.
1973   *Synchronicity: An Acausal Connecting Principle.* Princeton: Bollingen.
1976   *The Archetypes and the Collective Unconscious.* Princeton: Princeton University Press.
1977   *Psychology and the Occult.* Princeton: Princeton University Press.
1978   *Man and His Symbols.* New York: Doubleday.

Kakar, S.
1982   *Shamans, Mystics and Doctors: A Psychological Inquiry into India and Its Healing Traditions.* New York: Alfred A. Knopf.

Keesing, R. M.
1982   *Kwaio Religion.* New York: Columbia University Press.
1987   "Anthropology as Interpretive Quest." *Current Anthropology* 28:161–176.

Kennedy, J. G., and Langness, L. L.
1981   "Introduction." *Ethos* 9:249–257.

Kiev, A. (ed.)
1964   *Magic, Faith, and Healing: Studies in Primitive Psychiatry Today.* New York: The Free Press of Glencoe.

Kilbourne, B. J.
1981a   "Pattern, Structure, and Style in Anthropological Studies of Dreams." *Ethos* 9:165–185.
1981b   "Moroccan Dream Interpretation and Culturally Constituted Defense Mechanisms." *Ethos* 9:294–312.
1987   "On Classifying Dreams." In Tedlock 1987b:171–193.

Kline, M. V. (ed.)
1956   *A Scientific Report on the Search for Bridey Murphy.* New York: Julian Press.

Knauft, B.
1985   *Good Company and Violence: Sorcery and Social Action in a Lowland New Guinea Society.* Berkeley and Los Angeles: University of California Press.
1989   "Imagery, Pronouncement, and the Aesthetics of Reception in Gebusi Spirit Mediumship." In Herdt and Stephen 1989:67–98.

Koestler, A.
1964   *The Act of Creation.* New York: Macmillan.

Kohut, H.
1971   *The Analysis of the Self.* New York: International Universities Press.
1977   *The Restoration of the Self.* New York: International Universities Press.
1985   *Self Psychology and the Humanities: Reflections on a New Psychoanalytic Approach.* New York: W. W. Norton.

Kracke, W. H.
1981   "Kagwahiv Mourning: Dreams of a Bereaved Father." *Ethos* 9:258–275.
1987   "Myths in Dreams, Thought in Images: An Amazonian Contribution to the Psychoanalytic Theory of Primary Process." In Tedlock 1987b:31–54.

Kramer, M. (ed.)
1969   *Dream Psychology and the New Biology of Dreaming.* Springfield, Ill.: Charles C. Thomas.

Kramer, Y.
1988   "In the Visions of the Night: Perspectives on the Work of Jacob A. Arlow." In H. P. Blum., Y. Kramer, A. K. Richards, and A. D. Richards (eds.), *Fantasy, Myth, and Reality: Essays in Honour of Jacob A. Arlow, M.D.* Madison, Conn.: International Universities Press, Inc.

Krippner, S., and Hughes, W.
1970   "Dreams and Human Potential." *Journal of Humanistic Psychology* 10: 1–20.

Laing, R. D.
1965   *The Divided Self: An Existential Study in Sanity and Madness.* Harmondsworth: Penguin Books.

Lattas, A.
1992   "Skin, Personhood, and Redemption: The Doubled Self in West New Britain Cargo Cults." *Oceania* 63:27–54.

Lawrence, P.
1964   *Road Belong Cargo: A Study of the Cargo Movement in the Southern Madang District New Guinea.* Manchester, Carlton: University of Manchester and Melbourne University Presses.
1973   "Religion and Magic." In Hogbin 1973:201–226.
1984   *The Garia: An Ethnography of a Traditional Cosmic System in Papua New Guinea.* Carlton: Melbourne University Press.
1987   "De Rerum Natura: The Garia View of Sorcery." In Stephen 1987c:17–40.

Lawrence, P., and Meggitt, M.
1965   *Gods, Ghosts and Men in Melanesia: Some Religions of Australian New Guinea and the New Hebrides.* Melbourne: Oxford University Press.

Leach, E.
1976   *Culture and Communication: The Logic By Which Symbols Are Connected.* Cambridge: Cambridge University Press.

Lederman, R.
1981   "Sorcery and Social Change in Mendi." *Social Analysis* 8:15–27.

Leenhardt, M.
1979   *Do Kamo.* Trans. Basia M. Gulati. Chicago: University of Chicago Press.

LeVine, R. A.
1984   "Properties of Culture: An Ethnographic View." In Shweder and LeVine 1984:67–87.

LeVine, S.
1981   "Dreams of the Informant about the Researcher: Some Difficulties Inherent in the Research Relationship." *Ethos* 9:276–293.

Lévi-Strauss, C.
1972a   "The Sorcerer and His Magic." In C. Lévi-Strauss, *Structural Anthropology,* 167–185. Harmondsworth: Penguin Books.

1972b   "The Effectiveness of Symbols." In C. Lévi-Strauss, *Structural Anthropology,* 186–205. Harmondsworth: Penguin Books.

Lewis, I. M.
1971   *Ecstatic Religion: An Anthropological Study of Spirit Possession and Shamanism.* Harmondsworth: Penguin Books.

1986   *Religion in Context: Cults and Charisma.* Cambridge: Cambridge University Press.

Lincoln, J. S.
1935   *The Dream in Primitive Cultures.* Baltimore: Williams and Wilkins.

Lindenbaum, S.
1979   *Kuru Sorcery: Disease and Danger in the New Guinea Highlands.* Palo Alto, Calif.: Mayfield Publishing Company.

Lindstrom, L.
1984   "Doctor, Lawyer, Wise Man, Priest: Big-Men and Knowledge in Melanesia." *Man* (n.s.) 19:291–309.

Locke, R. G., and Kelly, E. F.
1985   "A Preliminary Model of the Cross-Cultural Analysis of Altered States of Consciousness." *Ethos* 13:3–55.

Ludwig, A. M.
1969   "Altered States of Consciousness." In Tart 1969a:11–24.

Luhrmann, T. M.
1989   "The Magic of Secrecy." *Ethos* 17:131–165.

Lukes, S.
1973   *Individualism.* Oxford: Basil Blackwell.

Malinowski, B.
1932   *The Sexual Life of Savages in North-Western Melanesia: An Ethnographic Account of Courtship, Marriage, and Family Life Among the Natives of*

the *Trobriand Islands, British New Guinea.* London: Routledge and Kegan
Paul.

1935   *Coral Gardens and Their Magic.* 2 vols. Bloomington: Indiana University
Press.

1961   *Argonauts of the Western Pacific.* New York: Dutton.

1974   *Magic, Science, and Religion: And Other Essays.* London: Souvenir Press.

Marcus, G. E., and Cushman, D.

1982   "Ethnographies as Text." *Annual Review of Anthropology* 11:25–69.

Marcus, G. E., and Fischer, M. J.

1986   *Anthropology as Cultural Critique: An Experimental Moment in the Human Sciences.* Chicago: University of Chicago Press.

Marcuse, H.

1969   *Eros and Civilization: A Philosophical Inquiry into Freud.* Trowbridge:
Redwood Press.

Marriot, M.

1976   "Interpreting Indian Society: A Monistic Alternative to Dumont's Dualism." *Journal of Asian Studies* 36:189–195.

Marwick, M. G.

1964   "Witchcraft as a Social-Strain Gauge." *Australian Journal of Science*
26:263–268.

1965   *Sorcery in Its Social Setting: A Study of the Northern Rhodesian Cewa.*
Manchester: Manchester University Press.

Mauss, M.

1938   "Une Catégorie de L'esprit Humaine: La Notion de Personne, Celle de
'Moi.'" *Journal of the Royal Anthropological Institute* 68:263–281.

1966   *The Gift: Forms and Functions of Exchange in Archaic Societies.* Trans.
[1902]   I. Cunnison. London: Cohen and West.

1972   *A General Theory of Magic.* Trans. R. Brain. London: Routledge and
Kegan Paul.

McHugh, E. L.

1989   "Concepts of the Person among the Gurungs of Nepal." *American Ethnologist* 16:75–86.

Meichenbaum, D.

1978   "Why Does Using Imagery in Psychotherapy Lead to Change?" In Singer
and Pope 1978a:381–394.

Meigs, A. S.

1984   *Food, Sex, and Pollution: A New Guinea Religion.* New Brunswick, N.J.:
Rutgers University Press.

Middleton, J. (ed.)

1967   *Magic, Witchcraft, and Curing.* New York: The Natural History Press.

Moerman, D. E.

1979   "Anthropology of Symbolic Healing." *Current Anthropology* 20:59–66,
75–80.

Monsell-Davis, M. D.

1981   "Nabuapaka: Social Change in a Roro Community." Unpublished Ph.D.
thesis, Macquarie University, Sydney.

Moore, B., Jr.
1984   *Privacy: Studies in Social and Cultural History.* Armonk, New York, and
         London: M. E. Sharpe Inc.

Mosko, M. S.
1985   *Quadripartite Structures: Categories, Relations, and Homologies in Bush
         Mekeo Culture.* Cambridge: Cambridge University Press.

Nemeroff, C., and Rozin, R.
1989   "'You Are What You Eat': Applying the Demand-Free 'Impressions'
         Technique to an Unacknowledged Belief." *Ethos* 17:50–69.
1990   "The Laws of Sympathetic Magic: A Psychological Analysis of Similarity
         and Contagion." In Stigler, Shweder, and Herdt 1990:205–232.
1992   "Sympathetic Magical Beliefs and Kosher Dietary Practice: The Inter-
         action of Rules and Feelings." *Ethos* 20:96–115.

Noll, R.
1985   "Mental Imagery Cultivation as a Cultural Phenomenon: The Role of
         Visions in Shamanism." *Current Anthropology* 26:443–461.

Noy, P.
1969   "A Revision of the Psychoanalytic Theory of Primary Process." *Inter-
         national Journal of Psycho-Analysis* 59:155–178.
1979   "Form Creation in Art: An Ego-Psychological Approach to Creativity."
         The Psychoanalytic Quarterly 48:229–256.

Obeyesekere, G.
1977   "Sorcery, Premeditated Murder, and the Canalization of Aggression in Sri
         Lanka." *Ethnology* 14:1–23.
1981   *Medusa's Hair.* Chicago: University of Chicago Press.

Oliver, D. L.
1955   *A Solomon Island Society: Kinship and Leadership Among the Siuai of
         Bouganville.* Cambridge, Mass.: Harvard University Press.

O'Nell, C. W.
1976   *Dreams, Culture, and the Individual.* San Francisco: Chandler and Sharp.

Orne, M. T.
1965   "The Nature of Hypnosis: Artifact and Essence." In Shor and Orne
         1965:89–123.
1979   "On the Simulating Subject as a Quasi-Control Group in Hypnosis
         Research: What, Why, and How." In Fromm and Shor 1979b:519–
         565.

Ortner, S.
1973   "On Key Symbols." *American Anthropologist* 75:1338–1346.

Paivio, A.
1971   *Imagery and Verbal Processes.* New York: Holt, Rinehart and Winston.

Panoff, M.
1968   "The Notion of the Double Self Among the Maenge." *Journal of the
         Polynesian Society* 77:275–295.

Papua New Guinea National Census
1980   National Statistics Office, Central Province, Preliminary Field Counts.
         Port Moresby: Government Printer.

Patterson, M.
1975   "Sorcery and Witchcraft in Melanesia." *Oceania* 45:132–160, 212–234.

Paul, R. A.
1989   "Psychoanalytic Anthropology." *Annual Review of Anthropology* 18: 177–202.

Paz, O.
1973   *The Bow and the Lyre: The Poem, the Poetic Revelation, Poetry and History.* Austin: University of Texas Press.
1976   *The Siren and the Seashell: And Other Essays on Poets and Poetry.* Austin: University of Texas Press.

Pearlman, C.
1970   "The Adaptive Function of Dreaming." In Hartmann 1970:329–334.

Peters, L. G., and Price-Williams, D.
1980   "Towards an Experiential Analysis of Shamanism." *American Ethnologist* 7:397–418.
1983   "A Phenomenological Overview of Trance." *Transcultural Psychiatric Research Review* 20:5–39.

Pontalis, J.-B.
1981   "Between the Dream as Object and the Dream-Text." In J.-B. Pontalis, *Frontiers in Psychoanalysis: Between the Dream and Psychic Pain,* 23–55. London: Hogarth.

Pribram, K. H.
1980   "Mind, Brain, and Consciousness: The Organisation of Competence and Conduct." In Davidson and Davidson 1980:47–64.

Price-Williams, D.
1975   *Explorations in Cross-Cultural Psychology.* Los Angeles: University of California.
1987   "The Waking Dream in Ethnographic Perspective." In Tedlock 1987b: 246–262.

Rabinow, P.
1977   *Reflections on Field Work in Morocco.* Berkeley and Los Angeles: University of California Press.

Reay, M.
1987   "The Magico-Religious Foundations of New Guinea Highlands Warfare." In Stephen 1987c:83–120.

Ricoeur, P.
1970   *Freud and Philosophy: An Essay on Interpretation.* New Haven: Yale University Press.

Riebe, I.
1987   "Kalam Witchcraft: A Historical Perspective." In Stephen 1987c:211–245.

Roheim, G.
1955   *Magic and Schizophrenia.* New York: International Universities Press.

Roseman, M.
1990   ''Head, Heart, Odor, and Shadow: The Structure of the Self, the Emotional World, and Ritual Performance Among Senoi Temiar.'' *Ethos* 18:227–250.

Rothenberg, A.
1979   *The Emerging Goddess: The Creative Process in Art, Science, and Other Fields.* Chicago: University of Chicago Press.

Rycroft, C.
1968   *Imagination and Reality: Psycho-Analytic Essays 1951–1961.* London: The Hogarth Press.

1972   *A Critical Dictionary of Psychoanalysis.* Harmondsworth: Penguin Books.

1979   *The Innocence of Dreams.* New York: Pantheon.

Sahlins, M.
1981   *Historical Metaphors and Mythic Realities: Structure in the Early History of the Sandwich Island Kingdom.* Ann Arbor: University of Michigan Press.

Said, E.
1978   *Orientalism.* New York: Pantheon.

Sarbin, T. R., and Slagle, R. W.
1979   ''Hypnosis and Psychophysiological Outcomes.'' In Fromm and Shor 1979b:273–303.

Sartre, J.-P.
1969   *Being and Nothingness: An Essay on Phenomenological Ontology.* London: Methuen.

Schenchner, R.
1986   ''Magnitudes of Performance.'' In V. W. Turner and E. M. Bruner (eds), *The Anthropology of Experience,* 344–369. Chicago: University of Illinois Press.

Schieffelin, E. L.
1977   *The Sorrow of the Lonely and the Burning of the Dancers.* St. Lucia: Queensland University Press.

Schneider, D. M.
1968   *American Kinship: A Cultural Account.* Englewood Cliffs, N.J.: Prentice Hall.

Seligman, C. G.
1910   *The Melanesians of British New Guinea.* Cambridge: Cambridge University Press.

Shaw, R. D.
1990   *Kandila: Samo Ceremonialism and Interpersonal Relationships.* Ann Arbor: University of Michigan Press.

Sheehan, P. W.
1979   ''Hypnosis and the Processes of Imagination.'' In Fromm and Shor 1979b: 381–411.

Sheehan, P. W., and McConkey, K. M.
1982   *Hypnosis and Experience: The Exploration of Phenomena and Process.* Hillsdale, N. J.: Lawrence Erlbaum Associates.

Shor, R. E.
1965   "Hypnosis and the Concept of the Generalized Reality-Orientation." In Shor and Orne 1965:288–305.
Shor, R. E., and Orne, M. T. (eds.)
1965   *The Nature of Hypnosis: Selected Basic Readings.* New York, Chicago: Holt, Rinehart and Winston.
Shweder, R. A.
1977   "Likeness and Likelihood in Everyday Thought: Magical Thinking in Judgements about Personality." *Current Anthropology* 18:637–658.
1990   "Cultural Psychology—What Is It?" In J. W. Stigler, R. A. Shweder, and G. Herdt (eds.), *Cultural Psychology: Essays on Comparative Human Development,* 1–43.
Shweder, R. A., and Bourne, E. J.
1984   "Does the Concept of the Person Vary Cross-Culturally?" In Shweder and LeVine 1984:158–199.
Shweder, R. A., and LeVine, R. A. (eds.)
1984   *Culture Theory: Essays on Mind, Self, and Emotion.* Cambridge, London, New York, and New Rochelle: Cambridge University Press.
Siegel, R. K., and West, L. J. (eds.)
1975   *Hallucinations: Behaviour, Experience, and Theory.* New York: John Wiley and Sons, Inc.
Singer, J. L.
1974   *Imagery and Daydream Methods in Psychotherapy and Behaviour Modification.* New York and San Francisco: Academic Press.
1976   *Daydreaming and Fantasy.* London: George Allen and Unwin Ltd.
1977   "Ongoing Thought: The Normative Baseline for Alternate States of Consciousness." In Zinberg 1977:89–120.
Singer, J. L., and Pope, K. S.
1978   "The Use of Imagery and Fantasy Techniques in Psychotherapy." In Singer and Pope 1978a:3–34.
Singer, J. L., and Pope, K. S. (eds.)
1978a   *The Power of Human Imagination: New Methods in Psychotherapy.* New York and London: Plenum Press.
1978b   *The Stream of Consciousness: Scientific Investigations into the Flow of Human Experience.* Chichester and New York: John Wiley and Sons.
Sørum, A.
1980   "In Search of the Lost Soul: Bedamini Spirit Seances and Curing Rites." *Oceania* 50:273–295.
Sperber, D.
1975   *Rethinking Symbolism.* Trans. A. L. Morton. Cambridge: Cambridge University Press.
Spiro, M.
1984   "Some Reflections on Cultural Determinism and Relativism with Special Reference to Emotion and Reason." In Shweder and LeVine 1984:323–346.

Springer, S. P., and Deutsch, G.
1981   *Left Brain, Right Brain.* San Francisco: W. H. Freeman and Company.

Stephen, M.
1974   "Continuity and Change in Mekeo Society 1890–1971." Unpublished Ph.D. thesis, Australian National University.
1977   "Cargo Cult 'Hysteria': Symptom of Despair or Technique of Ecstacy?" Occasional paper, Research Centre for South-West Pacific Studies, La Trobe University.
1979a   "Dreams of Change: The Innovative Role of Altered States of Consciousness in Traditional Melanesian Religion." *Oceania* 50:3–22.
1979b   "Sorcery, Magic, and the Mekeo World View." In N. Habel (ed.), *Powers, Plumes and Piglets: Phenomena of Melanesian Religion.* Bedford Park, South Australia: Australian Association for the Study of Religions.
1979c   "An Honourable Man: Mekeo Views of the Village Constable." *Journal of Pacific History* 14:85–99.
1981   "Dreaming Is Another Power!: The Social Significance of Dreams among the Mekeo of Papua New Guinea." *Oceania* 53:106–122.
1987a   "Master of Souls: The Mekeo Sorcerer." In Stephen 1987c:41–80.
1987b   "Contrasting Images of Power." In Stephen 1987c:249–304.
1989a   "Self, the Sacred Other, and Autonomous Imagination." In Herdt and Stephen 1989:41–64.
1989b   "Dreaming and the Hidden Self: Mekeo Definitions of Consciousness." In Herdt and Stephen 1989:160–186.
1989c   "Constructing Sacred Worlds and Autonomous Imagining in New Guinea." In Herdt and Stephen 1989:211–236.

Stephen, M. (ed.).
1987c   *Sorcerer and Witch in Melanesia.* New Brunswick, N.J.: Rutgers University Press.

Stephen, M., and Herdt, G.
1989   "Introduction." In Herdt and Stephen 1989:1–11.

Stigler, J. W., Shweder, R. A., and Herdt, G. (eds.)
1990   *Cultural Psychology: Essays on Comparative Human Development.* Cambridge: Cambridge University Press.

Strathern, A. J.
1977   "Why is Shame on the Skin?" *Ethnology* 14:347–356.

Strathern, M.
1988   *The Gender of the Gift.* Berkeley and Los Angeles: University of California Press.

Tambiah, S. J.
1990   *Magic, Science, Religion, and the Scope of Rationality.* Cambridge: Cambridge University Press.

Tart, C. T. (ed.)
1969a   *Altered States of Consciousness.* New York: John Wiley and Sons.

1969b   "Towards the Experimental Control of Dreaming: A Review of the Lit-
            erature." In Tart 1969a:133–144.
Taylor, E.
1978   "Asian Interpretations: Transcending the Stream of Consciousness." In
            Singer and Pope 1978b:31–54.
Tedlock, B.
1981   "Quiché Maya Dream Interpretation." *Ethos* 9:313–330.
1987a   "Dreaming and Dream Research." In Tedlock 1987b:1–30.
Tedlock, B. (ed.)
1987b   *Dreaming: Anthropological and Psychological Interpretations.* Cam-
            bridge: Cambridge University Press.
Thomas, K.
1971   *Religion and the Decline of Magic.* New York: Scribner.
Turner, V. W.
1957   *Schism and Continuity in an African Society.* Manchester: Manchester
            University Press.
1967   *The Forest of Symbols: Aspects of Ndembu Ritual.* Ithaca, N.Y.: Cornell
            University Press.
1969   *The Ritual Process.* Chicago: Aldine Publishing Company.
Turner, V. W., and Bruner, E. M. (eds.)
1986   *The Anthropology of Experience.* Urbana and Chicago: University of
            Illinois Press.
Tuzin, D. F.
1975   "The Breath of a Ghost: Dreams and the Fear of the Dead." *Ethos*
            3:555–578.
1980   *The Voice of the Tambaran: Truth and Illusion in Ilahita Arapesh Religion.*
            Berkeley and Los Angeles: University of California Press.
1989   "Visions, Prophecies, and the Rise of Christian Consciousness." In Herdt
            and Stephen 1989:187–208.
Ullman, M., and Zimmerman, N.
1979   *Working With Dreams.* London: Hutchinson.
Valeri, V.
1985   *Kingship and Sacrifice: Ritual and Society in Ancient Hawaii.* Chicago:
            University of Chicago Press.
Von Grunebaum, G. D., and Caillois, R.
1967   *The Dream and Human Societies.* Berkeley and Los Angeles: University
            of California Press.
Wagner, R.
1972   *Habu: The Innovation of Meaning in Daribi Religion.* Chicago and Lon-
            don: University of Chicago Press.
1975   *The Invention of Culture.* Chicago: University of Chicago Press.
Wallace, A. F. C.
1972   "Revitalization Movements." In W. A. Lessa and E. Z. Vogt (eds.),
            Reader in Comparative Religion: An Anthropological Approach, 503–
            512. New York: Harper and Row.
Watkins, M.
1984   *Waking Dreams.* Dallas, Tex.: Spring Publications, Inc.

Weber, M.
  1983   *Max Weber on Capitalism, Bureaucracy, and Religion: A Selection of Texts.* Ed. S. Andreski. London: Allen and Unwin.
West, L. J.
  1975   "A Clinical and Theoretical Overview of Hallucinatory Phenomena." In Siegel and West 1975:287–311.
White, G. M., and Kirkpatrick, J. (eds.)
  1985   *Person, Self, and Experience.* Berkeley and Los Angeles: University of California Press.
Whittaker, E.
  1992   "The Birth of the Anthropological Self and Its Career." *Ethos* 20:191–219.
Wikan, U.
  1982   *Behind the Veil in Arabia: Women in Oman.* Chicago: University of Chicago Press.
  1989   "Managing the Heart to Brighten Face and Soul: Emotions in Balinese Morality and Health Care." *American Ethnologist* 17:294–310.
  1990   *Managing Turbulent Hearts: A Balinese Formula for Living.* Chicago: University of Chicago Press.
Williamson, R. W.
  1913   "Some Unrecorded Customs of the Mekeo People of British New Guinea." *Journal of the Royal Anthropological Institute of Great Britain and Ireland* 43:268–290.
Wilson, M.
  1975   "Kinsman of Aruapaka." Unpublished M.A. thesis, University of Papua New Guinea.
Winkleman, M.
  1979   "Magic: A Theoretical Reassessment." *Current Anthropology* 23:37–66.
Winters, W. D.
  1975   "The Continuum of CNS Excitory States and Hallucinosis." In Siegel and West 1975:53–70.
Young, M. W.
  1983   *Magicians of Manumanua: Living Myth in Kalauna.* Berkeley and Los Angeles: University of California Press.
Zelenietz, M.
  1981   "Sorcery and Social Change: An Introduction." *Social Analysis* 8:3–14.
Zinberg, N. E. (eds.)
  1977   *Alternate States of Consciousness.* New York: Free Press.

Subject Index

A'aisa: body dirt of, 260; compared with
Christian God, 53, 57–59, 213; gifts of, 4,
307–308; myth, 3–4, 16, 41, 56–57, 137–
139, 148, 179, 241; myth, esoteric version
of, 261, 301–302, 305–306; as shape
changer, 304; sightings of, 249–250, 255;
takes form of *augama* snake, 249–250,
292; as trickster, 59, 136–137, 245, 263,
304, 329
Active imagination, 99
Adolescence, 12
Affines (*ipa gava*), 21–22, 272; and sorcery
fears, 42–43, 85, 257, 276
Aipeana, 86, 164
Aisaga, 65, 67–70, 72–73, 78, 177, 181–182,
187, 190, 229, 321; accusations against,
234, 274; anger of, 273–280, 285–287,
288–291; as man of knowledge, 231; as
head of lineage, 237, 271–273, 280; concealed nature of beneficent role, 238; control over hidden self, 240, 262; daily activities of, 232–239; dangers of his role,
236, 238, 239–240, 283, 287–288; deception by, 238–239, 251, 253, 258, 262,
278, 279; disguises of, 245; dream of being photographed, 288–289; dream of being rebuked, 286; dream of broken tractor,
268, 284; dream of Matthew dancing, 276;
dreams of, 240, 244, 261; dual role of,
194–195, 270–271; garden of, 232, 241;
gove of, 232; healing performed by, 232–
233, 235–236, 254–256, 276; and his family, 266–270; identification with the dead,

244–245, 279–280, 292; implacable will
of, 291–292, 321; installation of new man
of kindness, 247–249, 252–254; interaction with spirit realm, 239–244, 278–280,
287, 291–292; love rituals performed by,
233–234; methods of teaching esoteric
knowledge, 232–238, 246–263, 288;
painted face of, 247; payments to appease
anger of hidden self of, 285; and Philo's
illness, 249–258; possess relics of the
dead, 242, 279–280; relationship with eldest son, 267–268, 280–292; relationship
with George, 219, 221–222; relationship
with Henry, 271, 279–280, 284; relationship with Joe, 272–273, 280; reveals objects used for *ugauga* sorcery, 69–70; ritual regimen of, 242–243; role in Ruth's
death, 80–91, 234; secrecy of, 80, 83, 235,
237, 279; shaping of the self an heroic
task, 321; threats against, 87; wealth derived from ritual practice, 272; and wider
community, 270–273
Aisomo and Kopomo, 89, 243
Alcohol, effects on community of, 37, 87,
90, 156, 161, 267, 273, 275, 280
Alex, 72, 131, 158, 210–223, 229; descriptions of *kinapui* and *faifai* rituals by, 212–
220; dream of Ruth's death, 82, 93, 113;
role in Ruth's death, 79–85, 87–88
Alice, 151, 165, 169–170
Altered states of consciousness, 105–107;
and healing, 105–106; and suggestibility,
105

Author Index

Printed in the United States
2862

9 780520 088290